BLACKS IN THE MILITARY
ESSENTIAL DOCUMENTS

BLACKS
IN THE
MILITARY
ESSENTIAL DOCUMENTS

Edited by
Bernard C. Nalty and
Morris J. MacGregor

SR *Scholarly Resources Inc.*
104 Greenhill Avenue · Wilmington, Delaware 19805

PUBLISHER'S NOTE

The editors at Scholarly Resources Inc. have undertaken to establish a consistent style throughout the volume. To accomplish this, they have employed a system of abbreviation and capitalization based on the University of Chicago's style manual and applied it not only to source notes but also to the explanatory or introductory passages and to the documents themselves. Long quotes within the documents have been set in italics. Statements in italics in the original documents are so labeled.

Scholarly Resources Inc.
104 Greenhill Avenue
Wilmington, Delaware 19805

Library of Congress Cataloging in Publication Data
Main entry under title:

Blacks in the military.

Includes index.
1. Afro-American soldiers—History—Sources
I. Nalty, Bernard C.   II. MacGregor, Morris J.,
1931–
UB418.A47B55   355.1′08996073   80-54664
ISBN 0-8420-2183-3   AACR2

CONTENTS

vi

PREFACE

This one-volume work, using certain key documents or selections from them, sketches the changing status of blacks in the military service first of the American colonies and then of the United States. Space does not permit an exhaustive treatment; as a result, we have supplied explanations and interpretations to supplement the information found in the materials we have selected. This new, brief compilation should prove valuable to anyone interested in the contributions of blacks to American military history, whether he be student or teacher, serviceman or civilian, writer of history or curious reader.

In choosing passages or whole documents, we have sought to show how a disciplined institution, the armed forces, figured in the attainment by black Americans of the rights and obligations of full citizenship, especially the right to just and impartial treatment while fulfilling the obligation of military service. Instead of demonstrating the obvious existence of racial discrimination or recounting the efforts of blacks and their white allies to change American society, we have restricted ourselves to tracing the evolving racial policies of the army, navy, air force, and Marine Corps. Segregation and the reaction of blacks to this cruel and deeply rooted injustice, however, could not be ignored; as a result, we have included statements by various individuals, whether observers or the victims themselves, testifying to the corrosive effect of racism upon military efficiency.

We have chosen our materials from a number of published sources, collections, and depositories. The files of the National Association for the Advancement of Colored People, for example, chart the increasing influence of the black community in the decades following the first World War. The Military Archives Division of the National Archives and Records Service contains the official records generated before 1950 on the topic of blacks in the armed services. Material on the early years may be found in *The Negro in the Military Service of the United States, 1639–1886*, collected under the direction of Elon A. Woodward, chief of the Colored Troops Division, Adjutant General's Office. Now available on microfilm, the collection contains some 5000 pages, including handwritten and typed copies as well as original documents. Among the holdings of the Harry S Truman Library, Independence, Missouri, are such essential items as the report of the President's Committee on Equality of Treatment and Opportunity in the Armed Services, with its mass of testimony on racial policies during World War II and immediately afterward.

Since space is at a premium in this volume, we have incorporated the heading of a document—the sender, intended recipient, subject, and date—in a source note that identifies and follows the entry. Since the original orthography lent neither charm nor authenticity, we have used modern spelling throughout the selections. We have altered the punctuation only when necessary to clarify the meaning of the document.

We are grateful to a host of organizations and individuals that helped us obtain the documents reprinted or quoted in this volume. We wish to express special thanks to the Massachusetts Historical Society for permission to quote from its manuscript holdings and printed collections. The National Association for the Advancement of Colored People generously allowed us to make use of its correspondence files and to draw upon materials in its journal, *The Crisis*. Our research also benefited from the enthusiastic cooperation of the staffs of the National Archives and Records Service, the Manuscripts Division of the Library of Congress, the Navy Department Library, the US Army Military History Research Collection, the Harry S Truman Library, the Franklin D. Roosevelt Library, and the historical offices of the military services, the US Coast Guard, and the Joint Chiefs of Staff.

Deserving individual thanks are William H. Cunliffe, Timothy K. Nenninger, Gibson B. Smith, and Carrie B. Lee of the National Archives and Records Service; Dale E. Floyd, now a historian for the US Army Corps of Engineers; and John A. Slonaker of the Army's Military History Research Collection. We would never have begun the book, let alone finished it, except for the encouragement and technical skill of Daniel C. Helmstadter and James L. Preston of Scholarly Resources Inc. Philip G. Johnson chose the format and an editorial style that has brought consistency to documents, footnotes, and narrative. The task he began has been completed by Ann M. Aydelotte, his colleague at Scholarly Resources. Finally, the project depended to a great extent on the patience, good humor, and attention to detail of Barbara Nalty, wife of one of the collaborators.

INTRODUCTION

The history of blacks in the United States armed forces reflects their progress within American society, with certain differences. Members of the military and naval service form a distinct class that is bound by a discipline not found in most other vocations. Although a soldier may find the shovel as important as the rifle, the infantryman has never been a mere laborer who happens to carry a weapon. He belongs to a specific group with its own identifiable rules, customs, and interests. He may perceive himself as a member of a profession, one that has only gradually welcomed black Americans, or he may believe that he is temporarily fulfilling an obligation of citizenship, a duty that blacks have at times not been allowed to perform.

From the colonial era until the Vietnam War, American blacks progressed from slavery to freedom and then from nominal citizenship to the full exercise of the civil rights guaranteed to all citizens. In the armed services, which tend to reflect the strengths and failings of the nation they defend, blacks had to make a transition from auxiliaries, useful only in an emergency, to combat soldiers who were entrusted with the most complex and deadly weapons.

Progress from exclusion to full participation has proved uneven. At times it has been slowed or hastened by varied and conflicting pressures such as idealism, racial prejudice, and a recurring shortage of military manpower. Although Gunnar Myrdal, a celebrated student of black America, has observed that ideals always have played a dominant role in the nation's social dynamics, not every improvement in the status of blacks has represented a triumph of the democratic spirit. At one time, a need for manpower may have contributed to progress; at another, unreasoning prejudice may have turned advance into retreat, thus causing the nation to ignore a potentially valuable source of recruits.

Democracy, as embodied in the American Revolution, no doubt helped open the Continental Army to many blacks and held out to them a promise of freedom. Yet, at the same time the presence of both slaves and free blacks in the revolutionary army and navy was a pragmatic response to a pressing need for fighting men and military laborers. To American military and naval officers of that era, as indeed to their British enemies, blacks represented a manpower pool to be tapped in time of acute danger. This view prevailed throughout the War of 1812, when free blacks fought on land and sea, and later moved Union leaders to begin enlisting former slaves and other free Negroes during the Civil War.

With the outbreak of war between the Union and Confederacy, northern idealism gradually moved to the fore. Persons interested in the welfare of freed blacks believed that military service afforded a means of education and discipline that would ease the transition from servitude to freedom. By the time the South surrendered, some two hundred thousand blacks had served the Union cause, and their presence in uniform testified to the successful blend of the abolitionist's idealism and the recruiter's pragmatism.

Although their numbers were few and their prospects for advancement limited, blacks were now accepted as peacetime professionals, whether soldiers or seamen. Following the Civil War, the abolitionist impulse that formed the heart of the Radical Republican cause brought about the creation of four black regiments in the peacetime American army, while the navy continued to recruit blacks, assigning them throughout the service rather than grouping them in segregated units as the army did. The Marine Corps adhered to its policy of excluding blacks, but members of the race serving in the army or navy could attain noncommissioned rank. The postwar navy had no black officers, however, and the army had just three.

Idealism could not have prevailed had the black soldier and sailor not performed with distinction. Whether on the Civil War battlefield or in pursuit of the Apache in the wilds of the Southwest, black troops fought bravely, earning the respect of their comrades. Such accomplishments did not bring equal treatment. Segregation persisted in the army, and the War Department kept its black units on the frontier, refusing to transfer them to more desirable posts, especially those located in the South.

The war with Spain brought a tide of black volunteers and militiamen, including a few officers, into the army, but this phenomenon did not reflect the spirit of the times. A mantle of racial oppression was descending upon the land, and northern as well as southern cities and states enacted Jim Crow laws designed to limit the rights of black Americans. The few nationally prominent black leaders of that era tried to enlist politicians in the struggle against racism, but Negro citizens, many of them effectively disenfranchised, lacked sufficient influence in government to bring about change.

Not until the eve of World War II did the black community become powerful enough to influence political leaders. Men like Charles Houston, embittered by his treatment while an officer in World War I, Rayford Logan, Walter White, and A. Philip Randolph took advantage of the importance of black votes and the need for black manpower to obtain concessions within the military services, such as the acceptance of blacks for flight training, and greater opportunities for civilian employment in defense industry. These leaders, however, could not marshal adequate strength to end racial segregation in the armed forces, much less in society as a whole.

Allied ideology in World War II gave American blacks a powerful psychological weapon against racism, a moral instrument to be used in conjunction with a growing political strength and awareness. The conflict pitted the United States, as the champion of freedom and human dignity, against the forces of tyranny. The myth of racial supremacy, a lie that slaughtered millions, had not saved Nazi Germany from a crushing defeat. Throughout the world, American propagandists sought to rally the very races that the Nazis detested, and, in the United States, films and radio broadcasts urged that all citizens put aside differences of race, creed, or economic class to do battle against fascism and oppression. The flame of idealism thus kindled was not extinguished with the coming of peace.

The armed forces, however, did seem surprisingly resistant to these high-minded wartime goals. Once the fighting ended, the army and navy tried to retain segregation, maintaining as they had in the past that racial separation ensured efficiency and that blacks and whites differed so radically in talents and character that neither felt comfortable with the other. In this instance, the argument could not prevail, for efficiency demanded racial integration. In a period of persistent international tension, the United States could not afford the waste of manpower that resulted from maintaining segregated units with their separate training facilities and replacement systems.

World War II gave way to a cold war that saw the United States competing with the Soviet Union for moral and military ascendancy throughout the globe. Could the leader of the free world risk undermining its position by condoning racial segregation? Would the United States, by discriminating against minorities, risk forfeiting the respect of emerging nations whose citizens recently had experienced repression by colonial masters? Once again, the world situation worked to the advantage of black Americans.

During the 1950s, against this backdrop of East-West competition, overt racial segregation came to an end in the US armed forces, although not in civilian society. Several factors influenced this change: thoughtful citizens, Pres. Harry S Truman among them, had become disgusted by the violence spawned by racial discrimination; black votes became crucial to Truman's reelection campaign; and the cold war turned hot in Korea, and men were needed for that conflict.

Once the armed forces began reaping dividends from their integration policies, in terms of increased efficiency and racial harmony, they became reluctant agents of the civil rights crusade that engulfed the nation in the early 1960s. Under the leadership of Martin Luther King, Jr., and others who sought to prick the nation's conscience through peaceful resistance, the civil rights movement won impressive victories in the passage of new and powerful legislation that challenged racism in every aspect of society. Many senior service officials resisted joining in the crusade, arguing that the fight for equal treatment and opportunity outside the gates of the military compound should be led by others. These individuals came to be persuaded that segregation in the local community affected the morale and therefore the performance of approximately 10 percent of the armed forces. As a result, the military began taking action against racial discrimination in housing, schools, and public accommodations available in communities near military bases or naval installations. Consequently, when the pace of civil rights reform quickened later in the decade, the nation found its armed forces marching in the vanguard.

Then came the Vietnam War, during which a disproportionately large number of blacks appeared to be serving in combat units. As a result, Dr. King found himself in conflict with the military establishment that had played such an important role in the achievement of full citizenship by America's blacks. Although much had been gained, complete equality remained an unrealized ideal in the early 1970s. Since the Vietnam conflict serves as a watershed in terms of the national economy, the composition of the defense forces, and possibly the field of race relations as well, it is a convenient point for ending this study.

Bernard C. Nalty
Morris J. MacGregor

CHAPTER ONE
A TIME OF SLAVERY

Britain's North American colonies faced two military threats throughout most of the seventeenth and eighteenth centuries. In the event of war in Europe, the armed forces of France or Spain might attack in the New World; at any time, the Indian tribes might lash out, incited by resentment of white settlers or by England's continental enemies. Defense against these threats proved difficult, especially in those southern colonies where a plantation system prevailed, masses of slaves tilled the soil, and few free whites were available to bear arms. In these circumstances, colonial governments sought to obtain some form of military service from the slave population.

In doing so, the southern colonies faced the problem of servile insurrection alluded to by North Carolina's colonial agent and his merchant colleagues. When confronted by an Indian uprising, apparently fomented by the Spanish, these leaders thought of issuing weapons to slaves, only to decide that "there must be great caution used, lest our slaves when arm'd might become our masters."

Because of this danger, most slave-holding colonies followed the example of Virginia in excluding blacks from military service, although the assembly there finally conceded that "free mulattoes, Negroes, and Indians" might serve as noncombatant laborers or musicians. In contrast to Virginia and her imitators, South Carolina's legislators proposed arming the most trusted slaves in time of danger, and on at least one occasion actually did so. As slaves came to outnumber free men in the colony, the specter of a servile uprising grew more frightening, until Indian attack or foreign invasion seemed lesser perils. As a result, the colonial government chose to ignore the slave populace as a source of militiamen.

In general, only free men were eligible for military service, prior to the American Revolution. If white, the free colonist bore arms, which he usually supplied himself; if black, his status varied from one place to another. Where there were large numbers of slaves, the free black would be, at most, an unarmed auxiliary, but in a colony like Massachusetts, where slaves were few, he might serve as a combat soldier or ship's crewman, provided the emergency seemed grave enough.

Early in the revolution, free blacks, mostly from Massachusetts, saw service with the Continental forces besieging Boston. No real effort would have been made to recruit more of these men except for two developments. First, the enemy enjoyed some success in convincing slaves to run away and enter the armies of King George III, thus ensuring

1

their freedom. Second, the long conflict required increasing numbers of men, and war-weary free whites proved reluctant to spend long periods away from family, farm, or trade.

Although some slave states formally banned the recruiting of blacks, a good many slaves found their way into the Continental service, as it became more and more difficult to meet recruiting goals. Virginia, for example, enlisted enough slaves to justify granting freedom to those who had served. As many as five thousand blacks, most of them free men, enlisted in the revolutionary cause during the conflict.

With the emergency past, black veterans of the revolution found no welcome in either the state militias or the armed forces of the new nation. The military and naval services of the United States were so small that little recruiting was necessary; tapping the reservoir of black manpower simply was not necessary. Militia units remained a white man's preserve largely because they had social and political, as well as military, functions. The policy of black exclusion became the law of the land.

The War of 1812, frustrating and unpopular, produced a manpower crisis that compelled the American armed forces to call upon free blacks to sustain their ranks. First to do so was the US Navy, and this improvised recruiting was almost immediately authorized by law. In the army, blacks served under Maj. Gen. Andrew Jackson in the successful defense of New Orleans. The United States military and naval services did not recruit slaves. The British had scant opportunity to do so, except during the 1814 Chesapeake Bay expedition, when some two hundred escaped slaves took part in the campaign that culminated in the British sack of Washington.

With the return of peace, only the navy continued to enlist blacks, establishing a 5 percent recruiting quota. Only whites served in the Marine Corps, the army, and most state militias. In Louisiana, however, free black militia units survived. Tracing their lineage back beyond the Battle of New Orleans to the period of Spanish rule, they were active in 1861 when the Civil War began.

*This act codified the practice of excluding slaves
from militia service.*

All persons except Negroes to be provided with arms and ammunition or be fined at pleasure of the governor and council.

[An Act of the General Assembly of Virginia, 6 January 1639, William Hening, *Statutes at Large of Virginia*, vol. I, p. 224 in *The Negro in the Military Service of the United States, 1639–1886*, Microfilm M858, National Archives, Washington, DC.]

●

*With a slave population rapidly exceeding the number of
free citizens, the colony planned to arm certain slaves in case
of war, and black militiamen helped defeat the Yamassee Indian
tribe in 1715. Presumably some of these slaves received their
freedom in return for taking part in the campaign. Slaves may
have been mustered also into service to meet a threatened
Spanish invasion, but a slave uprising in 1739 convinced
authorities that this means of raising soldiers was too
dangerous. Stricken from the statute books but later reinstated,
the law was never again invoked.*

XXIII. Whereas, it is necessary for the safety of this colony in case of actual invasions, to have the assistance of our trusty slaves to assist us against our enemies, and it being reasonable that the said slave should be rewarded for the good service they may do us, be it therefore enacted . . . that if any slave shall, in actual invasion, kill or take one or more of our enemies, and the same shall prove by any white person to be done by him, shall, for his reward, at the charge of the public have and enjoy his freedom. . . ; and the master or owner of such slave shall be paid and satisfied by the public. . . ; and if any of said slaves happen to be killed in actual service of province by the enemy, then the master or owner shall be paid and satisfied for him. . . .

XXIV. And be it further enacted . . . that if any slave aforesaid is wounded in the service aforesaid, so that he is disabled for service to his master or owner, then such slave so disabled shall be set free at the charge of the public . . . and shall also be maintained at the charge of the said public.

XXV. And be it further enacted by the authority aforesaid, that it shall and may be lawful for any master or owner of any slave, in actual invasion, to arm and equip any slave or slaves, with such arms and ammunition as any other person by the act of militia are appointed to appear at muster or alarms.

[An Act of the General Assembly of the Province of South Carolina, 23 December 1703, *Statutes at Large of South Carolina* (1840), vol. VII, p. 33 in *The Negro in the Military Service of the United States, 1639–1886,* Microfilm M858, National Archives, Washington, DC.]

Massachusetts accepted free blacks for military service, a policy
common among the northern colonies.

And be it further enacted that all free male Negroes or mulattos, of the age of sixteen years and upwards, able of body, in case of alarm, shall make their appearance at the parade of the militia company of the precinct wherein they dwell, and attend such service as the first commission[ed] officer of such company shall direct, during the time the company continues in arms, on pain of forfeiting the sum of twenty shillings to the use of the company, or performing eight days labor as aforesaid, without reasonable excuse made and accepted for not attending.

[Section 3, An Act of the General Court of Massachusetts, 12 June 1707, *Acts and Resolves of the Province of Massachusetts Bay*, vol. I, p. 607 in *The Negro in the Military Service of the United States, 1639–1886,* Microfilm M858, National Archives, Washington, DC.]

●

Maryland excluded both slaves and free blacks from its militia.

And be it enacted by the authority aforesaid, that all Negroes and slaves whatsoever shall be exempted from the duty of training or other military service.

[An Act of the Assembly of the Province of Maryland, 3 June 1715, Bacon, *Laws of Maryland at Large* (1715) in *The Negro in the Military Service of the United States, 1639–1886*, Microfilm M858, National Archives, Washington, DC.]

●

Free blacks could serve as laborers or musicians, thereby
releasing whites for actual combat.

Provided always that such free Negroes, mulattoes, and Indians as are capable may be listed and emplaced as drummers or trumpeters; and that upon any invasion, insurrection, or rebellion, all free Negroes, mulattoes, or Indians shall be obliged to attend on and march with the military and to do the duty of pioneers, or such other servile labor as they shall be directed to perform.

[Section 5, An Act of the General Assembly of Virginia, 9 May 1723, *The Negro in the Military Service of the United States, 1639–1886*, Microfilm M858, National Archives, Washington, DC.]

This ambitious plan, which sought to make use of both free
blacks and slaves volunteered by their owners, never came to
fruition.

2. Now for the encouragement of 500 freemen, or native well-affected Indians, to enlist within this colony, as soldiers, for the said service, and for answering his majesty's just expectations, as to the supplying them with provisions . . . it is hereby enacted . . . that there shall be paid to every freeman, or native well-affected Indian, who shall enlist either as sergeant, corporal, drummer, or private soldier, the sum of six pounds proclamation money, over and above his majesty's pay. . . .

5. And be it enacted by the authority aforesaid, that it shall not be lawful to enlist any young men under the age of twenty-one years, or any slaves who are so for term of life, bought servants, or apprentices, without the express leave in writing of their parents or guardians, masters or mistresses, first had and obtained. . . .

[Act Passed by the General Assembly of New Jersey at Perth Amboy, 28 June 1746, Nevill, *Acts of New Jersey*, vol. I, pp. 314, 316 in *The Negro in the Military Service of the United States, 1639–1886*, Microfilm M858, National Archives, Washington, DC.]

●

This typical grant bestowed a pension on a black who had
served in the French-Indian War.

To the great and general court now setting in Boston.
We your honors petitioners humbly show that whereas one George Gire a Negro man living in Grafton became infirm by reason of the hard service in the French war[,] the General Court settled a pension on him of forty shillings per year during said court's pleasure and he hath drawn that sum or near the value thereof to June 1779. Said George still remains infirm. Therefore we your honors petitioners humbly pray to have said George's circumstances taken into your wise consideration and allow George for one year from June 1779. . . .

[Pension Grant to George Gire, 14 December 1780, *Manuscript Archives of Massachusetts*, vol. 231, p. 293 in *The Negro in the Military Service of the United States, 1639–1886*, Microfilm M858, National Archives, Washington, DC.]

*The colony retained the policy of recruiting free blacks, though
not slaves, in this case for service in the Continental Army.*

Resolved, that it is the opinion of this committee, as the contest now between Great Britain and the colonies respects the liberties and privileges of the latter, which the colonies are determined to maintain, that the admission of any persons as soldiers into the army now raising, but only such as are freemen, will be inconsistent with the principles that are to be supported, and reflect dishonor on this colony; and that no slaves be admitted into this army upon any consideration whatever.

[Resolution, Massachusetts Committee of Safety, 20 May 1775, Peter Force, *American Archives*, Series IV.]

•

*This offer of freedom to those escaped slaves willing to take up
arms on behalf of King George III attracted some three hundred
volunteers. On 9 July 1776, Virginia rebels defeated Dunmore's
force, which included the black troops.*

And I do hereby further declare all indented servants, Negroes, or others, (appertaining to rebels,) free, that are able and willing to bear arms, they joining His Majesty's troops, as soon as may be, for the more speedily reducing this colony to a proper sense of their duty to His Majesty's crown and dignity.

[Proclamation by the Governor of Virginia (John, Earl of Dunmore), 17 November 1775, Peter Force, *American Archives*, Series IV.]

•

*General Clinton began enlisting fugitive slaves to work on
fortifications and perform other labor. An estimated 1,000 men,
including those recruited by Lord Dunmore, served with
British forces in order to gain their freedom.*

Forty or fifty Negroes had also found means to get on board the shipping in this [Cape Fear] River previous to my arrival and as I conceived they might be very useful to us for many purposes in these climates I have determined to form a company of them with an intention of employing them as pioneers and on working parties. . . .

[Letter, Maj. Gen. Henry Clinton to Maj. Gen. William Howe, 20 April 1776, William Bell Clark and William James Morgan, eds., *Naval Documents of the American Revolution, 1775–1776*, Washington, DC, 1964–72.]

*The Continental Army adopted a restrictive policy that
disappointed those blacks who already had enlisted.*

10th. Whether it will be advisable to enlist any Negroes in the new army? or whether
there be a distinction between such as are slaves and those who are free?

Agreed, unanimously, to reject all slaves, and, by a great majority, to reject
Negroes altogether.

[Agenda Item, Council of War of the Continental Army, 8 October 1775, Peter Force, *American
Archives*, Series IV.]

●

*Although the slaveholding colonies might object, Massachusetts
had enlisted free blacks as Continental soldiers.*

I am sorry to hear that any prejudice should take place in any of the southern
colonies with respect to the troops raised in this; I am certain the insinuations you
mention are injurious; if we consider with what precipitation we were obliged to collect
an army. The regiments at Roxbury, the privates are equal to any that I served with in
the last war, very few old men, and in the ranks are few boys, our fifers are many of them
boys, we have some Negroes, but I look on them in general equally serviceable with
other men, for fatigue and in action. . . .

[Letter, Brig. Gen. John Thomas to John Adams, 24 October 1775, John Adams Papers, Massachusetts
Historical Society, reprinted courtesy of the Massachusetts Historical Society.]

●

*South Carolina approved the use of slaves as military laborers.
During the following summer, slaves helped construct
fortifications to defend Charleston and were "employed without
arms" at the batteries defending the city.*

On motion, resolved, that the colonels of the several regiments of militia throughout
the colony have leave to enroll such a number of able male slaves, to be employed as
pioneers and laborers, as public exigencies may require; and that a daily pay of seven
shillings and six pence be allowed for the service of each such slave while actually
employed.

[Resolution of the Provincial Congress of South Carolina, 20 November 1775, Peter Force, *American
Archives*, Series IV.]

*As promised, Lt. Gen. George Washington wrote the
Continental Congress on the following day, advising that he
would begin recruiting free blacks and reenlisting those
"discarded" as a result of the recent ban on accepting Negroes.
Some recruiters apparently signed up slaves as well as free
blacks, for an order specifically banning the enlistment of
"Boys—Old Men—or Slaves" was issued in February 1776.*

As the general is informed, that numbers of free Negroes are desirous of enlisting, he gives leave to the recruiting officers to entertain them, and promises to lay the matter before the Congress, who he doubts not will approve of it.

[General Orders, Headquarters of the Continental Army, 30 December 1775, John C. Fitzpatrick, ed., *The Writings of Washington from the Original Manuscript Sources,* Washington, DC, 1931–41.]

●

*Although Lord Stirling, a Continental general, sought only
the services of black laborers, the New York legislature in 1781
authorized the enlistment even of slaves in Continental Army
units to be raised for the defense of the northern frontier.*

The commanding officer of every corps of the troops in this city, by whatever denomination they are distinguished, are to parade tomorrow morning at nine o'clock, in the common, without firearms, but with all the shovels, spades, pickaxes, and hoes, they can provide themselves with. All the male Negroes in town are to parade at the same time and place.

It is intended to employ one-half of the inhabitants every other day, changing, at the works for the defense of this city; and the whole of the slaves every day, until this place is put in a proper posture of defense.

[Report, William Alexander, Lord Stirling, to the president of Congress (John Hancock), 14 March 1776, Peter Force, *American Archives*, Series IV.]

●

*Although the committee recommended the creation of a black
Continental regiment, the council rejected the plan.*

That there be one regiment of volunteers raised to serve during the war as soon as possible, to consist of the same number of officers and privates as those of a Continental regiment: that one sergeant in each and every company, and every higher officer in said

[Report of the Joint Legislative Committee, State of Massachusetts Bay, 18 April 1778, Manuscript Archives of Massachusetts, vol. 199, p. 85 in *The Negro in the Military Service of the United States, 1639–1886*, Microfilm M858, National Archives, Washington, DC.]

regiment, shall be white men, that all the other sergeants, inferior officers, and privates shall be Negroes, mulattoes, or Indians: that no men shall be enlisted, but only such as are able bodied: that every servant, as well as others, so enlisting, and having liberty from his master or mistress so to do, shall be entitled to and receive all the bounties, wages, and encouragements allowed by the Congress to any soldiers. . . ; and shall, upon passing muster, be from the service of his master or mistress . . . absolutely free. . . ; and in case such servant shall by sickness or otherwise be rendered unable to maintain himself, he shall not be chargeable to his master or mistress, but shall be supported at the expense of this state. That all such masters and mistresses, giving liberty as aforesaid to his or her servant to enlist, and who shall enlist as aforesaid, shall be allowed . . . a sum not exceeding for the most valuable servant, and in just proportion for others of less value.

●

Although accepting individual blacks for Continental service, Massachusetts now barred them from the militia, an act that possibly reflected the increasing social and political role of the militia muster. By the end of the war, the battleground had shifted southward, and Massachusetts no longer found it necessary to recruit extensively among blacks.

And be it further enacted by the authority aforesaid, that that part of the militia of this commonwealth commonly called the Training Band, shall be constituted of all the able-bodied male persons therein, from sixteen years old to fifty, excepting . . . Negroes, Indians, and mulattoes . . . that all the male persons from sixteen years of age to sixty-five, not included in that part of the militia called the Training Band, and exempted . . . from common and ordinary training, shall constitute an alarm list in the commonwealth; excepting . . . Negroes and mulattoes.

[Act of the General Court of Massachusetts, 3 March 1781, *Acts and Laws of the Commonwealth of Massachusetts* in *The Negro in the Military Service of the United States, 1639–1886*, Microfilm M858, National Archives, Washington, DC.]

In his letter to Jones, a Virginia judge and member of the
Continental Congress, Madison recommended that the
commonwealth, besides using blacks as drummers and fifers to
help recruit whites, should offer freedom to those slaves willing
to fight.

I am glad to find the legislature persist in their resolution to recruit their line of the army for the war; though without deciding on the expediency of the mode under their consideration, would it not be as well to liberate and make soldiers at once of the blacks themselves, as to make them instruments for enlisting white soldiers? It would certainly be more consonant to the principles of liberty, which ought never to be lost sight of in a contest for liberty; and with white officers and a majority of white soldiers, no imaginable danger could be feared from themselves, as there certainly could be none from the effect of the example on those who should remain in bondage; experience having shown that a freedman immediately loses all attachment and sympathy with his former fellow slaves.

[Letter, James Madison to Joseph Jones, 28 November 1780, *Madison Papers*, vol. 1, p. 68 in *The Negro in the Military Service of the United States, 1639–1886*, Microfilm M858, National Archives, Washington, DC.]

•

Although large-scale recruiting of slaves proved too radical a
measure, some Virginia units either enlisted slaves, with
permission of their masters, or accepted them as substitutes
for whites. Those slaves who entered military service in this
manner gained their freedom.

Whereas it hath been represented to the present General Assembly, that during the course of the war, many persons in this state had caused their slaves to enlist in certain regiments or corps raised within the same, having tendered such slaves to the officers appointed to recruit forces within the state, as substitutes for free persons, whose lot or duty it was to serve in such regiments or corps, at the same time representing to such recruiting officers that the slaves so enlisted by their direction and concurrence, were free men; and it appearing further to this assembly, that on the expiration of the term of enlistment of such slaves, that the former owners have attempted again to force them to return to a state of servitude, contrary to the principles of justice, and to their own solemn promise. And whereas it appears just and reasonable that all persons enlisted as aforesaid, who have faithfully served agreeable to the terms of their enlistment, and have thereby contributed towards the establishment of American liberty and independence should enjoy the blessings of freedom as a reward for their toils and labors.

[Section 1, Act of Virginia Legislature at Session begun 20 October 1783, Jefferson, *The Laws of Virginia*, vol. 6, Session October, 1783, pp. 6–7 in *The Negro in the Military Service of the United States, 1639–1886*, Microfilm M858, National Archives, Washington, DC.]

The Rhode Island black battalion of some two hundred men, commanded by Col. Christopher Greene, a white officer, served from July 1778 until June 1780. At that time, the unit was disbanded and the soldiers reassigned either to a black company or to other line organizations. An objection to enlisting slaves that was raised by some legislators did not prevail. Those slaves who served received their freedom.

It is voted and resolved, that every able-bodied Negro, mulatto, or Indian man-slave, in this state, may enlist into either of the said two battalions, to serve during the continuance of the present war with Great Britain. That every slave so enlisting shall be entitled tò and receive, all the bounties, wages, and encouragements allowed by the Continental Congress, to any soldier enlisting into their service.

It is further voted and resolved, that every slave, so enlisting shall . . . immediately be discharged from the service of his master or mistress, and be absolutely free, as though he had never been encumbered with any kind of servitude or slavery. And in case such slave shall, by sickness or otherwise, be rendered unable to care for himself, he shall not be chargeable to his master or mistress; but shall be supported at the expense of the state. . . .

It is further voted and resolved, that there be allowed, and paid by this state, to the owner, for every slave so enlisting, a sum according to his worth. . . .

[Proceedings of the General Assembly of the State of Rhode Island and Providence Plantations, February Session, 1778, *Rhode Island Colonial Records*, vol. 8, p. 358 in *The Negro in the Military Service of the United States, 1639–1886*, Microfilm M858, National Archives, Washington, DC.]

●

Connecticut refused to follow the example of Rhode Island in forming black units but instead recruited hundreds of individual blacks, free and slave, to serve in militia or Continental forces.

You will see by the report of [the General Assembly] committee, May, 1777, that Gen. [James M.] Varnum's plan for the enlistment of slaves had been anticipated in Connecticut; with this difference, that Rhode Island adopted it, while Connecticut did not.

The two states reached nearly the same results by different methods. . . .

In point of fact, some hundreds of blacks—slaves and freemen—were enlisted in the regiments of the state troops and of the Connecticut line. How many, it is impossible to tell; for from first to last, the company or regimental rolls indicate no distinction of color.

[Statement, J. Hammond Trumbull, ed., *Public Records of the Colony of Connecticut*, quoted in Livermore, *An Historical Research*, in *The Negro in the Military Service of the United States, 1639–1886*, Microfilm M858, National Archives, Washington, DC.]

*Congress proposed that Georgia and South Carolina recruit
slaves, who seemed more likely than free whites to serve for long
periods with Continental forces. Although neither state would
agree to the plan, a few slaves from each of the two states did
enter the Continental Army through arrangements between their
masters and the recruiters.*

The committee . . . appointed to take into consideration the circumstances of the southern states, and the ways and means for their safety and defense, report—

That the circumstances of the army will not admit of the detaching of any force for the defense of South Carolina and Georgia. That the continental battalions of those two states are not adequate to their defense. That the three battalions of North Carolina Continental troops, now on the southern service, are composed of drafts from the militia for nine months only, which terms, with respect to a great part of them, will expire before the end of the campaign. That all the other force now employed for the defense of the said states consists of militia who, from the remoteness of their habitations and the difficulties attending their service, ought not to be relied on for continued exertions, and a protracted war. That the state of South Carolina, as represented by the delegates of the said state, and by Mr. [John] Huger [a member of the South Carolina Committee of Safety], who has hither at the request of the governor of the said state, on purpose to explain the particular circumstances thereof, is unable to make any effectual efforts with militia, by reason of the great proportion of citizens necessary to remain at home, to prevent insurrections among the Negroes, and to prevent the desertion of them to the enemy. That the state of the country, and the great numbers of those people among them, expose the inhabitants to great danger from the endeavors of the enemy to excite them either to revolt or desert. That it is suggested by the delegates of the said state, and by Mr. Huger, that a force might be raised in the said state from among the Negroes, which would not only be formidable to the enemy, from their numbers and the discipline of which they readily admit, but would also lessen the danger from revolts and desertions, by detaching the most vigorous and enterprising from among the Negroes. That as this measure may involve inconvenience peculiarly affecting the states of South Carolina and Georgia, the committee are of opinion that the same should be submitted to the governing powers of the said states; and if the said powers shall judge it expedient to raise such a force, that the United States ought to defray the expense thereof. . . .

[Proceedings of the Continental Congress, 29 March 1779, *Secret Journals of Congress, Domestick Affairs, 1775–1788*, p. 107 in *The Negro in the Military Service of the United States, 1639–1886*, Microfilm M858, National Archives, Washington, DC.]

*Maryland abandoned a plan to recruit 750 blacks, free and
slave, in a special regiment. Individual blacks continued to enlist,
however, and also to serve as pilots or crew members on board
ships sailing in coastal waters.*

The Assembly is up and abandoned the design of raising a regiment of blacks, if the
assembly had adopted that plan of defense, we should have paid the greatest
deference to your recommendation of Major McPherson [as a regimental officer].

[Letter, Maryland Council to Marquis de Lafayette, 3 July 1781, William H Browne *et al*., eds.,
Archives of Maryland, Baltimore, 1883–1952.]

●

*A number of blacks, free and slave, served in Continental
or state warships or on board privateers. Also, black pilots
sometimes guided American ships through coastal waters,
especially among the rivers, creeks, and inlets of
Chesapeake Bay.*

Whereas information has been given to this board that there are five Negroes lately
captured and carried into Plymouth who are willing to serve this state in one of the
state vessels, as also a Negro man called Jack now on board the guard ship within this
harbor, therefore ordered that Captain Hallet commander of the brigantine *Active* be
and hereby is directed to send some officer to Plymouth for the purpose of enlisting
those five Negroes provided said Negroes are yet free and willing to enlist on board
said brigantine as seamen, as also, the Negro man Jack a prisoner on board the guard
ship provided he is also willing to serve on board said brigantine and if he shall so
incline the commissary of prisoners is hereby directed to liberate him.

[Instructions, Council of the State of Massachusetts Bay, 18 May 1779, *Massachusetts Muster Rolls*,
vol. 40, p. 24 in *The Negro in the Military Service of the United States, 1639–1886*, Microfilm M858, National
Archives, Washington, DC.]

●

*The limitations of membership in the militia to adult, white
males reflected the traditional relationship between military
service and citizenship.*

That each and every free able-bodied white male citizen of the respective states,
resident therein, who is or shall be of the age of eighteen years and under the age of
forty-five years ... shall severally and respectively be enrolled in the militia by the
captain or commanding officer of the company, within whose bounds such citizen
shall reside....

[Militia Act of 8 May 1792, c. 33, U.S., *Statutes at Large*, vol. 1, p. 272.]

The following was part of the recruiting instructions issued for
the Marine Corps in 1798. The marines remained a racially
exclusive service until World War II.

3. No Negro, mulatto[,] or Indian to be enlisted nor any description of men except natives of fair conduct or foreigners of unequivocal characters for sobriety and fidelity. (Any recruiting officer enlisting a vagrant transient person, who shall desert, shall reimburse out of his pay the loss sustained by such desertion.)

[Letter, Sec. of War Henry Knox to lieutenant of marines, frigate *Constellation*, 16 March 1798, *Naval Documents Related to the Quasi War between the United States and France*, Washington, DC, 1935.]

●

The naval war with France did not create a recruiting problem
sufficient to justify tapping the reservoir of black manpower.

As you have been appointed a lieutenant of the schooner *Retaliation*, now preparing for a cruise, it is necessary that you should recruit with all possible expedition, the requisite number of men, say thirty able seamen and twenty landsmen and boys. You will be careful not to enlist any but healthy[,] sound people, and that no indirect or forcible measures be used to induce them to enter into the service. No Negroes or mulattoes are to be admitted, and as far as you can judge, you must be cautious to exclude all persons whose characters are suspicious.

[Letter, Sec. of the Navy Benjamin Stoddert to Lt. Henry Kenyon, US Navy, 8 August 1798, *Naval Documents Related to the Quasi War between the United States and France*, Washington, DC, 1935.]

●

Louisiana had maintained three companies of black militia,
totaling about three hundred free men during Spanish rule.
Following the rapid transition from Spanish to French to
American administration, some members of these units applied
for similar service under the flag of the United States. Black
militia companies survived in the American territory of
Louisiana until 1805, when they were omitted from the militia
list, allegedly because of poor discipline.

To His Excellency William C. C. Claiborne: Governor General and Intendant of Louisiana.

We the subscribers [fifty-five in number], free citizens of Louisiana beg leave to approach your excellency with sentiments of respect and esteem and sincere attachment to the government of the United States.

[Address from the Free People of Color, January 1804, *Territorial Papers of the United States, Territory of Orleans, 1805–1812*, Washington, DC, 1940.]

We are natives of this province and our dearest interests are connected with its welfare. We therefore feel a lively joy that the sovereignty of the country is at length united with that of the American republic. We are duly sensible that our personal and political freedom is thereby assured to us for ever, and we are also impressed with the fullest confidence in the justice and liberality of the government towards every class of citizens which they have here taken under their protection.

We were employed in the military service of the late government, and we hope we may be permitted to say, that our conduct in that service has ever been distinguished by a ready attention to the duties required of us. Should we be in like manner honored by the American government, to which every principle of interest as well as affection attaches us, permit us to assure your excellency that we shall serve with fidelity and zeal. We therefore respectfully offer our services to the government as a corps of volunteers agreeable to any arrangement which may be thought expedient.

We request your excellency to accept our congratulations on the happy event which has placed you at the head of this government, and promises so much real prosperity to the country.

New Orleans[,] January 1804

●

War between the United States and Great Britain again
made black free men an attractive source of military manpower.

Be it enacted by the Senate and House of Representatives of the state of Louisiana in General Assembly convened, that the governor of the state of Louisiana is authorized by virtue of the present act, to organize a corps of militia, as soon as he may judge proper, for the defense of this state, certain free men of color, to be chosen from among the creoles, and from among such as shall have paid a state tax. The commander in chief shall provide for the choice of their officers; provided, however, that their commanding officer shall be a white man; and for the manner of arming them, and he shall prescribe the kind of discipline which to him may appear most conducive to the success and good order of the said corps; provided, always, that the said corps shall not consist of more than four companies, each of which, officers included, shall not consist of more than sixty-four men, and that such as shall enter into said corps must have been for two years previous thereto owners of landed property of at least the value of three hundred dollars.

[An Act to organize a corps of militia for service of the state of Louisiana, as well for its defense as for its police, a certain portion of the chosen men from among the free men of color, 6 September 1812, *Acts of the General Assembly of Louisiana*, first session, 1812, in *The Negro in the Military Service of the United States, 1639–1886*, Microfilm M858, National Archives, Washington, DC.]

*The "two corps of colored volunteers" that responded to
Andrew Jackson's proclamation and helped defend New
Orleans did not "disappoint the high hopes that were formed
of their courage and perseverance in the performance of their
duty." General Jackson addressed his call to all free blacks
rather than to the propertied few who were eligible for the
militia.*

Through a mistaken policy you have heretofore been deprived of participation in the glorious struggle for national rights in which our country is engaged. This shall no longer exist.

As sons of freedom you are now called upon to defend our most inestimable blessing. As Americans your country looks with confidence to her adopted children for a valorous support, as a faithful return for the advantages enjoyed under her mild and equitable government. As fathers, husbands, and brothers, you are summoned to rally round the standard of the eagle, to defend all which is dear in existence.

Your country, although calling for your exertions, does not wish to engage you in her cause without amply remunerating you for the services rendered. Your intelligent minds are not to be led away by false representations. Your love of honor would cause you to despise the man who should attempt to deceive you. In the sincerity of a soldier, and the language of truth I address you.

To every noble hearted, generous, freeman of color, volunteering to serve during the present contest with Great Britain, and no longer, there will be paid the same bounty in money and lands now received by the white soldiers of the United States, viz: $124 in money, and 160 acres of land. The noncommissioned officers and privates will also be entitled to the same monthly pay and daily rations and clothes furnished to any American soldier.

On enrolling yourselves in companies, the major general commanding will select officers for your government, from your white fellow citizens. Your noncommissioned officers will be appointed from among yourselves.

Due regard will be paid to the feelings of freemen and soldiers. You will not, by being associated with white men, in the same corps, be exposed to improper comparisons or unjust sarcasm. As a distinct independent battalion or regiment, pursuing the path of glory, you will, undivided, receive the applause and gratitude of your countrymen.

To assure you of the sincerity of my intentions and my anxiety to engage your invaluable services to our country, I have communicated my wishes to the governor of Louisiana, who is fully informed as to the manner of enrollment, and will give you every necessary information on the subject of this address.

[Proclamation to the free colored inhabitants of Louisiana, 21 September 1814, *Niles' Weekly Register*, 3 December 1814 in *The Negro in the Military Service of the United States, 1639–1886*, Microfilm M858, National Archives, Washington, DC.]

Since warships and privateers bore the brunt of the early fighting,
blacks were needed to fill out crews. The regulation reflected
shipboard reality.

Be it enacted by the Senate and House of Representatives of the United States of America in Congress assembled, that from and after the termination of the war in which the United States are now engaged with Great Britain, it shall not be lawful to employ on board any of the public or private vessels of the United States any person or persons except citizens of the United States, or persons of color, natives of the United States.

[Section 1 of An Act for the regulation of seamen on board the public and private vessels of the United States of 3 March 1813, c. 42, U.S., *Statutes at Large.*]

●

Besides banning slaves from naval vessels, the Board of Navy
Commissioners sought to prevent competition at shore
installations between slaves and free artisans.

No slaves or Negroes are to be employed in the navy yards of the United States, without express orders of the secretary of the navy or of the Board of Navy Commissioners.

Slaves are not to be borne on the books of the vessels of the United States; nor shall any person compose part of the crew of any vessel of the United States, who has not voluntarily entered the service.

[Rules, Regulations, and Instructions for the Naval Service, 20 April 1818, 15th Cong., 1st sess., *American State Papers, Naval Affairs.*]

●

This policy remained in effect until the Civil War. However,
hundreds of blacks, many of them slaves, were employed by
the military as laborers, teamsters, artisans, cooks, or officers'
servants at army posts and fortifications.

No Negro or mulatto will be received as a recruit of the army; . . .

[General Order, War Department, Adjutant and Inspector General's Office, 18 February 1820, *The Negro in the Military Service of the United States, 1639–1886*, Microfilm M858, National Archives, Washington, DC.]

The 5-percent quota, set forth by Acting Sec. of the Navy Isaac
Chauncey, remained official policy until the Civil War, though
probably exceeded in practice.

Frequent complaints having been made of the number of blacks and other colored persons entered at some of the recruiting stations, and the consequent underproportion of white persons transferred to seagoing vessels, it is deemed proper to call your attention to the subject, and to request that you will direct the recruiting officer at the station under your command, in future, not to enter a greater proportion of colored persons than 5 percent of the whole number of white persons entered by him weekly or monthly; and under no circumstances whatever to enter a slave.

[Circular, Department of the Navy, 13 September 1839, *Regulations, Circulars, Orders, and Decisions for the Guide of Officers of the Navy of the United States,* Washington, DC, 1851.]

CHAPTER TWO
CIVIL WAR AND EMANCIPATION

The Civil War again created a manpower crisis, which led to the enlistment of blacks—this time in large numbers—into the military and naval services. At first, Union authorities saw little military value in the black population and thousands of northern free blacks, responding to Pres. Abraham Lincoln's call to defend the republic, were rejected by recruiters. In part, this rejection was due to the fact that white volunteers seemed sufficient in both numbers and enthusiasm to defeat the rebellion. In part, it stemmed from the divisive nature of the slavery question in the north, where preserving the union, rather than freeing slaves, was the principal war aim at this time. Maj. Gen. John C. Frémont, commander of the Department of the West and an ardent abolitionist, sought to punish rebellion by freeing slaves owned by secessionists in the territory overrun by his troops. In contrast, Maj. Gen. Thomas W. Sherman, commanding Union troops at Port Royal, South Carolina, promised that his forces would not disturb the South's "peculiar institution."

Despite Tim Sherman's assurances, the advance of Union arms could not help but undermine slavery, creating legions of refugees, contraband of war at the disposal of the invaders. Though reluctantly in some instances, Union commanders came to welcome these persons as laborers, sources of military intelligence, and ultimately as combat troops.

From wielding a shovel or serving as scout to actually bearing arms proved a difficult transition for the black American. Even the navy, which had accepted free Negroes for about a half century, proved reluctant to enlist recently freed slaves, except for menial work at reduced pay. The Marine Corps persisted in its policy of enlisting whites only. Not until the summer of 1862, when a new call for volunteers proved disappointing and before the Union was willing to resort to conscription, did the Congress authorize the army to enlist blacks, paying them less than their white counterparts.

Among those to take advantage of the policy change were Maj. Gen. David Hunter, a professional soldier, and veteran abolitionists like Thomas Wentworth Higginson of Massachusetts and James Lane of Kansas. In occupied Louisiana, Maj. Gen. Ben Butler tried to resist, but Brig. Gen. Dan Ullman arrived from Washington with instructions to recruit blacks. These first black units fought with skill and gallantry on the St. Mary's River in Georgia, at Centre Creek, Missouri, or at Port Hudson, Mississippi, actions that encouraged further recruiting.

Of all these early units, the most celebrated was the 54th Massachusetts, a regiment raised by another of the abolitionists, Robert Gould Shaw. Killed in battle before Fort Wagner, South Carolina, in 1863, he would share a common grave with scores of his black soldiers.

Like Frémont in Missouri, General Hunter freed the slaves in that part of the South under his control. President Lincoln decided, however, that Hunter's general emancipation, announced in the spring of 1862, was ill-timed, since liberation of the slaves might yet cause the border states—where Union sentiment, though not support for abolition, remained strong—to cast their lot with the Confederacy. The battle of Antietam, fought in September, checked a southern invasion of Maryland and enabled Lincoln to follow the lead of Congress and emancipate the slaves in those states still in a state of rebellion on 1 January 1863.

The president's Emancipation Proclamation increased the tempo of recruitment among free blacks in the North and liberated slaves in the South. Except for Shaw's regiment and one other, all black units were administered by the War Department's new Bureau of Colored Troops. Within a year, soldiers, though not sailors, of equal rank were receiving equal pay, regardless of race. When the war ended, some two hundred thousand blacks had worn the uniform of the United States, most of them serving in combat units, though some were chaplains or medical orderlies. About thirty-eight thousand black soldiers died in battle or from disease or injury.

The wartime contributions of blacks did not gain acceptance for them, especially among urban workingmen. To these laborers, the freemen represented possible competition. When the Union cause resorted to a draft, war weariness and resentment toward the newly freed slaves combined to trigger the violence that rocked New York City in the summer of 1863.

Fear of armed blacks, whether free or slave, caused the Confederacy to ignore a potentially valuable source of manpower and adopt policies that would alienate public opinion outside the South. Although slaves served as military laborers prior to the bombardment of Fort Sumter, the Confederate States rejected any combat role for Negroes, spurning even the services of Louisiana's free black militia, which traced its origins beyond General Jackson's defense of New Orleans in the War of 1812. Indeed, since the invading black forces might inspire a slave uprising, the Confederate Congress vowed to enslave captured Negro soldiers and decreed the death penalty for white Union officers captured while leading black units. Following their successful attack on Fort Pillow, Tennessee, Confederate troops under Nathan Bedford Forrest, a former slave dealer, massacred black Union soldiers attempting to surrender, an outrage that not only failed to discourage Negro volunteers but caused widespread moral revulsion.

Early in 1864, Confederate Maj. Gen. Pat Cleburne challenged the conventional wisdom, urging that some slaves be granted freedom in return for military service. He believed that such a move, besides obtaining sorely needed manpower, would win the support of those elements in Britain and France that sympathized with the southern cause but hated slavery. A year passed before Confederate authorities could bring themselves to endorse so radical a scheme and, by that time, both secession and slavery were doomed.

Maj. Gen. John C. Frémont sought to suppress guerrilla warfare in Missouri by declaring martial law and freeing slaves belonging to supporters of the insurrection. Pres. Abraham Lincoln overruled this emancipation policy, because he felt that the intrusion of the issue of abolition would hinder his efforts to save the Union.

Whereas, Thomas L. Snead, of the city and county of St. Louis, state of Missouri, has been taking active part with the enemies of the United States, in the present insurrectionary movement against the government of the United States; now, therefore, I, John Charles Frémont, major general commanding the Western Department of the Army of the United States, by authority of law, and the power vested in me as such commanding general, declare Frank Lewis, heretofore held to "service or labor" by said Thomas L. Snead, to be free and forever discharged from the bonds of servitude, giving him full right and authority to have, use, and control his own labor, or service, as to him may seem proper, without any accountability whatever to said Thomas L. Snead, or any one to claim by, through, or under him. And this deed of manumission shall be respected and treated by all persons, and in all courts of justice, as the full and complete evidence of the freedom of said Frank Lewis.

In testimony whereof, this act is done at the headquarters of the Western Department of the Army of the United States, in the city of St. Louis, state of Missouri, on the 12th day of September, A.D. 1861, as is evidenced by the departmental seal hereto affixed by my order.

J. C. Frémont,
Major General Commanding

[Deed of manumission, Maj. Gen. John C. Frémont, 12 September 1861, Frank Moore, ed., *The Rebellion Record: A Diary of American Events*, New York, 1866.]

Unlike General Frémont, "Tim" Sherman promised to respect
southern institutions. Actually, Sec. of War Simon Cameron
had hoped that Sherman would emancipate and arm the slaves
in the territory his troops might overrun, but less radical counsels
prevailed, and slavery remained a secondary issue at this
stage of the conflict. Fugitive slaves were to become a problem,
however; within four months Sherman had to care for large
numbers of refugees, victims of "the absence and abandonment
of their disloyal guardians."

In obedience to the orders of the president of these United States of America, I have landed on your shores with a small force of national troops. The dictates of a duty which under the Constitution I owe to a great sovereign state and to a proud and hospitable people among whom I have passed some of the pleasantest days of my life, prompt me to proclaim that we come among you with no feelings of personal animosity; no desire to harm your citizens, destroy your property, or interfere with any of your lawful laws, rights, or your social and local institutions, beyond what the causes herein briefly alluded to, may render unavoidable.

[Proclamation to the People of South Carolina, Brig. Gen. Thomas W. Sherman, 8 November 1861, Frank Moore, ed., *The Rebellion Record: A Diary of American Events*, New York, 1866.]

●

Former slaves, now contraband of war, could be employed as
officers' servants or perform other duties.

All colored persons called "contrabands," employed as servants by officers or others residing within Fort Monroe, or outside of the fort, Camp Hamilton[,] and Camp Butler, will be furnished with their subsistence, and at least eight dollars per month for males, and four dollars per month for females, by the officers or others employing them.

So much of the above-named sums as may be necessary to furnish clothing, to be decided by the commanding officers of Fort Monroe, Camp Hamilton, and Camp Butler, will be applied for that purpose, and the remainder will be paid into the hands of the chief quartermaster, to create a fund for the support of those "contrabands" who are unable to work for their own support.

All able-bodied colored persons who are under the protection of the troops of this department, and who are not employed as servants, will immediately be put to work, in either the engineer's or quartermaster's departments.

By command of Maj. Gen. [John E.] Wool.

William D. Whipple,
Assistant Adjutant General

[Headquarters Department of Virginia, Special Orders No. 72, 14 October 1861, *War of Rebellion Records: A Compilation of the Official Records of the Union and Confederate Armies*, Washington, DC, 1880–91.]

*Because Kentucky was a slave state seeking to remain neutral
in the conflict and because Brig. Gen. William T. ("Cump")
Sherman was attempting to prevent the state's secession,
he attempted to prevent any interference with slavery in that
state. He ordered that slaves seeking refuge with Union forces
should be returned to their masters, pending receipt of orders
to the contrary.*

Headquarters Department of the Cumberland
Louisville, Kentucky, November 8, 1861

Brigadier General McCook, Camp Nevin:
   Sir: I have no instructions from government on the subject of Negroes. My opinion is that the laws of the state of Kentucky are in full force, and that Negroes must be surrendered on application of their masters or agents or delivered over to the sheriff of the county. We have nothing to do with them at all, and you should not let them take refuge in camp. It forms a source of misrepresentation by which Union men are estranged from our cause. I know it is almost impossible for you to ascertain in any case the owner of the Negro. But so it is; his word is not taken in evidence, and you will send them away.
   I am yours,

W. T. Sherman,
Brigadier General, Commanding

[Letter, Brig. Gen. William T. Sherman to Brig. Gen. Alexander McD. McCook, 8 November 1861, *War of Rebellion Records: A Compilation of the Official Records of the Union and Confederate Armies*, Washington, DC, 1880–91.]

●

*Fugitive slaves often served as a source of reliable intelligence
for Union forces operating in the South.*

   The Negroes are our only friends, and in two instances I owe my own safety to their faithfulness. I shall very soon have watchful guards among the slaves on the plantations bordering the [Tennessee] River from Bridgeport to Florence [Alabama], and all who communicate to me valuable information I have promised the protection of my government.

[Letter, Maj. Gen. O. M. Mitchel, commanding Third Division, Camp Taylor, Huntsville, Alabama, to Sec. of War Edwin M. Stanton, 4 May 1862, *War of Rebellion Records: A Compilation of the Official Records of the Union and Confederate Armies*, Washington, DC, 1880–91.]

Maj. Gen. David Hunter's decision to free the slaves in Florida,
Georgia, and South Carolina was judged premature by
President Lincoln, who declared the act "altogether void" and
reserved for himself the authority to emancipate.

The three states of Georgia, Florida[,] and South Carolina, comprising the Military Department of the South, having deliberately declared themselves no longer under the protection of the United States of America and having taken up arms against the said United States it becomes a military necessity to declare them under martial law. This was accordingly done on the 25th day of April, 1862. Slavery and martial law in a free country are altogether imcompatible; the persons in these three states—Georgia, Florida[,] and South Carolina—heretofore held as slaves are therefore declared forever free.

David Hunter
Major General, Commanding

[Headquarters, Department of the South, General Orders No. 11, 9 May 1862, *War of Rebellion Records: A Compilation of the Official Records of the Union and Confederate Armies*, Washington, DC, 1880–91.]

●

This act permitted the enlistment of blacks in the military service
of the United States. Public Law No. 166, passed at the same
time, fixed a lower rate of pay for blacks than for whites in the
same grade, a disparity that prevailed until 1864.

And be it further enacted, that the president of the United States is authorized to employ as many persons of African descent as he may deem necessary and proper for the suppression of this rebellion, and for this purpose he may organize and use them in such manner as he may judge best for the public welfare.

[Section 11 of Public Law No. 160, an Act to suppress insurrection, to punish treason and rebellion, to seize and confiscate the property of rebels, and for other purposes of 17 July 1862, U.S., *Statutes at Large.*]

*This order published President Lincoln's Emancipation
Proclamation. The recent Union victory at Antietam, Maryland,
checked a southern invasion, eased Confederate pressure of the
border states, and enabled the president to follow the lead
of Congress and free at least some slaves.*

I, Abraham Lincoln, president of the United States of America, and commander in chief of the army and navy thereof, do hereby proclaim and declare that hereafter, as heretofore, the war will be prosecuted for the object of practically restoring the constitutional relation between the United States and each of the states, and the people thereof, in which states that relation is or may be suspended or disturbed.

That it is my purpose, upon the next meeting of Congress, to again recommend the adoption of a practical measure tendering pecuniary aid to the free acceptance or rejection of all slave states, so called, the people whereof may not then be in rebellion against the United States, and which states may then have voluntarily adopted, or thereafter may voluntarily adopt, immediate or gradual abolishment of slavery within their respective limits; and that the effort to colonize persons of African descent, with their consent, upon this continent or elsewhere, with the previously obtained consent of the governments existing there, will be continued.

That on the first day of January, in the year of our Lord one thousand eight hundred and sixty-three, all persons held as slaves within any state or designated part of a state, the people whereof shall then be in rebellion against the United States, shall be then, thenceforward, and forever free; and the executive government of the United States, including the military and naval authority thereof, will recognize and maintain the freedom of such persons, and will do no act or acts to repress such persons, or any of them, in any efforts they may make for their actual freedom.

[War Department, Adjutant General's Office, General Orders No. 139, 24 September 1862, *The Negro in the Military Service of the United States, 1639–1886*, Microfilm M858, National Archives, Washington, DC.]

•

Along with Louisiana's Corps d'Afrique, *the 1st Kansas
Volunteers (redesignated as the 79th U.S. Colored Infantry) was
one of the first black units to enter the Union service.*

On the 4th day of August 1862, I was appointed, by the Hon. Sen. J. H. Lane, "a commissioner of recruiting for that portion of Kansas, lying north of the Kansas river," for the purpose of recruiting and organizing a regiment of infantry for the United States service, to be "composed of men of African descent." I accepted the appointment and immediately commenced the work of recruiting by securing the muster-in of recruiting

[Letter, Bvt. Brig. Gen. J. M. Williams to Gen. T. J. Anderson, adjutant general of Kansas, 1 January 1866, *The Negro in the Military Service of the United States, 1639–1886*, Microfilm M858, National Archives, Washington, DC.]

officers with the rank of second lieutenant, by procuring supplies from the Ordnance, Quartermaster's[,] and Commissary Departments, and by establishing in the vicinity of Leavenworth, a camp of rendezvous and instruction.

Capt. H. C. Seaman was about the same time commissioned with like authority, for that portion of Kansas lying south of the Kansas river. The work of recruiting went forward with rapidity; the intelligent portion of the colored people entering heartily into the work, and evincing by their actions a willing readiness to link their fate and share the perils with their white brethren. . . .

Within sixty days, in my district, 500 men were recruited and placed in camp, and I made a request that a battalion be mustered into the United States service. . . .

On the 28th day of October, 1862, a command, consisting of detachments from Captain Seaman's and my recruits, were ordered to Missouri. This force consisted of 225 men, commanded by Captain Seaman. At Island Mound, near Butler, Missouri, this detachment was attacked by a force of 500 rebels, commanded by Colonel Cockerel. After a severe engagement the rebels were defeated with severe loss. Our loss was 8 killed and 10 wounded. Among the killed was Capt. A. I. Crew, a gallant young officer. I joined the command the next morning with a small reinforcement and pursued the rebels for a considerable distance, however without further action. This was I believe the first engagement in the late war in which colored troops were engaged.

●

The War Department dispatched Brig. Gen. Daniel Ullman to
infuse a greater urgency into the recruitment of blacks in
Louisiana.

General: By direction of the secretary of war, you are hereby authorized to raise a battalion (six companies) of Louisiana Volunteer Infantry, to be used for scouting purposes; to be recruited in that state, and to serve for three years or during the war. . . . The recruitment will be conducted in accordance with the rules of the service, and the orders of the War Department, and by the said department all appointments of officers will be made. . . .

[Letter, Ass't. Adj. Gen. Thomas M. Vincent to Brig. Gen. Daniel Ullman, 24 March 1863, *The Negro in the Military Service of the United States, 1639–1886*, Microfilm M858, National Archives, Washington, DC.]

Writing almost a quarter-century after the war, Ullman
recounted, and quite possibly dramatized, his contributions
to Lincoln's Emancipation Proclamation and his role in
recruiting black troops for Louisiana's Corps d'Afrique.

Having a personal acquaintance with Mr. Lincoln, I considered it my duty to call upon the president soon after my arrival in Washington. Among other matters he desired very much to learn from me what the effect of his letter of the 22d of September [1862], respecting a proclamation of freedom, was upon the minds of that portion of Virginia which I had seen. I stated to him my opinions, so far as I had been able to form them from my limited means of observation. And yet I thought them to be correct as indicatory of general public sentiment. My opinions were simply that the effect had been to intensify their exasperated feelings, and some had declared that the sole basis of peace must be separation forever.

Noticing that the mind of the president was preoccupied, I soon took my leave, reserving for a future interview much on this subject which I intended to press upon his attention. Returning to the National Hotel, feeble and exhausted, I retired to my bed. About seven o'clock in the evening of the same day I was roused by a messenger at my door who said the president desired to see me immediately. Of course I reported to the Executive Mansion as soon as practicable, and found Mr. Lincoln waiting for me. The president said that at our interview earlier in the day his mind was so engrossed by other matters that he had not fully appreciated what I had said, and that he desired to have further conversation with me. Of course I went over the ground again and at greater length. My statements seemed to sink deeply into his mind and he questioned me closely. We then took up the subject of his issuing the Proclamation of Freedom on the ensuing 1st of January. I brought to his notice that I had heard that powerful influences were at work to prevent it. I also urged upon him the overruling necessity of arming the liberated slaves. After a long discussion of these points, I took my leave of him, satisfied that I had produced a serious impression on him. . . .

On the 12th of January, 1863, President Lincoln gave me a paper to hand to the secretary of war, Mr. [Edwin M.] Stanton, directing him to authorize me to raise and organize colored troops. Mr. [Hannibal] Hamlin, the vice president, and I immediately called at his office and discussed the subject at considerable length. He requested me to come in the next morning when the necessary papers would be prepared. I did so and he then wrote out a letter of appointment, promoting me to be a brigadier general, US Volunteers, dating it January 13th, 1863. In this he inserted an order directing me to raise and organize in Louisiana a brigade of four regiments of United States Volunteers! This I understand to be the first order ever issued by the government of the United States to organize colored men as soldiers in the Army of the US. Subsequently he gave me an order more explicit, and, at my request, added a fifth regiment of mounted scouts [probably the battalion mentioned in Vincent's letter to Ullman, 24 March 1863]. . . . Public sentiment was far from being ripe on the subject. Not a few officers and men of the volunteer army refused promotion in this service. I received friendly warnings to be on guard against a mob. . . . The work of organizing moved more slowly than was agreeable

---

[Letter, Bvt. Maj. Gen. Daniel Ullman to Adj. Gen. Richard C. Drum, 16 April 1887, *The Negro in the Military Service of the United States, 1639–1886*, Microfilm M858, National Archives, Washington, DC.]

because of the delay in some of the government bureaus in filling requisitions, etc. I required sharp letters from the secretary of war . . . to stimulate the action of several of them. . . . In all these matters Mr. Stanton was sympathetic and energetic. . . .

My officers were met with difficulties at every step [at New Orleans]. These came not only from planters. With a few very honorable exceptions, the whole mass of the officers, not only of the regular army, but where we did not expect it, of the volunteers, had an implacable prejudice, which led them to say and do many foolish things. These latter, however, finally abated their highly wrought feelings when they thought they discovered an opportunity for promotion in this direction. . . .

On the 10th of June, 1863, I issued my General Order, No. 7, . . . It was an appeal to the freedmen to enlist. The effect was very great, and we were proceeding very rapidly when we were brought to a standstill by an order from [Maj.] Gen. [Nathaniel P.] Banks, to forward all my enlisted men, armed and unarmed to Port Hudson, where they were employed on the trenches.

It is worthy of notice that in the assault on Port Hudson on the 27th of May, 1863, there were three regiments of colored troops engaged. They were on our extreme right where the ground was very broken and covered with an exceedingly entangled abattis. They made six or seven charges over the ground against the enemy's works. They were exposed to a terrible fire, and were dreadfully slaughtered. While it may be doubted whether it was wise to so expose them, all who witness these charges agree that their conduct was such as would do honor to any soldiers.

●

*A prewar abolitionist and pioneer in the organizing of black
units, Thomas W. Higginson reported on the role of his
command in the fighting along the St. Mary's River, Florida.
This regiment was redesignated the Thirty-third United States
Colored Infantry.*

I have the honor to report the safe return of the expedition under my command, consisting of 462 officers and men. . . , who left Beaufort [South Carolina] on January 23, on board the steamers *John Adams, Planter,* and *Ben De Ford*:

The expedition has carried the regimental flag and the president's [Emancipation] proclamation far into the interior of Georgia and Florida. The men have been repeatedly under fire; have had infantry, cavalry, and even artillery arrayed against them, and have in every instance come off not only with unblemished honor but with undisputed triumph.

At Township, Florida, a detachment of the expedition fought a cavalry company which met it unexpectedly on a midnight march through pine woods and which completely surrounded us. . . . So complete was our victory that the enemy scattered, and hid in the woods all night, not venturing back to his camp, which was five miles distant, until noon next day, a fact which was unfortunately unknown until too late to follow up our advantage. . . .

[Report, Col. T. W. Higginson, 1st South Carolina Infantry (Union), 1 February 1863, *War of Rebellion Records: A Compilation of the Official Records of the Union and Confederate Armies*, Washington, DC, 1880–91.]

On another occasion a detachment of about two hundred and fifty men, on board the *John Adams*, fought its way forty miles up and down a river regarded by naval commanders as the most dangerous in our department—the St. Mary's—a river left untraversed by our gunboats for many months, as it requires a boat built like the *John Adams* to ascend it successfully. The stream is narrow, swift, winding, and bordered at many places with high bluffs, which blazed with rifle shots. With our glasses, as we approached these points, we could see mounted men by the hundred galloping through the woods from point to point to await us, and though fearful of our shot and shell, they were so daring against musketry that one rebel actually sprang from the shore upon the large boat which was towed at our stern, where he was shot down by one of my sergeants. . . .

No officer in this regiment now doubts that the key to successful prosecution of this war lies in the unlimited employment of black troops. Their superiority lies simply in the fact that they know the country, while white troops do not, and, moreover, they have peculiarities of temperament, position, and motive which belong to them alone. Instead of leaving their homes and families to fight they are fighting for their homes and families, and they show the resolution and the sagacity which a personal purpose gives.

●

Maj. Gen. David Hunter, whose emancipation proclamation
had been rescinded by President Lincoln, reported favorably
on the value and acceptance of black units within the
Department of the South.

I find the colored regiments hardy, generous, temperate, strictly obedient, possessing remarkable aptitude for military training, and deeply imbued with that religious sentiment (call it fanaticism, such as like) which made the soldiers of Oliver Cromwell invincible. They are imbued with a burning faith that now is the time appointed by God, in His all-wise Providence, for the deliverance of their race; and under the incitement of this faith I believe them capable of courage and persistency of purpose which must in the end extort both victory and admiration. Their faith is childlike in its purity, fervor, and pathos. They accept with patience the slights and sneers occasionally thrown upon them by thoughtless or malignant hands, assured that in the day of trial or conflict they possess and stand ready to evince those qualities of true manhood and soldiership which must redeem, in the eyes of all just and generous men, however prejudiced, the misfortune of their darker skins and that condition of utter degradation out of which they feel themselves but now emerging.

And in this connection I am also happy to announce to you that the prejudices of certain of our white soldiers against these indispensable allies are rapidly softening or fading out. . . .

[Letter, Maj. Gen. David Hunter to Secretary of War Stanton, 30 April 1863, *War of Rebellion Records: A Compilation of the Official Records of the Union and Confederate Armies*, Washington, DC, 1880–91.]

Commissioners Robert Dale Owen, James McKaye, and
Samuel Howe surveyed the status of freedmen as refugees,
military laborers, and soldiers.

Section III. Negroes as military laborers.

Even under the present faulty or imperfect system of management, the refugee
Negroes furnish to the government in various localities, in the shape of military labor, the
full equivalent of the rations and the wages they and their wives and children receive. . . .
in all the localities visited by the commission, the demand for able-bodied Negroes as
laborers in the military service has greatly exceeded the supply.

Section IV. Negroes as soldiers.

Docility, earnestness, the instinct of obedience—these are qualities of the highest value
in a soldier—and these are characteristics, as a general rule, of the colored refugees who
enter our lines.

Another point in which these troops when brought under military rule show to
advantage, is in their neatness and care of their persons, uniforms, arms, and equipments,
and in the police of their encampments. Moreover, they are generally skillful cooks and
providers, and exhibit much resource in taking care of themselves in camp. . . .

The spiritual or religious sentiment also strongly characterizes the African race;
developed in somewhat rude phase, it is true, among southern slaves, especially rude in
the cotton states, but powerful, if appealed to by leaders who share it, as an element of
enthusiasm. If the officers of colored regiments themselves feel, and impart, as they
readily may, to their men the feeling that they are fighting in the cause of God and
liberty, there will be no portion of the army, the commission believe, more to be relied on
than Negro regiments.

But with these people, rather than with a more independent race, success depends
on whether their leaders are in sympathy with them, have gained their confidence, and
can arouse their devotion. . . .

In connection with the probabilities of our obtaining the above number [200,000]
of colored troops, it is the duty of the commission to report the fact that in too many
cases, not injustice only, but robbery and other crimes have been committed against
fugitives on first entering our lines. As an example, the assistant superintendent at
Suffolk, Virginia, informed the commission . . . of pickets who sometimes kept refugees
until their masters came for them, and sometimes sent them back, pocketing the reward.
The examples, however, of this offense were not numerous. He stated further that "in
hundreds of cases" the refugees had been robbed by the pickets, chiefly of money, but
occasionally of other articles. Valuable horses, too, and other property were taken from
them by the quartermaster without remuneration to the refugees who brought them in.

[Preliminary Report of the American Freedman's Inquiry Commission to Sec. of War Edwin M.
Stanton, 30 June 1863, *War of Rebellion Records: A Compilation of the Official Records of the Union and
Confederate Armies*, Washington, DC, 1880–91.]

This act provided that a master, if he could demonstrate loyalty
to the United States, would receive compensation for slaves
enrolled in the federal service.

And when a slave of a loyal master shall be drafted and mustered into the service of the United States, his master shall have a certificate thereof: and thereupon such slave shall be free, and the bounty of 100 dollars, now payable by law for each drafted man, shall be paid to the person to whom the drafted person was owing service or labor at the time of his muster into the service. . . . The secretary of war shall appoint a commission in each of the slave states represented in Congress, charged to award to each loyal person to whom a colored volunteer may owe service a just compensation, not exceeding 300 dollars, for each such colored volunteer . . . and every such colored volunteer on being mustered into the service shall be free.

[Section 24 of An Act of 24 February 1864 to amend an act entitled "An Act for enrolling and calling out the National Forces, and for other purposes," approved 3 March 1863, *The Negro in the Military Service of the United States, 1639–1886*, Microfilm M858, National Archives, Washington, DC.]

●

Designed to correct inequities in the treatment of black soldiers,
another act applied retroactively in matters of pay, allowances,
and equipment.

And be it further enacted, that all persons of color who have been or may be mustered into the military service of the United States shall receive the same uniform, clothing, arms, equipments, camp equipage, rations, medical and hospital attendance, pay and emoluments, other than bounty, as other soldiers of the regular or volunteer forces of the United States of like arm of the service, from and after the 1st day of January eighteen hundred and sixty-four; and that every person of color who shall hereafter be mustered into the service shall receive such sums in bounty as the president shall order in the different states and parts of the United States, not exceeding 100 dollars.

[Section 2 of An Act of 15 June 1864, U.S., *Statutes at Large.*]

In 1863, the Provost Marshal General's Bureau took charge
of the recruitment of blacks through the draft, either as
draftees or substitutes. The Bureau for Colored Troops,
however, retained responsibility for recruiting black volunteers.

On the 15th of July, 1865, the date on which the last organization of colored troops was mustered in, there were—
In the service of the United States
    120 regiments of infantry, numbering
        in the aggregate   98,938
Twelve regiments of heavy artillery   15,662
Ten companies of light artillery.   1,311
Seven regiments of cavalry   7,245
    Grand aggregate 123,156
    The foregoing is the largest number of colored troops in service at any one time during the war.
    The entire number of troops commissioned and enlisted in this branch of the service during the war is 186,017.

[Report, Provost Marshal General's Bureau, 17 March 1866, *War of Rebellion Records: A Compilation of the Official Records of the Union and Confederate Armies*, Washington, DC, 1880–91.]

●

Testifying before Commissioners Owen, McKaye, and Howe,
Nathaniel Paige of the New York Tribune *described the attack of*
the 54th Massachusetts, commanded by Colonel Robert Gould
Shaw, at Fort Wagner, South Carolina, 18 July 1863.

The bombardment of Fort Wagner commenced at 11 A.M. from the ironclad fleet and all the shore batteries; the action continued until about an hour before sunset, with occasional replies from Wagner and Sumter; [Maj.] Gen. [Truman] Seymour had command; [Maj.] Gen. [Quincy A.] Gillmore with his staff, the leading colonels, and the correspondents of the press, were on the observatory, two and one-half miles from Sumter and one and three-fourths [miles] from Wagner. An hour before sunset, General Gillmore (who had been most of the time on the observatory) came down and asked General Seymour (who was lying on the ground) if he thought the fort could be taken by assault. General Seymour replied: "I can run right over it. I can camp my whole command there in one night." Said General Gillmore: "Very well, If you think you can take it you have my permission to make the assault. How do you intend to organize your command?" General Seymour answered: "Well, I guess we will let [Brig. Gen. George C.] Strong lead and put those damned niggers from Massachusetts in the advance; we

---

[Testimony Accompanying the Final Report of the American Freedman's Inquiry Commission, 15 May 1864, *The Negro in the Military Service of the United States, 1639–1886*, Microfilm M858, National Archives, Washington, DC.]

may as well get rid of them one time as another. But," he said, "I would give more for my old company of regulars than for the whole damned crowd of volunteers." General Gillmore laughed, but ordered the movement to take place. General Seymour's command were soon formed in line of battle on the beach in front of the town; one and three-fourths miles from Wagner. The division was organized by placing General Strong in advance, Col. [Haldimond S.] Putnam second and [Brig.] Gen. [Thomas G.] Stevenson in reserve. The whole column moved together up to a house about a mile from Fort Wagner, in open daylight and in full view of the enemy from all the forts; there all halted but the brigade of General Strong; he marched up at double quick towards the fort, under a most terrific fire from Forts Gregg and Sumter and all the James Island batteries, losing on the way 150 killed and wounded. The First Brigade assaulted at dusk, the Fifty-fourth Massachusetts in the front. Col. [Robert Gould] Shaw was shot just as he mounted the parapet of the Fort. Notwithstanding the loss of their colonel, the regiment pushed forward, and more than one-half succeeded in reaching the inside of the fort. Three standard-bearers were shot, but the flag was held by the regiment until their retreat. The regiment went into action commanded by their colonel and a full staff of officers; it came out led by Second Lieutenant Higginson—a nephew of Col. H[igginson]—he being the highest officer left to command, all ranking being either killed or wounded. General Strong's brigade was led out by Maj. [Josiah] Plimpton of the Third New Hampshire. General Strong received a mortal wound almost at the commencement of the action; Colonel Shaw was killed, and all the other colonels severely wounded. The First Brigade having been repulsed with such severe loss, the Second Brigade was ordered to move. Colonel Putnam led his brigade into the fort, which he held for half an hour without being reinforced. The enemy succeeded in bringing to bear against him ten or twelve brass howitzers, loaded with grape and canister, when the slaughter became so terrible that he was forced to retire, having lost nearly all of his officers. About fifty of the Fifty-fourth Massachusetts were taken prisoners; none have been exchanged; I believe all reports as to harsh treatment of our colored prisoners are untrue; I have reason to think they are treated as prisoners of war. General Gillmore and staff ridiculed Negro troops; the evident purpose of putting the Negroes in advance was to dispose of the ideas that the Negroes could fight; Major Smith [Lt. Col. E. W. Smith] advised General Gillmore to put the Negroes at the head of the assaulting party and get rid of them. On the previous week [Maj.] Gen. [Alfred H.] Terry had made unfavorable mention of the Fifty-fourth Massachusetts for gallantry on James Island. Many of General Terry's officers spoke of them unfavorably before and favorably since the action referred to [the assault on Fort Wagner].

Slaves had sought refuge on the ships of the Union navy or at
naval installations ashore, prompting officers to seek some
means of putting them to work.

The department finds it necessary to adopt a regulation with respect to the large and increasing number of persons of color, commonly known as contraband, now subsusted at the navy yard and on board ships of war.

These can neither be expelled from the service to which they have resorted, nor can they be maintained unemployed, and it is not proper that they should be compelled to render necessary and regular services without a stated compensation. You are therefore authorized, when their services can be made useful, to enlist them for the naval service under the same forms and regulations as apply to other enlistments. They will be allowed, however, no higher rating than "boys," at a compensation of ten dollars per month and one ration a day.

[Order regarding enlistment of contrabands, Sec. of the Navy Gideon Welles to Flag Officer Louis M. Goldsborough, US Navy, commanding Atlantic Blockading Squadron, *Official Records of the Union and Confederate Navies in the War of Rebellion*, Washington, DC, 1894–1921.]

●

Robert Smalls, an escaped slave, organized and led the
capture of the steamer Planter, *which he handed over to the*
Union blockading squadron off Charleston, South Carolina.
He and his fellow refugees shared some nine thousand dollars
in prize money. Fittingly enough, Planter *soon was carrying*
black troops on expeditions along the coasts of Georgia and
Florida. During World War II, a training facility for black
sailors was named Camp Robert Smalls.

US Ship *Onward*
Off Charleston, SC, May 13, 1862

Sir: I have to report that this morning at sunrise I saw a steamer coming from the direction of Fort Sumter and steering directly for this ship. I immediately beat to quarters and sprung the ship around so as to enable me to bring her broadsides to bear, and had so far succeeded as to bring the port guns to bear, when I discovered that the steamer, now rapidly approaching, had a white flag set at the fore.

The steamer ran alongside and I immediately boarded her, hauled down the flag of truce, and hoisted an American ensign, and found that it was the steamer *Planter,* of

[Report, Acting Volunteer Lieutenant Nickels, US Navy, commanding the USS *Onward, Official Records of the Union and Confederate Navies in the War of Rebellion*, Washington, DC, 1894–1921.]

Charleston, and had successfully run past the forts and escaped. She was wholly manned by Negroes, representing themselves to be slaves.

I herewith place the steamer in your hands for disposition.

Very respectfully, your obedient servant,

> J. F. Nickels
> Acting Volunteer Lieutenant, Commanding
> US Ship *Onward*

Commander E. G. Parrott,
Senior Officer, Commanding Blockading Squadron
off Charleston

●

*Escaped or abandoned slaves might now qualify for a slightly
greater variety of duties in the navy.*

Persons known as "contrabands" will not be shipped or enlisted in the naval service with any higher rating than that of landsman; but if found qualified after being shipped may be advanced by the commanding officer of the vessel in which they serve to the rating of ordinary seaman, fireman, or coal heaver, if their services are needed in such ratings, and will be entitled to the corresponding pay. They will not be transferred from one vessel to another with a higher rating than that of landsman, but if discharged on termination of enlistment, or from a vessel going out of commission, will retain their advanced rating in the discharge.

[Circular regarding enlistment of contrabands, Sec. of the Navy Gideon Welles, 18 December 1862, *Official Records of the Union and Confederate Navies in the War of Rebellion*, Washington, DC, 1894–1921.]

●

*Former slaves enlisting in the Mississippi Squadron served in
the lower grades and performed arduous physical labor.*

> US Mississippi Squadron
> Flagship *Black Hawk,* off Vicksburg, July 26, 1863

Owing to the increasing sickness in the squadron, and the scarcity of men, it becomes necessary for the efficiency of the vessels to use the contrabands to a greater extent than heretofore. The white man cannot stand the southern sun, an exposure to

[Acting Rear Adm. David D. Porter, General Order No. 76 regarding the employment of Negroes on naval vessels, 26 July 1863, *Official Records of Union and Confederate Navies in the War of Rebellion*, Washington, DC, 1894–1921.]

which invariably brings on the disease of this climate, remittent fever. But while employed only on the ordinary duties of the vessels[,] I find that little or no disease exists. The blacks must therefore be used altogether as boats' crews, or for duty requiring exposure to the sun, every precaution being taken to keep them from being taken sick. The blacks must also be used to defend the vessels where there is a deficiency in the crew. This policy is dictated by necessity, and it is believed that in cases of emergency the blacks will make efficient men. It is desirable that none but the best class of Negroes should be taken into the service, and before being shipped they must undergo a physical examination by the surgeon. When qualified, they can be promoted to second-class firemen, coal heavers, landsmen, ordinary seamen, but not to petty officers. Only clothes enough will be issued to them to make them comfortable until they are out of debt, and in all cases they must be kept distinct from the rest of the crew. They can be stationed at guns when vacancies exist, to pass shot and powder, handle handspikes, at train-tackles and side-tackles, pumps, and fire buckets; and can be exercised separately at great guns and small arms.

Great attention will be necessary as respects the cleanliness of the blacks, as they are not naturally clean in their persons.

The policy of the government is to use the blacks, and every officer should do his utmost to carry this policy out.

> David D. Porter
> Acting Rear Admiral,
> Commanding, Mississippi Squadron

●

The Naval War Records Office tried to estimate the number
of blacks who enlisted in the United States Navy during the
Civil War.

There are no specific figures found in this office relating to the number of colored men enlisted in the US Navy, 1861–1865. The total number of enlistments in the navy from March 4, 1861, to May 1, 1865, was 118,044. During the War of 1812 and up to 1860 the proportion of colored men in the ships' crews varied from one-fourth to one-sixth and one-eighth of the total crew. During the Civil War the Negro was enlisted in the squadrons for one year. The regular enlistments at navy yards were for three years. In the absence of specific data it is suggested that as several vessels report during the Civil War having a crew of one-fourth Negroes that the actual number of enlistments must have been about one-fourth of the total number given above, or 29, 511.

[Letter, Sec. of the Navy John D. Long to Rep. C. E. Littlefield, 2 April 1902, Military Archives Division, National Archives, Washington, DC.]

*Black musicians were welcome in the Confederate army, and
slave labor proved valuable. At this early stage of the war,
however, arming either slaves or free blacks seemed too risky.*

The Congress of the Confederate States of America do enact, that whenever colored persons are employed as musicians in any regiment or company, they shall be entitled to the same pay now allowed by law to musicians regularly enlisted: Provided, that no such persons shall be so employed except by the consent of the commanding officer of the brigade to which said regiments or companies may belong.

[An Act of 15 April 1862 for the payment of musicians in the army not regularly enlisted, *War of Rebellion Records: A Compilation of the Official Records of the Union and Confederate Armies*, Washington, DC, 1880–91.]

●

*Although reluctant to arm even the free black militia of
Louisiana, with its long tradition of military service, the
Confederacy and its component states used slaves for military
labor.*

In accordance with an act passed by the legislature of Virginia October 3, 1862, I have the honor to call upon your excellency for 4,500 Negroes to be employed upon the fortifications. Enclosed you will find a letter from Lieutenant Colonel Gilmer, chief of the Engineer Bureau, suggesting the counties on which the call should be made and the apportionment of the draft among them, together with suggestions as to the manner of delivering the slaves to the Engineer Bureau, all of which is submitted for your consideration. It is unnecessary to call your excellency's attention to the importance of a prompt and efficient response to this call, in view of the necessity of completing the works for the defense of Richmond.

[Letter less enclosure, from Pres. Jefferson Davis, to Gov. John Letcher of Virginia, 10 October 1862, *War of Rebellion Records: A Compilation of the Official Records of the Union and Confederate Armies*, Washington, DC, 1880–91.]

A former United States congressman and secretary of the
treasury in the cabinet of Pres. James Buchanan, Cobb became
a leader in the secessionist movement. He warned of the
economic dangers of diverting slaves from agricultural to
military labor. Later, he would oppose the arming of slaves,
declaring that "you cannot make soldiers of slaves, nor slaves of
soldiers."

While writing I will refer to another matter that is creating some unpleasant feeling in our state [Georgia]. [Brig.] Gen. [Hugh] Mercer is impressing Negroes to complete the fortifications at Savannah, and is going to the plantations, where our planters give up their cotton crops to raise corn and provisions for the army and country, and he goes just at the time when they are saving their fodder and when all hands are required. Our planters very naturally say that we ought to take the Negroes working upon railroads, accustomed therefore to such work, and besides the railroads can wait. Corn and fodder cannot wait. In addition to this, the offer has been made to General Mercer to do the whole work by contract at less expense to the government. I mention this matter because it is creating much bad feeling. Our people are willing to make any and all sacrifices, but they like to see reason and common sense in the officials of government.

[Letter, Howell Cobb to Sec. of War George W. Randolph, 5 August 1862, *War of Rebellion Records: A Compilation of the Official Records of the Union and Confederate Armies*, Washington, DC, 1880–91.]

●

Sen. Benjamin Wade of Ohio and Rep. Daniel W. Gooch of
Massachusetts, serving as a subcommittee of the Joint
Committee on the Conduct of the War, investigated the
Confederate attack on Fort Pillow, Tennessee, 12 April 1864.
They concluded that the attackers—led by Lt. Gen. Nathan
Bedford Forrest, one of the founders of the postwar Ku Klux
Klan—took advantage of a flag of truce to move into position for
the assault that culminated in a massacre of black Union
soldiers.

Immediately after the second flag of truce retired, the rebels made a rush from the positions they had so treacherously gained and obtained possession of the fort, raising the cry of "No quarter!" But little opportunity was allowed for resistance. Our troops, black and white, threw down their arms, and sought to escape by running down the steep bluff near the fort, and secreting themselves behind trees and logs, in the bushes, and under the brush—some even jumping into the river, leaving only their heads above the water, as they crouched down under the bank.

Then followed a scene of cruelty and murder without a parallel in civilized warfare, which needed but the tomahawk and scalping knife to exceed the worst atrocities ever

[U.S., Congress, House, Report of the Joint Select Committee on the Conduct of the War, *Fort Pillow Massacre*, 38th Cong., 1st sess., 5 May 1864, H. Rept. no. 65.

committed by savages. The rebels commenced an indiscriminate slaughter, sparing neither age nor sex, white or black, soldier or civilian. The officers and men seemed to vie with each other in the devilish work; men, women, and even children, wherever found, were deliberately shot down, beaten, and hacked with sabers; some of the children not more than ten years old were forced to stand up and face their murderers while being shot; the sick and the wounded were butchered without mercy, the rebels even entering the hospital building and dragging them out to be shot, or killing them as they lay there unable to offer the least resistance. All over the hillside the work of murder was going on; numbers of our men were collected together in lines or groups and deliberately shot; some were shot while in the river, while others on the bank were shot and their bodies kicked into the water, many of them still living but unable to make any exertions to save themselves from drowning. Some of the rebels stood on the top of a hill or a short distance down its side, and called to our soldiers to come up to them, and as they approached, shot them down in cold blood; if their guns or pistols missed fire, forcing them to stand there until they were again prepared to fire. All around were heard cries of "No quarter! No quarter! Kill the damned niggers; shoot them down!" All who asked for mercy were answered by the most cruel taunts and sneers. Some were spared for a time, only to be murdered under circumstances of greater cruelty. . . .

•

Shortly after the capture of Fort Pillow, the Confederate
Congress declared that "to employ Negroes in war against the
Confederate States or to overthrow the institution of African
slavery and bring on servile war in these states" were
inconsistent with the usages of modern war and therefore
deserving of retaliation.

4. That every white person being a commissioned officer or acting as such who during the present war shall command Negroes or mulattoes in arms against the Confederate States or who shall arm, train, organize or prepare Negroes or mulattoes for military service against the Confederate States or who shall voluntarily aid Negroes or mulattoes in any military enterprise, attack or conflict in such service shall be deemed as inciting servile insurrection, and shall if captured be put to death or otherwise punished at the discretion of the court.

7. All Negroes and mulattoes who shall be engaged in war or be taken in arms against the Confederate States or shall give aid or comfort to the enemies of the Confederate States shall when captured in the Confederate States be delivered to the authorities of the state or states in which they shall be captured to be dealt with according to the present or future law of such state or states.

[Confederate States, Congress, Joint resolutions adopted on the subject of retaliation, 30 April–1 May 1863, *War of Rebellion Records: A Compilation of the Official Records of the Union and Confederate Armies,* Washington, DC, 1880–91.]

Maj. Gen. Pat Cleburne and his officers proposed arming the
most trustworthy slaves and emancipating all slaves who
remained loyal throughout the war. Pres. Jefferson Davis
spurned the proposal, however, declaring that such a suggestion
was "productive only of discouragement, destruction, and
dissension."

The president of the United States announces that "he has already in training an army of 100,000 Negroes as good as any troops," and every fresh raid he makes and new slice of territory he wrests from us will add to this force. Every soldier in our army already knows and feels our numerical inferiority to the enemy. Want of men in the field has prevented him from reaping the fruits of his victories and has prevented him from having the furlough he expected after the last reorganization, and when he turns from the wasting armies in the field to look at the source of supply, he finds nothing in the prospect to encourage him. Our single source of supply is that portion of our white men fit for duty and not now in the ranks. The enemy has three sources of supply: first, his own motley population; secondly, our slaves; and thirdly, Europeans whose hearts are fired into a crusade against us by the fictitious pictures of the atrocities of slavery, and who meet no hindrance from their governments in such enterprise, because these governments are equally antagonistic to the institution. In touching the third cause, the fact that slavery has become a military weakness, we may rouse prejudice and passion, but the time has come when it would be madness not to look at our danger from every point of view, and to probe it to the bottom. Apart from the assistance that home and foreign prejudice against slavery has given to the North, slavery is a source of great strength to the enemy in a purely military point of view, by supplying him with an army from our granaries; but it is our most vulnerable point, a continued embarrassment, and in some respects an insidious weakness. Wherever slavery is once seriously disturbed, whether by the actual presence or the approach of the enemy, or even by a cavalry raid, the whites can no longer with safety to their property openly sympathize with our cause. The fear of their slaves is continually haunting them, and from silence and apprehension many of these soon learn to wish the war stopped on any terms. The next step is to take the oath to save property, and they become dead to us, if not open enemies. To prevent raids we are forced to scatter our forces, and are not free to move and strike like the enemy; his vulnerable points are carefully selected and fortified depots. Ours are found wherever there is a slave to set free. All along the lines slavery is comparatively valueless to us for labor, but of great and increasing worth to the enemy for information. It is an omnipresent spy system. . . .

Adequately to meet the causes which are now threatening ruin to our country, we propose . . . that we retain in service for the war all troops now in service, and that we immediately commence training a large reserve of the most courageous of our slaves, and further that we guarantee freedom within a reasonable time to every slave in the South who shall remain true to the Confederacy in this war. As between the loss of independence and the loss of slavery, we assume that every patriot will freely give up the latter. . . .

[Memorial prepared by the commanding general, the corps, division, brigade, and regimental commanders of the Army of Tennessee, 2 January 1864, *War of Rebellion Records: A Compilation of the Official Records of the Union and Confederate Armies*, Washington, DC, 1880–91.]

One thing is certain, as soon as the great sacrifice to independence is made and known in foreign countries there will be a complete change of front in our favor of the sympathies of the world. The measure will deprive the North of the moral and material aid which it now derives from the bitter prejudices with which foreigners view the institution, and its war, if continued, will henceforth be so despicable in their eyes that the source of recruiting will be dried up. It will leave the enemy's Negro army no motive to fight for, and will exhaust the source from which it has been recruited. . . .

The immediate effect of the emancipation and enrollment of Negroes on the military strength of the South would be: to enable us to have armies numerically superior to those of the North, and a reserve of any size we might think necessary; to enable us to take the offensive, move forward, and forage on the enemy. It would open to us in prospective another and almost untouched source of supply, and furnish us with the means of preventing temporary disaster, and carrying on a protracted struggle. It would instantly remove all the vulnerability, embarrassment, and inherent weakness which result from slavery. . . . For many years, ever since the agitation of the subject of slavery commenced, the Negro has been dreaming of freedom, and his vivid imagination has surrounded that condition with so many gratifications that it has become the paradise of his hopes. To attain it he will tempt dangers and difficulties not exceeded by the bravest soldier in the field. The hope of freedom is perhaps the only moral incentive that can be applied to him in his present condition. It would be preposterous then to expect him to fight against it with any degree of enthusiasm, therefore we must bind him to our cause by no doubtful bonds; we must leave no possible loophole for treachery to creep in. The slaves are dangerous now, but armed, trained, and collected in an army they would be a thousand fold more dangerous; therefore when we make soldiers of them we must make free men of them beyond all question, and thus enlist their sympathies also. We can do this more effectually than the North can now do, for we can give the Negro not only his own freedom, but that of his wife and child, and can secure it to him in his old home. To do this we must immediately make his marriage and parental relations sacred in the eyes of the law and forbid their sale. . . . Give him as an earnest of our intentions such immediate immunities as will impress him with our sincerity and be in keeping with his new condition, enroll a portion of his class as soldiers of the Confederacy, and we change the race from a dreaded weakness to a position of strength.

●

The Confederate manpower shortage remained critical,
and the question of arming the slaves could not be ignored. At
last, Gen. Robert E. Lee reluctantly endorsed the idea, but, in
spite of his plea for haste, by the time such a plan went into
effect the war was lost.

Considering the relation of master and slave, controlled by humane laws and influenced by Christianity and an enlightened public sentiment, as the best that can exist between the white and black races while intermingled as at present in this country, I

[Letter. Gen. Robert E. Lee to Hon. Andrew Hunter, 11 January 1865, *War of Rebellion Records: A Compilation of the Official Records of the Union and Confederate Armies*, Washington, DC, 1880–91.]

would deprecate any sudden disturbance of that relation unless it be necessary to avert a greater calamity to both. . . .

I think, therefore, we must decide whether slavery shall be extinguished by our enemies and the slaves be used against us, or use them ourselves at the risk of the effects which may be produced upon our social institutions. My own opinion is that we should employ them without delay. . . .

We should not expect slaves to fight for prospective freedom when they can secure it at once by going to the enemy, in whose service they will incur no greater risk than in ours. The reasons that induce me to recommend the employment of Negro troops at all render the effect of the measures I have suggested upon slavery immaterial, and in my opinion the best means of securing the efficiency and fidelity of this auxiliary force would be to accompany the measure with a well-digested plan of gradual and general emancipation. . . .

I can only say in conclusion that whatever measures are to be adopted should be adopted at once. Every day's delay increases the difficulty. Much time will be required to organize and discipline the men, and action may be deferred until it is too late.

CHAPTER THREE
FREEDOM AND JIM CROW, 1865–1917

The defeat of the Confederacy signaled disbandment of the volunteer regiments that had won the war and their replacement by a small peacetime regular army. Except for the efforts of some Radical Republicans, determined that the freedmen should enjoy equality and share political power in the conquered South, blacks would have been excluded from this postwar force. Six black regiments—soon reduced to four, two of infantry and two of cavalry—were incorporated in the reorganized army. In this instance, the Congressional reformers had imposed their will on a nation largely indifferent to the needs and hopes of the Negro. The radicals proved far more successful in opening the army to blacks than in ensuring their political or social equality.

The black units, like the rest of the Indian-fighting army, endured boredom and battle at a succession of primitive frontier outposts, where the natural environment could prove as deadly as the enemy. Unlike other regiments, however, the black organizations—the Ninth and Tenth Cavalry and the Twenty-fourth and Twenty-fifth Infantry—rarely were assigned to the more desirable locations, Jefferson Barracks in Missouri, for example, or the permanent posts at New Orleans. The black soldier, moreover, might become the victim of racial violence anywhere from the Dakota Territory to the state of Texas. In an effort to improve conditions for black soldiers, General William Tecumseh Sherman suggested breaking up segregated units and reassigning the members throughout the service, as the navy was doing.

Although the navy accepted black recruits for general duty, it had no black officers. Only three black midshipmen entered the US Naval Academy during the three decades following emancipation, and none survived four years of harassment to graduate. Blacks had no greater opportunity to become officers in the regular army. By the end of the nineteenth century, just three black cadets had endured cruel hazing to emerge from the US Military Academy as second lieutenants. One of them, however, Charles Young, attained the grade of lieutenant colonel on the eve of World War I.

By the time the Spanish-American War broke out in 1898, the army had begun enlisting a few blacks in specialties other than infantry and cavalry. Responding to the call to arms were black militia units and wartime regiments of black volunteers. Ironically, the tripling of black strength in the army coincided with the widespread adoption of discriminatory legislation—the Jim Crow laws—throughout the United States. As a result, the very blacks who served in Cuba, Puerto Rico, or the Philippines may well have returned to find a more pervasive racism than they had known previously.

One result of this upsurge of racism was the wave of violence that began with attacks by civilian mobs on black troops during the Spanish-American War. In 1906, the Brownsville incident, in which citizens of that Texas city planted the evidence, resulted in the dismissal from service of 167 black infantrymen. The nadir came at Houston, Texas, during the summer of 1917, when black soldiers rebelled against local Jim Crow laws. This violent outburst, which cost the lives of sixteen whites and four of the soldiers, resulted in the execution for murder of nineteen members of the 24th Infantry.

The navy also felt the impact of Jim Crow, restricting blacks to duty in the boiler room or as servants in the wardroom. Although the navy regulations of the early 1900s did not reflect the change, blacks now served as stokers, boiler tenders, messmen, or stewards, usually eating and bunking separately from the rest of the crew. The navy thus became a segregated service, radically different from the one which General Sherman had proposed as a model for his army a generation earlier.

When the Civil War ended, the US Army stopped accepting
volunteer units, including those made up of blacks, and
contracted to a size compatible with its two immediate
missions—fighting Indians and maintaining federal authority
in the South. Black occupation forces proved unacceptable to
southern leaders, who demanded that all such garrisons be
withdrawn. Despite the inauspicious circumstances, a number
of congressmen, such as Sen. Henry Wilson of Massachusetts,
sought to incorporate black units in the postwar regular army
and asked the opinion of Lt. Gen. Ulysses S. Grant, only to find
him less enthusiastic than they.

Washington, January 12th, 1866

Hon. Henry Wilson
Chairman Military Committee, US S[enate]

In compliance with your request I have looked over your bill for the reorganization
of the army, and find that it differs in some respects from the recommendations I have
made. . . .

I have recommended that the president should be authorized to raise 20,000
colored troops if he deemed it necessary, but I did not recommend the permanent
employment of colored troops because our standing army in time of peace should have
the smallest possible numbers and the highest possible efficiency—aside from the
influence this consideration might have, I know of no objection to the use of colored
troops, and think they can be obtained more readily than white ones. I am not in favor of
colored artillery regiments, because I regard our artillery in time of peace merely as an
artillery school for time of war—in peace infantry can do all the duties of artillery—and
in time of peace I think the efficiency of the artillery as a school will be higher if
composed solely of white troops.

[Letter, Lt. Gen. Ulysses S. Grant to Sen. Henry Wilson, 12 January 1866, *The Negro in the Military
Service of the United States, 1639–1886*, Microfilm M858, National Archives, Washington, DC.]

•

Senator Wilson proposed the establishment of thirteen black
regiments—one of artillery (in spite of General Grant's specific
objections), two of cavalry, and ten of infantry. Among the
strongest objections to the plan were those voiced by Sen.
Willard Saulsbury of Delaware.

Cannot white men be found to enter your army and compose your regiments of cavalry and infantry? Are there not hundreds of thousands of white men in this country
who have for the last three or four years been engaged as soldiers in the army, some of

[U.S., Congress, Senate, *Congressional Globe*, 39th Cong., 1st sess., 9 July 1866.]

them as members of cavalry regiments, seeking employment every day? Time and again, since the commencement of this Congress, I have had white men who have been employed in the army come to me begging me to look for employment for them, that they might get bread and clothing. Do you suppose if the opportunity was given to those men to enter the army again that they would not prefer doing so to being starved or being kept out of employment? There are hundreds and thousands of white men who have been engaged in your army who would gladly accept the place of soldiers in the regular army. I presume there can be no doubt, if it was known generally to the men who have been soldiers that there would be an opportunity for them to enlist in the army under this bill, they would do so. If enlistment offices were opened throughout the United States plenty of such men would be found. It may be said there are offices open now. It may be so in some localities, but it is not so all over the United States. I undertake to say that in my own state a regiment of white soldiers can be found who would gladly enter the army, men out of employment, men seeking employment. . . .

What would be the effect if you were to send Negro regiments into the community in which I live to brandish their swords and exhibit their pistols and guns? Their very presence would be stench in the nostrils of the people from whom I come. A Negro soldier riding up and down the streets and through your country, dressed in a little brief authority, to insult white men! I have no objection to soldiers of the regular army being stationed in any community in which I live. In former years, when I was from home, in other states, I have been in the neighborhood of garrisons, and I have seen the soldiers generally well behaved; but if you were to send and quarter among white people a regiment of Negro soldiers, to march into their villages and to deport themselves as it is most likely they would, what would be the consequence? You must expect collisions. If gentlemen who are so anxious to have Negroes in the Army of the United States will take them among themselves, and provide in the bill that they shall be stationed in their section of the country, I have no objections; but if the object is to station them in my State, I object to it. . . .

Sir, it is peace that I want. I know that in some sections of this country, just as sure as you send these Negro soldiers among the people, there will be strife, ill blood, bad feeling; and that the sending of such soldiers into some communities will lead to nothing but outrage and bloodshed. If you want a standing army, large or small, give us white soldiers and there will be no complaint; but, sir, you must know that in many sections of this country sending Negro soldiers and quartering them in the midst of particular communities would engender strife, and in all probability would lead to bloodshed.

It may be said that I have an antipathy, a hatred to this class of people. It is not true. I do not speak from unkindness toward them. I believe I think as well of them as the rest of you do. I know them as well. But it is for peace, quietness, and the observance of public order that I want your army to be filled up with white men. It will be time enough when you cannot get white soldiers in your regular army to appeal to the patriotism of this superior Negro race; but until there is failure in procuring white soldiers, peace, harmony, and kind feeling demand that no Negroes should be incorporated into the regular army, but that it should be filled up from our own race. I do not wish to argue this question; I presume it would be of no use to do it; but I have felt it due to myself to make this objection.

*The Wilson bill resulted in the establishment of six black
regular army regiments, the Ninth and Tenth Cavalry and the
Thirty-eighth, Thirty-ninth, Fortieth, and Forty-first Infantry.
In March 1869, as part of an army-wide reorganization, the
infantry regiments were combined and redesignated the
Twenty-fourth and Twenty-fifth Infantry (Colored).*

Sec. 3. And be it further enacted, that to the six regiments of cavalry now in service there shall be added four regiments, two of which shall be composed of colored men. . . .

Sec. 4. And be it further enacted, that the forty-five regiments of infantry provided for by this act shall consist of the first ten regiments, of ten companies each, now in service; of twenty-seven regiments, of ten companies each, to be formed by adding two companies each to each battalion of the remaining nine regiments, and of eight new regiments, of ten companies each, four of which shall be composed of colored men. . . .

[War Department, Adjutant General's Office, General Orders No. 56, 1 August 1866, *The Negro in the Military Service of the United States, 1639–1886*, Microfilm M858, National Archives, Washington, DC.]

●

*Several regimental officers of the Tenth Cavalry, of them white
veterans of service on the frontier, anonymously submitted their
comments for use in a history of the unit.*

The employment of the colored man as a soldier, at first, was very discouraging. They lacked in many features so essential to the service, such as clerical ability, want of education, ability for skilled labor, and want of self-reliance. However, these defects were, in a measure, soon overcome, and they excelled in other good qualities. As a general rule, they are willing and obedient, easily disciplined and take pride in being soldiers. They are brave and exhibit patience and endurance under fire. On hard[,] tedious campaigns and forced marches without food or water they seldom, if ever, complain—which is so common among the white soldiers, but as a general thing appear happy and ready to rely upon their officers, and though they may be tired, they will always cheerfully attend to the wants of their officers without the slightest murmur or complaint. They show a pride in being trusted to perform any special duties that may require courage and good judgment, and no troops can be more determined or daring, nor are there any more deserving of the highest commendations. Any doubts as to their being made efficient and trustworthy soldiers should be eliminated. These men as soldiers, if properly officered, and properly handled, will prove second to none as staunch supporters and defenders of the government. The severe tests, to which they have been subjected in the past, and the determined manner in which they have faced the enemy, shows conclusively that they are a success as soldiers, and it is to be hoped that, in the future, their services may receive just recognition as soldiers of the United States Army, the

[Maj. John Bigelow, Jr. USA (retired), "Comments on Leading Colored Troops," *Historical Sketch of the Tenth Cavalry, 1866–1891*, Military Archives Division, National Archives, Washington, DC.]

same as other regiments, and not be referred to as *"Two colored troops of the 10th Cavalry were also engaged"*[1]—this was done at the Cheyenne Agency, I[ndian] T[erritory] when the colored men did all the fighting, sustained nearly all the casualties, and the white troops received the commendations. Many other similar cases have happened. I am now glad to say that I believe such things are of the past. I was once told to take my "Damned Hokes" and camp outside of the post. This was in 1867. This commanding officer was opposed to having a colored soldier sent to him with a verbal message. The colored soldier will follow wherever led, they will go without leading, and will stay with their leader throughout all danger, and never desert him.

An officer to make a successful commander of these men should be ready to listen to their complaints, explain to them the nature of the duties that may be required of them as soldiers, and he will then have no trouble enforcing discipline. All men as soldiers, white or colored, must be made to understand what is required of them, and they must know that obedience and discipline will be enforced in a proper and humane way, that their rights as soldiers will be protected and their personal welfare looked after. When this is done they will be found ready for all emergencies, on all occasions.

---

[1]Emphasis in the original.

●

In commenting for the secretary of war on a letter urging Rep. Ben Butler to muster support for retention of the four black regiments—whose existence was from time to time imperiled—General Sherman indicated that he preferred the navy method of recruiting blacks to serve alongside whites.

Hon. J. D. Cameron
Secretary of War
Washington, DC

FIRST ENDORSEMENT

Headquarters of the Army
Washington, February 21, 1877

Respectfully returned to the honorable secretary of war. I have watched with deep interest the experiment of using blacks as soldiers made in the army since the Civil War, and have on several occasions been thrown with them in Texas, New Mexico, and the plains. General Butler[1] misconstrues me as opposed to the blacks as soldiers for I claim for them equality in the ranks as in civil life—whereas they now constitute separate organizations with white officers. In my former paper on this subject I advised that the word "black" be obliterated from the statute book, that whites and blacks be enlisted

---

[Endorsement by Gen. W. T. Sherman to Sec. of War J. D. Cameron, 1 March 1877, of E. K. Davis to Hon. Benjamin F. Butler, 7 December 1876, *The Negro in the Military Service of the United States, 1639–1886*, Microfilm M858, National Archives, Washington, DC.]

[1]Benjamin F. Butler held the rank of major general, United States Volunteers, as of 16 May 1861.

and distributed alike in the army, as has been the usage in the navy for a hundred years.

General Butler pronounces the blacks a docile, temperate, rugged race peculiarly qualified for being soldiers. Now if soldiers were, as some presume, an idle, lazy set, contented to eat their rations and do nothing, he might be right. But our soldiers are not of that sort; some in our eastern forts may be, but if General Butler will accompany Col. [Nelson A.] Miles, or [Col. Ranald S.] MacKenzie or [Brig. Gen. David] Stanley in camp against the Sioux he will be convinced. We want and must have men of muscle, endurance, will, courage, and that wildness of nature that is liable unless properly directed to result in violence and crime, to combat the enemies of civilization, with whom we have to contend. I honestly think the white race is the best for this, but am willing to take black and white alike on equal terms, certainly a fairer rule than the present one of separating them into distinct organizations.

W. T. Sherman
General

●

In general, black units received assignment to the less desirable posts, as the army bent its knee before the prejudices of white communities. In this case, the Twenty-fourth Infantry exchanged cantonments with a regiment in the Dakota Territory rather than one in Louisiana, Georgia, or Arkansas.

Headquarters Department of the South
Newport Barracks, Kentucky, March 17, 1879

To the
Assistant Adjutant General
Headquarters Military Division Atlantic
Governors Island, N. Y. H. [New York Harbor]

Sir:
Referring to the letter of the adjutant general of the army of the 14th inst., a copy of which reached me this morning from your office and in which my views are desired as to the use of colored troops at New Orleans and Little Rock: I have respectfully to state that the Twenty-fourth Infantry is an excellent regiment and I am glad to learn that it is to have a change from its long and arduous service on the Rio Grande frontier; but I doubt if it would find a station at New Orleans or Little Rock agreeable to officers or men. However senseless and unreasonable it may be regarded, there is no doubt of the fact that a strong prejudice exists at the South against colored troops; and while I am very far from believing that the southern people would permit this prejudice to assume any outward and visible form still there is the danger always to be apprehended, that some reckless or drunken person may abuse one or a party of these soldiers in the streets, or elsewhere. In this event there would certainly be trouble, for these troops are easily

[Letter, with Endorsements, Brig. Gen. Christopher C. Auger to assistant adjutant general, Division of the Atlantic, 17 March 1879, *The Negro in the Military Service of the United States, 1639–1886*, Microfilm M858, National Archives, Washington, DC.]

excited and thoroughly united on any question of insult to their race. I had two very serious disturbances in Texas among the colored troops growing out of these questions and they are liable to occur at any time in the South.

There is another and contingent danger which though more remote, should I think be considered. If quartered in localities where a very large proportion of the inhabitants are colored people and a difficulty of the character suggested above occurred, it would almost certainly involve very many of the colored inhabitants. I know this from experience, and further, in case of any difficulty between the white and colored population growing out of questions of race, and they are not unusual there, it is doubtful if the restraints of a vigorous discipline would wholly prevent the colored soldiers from becoming involved—so strong with them is this question of the rights of their race. While I am very far from suggesting that the government should be controlled in its right and duty to station troops wherever it thinks proper, I am still in doubt as to the wisdom, except in case of necessity, of stationing colored troops at the centers of population in the South; until the relations between the two races there are settled upon a firmer and more satisfactory basis than at present. I hope therefore that it may be decided to send the Twenty-fourth to healthier and pleasanter stations for them, than I believe any posts in the South would be.

Should it however be thought a necessity to send a colored regiment to this department, I believe it would be much better to send it as a whole to Atlanta, and send the headquarters and four companies of the Fifth Artillery to New Orleans.

Referring to General Sherman's suggestion as to sending six companies of the Twenty-fourth to Jackson Barracks [New Orleans] and four to Little Rock, I have respectfully to state that four companies and band are all that can be comfortably quartered at Jackson Barracks, and three companies all that can be comfortably quartered at Little Rock. Mount Vernon [Alabama] is available for ample quarters for two companies and a field officer.

I am,

> Very respectfully
> Your obedient servant
> C. C. Auger
> Brigadier General Commanding

FIRST ENDORSEMENT

Headquarters, Military Division of the Atlantic
Governors Island, N. Y. H. March 24, 1879

General Auger has covered the ground pretty fully and I concur in his views. I, however, give a little additional weight to the hardship that the colored troops themselves would be exposed to by posting them to Louisiana. In further support of the points mentioned by General Auger, I may say that they are, in a change of station, entitled to a change of climate. It would be no improvement in that respect, especially for the [white] officers, to move them from Texas to Louisiana.

> Winfield S. Hancock
> Major General Commanding

SECOND ENDORSEMENT

Headquarters of the Army
Washington, March 25, 1879

This communication is most respectfully submitted to the hon[orable] sec[retary] of war [George W. McCrary]—asking an authoritative decision.

The case is fairly and squarely presented. The Twenty-fourth Infantry has colored enlisted men and white officers [and] has been ten full years on the Rio Grande. Its station ought to be changed. The officers want a change. The men are not consulted. The Tenth Infantry, a white regiment, is to be changed next month for the reason that it has been ten years on the Rio Grande. Shall one rule apply to a white regiment, and another to a black? The Thirteenth Inf[antry] (white) is the only one which can interchange without excessive cost. . . .

W. T. Sherman
General

ENDORSEMENT

War Department April 1, 1879

Respectively referred to the general of the army [Sherman]. The president [Rutherford B. Hayes] is of the opinion that the colored troops should be kept on duty in the South and desires the views of the general as to what measures can be adopted to give their officers duty a part of the time in the north or west.

G. W. McCrary
Secretary of War

Quartermaster General's Office
Washington, DC, March 31, 1879

General W. T. Sherman
Headquarters Army of the US
Washington, DC

General:

I have caused the estimate of the cost of the contemplated movement of troops to be revised as you directed. . . .

Permit me to suggest that while I can well understand that there are political objections to placing the Twenty-fourth, a colored regiment, in mass in New Orleans at this time, [but] there are in the welfare of the men themselves very great objections to sending them to Dakota.

I cannot but think that orders to Dakota will prove to be the death knell of any colored regiment. The colored men will not enlist with the prospect of going to that rigorous climate and I do believe that the effect of the cold will be very injurious to the men whose terms of enlistment do not soon expire.

The only nonpolitical reason at this time for keeping a body of colored troops in the US Army that I know of is their comparative exemption from the epidemics and other diseases of the southern coast.

At Key West, Tortugas, the forts below New Orleans, Pensacola, and St. Augustine and as far up the Mississippi as the yellow fever is virulent, these troops can be very useful.

In Dakota for half the year I doubt whether they will be of any more value than an army of . . . hibernating animals. While their constitutions will not so well resist the influences of cold.

The race is from the tropics, for their ancestors were not brought from the northern or southern extremities of Africa but from the torrid zone almost entirely.

The southern climate suits the men and while the officers doubtless need change, that can better and more cheaply be accomplished by transferring the officers to other regiments, or the men themselves.

> Very respectfully
> Your obedient servant
> M. C. Meigs
> Quartermaster General
> US Army

•

Although three blacks—Henry O. Flipper (1877), John H. Alexander (1887), and Charles Young (1889))—succeeded in graduating from the US Military Academy, racial prejudice was the order of the day, as shown by the comments of Maj. Gen. John Schofield, who chose to blame the victim of a racially motivated hazing, Cadet Johnson C. Whittaker, and not his tormentors.

The outrage which was committed at the cadets' barracks on the 6th of last April, and which has occupied so much of the public attention, deserves notice here mainly for the purpose of correcting erroneous impressions which have prevailed respecting the investigation which followed it, and for the important lesson which that investigation teaches. That matter was promptly investigated by the commandant of cadets, under my direction, in the usual way, and in the only way provided by law or regulations. The fraudulent character of the outrage was fully demonstrated within a very few hours of its discovery. Indeed, the fraud was so transparent that it could not possibly have escaped almost immediate detection. The surgeon reported that he had found the cadet in full

---

[Maj. Gen. J. M. Schofield, Superintendent, United States Military Academy, "The Freedman at West Point and in the Army," *Annual Report of the Secretary of War, 1880.*]

possession of all his faculties, and yet *feigning*[1] unconsciousness when discovered. His alleged injuries from blows upon the nose and head and in his side had been found utterly fictitious. No such blows and no such injuries had been received. The alleged note of warning was at once discovered to be in the familiar and peculiar handwriting of the cadet himself. The resemblance in some parts was so striking as to suggest the possibility of skillful imitation. But closer inspection showed the parts bearing such resemblance to have been written in a natural hand, while some other parts were evidently disguised. There was ample ground for the conviction, *produced in the minds of all who saw the note,*[1] that the cadet himself was the author of it. That conviction, added to the glaring falsehoods and attempt at deception, in respect to the alleged blows and feigned condition of unconsciousness, fully justified the commandant's report to me that the cadet was a criminal participant in, if not the sole author of, the fraudulent outrage of which he had pretended to be the victim. . . .

While every lawful right of the colored cadets has been fully secured to them, and their official treatment has been not only just but very kind and indulgent, their social relations to their fellow cadets have not been what they appear to have been led to expect. Military discipline is not an effective method of promoting social intercourse or of overcoming social prejudice. On the contrary the enforced association of the white cadets with their colored companions, to which they had never been accustomed before they came from home, appears to have destroyed any disposition which before existed to indulge in such association. Doubtless, this was due in part to the bad personal character of some of the young colored men sent to West Point, and in part to the natural reaction against an attempt to govern social intercourse by military regulations. Personal merit may rapidly overcome unjust prejudice when all are free to regulate their own social habits. But when social intercourse is enforced in spite of prejudice on the one side and of personal demerit on the other, the result must be rather an increase than a diminution of the preexisting prejudice. For this reason, the Military Academy cannot be made a favorable place at which to first introduce social intercourse between the white and black man. West Point will, at the most, only be able to follow the example of the country at large in this respect. . . .

The difficulty surrounding this subject is aggravated by the somewhat common error of ascribing it to an unreasonable prejudice against race or color. The prevailing "prejudice" is rather a just aversion to qualities which the people of the United States have long been accustomed to associate with a state of slavery and intercourse without legal marriage, and of which color and its various shades are only the external signs. That feeling could not be removed by the simple act of enfranchising the slave. It can only be done by education and moral elevation of the race. That great work has only been commenced, and it must of necessity require much time. To send to West Point for a four years' competition a young man who was born in slavery is to assume that half a generation has been sufficient to raise a colored man to the social, moral, and intellectual level which the average white man has reached in several hundred years. As well might the common farmhorse be entered in a four-mile race against the best blood inherited from a long line of English racers.

---

[1]Emphasis in the original.

*Sec. of War Robert Todd Lincoln, the president's son,
reversed army policy and permitted a qualified black to enlist
in the Signal Service, rather than in one of the black line
regiments.*

War Department,
Office of the Chief Signal Officer,
Washington City, July 23, 1884

The Honorable the Secretary of War, Washington, DC

Sir: I have the honor to return this paper in the case of Mr. W. Hallet Greene, a colored graduate of the College of the City of New York, who asks to be enlisted in the Signal Corps, and wish to state that in its publication and the comments made in many cases upon my action, my feeling and views in the case have been entirely mis-represented. This seems to have been done because I stated the general policy of the government had been opposed to enlistments of colored men in any except the four colored regiments especially set apart by Congress for that purpose.

I have never had prejudice on account of color, having lived all my life in a section peculiarly free from such a prejudice, and I have been in full sympathy with the people there, and was one of the first officers in the regular army commissioned to command regular colored troops.

Mr. Greene has been notified to hold himself in readiness, and if the secretary of war so directs, he will be enlisted to enter the next class at Fort Myer, and he will receive from me every consideration due to every member of the Signal Corps.

I am informed by the recruiting officer that without this order of the secretary he would not feel legally authorized to make this enlistment.

Whatever my own feelings may be, I am still of the opinion that I was not in error in stating what the customs of the service were, because it is well known that, except for the 4 regiments specifically designated by Congress for colored men, the 40 regiments of the army, the engineer battalion, the ordnance detachment, the 150 hospital stewards, 148 commissary sergeants and 500 enlisted men of the Signal Corps, have all been closed to colored men up to the time this case came before the secretary of war.

I did not deem it in the province of a chief of any one of these branches of the army to depart from that general rule any more than for a colonel of any one of the thirty-six white regiments to have done so, but these publications lead to the inference that I, by a narrow prejudice, had gratuitously taken adverse action in Mr. Greene's case.

The appointment of colored civil officers, and of colored officers to the four colored regiments referred to, in the secretary's endorsement, are not of the class of cases to which this question applies.

The affirmative legislation creating the four colored regiments has always been construed to exclude colored enlisted men from other portions of the army, and this construction has always governed enlistments.

If it is intended that the Signal Corps shall be singled out as a separate branch of the army, where mixed enlistments may take place, I feel it a duty to the best interests of

["Colored Men in the Signal Service of the Army," *Army Navy Register*, 4 October 1884.]

the corps and the service to recommend that it not be done. It is due Mr. Greene to say that his preliminary examination papers place him near the head of all the applicants for enlistment to the Signal Corps.

Very respectfully, your obedient servant,

> W. B. Hazen
> Brigadier and Brevet Major General,
> Chief Signal Officer,
> US Army

FIRST ENDORSEMENT

> War Department
> Washington, DC, August 4, 1884

Respectfully returned to the chief signal officer. The secretary of war sees no reason to modify the views expressed in his endorsement of June 4, 1884, as to the admission of colored men to the Signal Service. It is not considered necessary to discuss the propriety of assigning colored recruits to the line of the army to other organization of the line than the four regiments required by law to be composed of colored men. Reasons which might be good against such action would not apply to the employment of colored men of good character and sufficient attainments in any other position under the War Department any more than to their employment under other departments. There is certainly not, in the view of the secretary, anything peculiar in the character of the organization or in the duties of the ordnance detachment, of the hospital stewards, the commissary sergeants, the ordnance sergeants or the Signal Service, or of the clerical force of the War Department which makes it proper to exclude competent colored men from employment in these organizations, and he knows of no law, regulation or decision by which any of them, as stated within, closed to colored men.

It is thought proper to say also that even if in those branches of the public service under the War Department which are essentially military there were valid reasons for the exclusion of colored men, the secretary does not think these reasons would apply to the Signal Service. In his opinion its military name and its military methods of administration do not affect the fact that all of the work done by its members is as essentially civil as that done by the clerks of the War Department; indeed, with the exception of a few telegraph operators at military posts, they have in fact as little to do with any branch of military duty as if they did not exist.

The secretary does not believe that any detriment to the interests of the public service in [the] charge of the chief signal officer will come from these views. Without referring to colored employees in places requiring less education, there are now twenty-two colored clerks in the War Department, and it is understood that their performance of duty calls for no criticism and invites no discrimination against them.

> Robert T. Lincoln,
> Secretary of War

SECOND ENDORSEMENT

Signal Office,
Washington City, August 12, 1884

Respectfully returned to the honorable the secretary of war, with the remark that his action in this endorsement does not overcome the difficulty.

The Signal Corps and the other organizations mentioned are all equally legal parts of the army, the men are all similarly enlisted, and the fact that no colored men have ever been enlisted in them, while four other regiments are exclusively colored, is of itself proof that there is either law, or in place of it a custom of service, which up to this time has exclusively controlled the subject and prevented mixed enlistments.

The recruiting officer has informed me that from this fact he does not feel authorized to enlist Mr. Greene, except upon order of the secretary of war.

In view of the foregoing endorsement of the secretary of war I withdraw all objection, if I ever had any, to Mr. Greene's enlistment in the Signal Corps.

W. B. Hazen,
Brigadier and Brevet Major General,
Chief Signal Officer, US Army

THIRD ENDORSEMENT

If the recruiting officer referred to in the preceding endorsement has been advised of the views of the secretary of war in this matter, and he declines to act in accordance therewith, his name will be reported to the department, to be relieved by an officer who will act in accordance with the views of the secretary.

By order of the secretary of war:

John Tweedale,
Chief Clerk
War Department, August 20, 1884

FOURTH ENDORSEMENT

Signal Office,
Washington City, August 23, 1884

Respectfully referred to Lt. B. M. Purssell, Signal Corps, US Army, recruiting officer.

W. B. Hazen,
Brigadier and Brevet Major General,
Chief Signal Officer, USA

FIFTH ENDORSEMENT

Signal Office,
Washington City, August 23, 1884

Respectfully returned. The recruiting officer has been fully advised of the views of the honorable secretary of war at each stage of this correspondence. The recruiting officer's personal feelings and sympathies are all in favor of allowing Greene to enlist in the Signal Corps or any other corps or regiment of the army, but he does not believe that he has the authority of law, custom or precedent to make the enlistment. He (the recruiting officer) will with pleasure enlist Greene at any time, provided he will be authorized by the honorable the secretary of war to write on the enlistment papers the words, "Enlisted by the authority of the Secretary of War," and I respectfully ask that he be authorized.

B. M. Purssell,
Second Lieutenant Signal Corps,
US Army, Recruiting Officer

SIXTH ENDORSEMENT

Signal Office,
Washington City, August 23, 1884

Respectfully returned to the honorable the secretary of war. The action of the recruiting officer is not in disrespect of the views of the secretary of war, but he simply believes, this being the first case of the kind, he has no right to make this enlistment, whatever the opinions of the secretary of war may be, without his specific written authority, and it appears to me he is correct.

W. B. Hazen,
Brigadier and Brevet Major General,
Chief Signal Officer, US Army

SEVENTH ENDORSEMENT

War Department,
Washington, DC, September 12, 1884

The signal officer of the army is hereby ordered to give such orders and instructions to the officers now or hereafter serving under him as recruiting officers for the Signal Corps of the army as will prohibit the rejection as a recruit by any such recruiting officer of any applicant for enlistment in the Signal Corps on account of the color, or on account of the African descent of such applicant. The chief signal officer will report to the secretary of war the action taken under this order, with special reference to the application of William Hallet Greene.

Robert T. Lincoln,
Secretary of War

●

Capt. P. H. Cooper's explanation of the problems that a black
midshipman would face goes far to explain why almost a half
century would pass before the first such individual graduated
from the Naval Academy.

United States Naval Academy
Annapolis, Maryland
May 11, 1897

Personal

Sir:

With reference to the subject of your unofficial letter of May 10, 1897, I have to state that it must be acknowledged that the law cannot discriminate against colored boys, if members of Congress will recommend them for appointment, If therefore the government entrusts the Naval Academy authorities with the responsibility of educating and protecting the boy who is to report for examination in September I hope that there will be no doubt in the mind of the secretary that the duty will be faithfully discharged.

I cannot think that it is desirable to make any special point with the cadets that the law must be observed in this case. Their entire training is preparing them for any event that may arise and there is not in my opinion the least fear to be apprehended after the young man enters the academy, if perchance he qualifies. He will have the same examination and the same opportunities as the other candidates; he will not be discriminated against, nor will he be especially guarded. The trouble to be apprehended will be that before he becomes a cadet he may have rough treatment from outsiders, but that is a matter for the civil authorities to handle.

I can foresee the life he will lead at the academy in part. He will not of course be persona grata with other cadets; he will lead a solitary and forlorn existence in social relations; in official matters he will be as the others are and have the countenance of the authorities. Within the walls of the academy he will have no associates of his color, for he cannot look to the servants and messengers for companionship and if he can stand four years of such life he will be rewarded with a certificate of proficiency.

The newspaper reports you have referred to have not been inspired at the Naval Academy and I trust you will be able to answer your anxious correspondents that you

---

[Letter, Capt. P. H. Cooper, superintendent, United States Naval Academy, to Sec. of the Navy John D. Long, 11 May 1897, Massachusetts Historical Society. Reprinted by permission.]

are confident that the officers and cadets will give the colored man every chance to make his record upon his merits.

Very respectfully,
P. H. Cooper

Honorable John D. Long
Secretary of the Navy
Navy Department
Washington, DC

●

The spirit of Jim Crow was abroad in the land, as evidenced by scattered instances of discrimination and even violence directed at black units mustered into service for the Spanish-American War. The "colored regiments of immunes"—the volunteers— "turned out very satisfactory," said Maj. Gen. John C. Breckenridge, and the "regular colored regiments," he continued, "won golden opinions in battle." Many of the militia units, however, that had seen federal service went into decline with the return of peace and the resurgence of racial segregation.

1. It appears from the official records in this office that the following named volunteer organizations, officered wholly or in part by colored officers and whose enlisted strength consisted of colored men, served in the war with Spain:

Third Regiment Alabama Infantry,
Eighth Regiment Illinois Infantry,
Companies A and B, First Regiment Indiana Infantry,
Company L, Sixth Regiment Massachusetts Infantry,
Twenty-third Regiment Kansas Infantry,
Third Regiment North Carolina Infantry,
Ninth Battalion Ohio Infantry,
Sixth Regiment Virginia Infantry,
Seventh Regiment United States Volunteer Infantry,
Eighth Regiment United States Volunteer Infantry,
Ninth Regiment United States Volunteer Infantry,
Tenth Regiment United States Volunteer Infantry.

2. According to the latest compilation, the number of colored volunteer troops in the service of the United States during the war with Spain was 10,189. This number does not include the four colored regiments of the regular army which had an average strength of 3,328 enlisted men during the calendar year 1898.

The enlisted strength of the four colored regiments of the regular army on February 28, 1899, near the date of the close of the war with Spain, was 3,339 men.

[Endorsement to Letter, War Department, Adjutant General's Office, to James W. Howard, National Memorial Association, 3 August 1916, Center of Military History, Washington, DC.]

Pres. Theodore Roosevelt approved mass punishment
recommended after an investigation into an alleged attack by
black troops on the citizens of Brownsville, Texas, in reaction
to the Jim Crow laws enforced there. A total of 167 men, 6 of
them holders of the Medal of Honor, received administrative
discharges that, though not categorized as dishonorable, barred
them from reenlisting or obtaining pensions.

I am very sorry to record a most serious breach of discipline and the commission of a heinous crime by certain members of a battalion of the Twenty-fifth Infantry, Companies B, C, and D, on the night of the 13th and the morning of the 14th of August, at Fort Brown, Brownsville, Texas. . . .

The battalion was . . . sent to Fort Brown in command of Maj. C. W. Penrose, and arrived there July 28, 1906. Soon after its arrival, unfortunate differences arose between the enlisted men and some townspeople. As is usual in such cases, there was contradictory evidence as to the cause for the troubles, though they were doubtless due primarily to the resentment of certain of the townspeople at the proximity of a Negro battalion. The instances of friction were numerous and notorious enough to be the cause of much discussion in the barracks rooms of the three companies. The feeling of the enlisted men was also aroused by a discrimination insisted upon in most of the saloons of the town, in which separate bars were provided for them. No serious injury was done to any of the colored soldiers, although one of them was knocked down by a government official named Tate with a clubbed revolver for jostling his wife, as he charged, and another was pushed off a gang plank by a customs inspector into the mud of the Rio Grande, because [he was] drunk and disorderly, as it was claimed.

On the 12th of August it was reported in Brownsville that a white woman was seized by the hair by a colored soldier and dragged on the ground. This report among the townspeople caused great bitterness and excitement of feeling, which gave such concern to the officers of the battalion that on the night of the same day they sent patrols into the town to bring back their soldiers to the fort. A few minutes after twelve o'clock midnight of the next day, August 13, i.e., on the morning of August 14, shots were fired in the fort toward the town from the neighborhood of each barrack of the three companies. The fort is really in the town and only separated from the houses by a wall. The first shots seem to have been fired in the air. Immediately afterwards a number of men, variously estimated from nine to twenty, climbed over the wall between the fort and the town. There was much direct evidence that these men were colored soldiers in khaki and blue shirts, carrying the new service rifle. From seventy-five to one hundred cartridge shells and used clips and some undischarged cartridges were found upon the streets of the town the next morning, and Major Penrose, commanding the battalion, then identified them as ammunition for the new service rifle and reluctantly admitted their conclusive weight that the shooting was done by some of his men. . . .

Insp. Gen. [Ernest A.] Garlington . . . was unable to elicit a single circumstance leading to the identification of the murderers [of a bartender, the sole fatality, though a policeman was wounded]. He became convinced that there was a conspiracy of silence in the battalion to protect the criminals, and while he conceded that there might be a number of men in the battalion innocent both of the crime and of suppression of

---

["Discipline: The Brownsville Affray," *Annual Report of the Secretary of War, 1906.*]

evidence, he deemed it necessary in the interest and for the good of the service to recommend the issuing of the order which by authority he had told the men would be made and enforced, unless evidence pointing to the criminals was forthcoming. The department concurred in General Garlington's recommendation, and the president then directed the discharge of certain-named members of the battalion, which included all the enlisted men of the battalion who were present at Fort Brown on the night in question, without honor, and forever barred from reenlisting in the Army or Navy of the United States, as well as from employment in any civil capacity under the government. The order of discharge has been duly executed. . . .

Much sympathy has been evoked for those who have been so long in the public service as some of the noncommissioned officers and others of this battalion of the Twenty-fifth Infantry. It is to be said with respect to these noncommissioned officers, that upon them especially falls the duty of maintaining the discipline of the companies and the battalion, and that by reason of their long service and from their official authority they have more influence over the men and more opportunity to learn the circumstances leading to a detection of the guilty in this case than any others connected with the regiment. Indeed, it was their peculiar duty to find out and disclose the facts, but they failed to do so. It may be said that they were not derelict in this. If not, then they had the misfortune to be associated with men whose conduct and immunity from detection required the government in the public service to exercise its reserved contract right of discharge against the entire body of which they were members.

The suggestion made in some quarters that this battalion has been treated in this way because the men are colored hardly merits notice. The fact of their color and the racial feeling aroused between them and the citizens of Brownsville may have been the cause and furnished the motive, but certainly not a justification, for the plot to murder men, women and children; but to this extent only in explanation of the circumstances is the fact of their color at all relevant.

●

Roosevelt's decision to punish the entire unit at Brownsville came during a surge of racism, typified by anti-Negro rioting in Atlanta and the legalization of racial segregation throughout the land.

Personal and Confidential

Secretary William H. Taft,
War Department, Washington, DC

My dear Secretary Taft:
     Will you not tell me whether it is the intention of the War Department to enlist additional colored soldiers to take the place of the three companies that were dismissed?
     I am also writing to say that I very much hope, by the time the president returns, some plan will have been thought out by which to do something that may change the

[Letter, Booker T. Washington, principal, Tuskegee Normal and Industrial Institute, to Sec. of War William Howard Taft, 20 November 1906, Manuscript Division, Library of Congress, Washington, DC.]

feeling of the colored people now as a whole have regarding the dismissal of the three colored companies. I have never in all my experience with the race, experienced a time when the entire people have the feeling that they have now in regard to the administration. The race is not so much resentful or angry, perhaps, as it feels hurt and disappointed. I am not excusing or justifying this feeling, because I do not know the detailed facts upon which the action was based, but I am simply putting a condition before you. In considering it, it must be borne in mind that this order came at a time when the race was experiencing deep trial on account of the Atlanta riots and when there was much to discourage the race in the atmosphere.

Yours truly,
Booker T. Washington

●

*Senators Joseph B. Foraker, an Ohio Republican, and Morgan
G. Bulkeley of Connecticut demonstrated that no soldiers of
the Twenty-fifth Infantry could have committed the Brownsville
outrage. Indeed, they argued quite plausibly that the evidence
which the army found so convincing may actually have been
planted by townspeople. The president, however, remained
unmoved by Foraker's logic, and not until 1972 did the army,
at the urging of Att. Gen. Richard Kleindienst, correct the records
of the men expelled in 1906 to indicate that they had deserved
honorable discharges.*

RECAPITULATION

To recapitulate, the testimony of the eyewitnesses against the soldiers is not reliable, because of the darkness of the night, which made it impossible to see with any distinctness, and because of the many contradictions of the testimony of the various witnesses. . . .

2. In the second place, the confirmatory or circumstantial evidence of the exploded shells that were picked up in the streets of Brownsville and put in evidence is shown by the microscopic inspection to be conclusive testimony in favor of the innocence of the soldiers.

3. The clips, the bandolier, and the bullets are not of themselves evidence of the guilt of the men, because in view of the testimony not inconsistent with their innocence.

The testimony in favor of the soldiers is—

1. Their good record as both men and soldiers, both before August 13, 1906, and since.

2. Their own testimony as to their innocence. . . . To refuse to believe them is to assert that as fine a body of soldiers and as truthful, according to all their officers, as can be found in the entire army are conspirators, murderers, and perjurers, and all this upon the uncertain, unreliable, and contradictory statements of witnesses who did not pretend to

[U.S., Congress, Senate, Minority Report of the Senate Committee on Military Affairs, *The Brownsville Affray*, 60th Cong., 1st sess., 11 March 1908, Sen. Doc. no. 389.]

give personal knowledge, but only conclusions based on what was necessarily uncertain observation.

3. The soldiers are confirmed in the claim that they are innocent by the fact that immediately after the firing their ammunition was verified and not a cartridge was missing, and the next morning as soon as it was light enough their guns were rigidly inspected and not one was found to show any evidence whatever of having been fired the night before. There is much testimony in the record in regard to the length of time required to properly clean a gun after it has been fired so that it would pass such an inspection as these guns were subjected to the following morning. The overwhelming weight of this testimony is that it would require from fifteen to thirty minutes to clean these guns so that they would pass such an inspection as that to which they were subjected, and that it would be impossible to clean them in the dark or by artificial light, and that the men had no opportunity to clean them that night.

This testimony was given not alone by the colored soldiers of the Twenty-fifth Infantry, but also by a large number of white soldiers from the Twenty-sixth Infantry.

4. So far as Company C is concerned, the testimony shows that they had only guard ammunition, lead bullets without steel jackets, and only 650 rounds of that, and that after the firing they were found to have every cartridge. No one pretends that any bullets of this character were found or that any such ammunition was used. . . .

5. As to the other two companies, the calling of the roll in Company B while the firing was yet in progress, and the personal inspection and verification of Company D by Capt. [Samuel P.] Lyon also while the firing was still in progress, coupled with the fact that every man of the company was present or accounted for, with not a missing cartridge or a dirty gun, would seem in any ordinary case to be enough to exonerate them, to say nothing of the unqualified, straightforward testimony that clears all of them. . . .

6. The testimony further shows that the first five or six shots fired were pistol or revolver shots. . . . The testimony is conclusive that the men of the battalion had no pistols or revolvers in their possession. The only revolvers that had been issued to these companies were still in the boxes in which they had come from the arsenal. If, therefore, the first shots were pistol shots, they could not have been fired by the soldiers. Immediately after these first five or six pistol shots all testify that there was firing from high-power guns, but whether they were Springfield rifles or Krag rifles or Krag carbines or Winchester rifles or Mauser rifles no one could tell from the sound. So far, therefore, as the *reports* or *sounds*[1] of the firing were concerned, they might have been made by the firing of Krag guns or Winchester guns or Mauser guns.

7. But assuming that because of the marks of the four lands on the bullets they were fired from either a Springfield or a Krag rifle or a Krag carbine, the testimony shows that a number of Krag rifles—four at least—with the numbers effaced had been sold to citizens of Brownsville by the quartermaster-sergeant of one of the companies of the Twenty-sixth Infantry only a short time before the Negro soldiers arrived here. In addition, Mayor Combe testified that the Texas Rangers were, until recently, armed with Krag carbines.

8. The bullets taken from houses and put in evidence, as already pointed out, may have been fired either from Krag carbines or Krag rifles, or they might have been fired from Mauser rifles.

9. The location of the six shells and five clips found by Capt. [E. A.] Macklin on a

---

[1]Emphasis in the original.

circular area not more than ten inches in diameter indicates that they must have been placed where he found them, and no one has suggested any purpose the soldiers could have had in placing them there.

10. The bullet cut from the post in front of [Vincente] Crixell's was not a soldier's bullet and could not have been fired from any gun the soldiers had.

11. The microscopic examination and report.

All these several points are absolutely inconsistent with the theory that the soldiers did the shooting. But in addition to what such evidence proves, there is the improbability of soldiers with such a record as these soldiers had forming and executing any such conspiracy, and especially in the way claimed.

In the first place, the formation and execution of such a conspiracy would require a higher order of ability than any of the men of the battalion possessed; but it is not possible that men capable of planning such a raid and so managing its execution as to defy detection would be so absurdly stupid as to commence their operations by firing from their own quarters and grounds, and then, after they had thus aroused the town and fixed their identity as soldiers, and not until then, jump over the wall and start on their errand of outrage and murder.

NO MOTIVE

In the second place, there was no sufficient motive. To begin with, the only motive suggested is one of revenge . . . because some of the saloons would not sell to the soldiers except at separate bars, and because one of the soldiers, Pvt. [James W.] Newton, was hit over the head with a revolver by Customs Officer Tate and knocked down and badly injured without any adequate excuse therefor, and because one or two others of the soldiers had been unfortunate enough to have some petty difficulty. As to this provocation, the testimony is conclusive that the soldiers made no complaint because they were denied the equal privileges of the saloons, and it is further shown that Newton showed no special resentment and took no steps beyond reporting his trouble to his commanding officer, who promised to have it investigated, with which Newton expressed himself as entirely satisfied.

●

The army's judge advocate general advised Secretary Taft
that the federal government lacked the power to intervene to
prevent disbandment of black militia units, some of them
mobilized for the Spanish-American War.

Personal

Secretary W. H. Taft,
War Department, Washington, DC

Sir:

If not inconsistent with the rules of your department, I wonder if you would inform me if it is legal for any states to refuse to give the colored people any recognition whatever

---

[Letter, Booker T. Washington to William Howard Taft, 3 March 1906, Center of Military History, Washington, DC.]

in the state militia and still draw their quota from the public fund toward support of the state militia.

Several of the southern states have recently mustered out all of the colored companies, and I should like to know what the ruling of the department is on the subject mentioned.

Yours truly,
Booker T. Washington

●

Although the Military Intelligence Division of the Army General Staff recommended the formation of an experimental black artillery unit, a dissenting opinion, presented by Maj. C. DeWitt Willcox, declared that to recruit black artillerymen would "open a running sore that may never heal." No black artillery unit was formed until World War I.

I have the honor to ask you to issue an order that six of the batteries of field artillery and not less than eighteen of the companies of the coast artillery added by act of Congress, approved January 25, 1907, be recruited with colored men.

I ask the above favor for my race for some of the reasons which follow:

1. Their bravery in the Civil War, in the Indian campaigns, in the war with Spain. In this latter war they fearlessly used four Hotchkiss mountain guns with good effect. . . .

2. Some of the best shots in the Army of the US are colored men belonging to the colored cavalry and infantry regiments. A man that can learn to shoot one gun can learn to shoot another.

3. They possess sufficient intelligence. Many of the men at present in the army are especially intelligent, alert and ambitious fellows. They do the most, or all, of the clerical work of their regiments.

4. There are not many desertions from the colored regiments. Cognizance has been taken of the fact that there is increased desertion by white soldiers from the army and navy, and the credit on this score is altogether with the colored soldiers.

5. Last but not least, our population and the progress we have made since slavery was abolished entitle us, we believe, to the recognition above sought. There has never been in the regular army a company of colored artillery, and as only men of superior intelligence are enlisted for that branch of the service, our most intelligent men deserve a chance to prove their ability and serve their country in the artillery branch of the service the same as white soldiers of similar qualifications do.

I have been informed that the War Department in the past has been of the opinion that colored men with sufficient intelligence to make good artillerymen cannot be found. This was doubtless true in the '60s and in the period immediately following, but does not hold good now as a trial, I am sure will show. Whenever given an opportunity, as at La Gausimas [Cuba] in 1898, they have acquitted themselves creditably.

[Letter, Emmett J. Scott, Tuskegee Normal and Industrial Institute, to Pres. Theodore Roosevelt, 8 March 1907, Military Archives Division, National Archives, Washington, DC.]

*Racial friction now surfaced in the navy, as segregation made
its appearance there.*

I served three years in the navy from 1892 to 1895, and while at that time there
may have been no "prejudice" against Negroes, there certainly was a very strong objection
against their presence in the ship. I served on four different ships and can testify that the
objection was equally strong on all of them; and by coming in personal contact with the
crews of other ships I know that it pervaded the entire navy. The presence of Negroes
was one of the most disagreeable features of naval service, and had as much to do with
causing desertions as any other feature.

Officials may think that because our white sailors do not break out in open mutiny
that they do not object to serving with Negroes. Others think that if they are dissatisfied
they would enter a formal complaint; but they should bear in mind that the enlisted men
of the navy are not of a legislative turn of mind. During my three years I never knew of an
official protest against Negroes, but I do know that the white men objected to them and
that the objection was strongest among men with the longest service. The presence of the
blacks was a constant source of dissatisfaction which often broke out in bloody fights. It
may not always have been the fault of the Negroes, but the fact remains that such a state
of affairs existed. I firmly believe that it exists today in spite of the fact that we hear no
complaints. . . .

I will not go so far as to say that every white man in the navy was opposed to
Negroes, but I will say that the overwhelming majority were, and that it was not confined
to men from the South. I joined the navy from a northern state with the impression that
the American Negro was more sinned against than sinning. Six months in the navy
worked a permanent cure. When I hear a man advocate abolishing the color line in the
army, a measure that would affect thousands of helpless enlisted men, I can't help
wishing he would try it on himself. Let him serve with Negroes as I have done; sling a
hammock among them on a hot night; eat at the same mess table with them; heave coal
for a Negro fireman. Then ask him his views on the color line.

[Letter, 1st Lt. George Steunenberg, Thirteenth Cavalry, to the editor, *Army and Navy Journal*,
5 January 1907, *Army and Navy Journal*, vol. 44, p. 563.]

Racism took hold in the navy, reflecting the rise of Jim Crow throughout the country. Before World War I, racial segregation had become firmly established in the naval service, with most blacks either banished to engine room or galley or assigned to wait on officers. Insofar as possible, berthing and messing became separate.

In response to a letter from Mr. Cleveland G. Allen, Allen's National News Bureau, New York, the secretary of the navy wrote April 17, 1913, saying:

I have the honor to acknowledge receipt of your communication of the 12th instant, concerning alleged discrimination against colored men in the naval service, and the subject matter therein will be given my careful consideration and you will be further informed thereon at a later date.

The complaint registered by Mr. Allen was as follows:

The reason that there were no Negro sailors in the naval parade is that the parade is made up of men from the deck force of the ships; in other words "the seaman branch of the service," and there are no colored men in this branch of the service, as the Navy Department no longer enlist [sic] them as such. At present the Negro recruits are allowed to enlist only in a certain branch termed "the messman branch," and are kept messmen, and never get promoted to a higher rank, save that of stewards, who do not rank with petty officers. They are discriminated against in that on account of their color they cannot enlist as real seamen and when serving on board ship they are deprived of the regular system of shore leave unlike the rest of the crew; they are barred from the ship's entertainment, such as smokers, etc., and are denied the privilege of the ship's library, and not allowed to perform the duty which the uniform they wear really represents. A number of these men desert the service from time to time, after finding out how much they are discriminated against and that they are sailors only in that they wear the uniform and that their duties are upon the waters. There are, however, still quite a number of colored petty officers and a few seamen remaining in the navy, but these are nearly old men who were enlisted during the Spanish-American War or a little later, and are now isolated to obscure places for duty. When these men shall have passed or retired from the service our navy will be entirely without colored sea fighters, unless some good Samaritans should expose widely this fact and take action against the matter, which the Navy Department has so far been successful in keeping a secret.

[An account of an exchange of letters between Cleveland G. Allen and Sec. of the Navy Josephus Daniels, April 1913, *Army and Navy Journal*, vol. 50, p. 1140.]

*Shortly after the United States entered World War I, black
troops stationed at Houston, Texas, rioted against local Jim
Crow laws, killing fifteen white civilians, four of them
policemen, and a National Guard officer. Of sixty-four soldiers
tried by courts martial, twenty-nine received the death penalty,
and only five were acquitted. Neither Sec. of War Newton D.
Baker nor Pres. Woodrow Wilson chose to review the sentences
of the first thirteen men condemned to death, on the grounds
that the local commander had absolute authority to punish
offenses committed in wartime. During the following year,
Secretary Baker persuaded the chief executive to reexamine the
other sixteen cases, and Mr. Wilson commuted the sentences of
ten. The others were hanged, however, bringing to nineteen
the total number of executions that resulted from the Houston
violence.*

2. From the evidence to this case, the following facts appear:

On July 29th, 1917, the Third Battalion, Twenty-fourth Infantry, Lt. Col. William
Newman, commanding, 7 officers and 645 enlisted men, 1 officer and 9 enlisted men
attached, arrived at Houston, Texas, to "be used for purposes of guarding cantonment
construction and to furnish the necessary guards when and where requested by the
constructing quartermaster." The camp selected for these troops was between the city
and Camp Logan located on Washington Street, the only avenue of approach to Camp
Logan from the city of Houston.

From the time these colored troops arrived at Houston, July 29th, until the
disorder, August 23rd, there were numerous incidents occurred indicative of conditions
between the Negro soldiers and the citizens of Houston. The following are examples:

Troubles on streetcars due to the Jim Crow laws. . . . Segregation signs would
frequently be removed and colored men take seats in white section; these men were
sometimes profane and abusive.

A motorman called a police officer and reported to him a "nigger" who wouldn't
comply with the law; the police officer said[,] " 'Nigger, you are violating the law here,'
and he says[,] 'I don't give a _____ about no law or anything else' and he had a big
knife and I knocked him in the head and took him to jail. . . ."

Another motorman stated that all the colored soldiers that rode the cars usually
seemed to have a hard feeling towards riding behind the screens [that separated the
passengers according to race].

Similar incidents indicating race antipathies occurred in the construction camp
where there was a daily guard from the Twenty-fourth Infantry of 140 men; separate
cans for drinking water were provided; the soldiers refused to drink from those labeled
"colored."

The white labor apparently lost no opportunity to refer to these guards from the
Twenty-fourth Infantry as "niggers"; the city police and people generally did the same;

[Memorandum, Col. G. C. Gross, assistant inspector general, to (Brig. Gen. James Parker) com-
manding general, Southern Department, 13 September 1917, subject: Investigation of trouble at Houston,
Texas, between Third Battalion, Twenty-fourth Infantry, and citizens of Houston, 23 August 1917, Military
Archives Division, National Archives, Washington, DC.]

the Negro soldier in uniform, whether on duty or not, was treated the same as any other individual of his race, and no efforts appear to have been made in any respect to discourage the use of this appellation until the afternoon of August 23rd when the chief of police promised . . . that he would require his police officers in the future to abstain from the use of the name "nigger." This word "nigger" appears in practically every case of disorder reported, and with the same result: a display of anger on the part of the soldier, with profane and abusive language and threats of vengeance. Another influence, the tendency of which was to arouse in the Negroes a desire for revenge was their belief that, while they were punished for these troubles, no corrective measures were applied to the citizen offender.

The colored population of Houston, the class frequenting dives and poolrooms in particular, and the women, appear also to have exerted their influence towards arousing the soldiers, to take measures that they supposed would secure better treatment for them all.

The removal of segregation signs, and other similar incidents demonstrate the fact that these soldiers, sworn to uphold the law, were not willing to comply with laws repugnant to them, and an overbearing spirit was shown in several cases where on slight provocation they threatened to shoot. One case was reported where a colored soldier on the streets of Houston and not on duty ordered a white soldier to salute him; this resulted in a fight between the white soldier and a Negro citizen friend of the colored soldier.

In order to prevent trouble between the civil and military, the commanding officer, Twenty-fourth Infantry, appointed sixteen of his best enlisted men to act as military police. According to the understanding [with local authorities] . . . these military police . . . as far as practicable were to handle soldiers who in any way offended against the laws while in Houston. . . .

This [Third] Battalion continued in the performance of the duty assigned to it until August 23rd. About eleven o'clock A.M. on this date city Police Officer Lee Sparks, on duty in the Fourth Ward, the colored section of Houston, broke up a game of craps being played by some Negro boys. These boys were followed into a house by Officer Sparks who later appeared with a colored woman who, it is reported, he was striking. A Negro soldier of the Twenty-fourth Infantry, reported to be somewhat under the influence of liquor, remonstrated with the officer for his treatment of the colored woman and in turn was beaten up by Officer Sparks and sent to the chief of police under the charge of interfering with an officer.

On the day in question Corporal Baltimore, a member of the military police on duty in the section where the man was earlier in the day arrested by Officer Sparks and, as part of the duty required of him, made inquiry of Officer Sparks as to the circumstances of the arrest of the soldier. There is disagreement between Officer Sparks and Corporal Baltimore as to the latter's manner in asking for this information. Officer Sparks claims Corporal Baltimore used profanity; Officer Daniels, Sparks' partner, present during the arrest, says he heard no profanity. Officer Sparks struck Corporal Baltimore with his pistol; Corporal Baltimore turned and ran; Officer Sparks fired three times, he states at the ground merely to frighten Corporal Baltimore, who ran into a house followed by Officer Sparks, who there overtook Corporal Baltimore and struck him over the head one or more times and sent him to police headquarters in arrest. It was soon reported in the Twenty-fourth Infantry camp that Corporal Baltimore had been shot by a policeman and considerable excitement followed. . . .

The rioters, variously estimated at from one hundred to one hundred fifty soldiers, left the camp following down Washington Street towards the city of Houston, east four blocks, thence south about a mile to San Felipe Street, thence east on San Felipe Street about two miles until those who remained together, numbering about thirty, arrived near [the] corner of San Felipe and Heiner Streets, where Captain Mattes, Illinois National Guard, a chauffeur, a policeman, and a soldier, traveling west on San Felipe Street in an automobile, were fired on by the rioters and Captain Mattes and two of the party were killed. After this the rioters appear to have dispersed, some returning to camp and others were rounded up by the National Guard and coast Artillery Corps troops called out. These rioters appear to have fired indiscriminately at whites. From among the civil population there were fifteen killed and twenty-one wounded; of the killed, four were policemen. Of the fifteen killed, seven were more or less mutilated by bayonets. Two soldiers were killed in Houston that night. Sergeant Henry and the guard, Pvt. Bryant Watson, Company I sentinel on post over which the rioters passed; one soldier, Pvt. Wiley Young, wounded in camp; a fourth, armed and undoubtedly one of the rioters, wounded near San Felipe Street; both have since died. . . .

CONCLUSIONS

1. That the clash between certain soldiers of the Twenty-fourth Infantry and the city of Houston on the night of August 23, 1917, was inherently racial and resulted from the following:

A. The general treatment and attitude of the citizens of Houston towards the Negro race; and the resentment of the Negroes to the enforcement of the so-called Jim Crow Laws.

B. The incompatibility between the handling of the Negro by the civil authorities of Houston, and the training of Negro soldiers as pursued in the service, where effort is made to increase his self-respect, his respect for the uniform and for the authority of the government, and where he is given to understand he may expect fairness and justice in the treatment accorded him.

C. The incompetency and inefficiency of the city administration of Houston, particularly in the police department. (Chief of Police C. L. Brock has since been removed from office.)

D. The brutal, unwarranted, and unjustified assault on Cpl. Charles W. Baltimore, a member of the military police, who at the time of the assault was in uniform and in the performance of his duty. (Police Officer Leo Sparks has since been indicted by the grand jury for his assault upon Cpl. Charles W. Baltimore.)

2. That Acting First Sergeant Henry, Company I, Cpl. Lammon J. Brown, Company I, and other men of the Third Battalion, Twenty-fourth Infantry, when they defied their officers, took their rifles and ammunition and left camp about 8:45 P.M. August 23rd and proceeded into the city of Houston, killing and wounding innocent white citizens, were guilty of mutiny, murder, and riot.

3. That members of the Third Battalion of the Twenty-fourth Infantry who remained in camp and who, due to the alarm "They are coming! The mob is coming to

camp!" and the darkness, which prevented their seeing beyond camp, became panic-stricken and who were obsessed with fear that a mob from Houston would attack them, were not a party to the mutiny and resulting murders.

4. That there was a prearranged plan for revenge, in all probability conceived in I Company, and assisted by a few men from each of the other companies, and that the alarm "They are coming! The mob is coming to camp!" was part of the plan, made with a view to involve the entire command. . . .

10. That the tendency of the Negro soldier, with fire arms in his possession, unless he is properly handled by officers who know the race is to become arrogant, overbearing, abusive and a menace to the community in which he happens to be stationed.

11. That so long as the people of Houston and the state of Texas maintain their present attitude towards the Negro, troubles more or less aggravated and similar to the affair at Houston, are likely to occur at any time Negro troops are stationed within the boundaries of the state.

CHAPTER FOUR
THE GREAT WAR AND AFTER, 1917–40

Shortly after the United States declared war on Germany in the spring of 1917, black leaders like J. E. Spingarn of the National Association for the Advancement of Colored People began urging that American Negroes become full partners in the war effort. The War Department laid plans to tap the reservoir of black manpower, but the spirit of Jim Crow permeated such efforts. Concessions made by the military to the black population proved so few and carefully circumscribed that, prior to the Armistice, some of the very leaders who had urged participation already despaired of advancing the status of blacks as a result of wartime service.

The army systematically denied equality to blacks during the war. Although the War Department accepted Negro officer candidates, these men trained at segregated camps for service in segregated units. Because he was in line for promotion to brigadier general in the wartime expansion, Lt. Col. Charles Young, the highest ranking black in the army, had to retire, only to be recalled to duty in the final days of the conflict. Some 380 thousand blacks entered the army during the World War, but no more than forty-two thousand served in combat units; the others were laborers in engineer, quartermaster, or pioneer battalions. Of those few who did see action in France, roughly half served with the French army, where they received better treatment than from their own countrymen.

After the war, both the army and navy evaluated their World War experience and sought to determine the future of the black soldier and sailor. Although some army officers believed that the black soldier, when properly trained and led, was the equal of the white, the War Department did not accept this view. In any future conflict, most black troops were again to be laborers. Also, the army sought to break up the four combat regiments that had been part of the regular establishment since the post-Civil War reorganization. The navy, its wartime ranks about 1 percent black, chose to accept members of this race solely for duty as messmen or stewards. The Marine Corps remained exclusively white.

An increasingly articulate black community protested racial discrimination within the peacetime armed services. Not until the eve of World War II, however, did it obtain the forum and the leverage it needed to effect even minor change. Congressional debate on military conscription enabled black spokesmen to present their grievances, but reform failed to materialize. The threat of a march on Washington, led by A. Philip Randolph of the Brotherhood of Sleeping Car Porters, and the possibility of black resistance to the draft prodded Pres. Franklin D. Roosevelt into broadening the opportunities for blacks both in the armed forces and in defense of industry. The threat of war led the president to side with those Negro leaders who urged that members of their race have an opportunity to serve in what remained a racially segregated army and navy. Perhaps the most encouraging result of this black agitation was the acceptance of blacks into the Army Air Corps, a symbolic triumph which directly affected comparatively few individuals.

*Dr. Joel E. Spingarn of the National Association for the
Advancement of Colored People had charged that the army
General Staff was yielding to pressure from southern
congressmen and arranging to exclude blacks from the World
War I draft.*

2. Dr. Spingarn is mistaken in his assumption that the General Staff of the army has advocated exclusion of the colored race from the proposed system of universal military training. Section four of the General Staff Universal Military Training and Service Bill clearly contemplates that colored men shall be trained for it provides expressly that:

White and colored enlisted or enrolled men shall not be organized in or assigned to the same company, battalion, or regiment.

3. This is in line with the existing policy in the regular army which limits the assignment of colored enlisted men to certain regiments, namely the Twenty-fourth and Twenty-fifth regiments of infantry and the Ninth and Tenth regiments of cavalry. The records of these regiments have demonstrated the fine soldierly qualities of our colored citizens. Their loyalty is not to be questioned.

A. G.

After the word "policy" in third paragraph above, insert the words "of Congress"; and after the word "in," in the same line, insert the words "respect to."

T. H. B.

[Memorandum, Maj. Gen. Tasker H. Bliss, assistant to the chief of staff, for the adjutant general, 14 April 1917, subject: Inclusion of colored citizens in proposed system of universal military training, Military Archives Division, National Archives, Washington, DC.]

●

*In commenting upon Secretary Baker's memorandum to
the army chief of staff, Brig. Gen. Joseph E. Kuhn, chief of the
General Staff's War College Division, pointed out that:
"Whether or not they [blacks] should be utilized as officers
is . . . more of a political than a military question, but in
general it is believed that our colored citizens make better
soldiers if commanded by white officers than they do under
officers of their own race." A policy of commissioning company-
grade black officers went into effect, however, with a training
camp at Fort Des Moines, Iowa, rather than at Howard
University, Washington, DC, as the secretary of war had
suggested.*

The operation of the selective conscription system will undoubtedly bring into the forces to be trained a substantial number of colored men. It will not be possible to officer these men entirely with white officers nor would it be desirable. Would it not be wise to

---

[Memorandum, Sec. of War Newton D. Baker for Gen. Hugh Scott, 6 May 1917, Military Archives Division, National Archives, Washington, DC.]

set up a separate training camp for colored in connection with Howard University? The authorities of that college tell me that they would be able to assemble probably a thousand graduates of their institution, and educated colored men from other places could be sent to the same camp.

•

The acceptance of blacks for officer training met an enthusiastic
response among Negro college men.

A reserve officers' training camp, accommodating 1,250, at Des Moines, Iowa, for colored men, to start June 15. Such was the official announcement of the War Department last Saturday, May 19.

Stop but a moment, brother, and realize what this means. At present, we have only three officers of the line in the army; in less than four months we shall have 1,250 officers. Our due recognition at last. But no one who was not in the fight knows what a fight we had to obtain the camp. Only a few of those in authority would support the project; most of them did not want to consider it; and the remainder were bitterly against it. "Why waste time trying to train Negroes to be officers?" they said, "when the Negro can't fight unless he is led by white officers?" The truth is the Negro has had no chance to fight under his own leadership. Now the chance has come; the greatest opportunity since the Civil War. But what if we fail? Eternal disgrace! Our enemies forever will say: "O yes, the Ninth and Tenth were uneducated men; but just as soon as the Negro gets a little education he becomes a coward." There is a terrible responsibility resting upon us. The government has challenged the Negro race to prove its worth, particularly the worth of its educated leaders. We must succeed and pour into camp in overwhelming numbers. Let no man slack.

Some few people have opposed the camp as a Jim Crow camp; they say we are sacrificing principles for policy. Let them talk. This camp is no more Jim Crow than our other institutions, our newspapers, our churches, our schools. In fact, it is less Jim Crow than any other institution, for here the government has assured us of exactly the same recognition, treatment, instruction and pay as men in any other camp get.

[Letter to the editor, "Officers' Training Camps," *Atlanta Independent*. 24 May 1917.]

Despite the idealistic beliefs of the black college men, not every
officer received the same treatment; race and political
connections remained powerful influences. The special
treatment given Lieutenant Dockery reflected a concern that
blacks—especially the senior black officer in the army, Lt. Col.
Charles Young—might command whites. Rather than
reprimand or transfer Dockery, the War Department placed
Young, who seemed likely to be promoted to general during the
wartime expansion, on the retired list, keeping him there until
the closing weeks of the conflict.

Sen. [John Sharp] Williams of Mississippi called my attention to a case the other day which involves some serious possibilities, and I am venturing to write you a confidential letter about it.

Albert B. Dockery, first lieutenant in the Tenth US Cavalry, now stationed at Fort Huachuca, Arizona, is a southerner and finds it not only distasteful but practically impossible to serve under a colored commander. The Tenth Cavalry is temporarily in command of Lt. Col. Charles Young, who recently relieved Col. D. C. Cabell, and I am afraid from what I have learned that there may be some serious and perhaps even tragical insubordination on Lieutenant Dockery's part if he is left under Colonel Young, who is a colored man. Is there not some way of relieving this situation by transfering Lieutenant Dockery and sending some man in his place who would not have equally intense prejudices?

[Letter, Pres. Woodrow Wilson to Sec. of War Newton D. Baker, 25 June 1917, Manuscripts Division, Library of Congress, Washington, DC.]

●

As indicated by this editorial, written by W. E. B. Du Bois,
black Americans supported the war as a crusade against
German tyranny.

This is the crisis of the world. For all the long years to come men will point to the year 1918 as the great Day of Decision, the day when the world decided whether it would submit to military despotism and an endless armed peace—if peace it could be called—or whether they would put down the menace of German militarism and inaugurate the United States of the World.

We of the colored race have no ordinary interest in the outcome. That which the German power represents today spells death to the aspirations of Negroes and all darker races for equality, freedom, and democracy. Let us not hesitate. Let us, while this war lasts, forget our special grievances and close our ranks shoulder to shoulder with our own white fellow citizens and the allied nations that are fighting for democracy. We make no ordinary sacrifice, but we make it gladly and willingly with our eyes lifted to the hills.

["Close Ranks," *The Crisis*, July 1918.]

*Instead of adhering to an earlier plan to organize several
combat regiments of black draftees, Secretary of War Baker
approved diverting most of these men into service or labor units
desperately needed for an American Expeditionary Force, under
the command of Gen. John J. Pershing.*

VI. The sixth and last, and in the opinion of the [General Staff] committee, the preferable plan with respect to the object of preventing racial trouble is to suspend for a little while the call for the colored draft; to call these men out as they are required for service with the Quartermaster Corps [or] Engineers. . . ; organizing and giving preliminary instruction in the localities where raised; and shipping them abroad as rapidly as possible.

General Pershing has been urgently calling for troops of this character as being absolutely necessary in connection with the service at the ports of debarkation in France, along the railway lines of communication, at the great depots of supplies, for service as forestry regiments etc. We require now some 46 service battalions of engineers or a total of 46,276 enlisted men. We require 46 service companies of 250 men each, or a total of 10,000 [11,500] men. We require a large number of forestry regiments and railroad construction regiments. In fact we already require more regiments organized for this sort of service than the entire colored draft will provide for. White regiments have been and are being organized for this same service.

COMMENTS

Plan VI It is believed to be the best. The regiments organized for the service mentioned in this plan (for which also many white regiments must be organized) calls for the minimum of training *under arms*.[1] In fact this part of the training can be deferred until these troops arrive in France. It will result in getting the colored draft abroad more quickly than any other plan; and when once abroad, we do not apprehend trouble arising from racial differences. Experience has shown that when troops are once in the field, these differences disappear.

> Tasker H. Bliss
> Major General,
> US Army

General Bliss
   Plan VI is approved. Please let me know how the details of it work out.

> Baker

[Memorandum, Maj. Gen. Tasker H. Bliss for Sec. of War Newton D. Baker, 24 August 1917, Military Archives Division, National Archives, Washington, DC.]

[1] Emphasis in the original.

General Bliss proposed forming one combat division of black draftees for service in France. The Ninety-second Division, formed in this manner, arrived in France in the summer of 1918 and fought in the Meuse-Argonne offensive and the Marbache Sector-Woevre Plain operation. Another black unit, the Ninety-third Division (Provisional) made up of both draftees and members of militia or National Guard organizations, lacked the artillery and other supporting elements of the standard US Army division. As they reached the front in the spring of 1918, the four infantry regiments of this provisional division were incorporated into French forces.

The 29,563 colored men that can be taken care of in the southern National Army cantonments can be formed into one division of troops, similar to the divisions which we now have organized and are sending to France.

I recommend that it be announced that after their preliminary training has been sufficiently completed we will form a combatant division of colored troops. The component parts of this division will remain in their respective cantonments until the time comes to prepare the division to go abroad. They can then be assembled at some National Guard camp, which by that time will have been abandoned. By that time the officers will know their men, the troops will have become accustomed to their officers, and should be fairly well disciplined.

At the same time we can proceed with the organization of the noncombatant Negro forces as rapidly as they are required, and as we are able to send them abroad.

The colored race, knowing that a combatant division is being formed, will realize that in the noncombatant service, they are doing no more than their share along with similar white troops, and there can be no reasonable cause for ill feeling.

In regard to the proposition to distribute 30,000 colored men among the northern army cantonments, it must be remembered that these cantonments have not been planned for this additional number, and instructions for the necessary work will have to be given without delay.

[Memorandum, Maj. Gen. Tasker H. Bliss, acting chief of staff, for Sec. of War Newton D. Baker, 3 September 1917, Military Archives Division, National Archives, Washington, DC.]

*Although the plan for token black participation in combat
resulted in sending one division and the infantry components
of another to the European battlefields, most Negro draftees
were destined for assignment to some variety of service or
labor unit.*

It is the policy to select those colored men of the best physical stamina, highest education and mental development for the combatant troops and there is every reason to believe that these specially selected men, the cream of the colored draft, will make first-class fighting troops. After this cream has been skimmed off, there remains a large percentage of colored men of the ignorant, illiterate, day-laborer class. These men have not, in a large percentage of cases, the physical stamina to withstand the hardships and exposure of hard field service, especially the damp, cold winters of France. The poorer class of backwoods Negro has not the mental stamina and moral sturdiness to put him in [the] line against German troops who consist of thoroughly trained men of high average education. It is feared that the enemy will concentrate on parts of the line held by inferior troops, break through and get in the rear of high-class troops who will be at a terrible disadvantage. . . .

  8. The War Plans Division is of the opinion:

  (a) That it should be the policy to utilize for combatant purposes the greatest possible proportion of colored drafted men, with the understanding that only fit and reliable men be so used. That future organizations of combatant colored troops should be in units no larger than regiments in accordance with the desire of General Pershing who contemplates their use in connection with similar colored organizations of the French army.

  (b) That the organization of fifty reserve labor battalions, Quartermaster Corps . . . should be authorized for service in the United States only . . . in addition to the labor battalions, Quartermaster Corps, stevedore regiments, Quartermaster Corps, Engineer Service battalions and pioneer regiments, now authorized or hereafter to be authorized.

  (c) That the colored draft should be absorbed for the present as above indicated. The mixture of colored and white men in the same unit, on account of difficulties of administration which would otherwise result, should not extend further than appointing white officers, and noncommissioned officers of the higher grades in such colored units.

[Memorandum, Brig. Gen. Lytle Brown, assistant chief of staff, director, War Plans Division, for the chief of staff, 12 June 1918, subject: Disposal of colored draft, Military Archives Division, National Archives, Washington, DC.]

*Although the War Department sought to use the Ninety-third
Division (Provisional) to provide replacements for the Ninety-
second, Gen. John J. Pershing, commander of the American
Expeditionary Force, arranged for the skeletal division's four
infantry regiments to serve with the French. Except for
replacements needed by the two units, Pershing believed that
blacks sent to France could render the greatest service as
laborers or members of service detachments.*

Cable to Pershing, No. A. 726   February 2, 1918

Paragraph 4 .... The 369th, 370th, 371st, and 372nd are National Guard regiments
not part of any real division. It is understood you are to use them as line-of-communication
and not combatant troops. There are no more Negro regiments here except in Ninety-
second Division and it is not desired to organize more. Replacements have been delayed
by quarantine on account of epidemics as well as by transportation and equipment
difficulties. Will try to send both February and March replacements this month.

Cable from Pershing, No. P. 592   February 11, 1918

Paragraph 8 .... These regiments are not to be used as labor troops but to be placed at
disposal of French for combat service in French divisions. This utilization [of] these
regiments already approved by War Department. In view of service these regiments are
to be engaged it will be necessary for them to have ample replacements available. . . .

Cable to Pershing, No. A. 800   February 16, 1918

Paragraph 3 .... All replacements including those for March now en route or being
assembled. Still considered undesirable to organize two new Negro regiments here. If it
meets your approval, will ship two regiments of Ninety-second Division for replacements. Later when Ninety-second Division is shipped, use 369th, 370th, 371st, and
372nd Infantry as replacements for Ninety-second Division.

Cable from Pershing, No. P. 692   March 7, 1918

Paragraph 3 .... Under approved arrangements with French these four Negro regiments are to be used as combat units with French divisions. As these regiments are
combat units they should be brought to full strength before being sent abroad and
maintained at such. . . . Therefore request 1800 men immediately as exceptional
replacements for 369th Infantry. Also request automatic replacements for all Negro
infantry at rate of 6 percent per month. . . .

Cable to Pershing, No. 1447   June 3, 1918

The question of the best use to make of the large number of Negroes being received
from the draft is under consideration. It is proposed to use these for labor and service
battalions, pioneer infantry regiments and to form the remainder into regiments of

[Cable Section, General Staff, *Cable History of the Subject of Colored Soldiers*, Military Archives
Division, National Archives, Washington, DC.]

infantry. The French say they can train and use all colored regiments of infantry we can supply. It is proposed to replace the white pioneer infantry regiments that will be sent you by colored regiments as soon as they are ready and to use the white regiments so replaced in forming new divisions. Colored pioneer infantry regiments also to be used for your Second Army. . . .

Cable from Pershing, No. 1265   June 8, 1918

. . . Considering your plan to use Negroes received from the draft for labor and service battalions, pioneer infantry regiments, and to form the remainder into regiments of infantry, provides best possible utilization of these men. I recommend that these troops be formed for use as part of American forces and that their training and use by the French not be considered. Instead of forming white pioneer infantry regiments into divisions, I believe it important that they be utilized for training replacements, my needs for which will constantly increase.

●

Prior to entering combat, the 369th, 370th, 371st, and 372d Infantry of the Ninety-third Division (Provisional) seemed in generally good condition. The French instructors expressed satisfaction with the black Americans, who displayed firm discipline and high morale.

1. . . . I inspected the billets and the personnel of the 372d Infantry. . . . The appearance of officers and men is excellent. Discipline is reported to be excellent. The French officers on duty with the regiment as well as civilians express themselves as highly pleased with the conduct of the men, their discipline, and their aptness under instruction. This was rather remarkably emphasized on several occasions. A civilian informed me that when it was first learned that colored troops were to be stationed in the village that the inhabitants were quite concerned, but that after the short sojourn by the present, they now prefer them, even to their own troops. This seems such a remarkable statement that it is deemed worth quoting. . . .

4. 371st Infantry. . . . I found the same state of contentment existing among the attached French officers and civil population with the conduct and discipline of the regiment. The appearance of the men as to health is excellent. It is a new regiment formed of men obtained from the draft and the majority of them with no former military experience or training. They are reported to be progressing very rapidly. . . .

5. 369th Infantry. . . . The same enthusiasm on the part of the French instructors was evident in this regiment. I met the divisional commander and a number of other officers of adjoining sectors and all were enthusiastic in their comments about the progress and bearing of the 369th.

[Memorandum, Col. T. A. Roberts for chief of staff, American Expeditionary Force, 8 May 1918, Military Archives Division, National Archives, Washington, DC.]

6. 370th Infantry. . . . Appearance of officers and men is excellent. Discipline is reported to be also excellent. Reports from the French instructors and from civilians indicates [*sic*] the same contentment with their progress and with their conduct. A very marked improvement in general cleanliness over adjoining villages is evident in this town, due to the interest and industry of the officers and men of this regiment and has produced the same feeling of gratification among the inhabitants.

●

Pershing had requested that Foch, commander in chief of the allied armies, arrange the release from French control of the four regiments of the Ninety-third Division (Provisional). Once under American control, they would be reorganized as pioneer infantry units for field engineering duty.

That measure would have, just now, serious consequences. Two of these regiments, in fact, form a part as combatant units of a French division and the two others should shortly be assigned in the same way to two of our divisions.

If then, your suggestion were followed, the general commanding the French Armies of the North and North East would be under the necessity of immediately suppressing two of his divisions—through the inability of the moment to fill them up—which could not now be considered.

In presenting this situation to you I have no doubt that you will recognize with me that any modification made today in the employment of these colored regiments of the Ninety-third Division, instructed and used as combatants, would have troublesome consequences which could not be weighed with the slight advantage which the American army would gain in withdrawing them for labor troops.

[Letter (translation), Marshal Ferdinand Foch to Gen. John J. Pershing, 26 August 1918, Military Archives Division, National Archives, Washington, DC.]

●

The strain of combat and the resultant casualties eroded the strength of the 369th Infantry. Compounding the impact of sustained fighting were shortages of French-supplied equipment, the arrival of ill-trained replacements, the lack of decorations or other deserved recognition, absence of a leave policy, and losses among the officers.

11. During the recent offensive, in which this regiment participated as the center regiment of the 161st Division, and in which the heights and ridges of Champagne lying between Butte de Mesnil and Main Massiges were stormed, a large percentage of the

[Report, Col. William Hayward, commanding officer, 369th Infantry, to commander in chief, General Headquarters, American Expeditionary Force, 9 October 1918, subject: Condition of the regiment and request for advice and instructions, Military Archives Division, National Archives, Washington, DC.]

personnel of the regiment conducted itself in the most heroic manner, standing the terrific losses inflicted without yielding. To the disgrace of the regiment, the Negro race, and the American army, it must be said that a large number of enlisted men of this regiment conducted themselves in the most cowardly and disgraceful manner. They absented themselves without leave prior to each of the battles, stealing away in the night, throwing away their equipment, lurking and hiding in dugouts, and in some cases traveling many, many kilometers from the battlefield. This result did not come from any condition of general panic, as the regiment was never attacked, but on the contrary itself attacked the enemy each day. The result was that practically all of the heavy casualties were suffered by the older and better men of the regiment, and of course, among the officers. The situation now is such that it is not believed the remainder of the regiment can be made to attack again if the cowardly offenders escape punishment. Large numbers should be tried for misconduct in the face of the enemy. There should be wholesale executions following convictions. With all rewards in the form of citations denied this regiment and no punishment for gross cowardice inflicted, the unit cannot be made a fighting unit. . . .

●

As a temporary major general in command of the Ninety-second Division, Colonel Ballou had assured General Pershing that members of the black unit would "prove the best close in fighters in your Army, which means the best in the world." The division, however, failed to attain this high standard, ruining Ballou's prospects for advancement. An advocate of appointing black officers, he tended after the war to blame the failure, at least in part, on the policy he had recommended. In spite of his understandable disappointment, he acknowledged that white leadership and pervasive racial discrimination contributed to the problems his troops had encountered.

The colored company officer was slothful and negligent. The platoon commanders were prone to leave the frontline trenches and loaf around the kitchens. The conditions that demanded a most rigid discipline to counteract the evil effects of dispersion on a twenty-mile front were too often utilized as an opportunity for laxity and neglect. Work in front of the lines, especially night patrolling, was a farce. . . .

Viewed from a purely military point of view, which considers only military efficiency, all experience indicates that, in their present state of education and development, colored troops to compare favorably with white troops must have an even better leadership than the whites. With an inferior leadership they will surely fall below the average of the white troops.

It is probable that philanthropic considerations, or at any rate considerations not purely military, influenced decisions regarding the use of Negro officers; but even so it is

[Memorandum, Col. C. C. Ballou to the assistant commandant, General Staff College, 14 March 1920, subject: Use to be made of Negroes in the US military service, appendix 26, Army War College, *History of Negro Troops in the World War, 1917–1918,* Military Archives Division, National Archives, Washington, DC.]

believed that the decisions were erroneous. No good came, nor could come, to the colored race from imposing upon it responsibilities and burdens it could not creditably sustain. Such action was unfair to the race, and unfair to the handful of white officers whose reputations were bound up with the achievements of the colored troops.

The first fault in the making of the Ninety-second Division lay in the plan pursued in obtaining its officers. To officer a division in which the best possible leadership was required, only one-half as many students were summoned to the training camp as were summoned from which to select the officers of a white division. And, whereas candidates for commissions in the white camps were required to be college graduates, only high school educations were required for admission to the colored camp. And in many cases these high school educations would have been a disgrace to any grammar school.

For the parts of a machine requiring the finest steel, pot metal was provided.

Another serious fault was in providing that certain officers should be black, and certain others white. This barred the blacks from all hope of promotion, except as a captain or first lieutenant was eliminated, and a junior advanced in his place. The colored officers never could understand this, and attributed it all to the injustice of their division commander. It made no end of trouble. . . .

The colored man is entitled to *equality of opportunity*[1]—nothing more and nothing less. A dual code of opportunity based upon color is iniquitous as is our dual moral code, based on sex. Neither has a proper place in a civilized country. . . .

It was my misfortune to be handicapped by many white officers who were rabidly hostile to the idea of a colored officer, and who continually conveyed misinformation to the staff of the superior units, and generally created much trouble and discontent. Such men will never give the Negro the square deal that is his just due.

---

[1]Emphasis in the original.

●

The large number of black draftees—a projected 56,871 for May and June 1918—could not be absorbed by labor and service units, to which more than a hundred thousand blacks had already been assigned. This surplus of manpower, along with savage fighting on the western front, prompted the War Department to approve the organization of additional black infantry regiments, none of which was available before the Armistice.

1. Under authority conferred by sections one, two, and three of the act of Congress "authorizing the president to increase temporarily the military establishment of the United States" approved May 18, 1917, the president directs that there be organized, for the period of the existing emergency, the enlisted strength being raised and

---

[Memorandum, Brig. Gen. Henry Jervey, acting director of operations, for the adjutant general, 18 May 1918, subject: Organization of eight regiments of colored infantry, Military Archives Division, National Archives, Washington, DC.]

maintained by voluntary enlistment or draft, eight regiments of colored infantry, National Army. . . .

3. That field officers for these regiments be selected from the regular army and National Army and assigned to these regiments. . . . Company and staff officers will be selected from the National Army or reserve and will be white officers entirely.

●

In spite of a complaint by Emmett J. Scott, a Tuskegee Institute
educator and special representative of the secretary of war, the
army restricted blacks to the lower noncommissioned grades in
the newly organized black units.

1. . . . Mr. Scott states that this question was raised last winter and that he believes it was stated or intimated that later regiments would have colored noncommissioned officers. . . .

3. . . . It will be seen that only a small proportion of the noncommissioned-officer grades in colored organizations are reserved to white soldiers. . . .

This approved recommendation to appoint white noncommissioned officers to the higher grades only in colored units has been carried out. It would seem that no "Dead Line" exists except possibly in reserve labor battalions and in provisional and temporary organizations.

It must be remembered that the more intelligent, reliable colored men are placed in our combatant forces, in the engineer service battalions, stevedore regiments or labor battalions, where opportunity is given for advancement. Reserve labor battalions are composed of colored soldiers who, on account of their lack of intelligence, are not capable of performing any other class of duty. They are organized for domestic service only, being composed of laborers, a very large percentage of whom cannot read nor write. In order to remove the so-called "Dead Line" in reserve labor battalions and in provisional and temporary organizations, it would be necessary to include in their organization colored men capable of performing duty with combatant troops, engineer service battalions, stevedore regiments or labor battalions with the AEF. This would seem to be impracticable.

[Memorandum, War Plans Division for the adjutant general, 9 August 1918, subject: Request to remove the "Dead Line" which operates to prevent colored men from serving as noncommissioned officers, Military Archives Division, National Archives, Washington, DC.]

News of discriminatory policies, such as those announced by
order of Maj. Gen. Charles C. Ballou, helped alienate black
public opinion.

2. To avoid such [racial] conflicts the division commander has repeatedly urged that all colored members of his command, and especially the officers and noncommissioned officers, should refrain from going where their presence will be resented. In spite of this injunction, one of the sergeants of the Medical Department has recently precipitated the precise trouble that should be avoided, and then called upon the division commander to take sides in a row that should never have occurred, and would not have occurred had the sergeant placed the general good above his personal pleasure and convenience. The sergeant entered a theater, as he undoubtedly had a legal right to do, and precipitated trouble by making it possible to allege race discrimination in the seat he was given. He is strictly within his legal rights in this matter, and the theater manager is legally wrong. Nevertheless the sergeant is guilty of the greater wrong in doing *anything,*[1] no matter how *legally*[1] correct, that will provoke race animosity.

3. The division commander repeats that the success of the division, with all that success implies, is dependent upon the goodwill of the public. That public is nine-tenths white. White men made the division, and they can break it just as easily if it becomes a troublemaker.

4. All concerned are again enjoined to place the general interest of the division above personal pride and gratification. Avoid every situation that can give rise to racial ill will. Attend quietly and faithfully to your duties, and don't go where your presence is not desired.

[Headquarters Ninety-second Division, Bulletin No. 35, 28 March 1918, Military Archives Division, National Archives, Washington, DC.]

[1]Emphasis in the original.

●

The reality of Jim Crow, enforced by American authorities,
followed the division overseas and persisted after the Armistice
of 11 November 1918.

5. It is expected that a local military police detachment will be stationed in every town billeted by organizations of this division, this force will be augmented by the necessary details from the military police of this division so that there will be sufficient force in each town to maintain the strictest order and discipline at all times, day and night. In addition, the commanding officer of each town will employ the necessary sentinels to prevent men from leaving the town in which billeted without written

---

[Headquarters, Ninety-second Division, General Orders No. 40, 26 December 1918, Military Archives Division, National Archives, Washington, DC.]

permission. The especial duties with which the military police and sentinels are charged are:

(a) To ensure order and proper behavior by enlisted men at all times.

(b) To prevent them from loitering on streets and congregating in groups.

(c) To enforce proper dress and saluting by enlisted men.

(d) To prevent enlisted men from leaving the town in which billeted without permission.

(e) To prevent enlisted men from addressing or holding conversation with the women inhabitants of the town.

(f) To prevent enlisted men entering any building other than their respective billets with the exception of stores, places of amusement and cafes.

6. The commanding officer of each town in which troops are billeted will station a military police or n.c. [non-commissioned] officer in each cafe whenever they are opened for trade with enlisted men to enforce order at all time and ensure compliance with orders relative to the sale of liquor, etc. No enlisted man will be allowed in any room of the building except the cafe. In the event of misbehavior in any cafe in any town, the commanding officer will at once close all cafes in that town to soldiers, and will keep them so closed until the conduct of every man of his command is a guarantee of future good order. This is punishing the many for the sins of the few but is a necessary measure until the many will assist the authorities in getting rid of the few who are a menace to the public and to the good name and reputation.

●

W. E. B. Du Bois collected and published a series of documents that revealed the treatment black soldiers received during World War I. Even though the fighting had ended, the US Post Office Department refused to accept this issue of his magazine, an action that lent further credibility to the evidence that Du Bois presented. In August 1918, The Crisis *had declared that "the American Negro . . . is more than willing to do his full share in helping to win this war for democracy and he expects his full share of the fruits thereof. . . ." The contribution of black America, however, was scarcely appreciated and not rewarded.*

French Military Mission
Stationed with the American Army
August 7, 1918

Secret Information Concerning Black American Troops

CONCLUSION

1. We must prevent the rise of any pronounced degree of intimacy between French officers and black officers. We may be courteous and amiable with these last, but we cannot deal with them on the same plane as with white American officers without

["Documents of the War," *The Crisis*, May 1919.]

deeply wounding the latter. We must not eat with them, must not shake hands or seek to talk or meet with them outside of the requirements of military service.

2. We must not commend too highly the black American troops, particularly in the presence of [white] Americans. It is all right to recognize their good qualities and their services, but only in moderate terms, strictly in keeping with the truth.

3. Make a point of keeping the native cantonment population from "spoiling" the Negroes. [White] Americans become greatly incensed at any public expression of intimacy between white women and black men. . . . Familiarity on the part of white women with black men is furthermore a source of profound regret to our experienced colonials who see in it an overweening menace to the prestige of the white race.

Military authority cannot intervene directly in this question but it can through the civil authorities exercise some influence on the population.

•

The army had a low opinion of the Ninety-second and Ninety-third Divisions, with black officers more likely to be criticized than the noncommissioned officers—many of them veterans of the four black regular army regiments—or the enlisted men. The evidence, had the army been more willing to heed it, indicated that the problems experienced by the two units resulted largely from piecemeal or incomplete training.

The colored troops used by the United States included, besides the old regular regiments, one complete division, the Ninety-second; four infantry regiments, intended as the nucleus of an additional division, the Ninety-third; and numerous labor units of various kinds. Those who went abroad were the Ninety-second and Ninety-third Divisions, and labor troops.

Approximately, 350,000 colored men were drafted into the service, besides the comparatively small number of volunteers. Some 140,000 were sent to France, of whom 40,000 were combat troops, the rest labor units. They formed 9 percent of the strength of the army, 8.15 percent of the AEF, and 2.87 percent of its combat strength.

The Ninety-second was a National Army division, mostly of drafted men; the Ninety-third was formed from National Guard regiments, reorganized and redesignated as federal troops. Neither division was assembled for training, but both were scattered by detachments in various training camps. In general, the original company officers were colored, field and staff [officers] white. Many of the colored officers were members of the National Guard regiments incorporated; many others were old noncommissioned officers of the regular regiments; some few were graduates of officers' training schools such as those at Fort Knox [Kentucky] and Fort Sill [Oklahoma], and a special training school for colored officers at Fort Des Moines [Iowa]. It is noteworthy in this connection, that at the various schools very few [black] candidates qualified.

It is interesting to note that the commandant of this Fort Des Moines school was

[Army War College, *History of Negro Troops in the World War, 1917–1918,* Military Archives Division, National Archives, Washington, DC.]

Col. Charles C. Ballou, later major general commanding the Ninety-second Division. . . . General Ballou retained his command without intermission during the entire period of training and service in France—a piece of good fortune which came to few divisions.

The Ninety-second served as a complete division in France. The Ninety-third was never completed; its four regiments were distributed among various French divisions, where they were often transferred from one command to another, were equipped as French troops, and served as such. By reason of this use, it is impossible to give any complete estimate of the training received in France by these four regiments, but evidently it must have been sketchy. . . . A detailed analysis of the training of the Ninety-second as compared with a white division which had approximately the same time . . . shows that all the circumstances hampered the work of the Ninety-second more than that of the other. . . .

●

In spite of the complaints about the performance of black divisions in World War I, the army, as indicated by the results of this poll of Army War College students and staff, was not yet ready to bar blacks from its wartime ranks. Easily the most surprising response was a proposal to abolish segregated black combat units, replacing them with integrated organizations about 10 percent black.

In May, 1924, the Army War College, in one of its courses, asked each member of the faculty and class to answer a detailed questionnaire giving their opinions on the use of Negro troops in the army. The replies, coming from officers of considerable army experience and in some cases men who had had direct contact with Negro troops in one way or another, showed seventy-six favoring the use of Negroes in combatant organizations, compared to eight who did NOT[1] favor such use. The eight thought Negro manpower should be used only for labor purposes. Of those that favored combat use, thirty-nine said no combat branches should be excluded from getting a proportionate share of Negroes, thirty-seven said technical arms should be excluded, such as the Air Corps.

Fifty-nine said that for infantry and cavalry the regiment should be the largest unit in which Negroes are organized, thirteen thought the battalion should be the largest, and two thought there should be no colored organizations at all but that all colored manpower should be absorbed into white organizations.

In answer to the question whether Negro officers should be used if Negro combatant organizations are authorized, fifty-three officers thought there should be a minimum number of Negro officers used, generally in company grade, and that their appointment should be under [the] same physical, mental and moral qualifications as

---

[Memorandum for the commandant, Army War College, 24 August 1924, Military Archives Division, National Archives, Washington, DC.]

[1]Capitalized in the original.

whites. . . . About fifteen considered there should be no Negro officers commissioned in any combatant arms but only in service organizations. . . .

Col. James K. Parsons of the infantry, one of those favoring the use of Negro troops in combat units, opposed any all-Negro combat units. He said this was not because Negro combat units could not be made as efficient as white—he thought they could in units as large as brigade—but because of the "racial antagonism that will develop between white and negro [sic] units." His recommendation was to assign individual Negroes at a ratio of about two thousand to a division, three hundred to a regiment, twenty to a rifle company and one to a squad (infantry). He felt this plan would "reduce racial antagonisms to a minimum," permit like organization of all units so failure of any one could not be charged to the fact that it contained a Negro outfit, and cause [the] Negro to bear his proper share of combat losses. He predicted it would not meet opposition from whites because "even in the south [sic] white men work along side of the Negro without objecting, and it is reasonable to suppose that if he will do this, he will not object to serving alongside of him in time of war." He was, however, against putting Negro officers or noncoms over white men. . . .

●

The percentage of blacks in the navy during World War I was the lowest in any American war. The highest percentage was reached during the Civil War, when an estimated 25 percent of all sailors were Negroes. Estimates for the Revolutionary War and War of 1812 were 10 percent, about 8 percent for the Mexican War, and 8 percent for the Spanish-American War.

During the European war, total enlistments in the navy, 435,398, of which 5,328 were Negroes. The latter were divided as follows:

US Navy 3,203
US Naval Reserve. 2,099
National Naval Volunteers. 26
                                                                                  5,328

[Letter, superintendent, Office of Naval Records and Library, Navy Department, to librarian, Army War College, 10 December 1924, Military Archives Division, National Archives, Washington, DC.]

Following World War I, as the size of the army contracted, the
War Department imposed restrictions on the enlistment of
blacks, though men with previous service were later allowed
to enlist in cavalry units.

1. Only colored men who have had previous military (army federal) service will be accepted for enlistment. Students' Army Training Corps service will not be considered as previous service for purpose of such enlistment.

2. For the present, colored men will be accepted for infantry only, except in special cases as provided as follows:

a. For Quartermaster Corps, Medical Department, and Ordnance Corps only on the specific recommendation of the chief of the corps or department concerned.

b. For Motor Transport Corps only as authorized in the letter . . . which granted specific authority for the enlistment of 176 colored men, on recommendation of the chief of the Motor Transport Corps in each case.

3. Enlistments for and assignments to detachments at service schools will only be made by authority from the adjutant general of the army.

4. Enlistment for colored cavalry, Philippine Islands, were discontinued May 22, 1919. . . .

5. Enlistments for colored cavalry in general were discontinued July 16, 1919. . . .

[War Department Circular No. 365, 22 July 1919, US Army Military History Research Collection, Carlisle Barracks, PA.]

●

As the army shrank to postwar size, staff officers suggested
finding some legal means of reducing the black regiments to
permit the recruitment of more whites.

11. Having in mind the legislative and administrative action covering almost sixty years of our national existence, the following practical solutions are suggested—

(a) Portions of certain colored regiments might be made inactive, that is, one or more of the colored regiments of infantry and cavalry might be reduced to a headquarters, and one or two squadrons or battalions, the remaining squadrons and battalions made inactive. Such action has been taken with reference to certain regiments of white troops. . . .

(b) Certain miscellaneous detachments of colored enlisted men, such as the Cavalry School detachment at Ft. Riley [Kansas], the detachment at the Field Artillery School at Camp Knox [Kentucky], the detachment at the headquarters, District of Washington (Ft. Meyer [Virginia]); the detachment at the US Military Academy, and the

[Memorandum, acting judge advocate general for the deputy chief of staff, 15 March 1922, subject: Colored regiments in the United States Army, Military Archives Division, National Archives, Washington, DC.]

detachment at the General Service Schools, as well as others, amounting to considerably more than one thousand men, might be incorporated in and made a part of the colored regiments of infantry or cavalry.

●

Although unable to disband the black regiments, the War Department reduced their strength and designated certain small detachments as housekeeping troops at several installations. Blacks like Walter White complained that these changes served primarily to permit expansion of the Air Corps, which barred Negroes. By way of defense, the army pointed out that several large white units had been disbanded for this reason and that others had undergone reductions in strength.

It is not the intention of the War Department to abolish any one of the four present colored regiments, viz., the Twenty-fourth Infantry, Twenty-fifth Infantry, the Ninth Cavalry, and the Tenth Cavalry.

It is, however, necessary at the present time to restation the elements of the Tenth Cavalry and two companies of the Twenty-fifth Infantry in connection with troop movements now in progress involving many regiments of the army. These troop movements are necessary in order to distribute more effectively the troops of the reduced regular army and to effect economies in the housing program therefor.

It is also necessary at this time to effect a limited reduction in the number of colored enlisted men in the regular army. No colored units have been made inactive to date for the increments of the Air Corps. . . .

The reduction in strength and the rendering inactive of units of the regular army to permit the execution of the Air Corps Act of July 2, 1926, has been unavoidable. The reductions now contemplated in colored units are necessary to assist in providing the . . . last Air Corps increment.

———————

[Letter, F. B. Payne, acting secretary of war to Walter White, secretary, National Association for the Advancement of Colored People, 11 August 1931, Military Archives Division, National Archives, Washington, DC.]

The exclusion of blacks from the Air Corps remained a sore point
with the National Association for the Advancement of Colored
People, especially since the old black regiments were being
reduced in strength to facilitate expansion of the air arm.

White enlisted men are not permitted to enlist in the four colored regiments. They are kept exclusively for colored applicants. The Congress having thus expressed its will, the War Department has labored under the belief that it was the general intent of Congress not to mix the white and colored enlisted men in the same organization. Thus troops, batteries and companies throughout the service are made up entirely of white enlisted men or colored enlisted men. That is, there has been no mixing in these minor units. There have been a few exceptional cases where both white and colored applicants have been enlisted in the Medical Corps or the Quartermaster Corps. Generally, these men serve in an individual capacity rather than as a member of an organization. Colored men so enlisted are as a rule attached to colored organizations for duty, and corresponding white men are attached to white organizations.

You inquired about the Air Corps in particular. As far as I can discover, the question of enlisting colored men in the Air Corps has never been an issue before the War Department. Following its long-established policy, the War Department would not feel justified in mixing colored and white enlisted men in the same squadrons of the Air Corps. To do so would also violate what we believe was the intent of Congress when it prescribed that four regiments should be composed of colored enlisted men.

[Letter, Maj. Gen. George Van Horn Moseley, acting chief of staff, to Walter White, secretary, National Association for the Advancement of Colored People, 21 September 1931, Military Archives Division, National Archives, Washington, DC.]

●

The navy was now accepting blacks exclusively for duty as mess
attendants, and openings were very few.

1. A standard monthly quota of Negro mess attendants third class is assigned to each of the following recruiting districts:

Macon, Ga...................	5	Birmingham, Ala...............	5
Raleigh, NC	5	Little Rock, Ark.	5
Richmond, Va.	5	Nashville, Tenn...............	5

Total—30

2. The quota for December 1933 and the quota for January 1934 is set at the standard listed above.

[Navy Department, Bureau of Navigation Circular Letter no. 61-33, 16 November 1933, Navy Department Library, Washington, DC.]

*Charles H. Houston, an officer during World War I and a
Washington attorney, belonged to a growing number of blacks
actively seeking fundamental changes in race relations in the
United States. At one point, Pres. Herbert Hoover had taken stock
of the complaints from black attorneys, journalists, and other
leaders about the breakup of the Negro regiments and complained
that: "We do not seem to be able to get this thing quiet." In
the case of this Houston letter, the chief of staff refused to
acknowledge that a racial problem existed in the army, replying
that "there has been and will be no discrimination against the
colored race in the training of the national forces."*

In connection with the test mobilization and maneuvers of the army announced for this month and September, as a Negro veteran and former reserve officer I tender you in this open letter some plain but friendly advice about the attitude of Negroes toward the national defense. Negroes keenly resent the present policy of the War Department which excludes them from the newer arms of the service, which has eliminated Negro officers from duty with troops and has reduced three of the four Negro regiments in the regular army to the practical status of service battalions. The army cannot ignore and reject the Negro in time of peace and expect him to function with 100 percent efficiency in time of war. . . .

Negroes are willing to accept the full responsibility of their citizenship in the national defense, but they insist upon being integrated into the armed forces in time of peace with equal opportunity in all arms according to merit, and not according to preconceived prejudices. Negro troops and Negro officers have demonstrated their loyalty and ability wherever they have been given a fair chance. The Negro has a record of faithful and efficient military service reaching back to colonial days.

I therefore urge you to use your influence in lifting the ban of discrimination against Negroes in the army, and to see that Negroes are accorded full representation in all arms of the service with equal opportunity for advancement according to their ability.

[Letter, Charles H. Houston to General Douglas MacArthur, chief of staff, US Army, 9 August 1934, National Association for the Advancement of Colored People.]

•

*This letter, inspired by President Roosevelt's speech proposing a
quarantine of aggressor nations, raised the question of how the
United States could aspire to moral leadership abroad while
permitting racial discrimination at home.*

In view of your Chicago speech this week warning the United States of the dangers it faces in common with the rest of the world on account of the strife and warfare stirred up by aggressor nations, we again bring to your attention the bans and discriminations against

[Letter, Charles H. Houston to Pres. Franklin D. Roosevelt, 8 October 1937, National Association for the Advancement of Colored People.]

Negro citizens in the service of the armed forces. Our Negro population is the most loyal element in the country, and as 10 percent of the total population its loyalty and support are indispensable to the United States in any major war.

During the World War the patriotism and devotion of the Negroes in the armed forces were sorely tried by all the devilish insults and discriminations which prejudice could devise. We pray that the Negro population will always remain loyal, but it will not again silently endure the insults and discrimination imposed on its soldiers in the course of the last war.

We respectfully ask you then as commander in chief of the armed forces to issue whatever orders may be necessary to remove race discrimination in all branches of the armed forces on land, sea, and in the air, and to give Negro citizens the same right to serve their country as any other citizen, and on the same basis.

●

Two black aviators risked their lives to prove that members of their race could become successful pilots and were therefore worthy of acceptance in federal pilot training programs.

1. Chauncey E. Spencer and Dale L. White, both officers of and representing The National Airmen's Association of America, an organization which had its beginning in February 1939 . . . on 8 May 1939 made a cross-country flight of approximately three thousand miles for three purposes: (1) To meet with congressional representatives in Washington DC and to request their support to enact into the national law that Negroes be accepted into the, then, United States Air Corps, as pilots, mechanics and other related fields of aviation. (2) That a clause be inserted in section four of the House of Representatives Bill 3791 to authorize the secretary of war. . . . "to lend [equipment] to accredited civilian aviation schools, one or more of which would be designated by the CAA[1] for the training of any Negro air pilot . . ." (3) To attempt to stimulate interest in aviation among the youth of America by visiting Negro colleges and universities[,] giving talks on the proposed legislation and publicizing an air conference and air show . . . in which Negro airmen would participate.

2. Sen. James Slattery (Illinois), successor to the late James Hamilton Lewis, who championed the initial move to include Negroes for training under the National Defense Act, along with, and supported by Rep. Emmett O'Neil (Kentucky), Sen. Harry S Truman (Missouri) and Cong. Everett McKinley Dirksen (Illinois). Dirksen introduced the amendment to the Civil Aeronautics Bill in the House of Representatives prohibiting discrimination on account of race, creed, color or national origin . . . which resulted in Negro colleges and universities being designated by the CAA to train Negro youths under the Civilian Pilot Training Act. . . . The first two Negro schools certified by the CAA were West Virginia State College . . . and North Carolina's Agricultural and Technical College. . . . In 1941, the first Negroes began training to qualify as pilots with the United

---

[Letter, Chauncey E. Spencer to Lee Nichols, 19 June 1953, Center of Military History, Washington, DC.]

[1]Civil Aeronautics Authority.

States Air Corps, later to become pilots in the all Negro 99th and 100th Pursuit Squadrons at Tuskegee, Alabama. . . .

6. On 8 May 1939 while flying over Sherwood, Ohio, en route to Washington, DC for prearranged conferences with congressmen regarding the inclusion of Negroes in the National Aviation Programs, Spencer and White were forced to land their obsolete plane in a farmer's backyard due to a broken crankshaft. After two days and one night of repairing the damage they continued their flight toward Washington, however, darkness overtook them between Morgantown, West Virginia, and Pittsburgh, Pennsylvania, with no navigation instruments, means of communication with the tower or lights, they were guided into the Pittsburgh County Airport by its beacon light. After circling the airport several times attempting to attract attention of the tower operators, they noted a Pennsylvania Central Airline, commercial transport, coming in for a landing. They circled once more and lined up their frail ship behind it in order that they could "feel" their way down as its experienced pilot set the big transport on the runway . . . they made it but were immediately ushered to the tower officials and Insp. E. A. Goff, Jr. and asked to explain why they had violated established flight regulations, thereby endangering their lives and the lives of the passengers on board the PCA transport, in that they were flying after dark without the proper equipment and clearance. They explained that the attendants at Morgantown had refused to allow them to stay overnight and had directed them into Pittsburgh. They were grounded by the inspector but early the following morning he called to inform them that the results of the investigation cleared them and he commended them on a fine landing under such emergency conditions. Little did they realize it at the time but this incident played an important part, on their behalf, when it was related to the congressional representatives.

●

Sen. Harry H. Schwartz of Wyoming was instrumental in prodding the Congress into ending racial discrimination in federally sponsored civilian pilot training. He also addressed the problem of finding a place in the Army Air Corps for black airmen. His negotiations with Maj. Gen. Henry H. Arnold, chief of the Air Corps, led to the establishment in the spring of 1941 of a military training field at Tuskegee Institute, Alabama, where "social conditions" would not be embarrassing.

Mr. Chairman. . . . I have talked to Gen. [Barton K.] Yount [in charge of Air Corps training] several times and also with General Arnold. They have stated difficulties of one kind or another that they are encountering.

It is my considered judgment that those difficulties can be overcome. . . .

Of course, you understand the same as I do, whether we want to admit it or not, that

[Statement of Hon. H. H. Schwartz, United States senator from Wyoming, U.S., Congress, House, Subcommittee of the Committee on Appropriations, *Hearings on Supplemental Appropriation Bill for 1940*, 76th Cong., 1st sess.]

back under this is a feeling in the army and in the navy that bringing these Negro pilots and giving them this opportunity will result in some embarrassment one way or another on account of social or economic conditions.

I am not trying to change those conditions. . . . But I do believe that that trouble need not occur at all.

When I talked with General Arnold, he went this far. He said he thought that without trouble they could give approximately ninety-days' training at one of the flying schools, ninety days at Randolph Field [Texas] and ninety days at Kelly Field [Texas]. Of course, the trouble they expected to encounter from social conditions would be encountered at Randolph Field and at Kelly Field.

I suggested to General Arnold that that might be worked out, and he said he thought that it might be worked out. He said in his judgment a school could be designated by the War Department for this primary work. . . .

Then he said that he was of the opinion that the instruction at these schools, where they had colored students, insofar as it applied to instruction given at Randolph, that that also could be given there.

Then, when we got to the question of considering Kelly Field, the difficulty there was that there they are flying in squadrons, and in that case there would be a question of whether or not a white mechanic wanted to fly with a colored soldier, or whether a colored officer and a white officer could get along agreeably, or whether the social conditions might be embarrassing.

●

Although Congress forced the War Department to cooperate in the training of black aviators, Sec. of War Harry H. Woodring showed scant enthusiasm for accepting into the Air Corps graduates of this instruction program.

Mr. [D. Lane] Powers [of New Jersey]. Mr. Secretary, you are no doubt very familiar with Public Act No. 18, Seventy-sixth Congress, an act to provide more effectively for the national defense by carrying out the recommendations of the president in his message of January 12, 1939 to the Congress.

I wish to refer particularly to Section 4 of this act, which provides:

The secretary of war is hereby authorized, in his discretion and under rules, regulations, and limitations to be prescribed by him, to lend to accredited civilian aviation schools, one or more of which shall be designated by the Civil Aeronautics Authority for the training of any Negro air pilot, at which personnel of the military establishment are pursuing a course of education and instruction pursuant to detail thereto under competent orders of the War Department, out of aircraft, aircraft parts, aeronautical equipment and accessories for the Air Corps, on hand and belonging to the government, such articles as may appear to be required for instruction, training, and maintenance purposes.

["Training Negro Pilots," U.S., Congress, House, Subcommittee of the Committee on Appropriations, *Hearings on Supplemental Appropriation for 1940,* 76th Cong., 1st sess.]

I am wondering whether or not one of these schools will be designated for the training of Negro pilots.

Sec. [of War Harry H.] Woodring. We are considering that now. We are trying to work out a plan whereby we shall have a program under which Negroes can be trained. At the same time we are trying to avoid any situation that might be embarrassing either to the colored or to the white race. It is a very difficult problem, as you know.

We are trying to work this out in fairness to those colored men who are rightfully entitled to the training.

We are going to try to work this out honestly in the interests of every citizen of the United States.

●

A black historian cited the treatment accorded his race by the
US Army and asked that guarantees of equal treatment be
included in the draft law.

According to the 1930 census the Negro population was 11,891,143, or 9.7 percent of the total population. This constitutes a considerable reservoir of manpower. Nevertheless, both the army and the navy have declined to enlist this manpower except to a very limited extent. According to the adjutant general, the total strength of the colored personnel of the regular army on February 29 [1940] numbered 4,451, including 5 commissioned officers, 11 warrant officers, and 4,435 enlisted men, or 1.5 percent of the actual strength. . . .

At that time, the actual strength was approximately 229,636 men of whom 13,350 were officers.

In May and June, while the army was seeking 15,000 additional men, the quota of additional colored enlisted men authorized was 314. Currently, the army is enlisting 304 additional colored men. . . . under the expansion program of the army to 375,000 through voluntary enlistment the number of Negroes will be approximately 8,464 or 2.25 percent.

Of the five Negro officers, only two are line officers and neither one of them is serving with the regular army. Col. Benjamin O. Davis is the commanding officer of the 369th Infantry, New York National Guard. His son, 1st Lt. Benjamin O. Davis, a graduate of the United States Military Academy, is detailed to duty with a junior [senior high school] unit of the Reserve Officers' Training Corps. The other three Negro officers are chaplains. There is not a Negro doctor in the Medical Corps and not a Negro dentist in the Dental Corps.

And I respectfully invite the particular attention of the committee to this:

Congress thought it was providing for the training of Negro youths as army pilots when it enacted Public [Law] No. 18, Seventy-sixth Congress, approved April 3, 1939. . . .

Pursuant to that. . . , the Civil Aeronautics Authority designated the Chicago

[Statement of Rayford W. Logan, chairman, Committee on the Participation of Negroes in the National Defense Program, U.S., Congress, House, Committee on Military Affairs, *Selective Compulsory Military Training*, 76th Cong., 3d sess.]

School of Aeronautics at Glenview, Illinois, for the training of Negro pilots, and the secretary of war lent equipment to that school, but no Negro applicant has yet been accepted as a flying cadet and sent to that school for primary training. . . .

In order that the persons who will administer the compulsory military training law, if it is enacted, may know the intent of Congress with respect to the selection and training of Negroes, our committee is asking this committee to amend H. R. 10132 by changing Subsection (c) of Section 12, pages 12 and 13, to Subsection (d) and inserting a new Subsection (c) to read as follows:

No provision of this act shall be construed or administered so as to discriminate against any person on account of race, creed, or color.

or, in the alternative, as follows:

In the selection and training of men as well as in the interpretation and execution of the provisions of this act there shall be no discrimination against any person on account of race, creed, or color.

●

Sen. Tom Connally of Texas cited the Houston Riot of 1917 and the Brownsville Incident of 1906 in opposing the antidiscrimination amendment, offered by Sen. Robert H. Wagner of New York, to the Selective Training and Service Act.

I think I know as much about the colored race as does the senator from New York, and I think I serve them fully as well as does the senator from New York. I was raised with colored people, and played with colored boys when I was a boy, and I worked with them side by side in the cotton fields and other places. I am ready to fight for the right of the colored man under the Constitution, not simply during election time, as the senator from New York is. [Laughter in the galleries.]

But I realize better perhaps than the senator from New York that constitutional and legal rights are one thing, and the right to select one's associates socially is another thing. There is something in the Anglo-Saxon written in the constitution of the race, there is something written in the statutes of our blood, "Do not compel me to accept any man, whether he is white or black or yellow or red, as my social companion and equal, if I do not want to accept him. . . ."

In my state in 1916, I believe it was, or shortly before the World War, two regiments of colored regular infantry were stationed at Houston, Texas. What happened? There was a riot. There was some little social disturbance in the beginning. A policeman or someone reproached one of the colored soldiers for misconduct. I cannot give the details, but they are all in the official records. What happened? Those colored soldiers went out upon the streets of Houston and shot down and murdered a large number of inoffensive citizens, simply because agitators, social climbers, and others, for their own selfish and political profit, wanted to stir up the colored people. The lowest depths of their passions and prejudices were stirred up. They murdered countless white citizens going about their peaceful vocations.

[U.S., Congress, Senate, *Congressional Record*, 76th Cong., 3d sess., 1940.]

When Theodore Roosevelt was president of the United States, colored troops were stationed at Fort Brown, Brownsville, Texas. There was a riot and mutiny. The troops went about destroying property, and things of that kind. What did President Roosevelt do? Courageous man that he was, he ordered the discharge from the army of every member of that organization because of the mutinous conduct. As I remember—it was long before I came to Washington—Senator Foraker, trying to get a few votes, stir up everybody's passions, and collect dividends at election time, bitterly assailed President Roosevelt. However, the country sustained President Roosevelt. The investigation of the congressional committees vindicated him.

●

Dr. Rayford Logan championed views diametrically opposed to those of Senator Connally; a "third attitude" prevailed and the Selective Service Act prohibited racial discrimination in its application. In this instance the coalition of black organizations that Logan represented could not obtain a specific amount of money earmarked for the training of Negro National Guardsmen.

There are three prevailing attitudes among the Negro citizens of this country. One is that Negroes should be integrated into all branches of the military establishment without regard to race or color. A second attitude holds that since Negroes are the victims of many forms of oppression and discrimination comparable to those which this government has condemned in foreign countries, they should refrain from any participation in the armed forces of the United States. The third attitude. . . , while deploring this discrimination, insists that Negroes be given the opportunity to exercise their rights and perform their obligations as American citizens so that the United States will be morally as well as physically strengthened by a fair proportion of all her citizens in defending the principles upon which this nation was founded.

[Statement of Dr. Rayford Logan, U.S., Congress, Senate, Subcommittee of the Committee on Appropriations, *Military Establishment Appropriations Bill, 1941*, 76th Cong., 3d sess.]

●

Blacks in the navy remained few, and were segregated by race and assignment.

2. . . . the following information is furnished relative to Negroes in the US Navy. . . .
According to statistics compiled as of 30 June 1940, there were 4,007 Negroes in the US Navy. The majority hold ratings in the messmen branch and are stationed on the various ships and stations.

[Memorandum, Capt. H. A. Badt, USN to the officer in charge, Public Relations, 24 July 1940, subject: Negroes in the navy, Military Archives Division, National Archives, Washington, DC.]

The records do not show that a Negro has ever held a commission rank in the naval service. However, the highest rating held by a Negro is that of a chief petty officer, which is the highest enlisted rate obtainable.

The records show that five Negroes have been appointed to the US Naval Academy, but not [*sic*] have ever graduated.

CHAPTER FIVE
BLACK SOLDIERS IN WORLD WAR II

The United States raised the largest racially segregated army in the nation's history during World War II. The nondiscrimination clause of the Selective Service Act of 1940 banned racial discrimination only insofar as ensuring that every tenth man inducted into the armed forces would be a black. The army resisted even this gesture at first, arguing that it did not have appropriate units and facilities—appropriate meaning segregated—to absorb so many blacks. As in other wars, however, a worsening manpower shortage compelled the military to draw on the resources of the black community. By the time Japan surrendered, almost 700 thousand blacks were serving in the army throughout the world.

Black leaders and civil rights advocates urged that Negroes participate in the defense effort in order to combat both the foreign enemy and domestic segregation and discrimination. The name given this effort was the Double V campaign: victory against fascism abroad and discrimination at home. Although these leaders seemed to concentrate upon enlarging the role of the black soldier and sailor and ameliorating the blatant injustice that Negroes in uniform had to endure, they never forgot that segregation itself, which permeated American society, was the basic form of discrimination. They insisted that justice and the law demanded that black soldiers should serve alongside whites in all arms and branches of the service. These arguments failed to convince the Army General Staff. Couching its arguments in terms of military efficiency, the General Staff cited the army's experience in World War I and warned that social experimentation could undermine the war effort. The military leadership endorsed continued segregation and declared that blacks should serve where it considered them most useful—driving trucks or performing unskilled labor.

President Roosevelt, who sought to retain the support of black voters, arranged a compromise between the activists and the army. The army would remain segregated, though it would create black units in all its branches, both combat and service. The president also appointed a few Negroes to important and highly visible posts. Col. Benjamin O. Davis became the first black general, and William H. Hastie, dean of the Howard University School of Law, became the War Department's principal adviser on racial matters.

Roosevelt's attempt at compromise failed for a number of reasons. From the beginning, the army found it impossible to assign blacks to separate units in all the various branches. The policy of segregation required that blacks, many of them poorly educated, had to fill every specialty, regardless of the necessary skills, in an entire unit—for instance as pilots, gunners, bombardiers, clerks, and mechanics in a segregated Air Forces squadron. Also the army could not procure and train enough black officers to lead these units and had to rely instead upon white officers, a few of them very capable but many of questionable ability and sensitivity. Because of these policies, more and more black soldiers found themselves doing menial labor with little hope of promotion and almost no sense of participation in the war effort. Moreover, segregation on military bases, often resulting in markedly inferior living conditions for black units, was reinforced by the Jim Crow laws that operated against black soldiers in nearby communities. These factors had combined by mid-war to produce severe morale problems in black units and an increasing number of racial incidents.

The task of bringing the reality of the army's racial practices more closely into line with its announced policy of separate-but-equal treatment fell to the Secretary of War's Committee on Negro Affairs. Under the chairmanship of Asst. Sec. John J. McCloy, a white, who worked closely with Judge Hastie's successor, Truman K. Gibson, Jr., the committee quickly assumed leadership in matters concerning the organization and assignment of black units. McCloy and Gibson urged the army to expand the role of the thousands of trained black soldiers whose potential was being wasted in camps throughout the United States. As a result of the committee's efforts, reluctant overseas commanders were made to accept black infantry divisions and other combat units, particularly in the Pacific and in Italy. Although some of the black soldiers, especially members of tank and artillery battalions, gained hard-earned recognition, most blacks assigned overseas found themselves still mired in thankless routine well behind the lines. The advisory committee also tried to eliminate on-post discrimination, concentrating on the use of recreational facilities. Convinced that much of the army's race problem stemmed from poor leadership in black units, the committee worked to obtain more black officers and to improve the quality of white officers in command of black organizations.

The actions inspired by McCloy and Gibson helped stem the tide of black complaints but could not solve the basic problem, which resulted from a refusal to recognize that segregation was the most demoralizing form of discrimination. The War Department was caught on the horns of a dilemma. It could not raise morale and obtain maximum efficiency from black units unless it broke up those very organizations and disavowed the very policy that had spawned them. The claims of justice aside, as a practical matter segregation concentrated a large group of poorly educated black soldiers in a small number of racially exclusive units. Conversely, this same racial policy condemned the most gifted blacks to segregated outfits, many of them labor or service battalions that had little use for their talents and offered less opportunity for their development. Defended in the name of efficiency, military segregation was inherently inefficient.

An indication that segregation might someday end appeared late in the war. The European command, short of manpower on the eve of the German counteroffensive in December 1944, decided to use platoons and companies of black volunteers within front-line divisions. This action, along with the practice of integrating officer training, represented a minor deviation from the army's segregationist tradition, but the successful incorporation of blacks into white divisions offered a precedent for future change.

*Assured by passage of the Selective Service Act that blacks
would be included in significant numbers in the coming
mobilization, civil rights leaders were nevertheless concerned
about the nature of that service. Would it, they wondered, be
limited to the narrow range of assignments available to black
soldiers and sailors in the 1930s? A highlight of the campaign to
win equal opportunity for black servicemen was the meeting
between black leaders A. Philip Randolph, T. Arnold Hill, Mary
McLeod Bethune, and Walter White with President Roosevelt
on 27 September 1940. The discussion quickly moved beyond
the subject of job opportunity to integration. Despite the cautious
optimism of the president and Asst. Sec. of War Robert P.
Patterson that the services would move gradually toward
integration, Walter White, the executive secretary of the NAACP
and author of this report on the meeting, remained skeptical.*

The president opened the conference by stating that he had been pleasantly surprised a few days before by the officials of the War Department stating to him, without solicitation on his part, that Negroes would be integrated into all branches of the armed service as well as service units.

The secretary of the NAACP having been designated as spokesman, asked the president, first, if this applied to officers as well as enlisted men and, second, if this meant that Negroes would be continued to be used only in separate units, and third, if this open door policy applied to the navy as well as to the army.

Mr. [Robert P.] Patterson stated that it was planned to call soon approximately six hundred Negroes who were reserve officers for use in the armed forces. And as to the further use of Negroes as officers he stated that the War Department is bound by legislation passed by Congress in 1920 limiting them to the use of officers who have had World War service or ROTC training. Patterson stated that the War Department was attempting to get Congress [to] change this act since officers with the above qualifications were not sufficient in number to handle the army which will be created by the draft. Mr. Patterson did not refer to officers trained at West Point from which Negroes are almost completely excluded, there having been only two Negro graduates from that institution since 1870.

Apparently no one of the conferees with the exception of Messrs. Randolph, Hill, and the secretary had even thought of nonsegregated units in the army. The president, however, was immediately receptive when the secretary called to his attention the fact that while there might be at the outset difficulties in putting white and Negro soldiers together in Mississippi and Georgia divisions or regiments; there was no reason to anticipate any difficulties as being unsurpassable in states like New York, Massachusetts, Pennsylvania, and Illinois, where Negroes and whites attend the same schools, play on the same athletic teams, and live in the same neighborhoods without difficulty. The

[Report on Conference at the White House, 27 September 1940, subject: Discrimination against Negroes in the armed forces of the United States, Papers of the National Association for the Advancement of Colored People, Manuscript Division, Library of Congress, Washington, DC.]

secretary emphasized that in [*sic*] an army fighting allegedly for democracy should be the last place in which to practice undemocratic segregation.

The president stated that it should not be difficult to have the Negro regiments next to the white regiments and the Negro battery next to the white battery in an army division; that in times of war replacements from one battery or regiment to another are the usual procedures; that through this continuity of Negro and white regiments and batteries the army could "back into" the formation of units without segregation.

Mr. Patterson stated to the secretary that the suggestion was one which the War Department had never thought of but that he personally thought that it was an experiment worth trying and one which might be made a success.

As to the navy, Col. [Frank] Knox [secretary of the navy] stated that while he was sympathetic, he felt that the problem there was almost unsolvable since men have to live together on ships. He stated that southern ships and northern ships are impossible.

The president, however, stated to Colonel Knox that since the navy was organizing new bands for ships, the navy should immediately organize Negro bands and place them on the ships. This would be an opening toward [*sic*] which in time might help to solve the problem since it would accustom white sailors to the presence of Negroes on ships. Colonel Knox promised to look into the possibilities of doing this.

At this point the . . . memorandum which had been prepared by the Messrs. Randolph, Hill, and White, with the assistance of Messrs. Houston, Hastie, and Weaver was presented to the president and Messrs. Knox and Patterson. Each of these individuals agreed to study the memorandum and to see what could be done about carrying it out. The president read the memorandum carefully before the conference ended.

The president stated to the War and Navy Department representatives that there should be someone in each of these departments to handle matters relating to the Negro. The secretary got the impression that the president had in mind only someone in an advisory capacity rather than one with authority such as would be vested in, for example, an assistant secretary of war, or an assistant to the assistant secretary of war, and a comparable position in the navy.

It will remain to be seen how far the two branches of the armed service will go. Emphasis was placed in eliminating discrimination in employment in the army arsenals, navy yards, and in the apprenticeship schools being conducted by the government. Because of the shortness of time, there was no opportunity to go into great detail in connection with this discrimination.

*In accordance with its agreement to provide blacks equal
opportunity for military service, the army prepared a statement
of policy that, with the president's approval, became the basis
of the service's racial practices during World War II. Contrary
to Assistant Secretary Patterson's speculations at the White
House on 27 September, the new policy firmly established
segregation as the army norm.*

Memorandum to the President.

As the result of a conference in your office on September 27, 1940, on the subject
of Negro participation in national defense, the attached statement of the policy of the
War Department with regard to Negroes has been prepared. This policy has been
approved informally by the secretary of war and the chief of staff. I believe that it
provides a fair and reasonable basis for the utilization of Negroes in the army expansion
program, and if you concur it will be made effective.

Robert P. Patterson,
The Assistant Secretary of War

[Noted on the original: "OK FDR"]

WAR DEPARTMENT POLICY IN REGARD TO NEGROES

It is the policy of the War Department that the services of Negroes will be utilized
on a fair and equitable basis. In line with this policy provision will be made as follows:

1. The strength of the Negro personnel of the Army of the United States will be
maintained on the general basis of proportion of the Negro population of the country.

2. Negro organizations will be established in each major branch of the service,
combatant as well as noncombatant.

3. Negro reserve officers eligible for active duty will be assigned to Negro units
officered by colored personnel.

4. When officer candidate schools are established, opportunity will be given to
Negroes to qualify for reserve commissions.

5. Negroes are being given aviation training as pilots, mechanics, and technical
specialists. This training will be accelerated. Negro aviation units will be formed as soon
as the necessary personnel has been trained.

6. At arsenals and army posts Negro civilians are accorded equal opportunity for
employment at work for which they are qualified by ability, education and experience.

[Memorandum, Asst. Sec. of War Robert P. Patterson to the president, 8 October 1940, Modern
Military Records Branch, National Archives, Washington, DC.]

7. The policy of the War Department is not to intermingle colored and white enlisted personnel in the same regimental organizations. This policy has been proven satisfactory over a long period of years and to make changes would produce situations destructive to morale and detrimental to the preparations for national defense. For similar reasons the department does not contemplate assigning colored reserve officers other than those of the Medical Corps and chaplains to existing Negro combat units of the regular army. These regular units are going concerns, accustomed through many years to the present system. Their morale is splendid, their rate of reenlistment is exceptionally high, and their field training is well advanced. It is the opinion of the War Department that no experiments should be tried with the organizational setup of these units at this critical time.

[Noted on the original: "Dear Bob I think this is now in fine shape. HLS"[1]]

---

[1]Henry L. Stimson, secretary of war, June 1940–September 1945.

●

The time had come when no responsible black leader could countenance a mobilization plan, no matter how progressive in other respects, that called for segregated units. A battle had been joined between the civil rights leaders and the army.

A statement from the White House, October 9, implying that a committee of three persons, including Walter White, secretary of the NAACP, had approved a policy of segregation for Negro units in the army, was repudiated and denounced October 10 in a prompt telegram of protest to President Roosevelt.

The United Press account of the White House statement declared:

White House Secretary Early said the segregation policy was approved after Mr. Roosevelt had conferred with Walter White, president of the National Association for the Advancement of Colored People, and two other Negro leaders, etc.

This phraseology in the press was characterized by the NAACP as a "trick" to give the impression that Negroes had approved of the army Jim Crow, and to remove the pressure from President Roosevelt as commander in chief of the army and navy.

The telegram, signed by Mr. White, A. Phillip [*sic*] Randolph, president of the Brotherhood of Sleeping Car Porters, and T. Arnold Hill, formerly industrial secretary of the National Urban League and at present an assistant in the National Youth Administration, declared "in a written memorandum we submitted we specifically repudiated segregation."

["White House Blesses Jim Crow," *The Crisis*, Nov. 1940, pp. 350–51 and back pages. Reprinted by permission.]

On the other points of policy enunciated by the White House statement, the telegram declared:

> *We most vigorously protest your approval of War Department policy regarding Negroes in armed forces which precludes Negro officers except chaplains and doctors in regular army units other than two National Guard regiments staffed by Negro officers. We deny statement that "at arsenals and army posts Negro civilians are accorded equal opportunity for employment."*
>
> *We ask proof that even one Negro is now being given aviation training as pilot in Army Air Corps. As recently as October 1, 1940 the adjutant general of the War Department wrote "applications from colored persons for flying cadet appointment or for enlistment in the Air Corps are not being accepted."*
>
> *We further vigorously question your statement that morale is splendid in existing Negro units of the regular army. Many enlisted men in these segregated units have made repeated protests at being forced to serve as hostlers and servants to white army officers. We further question that Jim Crow policy of army "has been proven satisfactory." It has never been satisfactory nor is it now to Negro Americans. Such segregation has been destructive of morale and has permitted prejudiced superiors to exercise their bigotry on defenseless Negro regiments.*
>
> *We are inexpressibly shocked that a president of the United States at a time of national peril should surrender so completely to enemies of democracy who would destroy national unity by advocating segregation. Official approval by the commander in chief of the army and navy of such discrimination and segregation is a stab in the back of democracy. It is a tragic coincidence that you issued your statement on the same day the coup de grace was given by Senate Majority Leader Alben Barkley to the Anti-Lynching bill. The two acts are a double blow at the patriotism of twelve million Negro citizens.*

The NAACP has sent a letter to its 600 branches, youth councils and college chapters urging active and continued protest against President Roosevelt's Jim Crow national defense policy. The letter asks action before election day to make the protests of Negro Americans most effective.

The NAACP announced that the whole section of policy dealing with Negro army officers was a plan to put Negro officers "on the skids" and eventually eliminate them altogether.

An important part of the NAACP protest and activity will be upon the employment of Negroes in arsenals, navy yards, and industrial plants which have been awarded contracts under the national defense program.

*A particular goal of the civil rights forces was providing blacks
with equal job opportunity in the glamorous Air Corps. In
accord with its newly announced policy, the army formed a
black squadron but provided for its segregated training, and,
incidentally, the only completely segregated officer training in
the service, at Tuskegee, Alabama.*

2. Although it is estimated that it will require approximately a year and a half to complete the project outlined in the following paragraphs[,] it is desired to strongly emphasize the fact that a much longer period of time will be required for key enlisted personnel to absorb the requisite technical skill and experience that is indispensable to the proper functioning of tactical air units. *A period of at least from three to five years is normally required before enlisted personnel are qualified as competent crew chiefs, line chiefs, and hangar chiefs. Corresponding intervals of time must elapse before personnel in this category will be able to function satisfactorily in units visualized in this project.*[1] In view of the foregoing, white noncommissioned officers must continue to act as inspectors, supervisors and instructors for an indefinite period of time.

3. There are attached "Plan for Technical Training," Enclosure 1,[2] and "Plan for Flying Training and Establishment of Pursuit Squadron (C) SE,"[3] Enclosure 2,[2] which set forth detailed requirements and the steps involved in accomplishing this project. The general plan provides for the training of the following personnel:

	EM	Officers
Pursuit Squadron, Single-Engine	210	33
Base Group Detachment	160	10
Weather & Communications	20	2
Services	39	2
	429	47

In addition to the foregoing, twelve officers (C) will be required in the event that it is intended to establish the flying training activity on a more or less permanent basis for the establishment of additional units and for the furnishing of replacements. Officer candidates are to be on flying cadet status during the training period. The 429 enlisted men and the 14 flying cadets (nonpilot) taking technical and administrative training are to be concentrated at Chanute Field thirty days after the approval of the project for the immediate initiation of the necessary technical training and the other specialized training concerned.

[Memorandum, Office of the Chief of the Air Corps for the adjutant general, 18 December 1940, subject: Training and establishment of pursuit squadron (colored) single-engine, Modern Military Records Branch, National Archives, Washington, DC.]

[1]Emphasis in the original.

[2]Not included.

[3]Pursuit Squadron (Colored) Single-engine.

4. Approximately twenty-four weeks after the initiation of technical training a nucleus of trained personnel will become available for the initiation of flying instruction where students will enter the basic phase of training. Advanced instruction and unit training will be initiated subsequently after students are qualified. Due to the impracticability of undertaking the elementary phase of instruction at civil flying schools[,] it is planned to obtain trainees by the enlistment of graduates of the CAA[4] secondary phase, as flying cadets. A number of qualified candidates are now available and approximately fifteen additional potential candidates for basic military flying instruction will become available each four months.

5. A summary of the funds required is set forth in Enclosure 3.[5] It is recommended that flying training be conducted at Tuskegee, Alabama, and that all facilities required in connection with this training and the establishment of the unit under consideration be installed at that place.

FIRST ENDORSEMENT

War Department, AGO, January 9, 1941.   TO: Chief of the Air Corps.

Approved.

By order of the secretary of war:
Adjutant General

---

[4]Civil Aeronautics Authority.
[5]Not included.

*After serving ten months as the secretary of war's principal
adviser on racial affairs, Judge William H. Hastie prepared a
comprehensive assessment of the status of blacks in the army
along with a lengthy list of recommendations for remedial
action. On the whole, his recommendations, representing
practical steps the army might take to provide more equitable
treatment of black soldiers, were generally ignored by the army
staff. His general indictment of the army's racial policy,
however, would serve as a prototype of the attacks against
segregation in the services for over a decade.*

I. INTRODUCTION

The Fundamental Error of Philosophy and Approach

The traditional mores of the South have been widely accepted and adopted by the army as the basis of policy and practice in matters affecting the Negro soldier.

In tactical organization, in physical location, in human contacts, the Negro soldier is separated from the white soldier as completely as possible. Again, it is all too generally accepted that the white officer reared in the southern tradition, "understands" Negroes. That assumption has often led to the deliberate selection of junior reserve officers direct from civilian life in the South to command and train Negro soldiers. While it is not intended to burden this paper with many illustrative cases, it seems worthwhile to note the example of a commanding officer of a Medical Corps replacement center, who, after speaking proudly of his policy of selecting officers from the South to train Negro troops because of their understanding of the Negro, a few minutes later justified the quartering of a Negro chaplain in the enlisted men's barracks on the ground that these same carefully selected officers threatened to sleep in their automobiles if the Negro chaplain should be permitted to share officers' quarters with them. The general unwillingness of the army to assign colored and white line officers to the same regiment reflects the same underlying philosophy. The recent establishment of colored wards in station hospitals, contrary to former policy, is a similar manifestation.

The same basic error appears in the handling of relations between the Negro soldier and the civilian community. Insufficient effort is directed toward persuading the southern community to accept and treat the Negro in uniform as a man and a soldier. On the other hand, pressure is too frequently put upon the Negro soldier to make him humble and subordinate in accepting the insulting and humiliating manifestations of the traditional southern concept of the Negro's place.

This philosophy and approach are not working. In civilian life in the South, the Negro is growing increasingly resentful of traditional mores. The northern Negro's resentment is expressed more freely, if not felt more deeply. In the army the Negro is taught to be a man, a fighting man; in brief, a soldier. It is impossible to create a dual

---

[Memorandum, civilian aide to the secretary of war for secretary of war, 22 September 1941, Modern Military Records Branch, National Archives, Washington, DC.]

personality which will be on the one hand a fighting man toward the foreign enemy, and on the other, a craven who will accept treatment as less than a man at home. One hears with increasing frequency from colored soldiers the sentiment that since they have been called to fight they might just as well do their fighting here and now. Only determined and persistent efforts by the War Department and by commanders in the field can change the soldier's belief that he has only himself to rely upon when he is faced with humiliation and insult.

The present approach is failing in another way. The isolation of Negro combat troops, the failure to make many of them parts of large combat teams, the refusal to mingle Negro officers—most of whom have had little opportunity to command and train soldiers—in units with experienced officers of the regular army, all are retarding the training of Negro soldiers. . . .

V. SEPARATE NEGRO UNITS

Many of the underlying problems of morale and administration discussed in this report are inherent in the fundamental scheme of separate units for colored soldiers. Difficulties begin in Selective Service calls where the requirements of separate units have led to separate calls for white and colored soldiers in violation of the spirit of the Selective Service lottery. It will be remembered that in at least one state local officials refused for a period to honor such racial calls. The danger of such rebellion is again imminent. Many of the problems of placing Negro soldiers according to training and ability result from the necessity for finding a separate Negro unit and a vacancy in such a unit before the soldier can be assigned to duty. Another by-product of this policy is the absence of adequate recreational facilities for some small units and the expensive necessity for dual recreational facilities in other cases. The problem of the tactical disposition of the separate Negro unit has already been discussed.

All of this will not be changed overnight. The disturbing thing, however, is that there is no apparent disposition to make a beginning or a trial of any different plan. The beginning of the training of Negro pilots for the Army Air Corps offered such an opportunity and still does. The Armored Force offers another opportunity for a fresh start along sound lines. For example, a substantial portion of the Armored Force is being trained at Pine Camp, New York, in an area where racial tensions are not serious. Integration of highly competent Negroes, selectees and volunteers for three-year enlistments, into such an organization would be an important first step in the desirable direction. It is strongly recommended that some such beginning be made in the Air Corps, in the Armored Force, or in any organization which in its nature requires carefully selected men of superior intelligence and special competence.

I believe the military authorities do not comprehend the amount of resentment among soldiers and civilians, white as well as black, over the rigid pattern of racial separation imposed by the army. Today, soldiers and civilians are more critical than they were twenty-five years ago, in their examination of our professed ideals. Insistence upon an inflexible policy of separating white and black soldiers is probably the most dramatic evidence of hypocrisy in our profession that we are girding ourselves for the preservation of democracy. . . .

VIII. CONCLUSION

The proposals herein advanced involve the devising of detailed plans and procedures for the accomplishment of specific corrective measures and the surmounting of
difficulties inherent in the decentralization of the vast military establishment. But more
than that and before that, they require a determination that the tremendous power of
"higher authority" in an army shall be exerted in a forthright and uncompromising effort.

I sincerely believe that much of the difficulty being experienced in arousing the
nation today is traceable to the fact that we have lost that passion for national ideals
which a people must have if it is to work and sacrifice for its own survival. We have lost
that motivating drive because we have let our own behavior become inconsistent with
our wordy professions. Whatever we may think of the ideals of Germany or Russia,
fascism on the one hand and communism on the other had to become a national
obsession, a driving force revealed in domestic behavior, before these nations could be
keyed to a great war effort for the preservation and extension of their ideologies.

Until the men in our army and civilians at home believe in and work for democracy
with similar fervor and determination, we will not be an effective nation in the face of a
foreign foe. So long as we condone and appease un-American attitudes and practices
within our own military and civilian life, we can never arouse ourselves to the exertion
which the present emergency requires.

Such, I believe is the key to morale in the army and behind the army. Thus, the
types of correctives suggested in this report are one important aspect of our job of making
democracy real to ourselves, before we can achieve a supreme, united effort on behalf of
democracy against foreign foes. . . .

●

*As it would for years to come, the army rejected the possibility of
integrating its troops. In rejecting Hastie's primary
recommendations, General George C. Marshall, the chief of
staff, recited the familiar arguments about race and military
efficiency and the necessity of relating its policies to the customs
and habits of American society in general.*

A solution of many of the issues presented by Judge Hastie in his memorandum to
you on "The Integration of the Negro Soldier into the Army," September 22, would be
tantamount to solving a social problem which has perplexed the American people
throughout the history of this nation. The army cannot accomplish such a solution, and

---

[Memorandum, chief of staff for secretary of war, 1 December, 1941, subject: Report of Judge William
H. Hastie, civilian aide to the secretary of war, dated 22 September 1941, Modern Military Records Branch,
National Archives, Washington, DC.]

should not be charged with the undertaking. The settlement of vexing racial problems cannot be permitted to complicate the tremendous task of the War Department and thereby jeopardize discipline and morale.

I have considered carefully Judge Hastie's memorandum. Many of the recommendations contained therein are sound. Corrective measures have been taken regarding certain issues, and similar measures will be taken in others. There remain issues in which it is believed that the possible consequences of the action recommended would be detrimental.

The problems presented with reference to utilizing Negro personnel in the army should be faced squarely. In doing so, the following facts must be recognized: first, that the War Department cannot ignore the social relationship between Negroes and whites which has been established by the American people through custom and habit; second, that either through lack of educational opportunities or other causes the level of intelligence and occupational skill of the Negro population is considerably below that of the white; third, that the army will attain its maximum strength only if its personnel is properly placed in accordance with the capabilities of individuals; and fourth, that experiments within the army in the solution of social problems are fraught with danger to efficiency, discipline, and morale.

On October 16, 1940, the War Department policy in regard to Negroes was published to the service. This policy had the approval of the president prior to its publication. It is my sincere belief that the department has wholeheartedly carried it out. I can see no reason why it should be changed in any respect.

General Bryden[1] is discussing the report in detail with the undersecretary.

---

[1]Maj. Gen. William P. Bryden, deputy chief of staff.

*The termination of volunteer enlistment for the vast majority of
Americans and the need for the services to rely exclusively on the
draft for the acquisition of manpower caused an immediate and
unprecedented increase in the number of black servicemen and
would be a significant factor in the eventual reform of the
services' racial policies.*

PROVIDING FOR THE MOST EFFECTIVE MOBILIZATION AND UTILIZATION OF THE NATIONAL MANPOWER AND TRANSFERRING THE SELECTIVE SERVICE SYSTEM TO THE WAR MANPOWER COMMISSION

4. After the effective date of this order no male person who has attained the eighteenth anniversary and has not attained the thirty-eighth anniversary of the day of his birth shall be inducted into the enlisted personnel of the armed forces (including reserve components), except, under provisions of the Selective Training and Service Act of 1940, as amended; but any such person who has, on or before the effective date of this order, submitted a bona fide application for voluntary enlistment may be enlisted within ten days after said date. . . .

13. This order shall take effect immediately and shall continue in force and effect until the termination of Title I of the First War Powers Act, 1941.

Franklin D. Roosevelt

[Executive Order 9276, 5 December 1942, *The Federal Register.*]

●

*Although only incidentally related to the provision of equal
treatment and opportunity for black servicemen, the decision to
segregate blood banks nevertheless significantly affected morale
in the black community and provided yet another cause for the
development of a universal and effective black protest in the
years to come.*

The following reply is made to your memorandum of August 30:
This office has never at any time given such orders as those referred to in recommendation (1). No army agency is concerned in the direct collection of blood in connection with the present military program.
When it was decided to establish a blood plasma bank, the American Red Cross volunteered to aid the army and navy, which participate equally in this effort, by procuring from voluntary donors blood in the required amounts, all expense to be borne

[Memorandum, Maj. Gen. James J. Magee, the surgeon general, for Ass't. Sec. of War John J. McCloy, 3 September 1941, Modern Military Records Branch, National Archives, Washington, DC.]

by the Red Cross up to the point of reception of the collected blood by the biological laboratories designated to process it. The collecting stations are operated by the Red Cross, at Red Cross expense and without interference from any army agency. The program already inaugurated is believed to be adequate for the combined needs of the army and navy.

The possibility that this worthy and necessary project might encounter opposition because of the interjection of racial differences did not at any time present itself until the occurrence of an incident recently in Baltimore. Since that time, this office has had correspondence with the chairman of the American Red Cross and conferences with representatives of his office. For reasons not biologically convincing but which are commonly recognized as psychologically important in America, it is not deemed advisable to collect and mix Caucasian and Negro blood indiscriminately for later administration to members of the military forces.

Consideration has been given to an alternative plan of establishing, in addition to the present chain of blood donor stations, a duplicate chain for the collection of Negro blood only, this to be processed separately and dispensed for use among Negro members of the military establishment. I am informed that the American Red Cross does not look with favor upon this proposal because of the added expense and administrative difficulties, and I have informed the chairman of that organization that, in my opinion, this additional expense would not be justified by the relatively small amount of Negro blood to be obtained under such a plan. It should be noted also that such a system of segregation of white and Negro blood plasma would entail many problems in connection with separate processing, while the effective administrative control of storage and shipment to the place of use would present very great difficulty.

The question raised in recommendation (1) of the enclosed letter from Mr. John P. Davis[1] apparently had its genesis in a laudable desire on the part of the group he represents to ensure full expression of the patriotic impulses of American Negroes. This sentiment undoubtedly has the full approbation of all our people and the matter may perhaps be looked upon as one of method only toward the furtherance of an important project. It seems that the most effective demonstration of Negro help in this case may be found in acquiescence in the present program of blood plasma procurement without insistence on the introduction of changes which would result in increased expense and administrative complications.

---

[1]Not included.

*Concerned with placing black demands for integration in what
he considered the proper context, Ass't. Sec. of War John J.
McCloy called for an abatement of criticism in the black
press and predicted, as army leaders had been predicting for
more than a century, that black performance during the war
would bring about black goals after the war.*

I have your note of June 30 and the editorials from *Fortune,* the *Chicago Defender*
and the *Philadelphia Tribune.* I like the editorial from the *Tribune.* I have yet to read the
article in *Fortune.*

I think I probably ought to state in writing what my attitude is. Of course, there is
no group in the country that should not agitate for the elimination of undemocratic
practices. Like sin, everyone is against undemocratic practices. What I urge upon the
Negro press is to lessen their emphasis upon discriminatory acts and color incidents
irrespective of whether the white or the colored man is responsible for starting them.
Frankly, I do not think that the basic issues of this war are involved in the question of
whether colored troops serve in segregated units or in mixed units and I doubt whether
you can convince the people of the United States that the basic issues of freedom are
involved in such a question. In its policy of playing up the incident of which I speak, I
believe that papers like the *Pittsburgh Courier* and, perhaps, some others, serve to take
the mind of the Negro soldier and the Negroes generally off what you term the basic
issues of this war. If the United States does not win this war, the lot of the Negro is going
to be far, far worse than it is today. Yet, there is, it seems to me, an alarmingly large
percentage of Negroes in and out of the army who do not seem to be vitally concerned
about winning the war. This, to my mind, indicates that some forces are at work
misleading the Negroes. I bespeak greater emphasis on the necessity for greater out-and-
out support of the war, particularly by the Negro press, and I feel certain that the
objects for which you aim will come much closer to achievement if the existing emphasis
is shifted than if it is not.

[Memorandum, Ass't. Sec. of War John J. McCloy for Judge Hastie, 2 July 1942, Modern Military
Records Branch, National Archives, Washington, DC.]

●

*Frustrated by the army's adamant opposition to what he
considered essential racial reforms, Hastie resigned. Whatever
else his resignation may have achieved, his protest stopped the
planned segregated training of black officer candidates in the
Army Air Forces.*

As you know, I have believed for some time that my presence in the War
Department is no longer essential to the maintenance of the several substantial gains

---

[Memorandum, William H. Hastie, civilian aide to secretary of war for secretary of war, 5 January
1943, Modern Military Records Branch, National Archives, Washington, DC.]

made during the past two years in the handling of racial issues and particular problems of Negro military and civilian personnel. At the same time I have believed that there remain areas in which changes of racial policy should be made but will not be made in response to advocacy within the department but only as a result of strong and manifest public opinion. I have believed that some of these changes involve questions of the sincerity and depth of our devotion to the basic issues of this war and thus have an important bearing, both on the fighting spirit of our own people and upon our ability as a nation to maintain leadership in the struggle for a free world. Segregation within army theaters, the blood plasma issue and the unvarying pattern of separate Negro units are such matters.

Therefore, it has seemed to me that my present and future usefulness is greater as a private citizen who can express himself freely and publicly upon such issues than as a member of the War Department under obligation to refrain from such public expression. Both the secretary of war and the undersecretary have felt that my view of this matter is mistaken. In deference to the judgment of men whom I respect and to whom I feel an obligation of personal loyalty I have remained at my post.

Compelling new considerations have now arisen. In one very important branch of the army, the Air Forces, where the handling of racial issues has been reactionary and unsatisfactory from the outset, further retrogression is now so apparent and recent occurrences are so objectionable and inexcusable that I have no alternative but to resign in protest and to give public expression to my views. This ultimate decision has been forced upon me by:

(a) the announcement just made of the establishment of a segregated officer candidate school to train Negro ground officers for the Air Forces, to open at Jefferson Barracks, Missouri, on January 15, 1943; and

(b) the humiliating and morale-shattering mistreatment which, with at least the tacit approval of the air command, continues to be imposed upon Negro military personnel at the Tuskegee Air Base, the principal training center of the Air Forces for Negro troops.

For convenient reference I will discuss these issues and related matters in numbered paragraphs. . . .

[2] c. A small deviation from the separate school program was made when one group of Negro soldiers received training as enlisted technicians and mechanics at Chanute Field [Illinois]. The results were excellent. The men did well. I urged the importance of repeating such training for subsequent groups on a continuous basis. However, the program stopped with the first group. Efforts were made by the Air Forces to set up segregated technical training at Tuskegee or elsewhere. Difficulties were encountered. In the meantime successive classes of Negro pilots were being trained, but no supporting technical schooling of ground crew members was in progress. Thus even the segregated program has gotten badly out of balance in the effort to accomplish its extension. The prospect is that in 1943 Negro pilots will be ready before and faster than adequate numbers of trained ground crews are available. . . .

3. The racial impositions upon Negro personnel at Tuskegee have become so severe and demoralizing that, in my judgment, they jeopardize the entire future of the Negro in combat aviation. Men cannot be humiliated over a long period of time without a shattering of morale and a destroying of combat efficiency. . . .

d. It is tragic irony that while the whole course of handling racial relations at Tuskegee is such as to destroy combat efficiency, the Air Forces are now undertaking an historical study to determine whether and where Negroes will fit into air combat functions. The answer to this question will not be found in such a study, but rather in such present and future handling of Negro soldiers that their pride and dignity and self-respect as men and as American soldiers will be preserved and heightened rather than destroyed.

●

Truman K. Gibson, Jr., succeeded Hastie as civilian aide in 1943. A lawyer with ties to the Democratic party in Chicago, Gibson adopted a different approach to the army's race problems. Enjoying close personal ties with Assistant Secretary McCloy, Gibson avoided a frontal attack on the army's policy, concentrating instead on winning piecemeal reforms. His efforts gained many practical reforms in the army's treatment of its black soldiers.

1. During the last two and one-half years, I have visited most of the army posts and stations throughout the country and have examined numerous records that have reported investigations of racial matters. On the basis of this experience, it is my opinion that there is a serious and immediate need for some expression calling attention to the responsibilities of commissioned personnel for the proper treatment of Negro officers and enlisted men.

2. Certainly the problem of race in America will not be solved by the army. Quite properly, the army should state that it does not possess the time or the facilities to solve both the social and military problems facing the country.

3. Unfortunately, racial attitudes are unpleasant facts that must be dealt with and met by the army. They cannot be dismissed as social problems. It is my conviction that in the army there is no satisfactory pattern of procedure that can serve as a uniform guide for the treatment of Negroes. There have been directives that have issued from time to time on various aspects of the problem that appear important at the moment. Because of the large number of such statements issued, generally experience has shown that little importance has been attached to those dealing with Negroes. In addition, since the issuance of these statements many officers have been commissioned. As result of these factors most officers do not know what the official policy and attitude should be toward Negroes. Consequently, the military pattern is as variegated as the one Negroes have met in civilian life. It is not surprising then that most officers, in view of the fact that they have to draw on their civilian experiences, tend to adopt the same approaches toward Negro soldiers as they used toward Negro civilians.

[Memorandum, Truman K. Gibson, Jr., acting civilian aide to assistant secretary of war, 14 May 1943, Modern Military Records Branch, National Archives, Washington, DC.]

4. This attitude has been unfortunate. Negro soldiers do not possess the regional cohesion and the general uniformity found in civilian communities. They enter the service from all parts of the United States. They have been instructed to regard themselves as soldiers. They have been exposed to the current preachments about democracy. They are, therefore, not conditioned to withstand the shock of attitudes within the army that relegate them to inferior positions. Certainly difficulty can be expected from such attitudes as evidenced by a memorandum dated May 8, 1941, that went out from the Air Forces where it was stated "there must and will be segregation." Honest confusion necessarily arises in the field as to just what is expected of commanders, particularly when the memorandum had to do not alone with unit segregation but with complete segregation in recreational facilities which in turn plays into the hands of Negro protagonists of equal rights who say that the army is attempting to impose the southern pattern of segregation throughout the continental United States and in fact throughout the world.

5. I do not believe that racial attitudes which have been firmly entrenched over a period of years can be radically changed in a short while by any general statement. The issue, in my opinion, is not one of changing fundamental attitudes. It is little more than getting the attitude across to our civilian army that all soldiers engaged in a common task should be treated as soldiers regardless of race. Racial prejudices from a point of view of military necessity must be shelved for the duration of the war at least by military personnel and when our country and democratic institutions are not so seriously threatened as they are now, we will all have opportunity to indulge ourselves in many luxuries including those of personal preferences and prejudices. . . .

●

Disturbed by reports of growing racial tension in the army in
1943, Secretary Stimson created the Advisory Committee on
Negro Troop Policies under Assistant Secretary McCloy to
investigate conditions and recommend reforms in the army's
racial practices. Truman Gibson worked closely with McCloy
(in time he would become an official member of the advisory
committee), and his influence can be seen in the tenor of the
committee's first recommendations.

1. Disaffection among Negro soldiers has spread to the extent that it constitutes an immediately serious problem. In recent weeks, there have been riots of a racial character at Camp Van Dorn, Mississippi; Camp Stewart, Georgia; March Field, California; Fort Bliss, Texas; Camp Breckinridge, Kentucky; San Luis Obispo, California. At many other stations there is a smouldering unrest which is quite likely to erupt at any time. . . .

[Memorandum, Ass't. Sec. of War John J. McCloy for chief of staff, 3 July 1943, subject: Negro troops, Modern Military Records Branch, National Archives, Washington, DC.]

2. Practically all of the reported disturbances have followed a fairly definite pattern. Unrest and disaffection begin with real or fancied incidents of discrimination and segregation. No positive action is taken to overcome the causes of irritation or unrest. Gossip or rumor, of a nature designed to excite the men, circulates among the units, and a minor incident brings on a general outbreak.

3. In the opinion of this committee, after a study of detailed reports of many such cases, there is general evidence of failure on the part of commanders in some echelons to appreciate the seriousness of the problem and their inherent responsibilities. Also apparent is the lack of appreciation for the urgent necessity of continuous and vigorous action to prevent incidents of discrimination and segregation and the spread of inflammatory gossip, and to take positive preventative measures to spike the impending general outbreak.

4. a. The committee recognizes that the principal function of the troop leader under present conditions is training, but leaders must nevertheless concern themselves adequately with discipline, morale, and welfare. It is important that there be no discrimination against Negro troops in the matter of privileges and accommodations. It is equally important that there be no discrimination in favor of Negro troops in the way of compromising disciplinary standards. Under no circumstances can there be a command attitude which makes allowances for the improper conduct of either white or Negro soldiers, among themselves or towards each other. Improper conduct cannot be justified on the basis of relative average intelligence. Discipline is not a matter of intelligence. Breaches of discipline must be handled firmly, legally, and without compromising any standards of conduct, and this is true whether the problem deals exclusively with white troops, exclusively with Negro troops, or with both classes. All men must be made to understand this and, if necessary, instruction must be adjusted to their respective temperaments and limitations.

b. Maintenance of proper discipline and good order among soldiers, and between soldiers and the civilian population, is a definite command responsibility. Mutinous conduct and violations of the principles of military discipline cannot be countenanced in any element of the army, and prompt and effective disciplinary measures must be taken to punish those guilty of such conduct.

c. Failure on the part of any commander to concern himself personally and vigorously with this problem, and to take proper action to prevent outbreaks of the type referred to in paragraph 1, should be considered as evidence of lack of capacity to properly fill the position to which he has been assigned.

5. The committee recommends:

a. That the chief of staff, either by memorandum or through oral instructions, bring the seriousness of the present situation and the responsibility of commanders of all echelons to the attention of the three principal commanders, to be conveyed by them to those under their jurisdiction. It should be impressed upon the commander of every unit or station at which Negro troops are located that the proper and intelligent treatment of this problem is one of his most difficult and important tasks. He must be required—

(1) To maintain close personal contact with the situation,

(2) To follow implicitly the War Department policies and instructions, in letter and spirit, with respect to discrimination and the provision of equal facilities,

(3) To take positive action to ensure early determination of the existence of unrest and disaffection among the troops and to remove the causes therefor, whether they result from conditions under his jurisdiction or from unsatisfactory relationships with the civilian population,

(4) To develop definite programs within his own jurisdiction for the elimination of causes of friction on military reservations,

(5) To maintain close relations with the civil authorities and secure cooperative action by them to remove or correct causes of friction between soldiers and the civil population.

(6) To discover and suppress inflammatory gossip, rumors, or propaganda among the troops, preferably by countermeasures to offset same. When unrest and the causes therefor are known to exist, he must see that the troops themselves are aware that he is so informed and are themselves informed as to the measures the commander is taking to remove the causes.

(7) When conditions so warrant and when it is apparent that the means under his jurisdiction are ineffectual to obtain corrective or remedial action, to immediately report all facts of the circumstances to his superior.

b. That the commanding generals of the Air, Ground, and Service Forces be directed to submit specific recommendations with regard to changes in War Department policy; treatment of Negro personnel; use of facilities; organization of Negro soldiers into units and employment of Negro units.

c. That Negro combat troops be dispatched to an active theater of operations at an early date. In the opinion of the committee, such action would be the most effective means of reducing tension among Negro troops.

d. That the three principal commanders be directed to report to the chief of staff the action taken by them to carry out this program.

●

*General Marshall acted quickly on the advisory committee's
first recommendation. Admitting that much of the racial unrest
in the army had been caused by discrimination, itself the result
of the failure of commanders to live up to their responsibilities,
Marshall ordered "vigorous action" to prevent incidents of
discrimination, to maintain discipline, and to move quickly
against mutinous conduct. At the same time, the chief of staff
ignored the committee's other proposals, one of which it
considered so important that it turned to the secretary of war for
help.*

1. The committee met in Mr. McCloy's office at 1000. All members were present except Col. J. H. McCormick, AAF, who was represented by Col. C. DuBosque, AAF.

[Minutes of meeting of Advisory Committee on Negro Troop Policies, 29 February 1944, Modern Military Records Branch, National Archives, Washington, DC.]

Gen. C. A. Russell, Lt. Col. H. A. Gerhardt and Mr. T. K. Gibson, Jr. were also present. Mr. McCloy was absent during the first few minutes of the meeting.

2. The following is a summary of the proceedings of the meetings:

a. The use of Negro combat troops against the enemy

Gen. [Miller G.] White asked General Russell to comment on the use of Negro combat troops in action against the enemy.

General Russell: There is little to discuss; we supply the means. It would be disastrous to impose rigidly on the theater commander without assuming responsibility.

General White: We must use available troops. We allot certain types.

General Russell: Theater commanders want so many of various types, air, ground, etc. Designated units are dispatched. They are selected according to fitness. After arrival in the theater, the theater commander decides their use. About 9 percent of the troops overseas are Negro, which is about the percentage of Negroes in the army.

General White: Despite this, only the Ninety-ninth Squadron and some antiaircraft units have been in action. In Italy all types of troops are present. Have you sent any colored infantry or artillery there?

General Russell: Can't say.

General White: Assume only the Ninety-second Division is available and we can't send it now. We can send a combat team similar to the Japanese. Sooner or later we will have to do it. We can't take 10 percent of the army from Negroes and not use any of them for combat troops.

Gen. [Benjamin O.] Davis: I think the War Department is subject to criticism because of lack of publicity about Negroes in the army. Some publicity has been given out recently. In movies, action scenes are shown but none of Negroes. For a speech recently the Bureau of Public Relations gave me information I had never seen. I don't believe the people realize the number of Negroes abroad.

General White: This is not the point. We will have to engage Negro combat units.

Mr. McCloy joined the meeting at this point and said in effect: In a talk with General Marshall and the secretary of war, I said I thought we ought to have on record the use of Negro combat troops in war. General Marshall asked if I suggested anything further.

The secretary of war said present it to the staff; we feel that we must use colored combat troops, put them to the gage of battle.

I would like to discuss the form of a recommendation for this committee to make.

General White: We have talked on the same line. Russell said 9 percent overseas are colored and the War Department can't dictate how theater commanders use troops. I feel and believe and [Maj. Gen. Ray] Porter agrees; organize combat teams and tell the theater commanders to use them.

Mr. McCloy: In some situations we have to dictate, as when national policy is involved. This is such a case. Ten percent of our people are colored and we have to use it. We make a farmer out of a clerk. It is a vital national policy to make a military asset out of that part of the population.

Mr. Gibson: I can't talk of the military side. However, West African troops are being used in Burma. The War Department sent an unfortunate letter to a Republican congressman. The present issue of conversion of troops is in the minds of civilians, both

Negro and white. The belief is that the War Department will not use Negroes in combat. At a recent Negro Republican meeting the subject of the keynote address was the nonuse of Negro troops. This is a real political issue. The War Department should not be involved, but is right in the middle of it. Many say it's the long-time War Department policy. I can't overemphasize the importance of this question. If things are done under pressure, no one will be satisfied.

General Porter: On that line—converting Negro units, I am forced to recommend conversion if Negro combat units aren't used in combat.

Mr. Gibson: Congressman [William L.] Dawson was going to act Monday, but I got him to hold off. I think some statement should be put out. The inconsistencies in the letter to Congressman [Hamilton] Fish, as the discussion of educational standards, appear to Negroes.

General White: If we are going to force theater commanders to take Negro combat units, we have to bring units up to efficient standards.

Mr. McCloy read a proposed recommendation to the secretary of war and requested comment (the final form of recommendation is stated later).

General Porter: We could provide combat teams from the Ninety-second Division.

General White: We should start off in a conservative manner.

General Russell: General Porter prepares them. The Ninety-third Division was under standard. If you are going to force the commander to use them, be sure of the efficiency of the unit. We were accused in the last war of using unprepared Negro units. I don't know the units; they are given to me.

Mr. McCloy read a revised statement of the proposed recommendation.

General Russell: They should be hand picked.

General White: I disagree. Take a normal unit and train it.

General Davis: Can we say our officers can't train our Negroes if West African troops are used? If the army makes up its mind, it can do it.

Mr. McCloy: Is the recommendation satisfactory?

General Dalton: I would make it stronger.

General Porter: It would take a directive of the chief of staff to enforce it.

General Dalton: I feel as strongly as anyone to give the theater commander what he wants.

Mr. McCloy: I feel the theater commanders have been given too much consideration.

Mr. Gibson: How about a statement to the public?

Mr. McCloy: I think it desirable. I will talk with the chief of staff and the Bureau of Public Relations.

General Porter: Publicity should be given to the Ninety-third Division after it arrives.

The committee then adopted the following recommendation to be submitted to the secretary of war:

It is the recommendation of this committee that, as soon as possible, colored infantry, field artillery, and other combat units be introduced into combat and that if present organizations or training schedules do not permit such prompt commitment, that steps be taken to reorganize any existing units or schedules so as to permit the introduction of qualified colored combat units, as promptly as possible, into battle.

The secretary of war ordered the commitment of black units to
battle. In this recommendation, McCloy spoke of the need to
change army training practices if current methods failed to
produce acceptable black combat units.

I enclose a formal copy of a resolution adopted by the Committee on Negro Troop Policies, which was appointed, as you know, over a year ago by the chief of staff. The committee is composed of the heads of the General Staff bureaus, representatives of the Ground Forces, the Air Forces, and the Army Service Forces, General Davis, and it is customary for Truman Gibson to sit in.

It is the feeling of the committee that colored units should be introduced in combat at the earliest practicable moment. There has been a tendency to allow the situation to develop where selections are made on the basis of efficiency with the result that the colored units are discarded for combat service, but little is done by way of studying new means to put them in shape for combat service.

With so large a portion of our population colored, with the example before us of the effective use of colored troops (of a much lower order of intelligence) by other nations, and with the many imponderables that are connected with the situation, we must, I think, be more affirmative about the use of our Negro troops. If present methods do not bring them to combat efficiency, we should change those methods. That is what this resolution purports to recommend.

[Noted on the original: "I concur with the recommendations. HLS"]

[Memorandum, Assistant Secretary of War McCloy for Secretary of War Stimson, 2 March 1944, Modern Military Records Branch, National Archives, Washington, DC.]

●

The adjutant general reiterated in specific terms the army's
order to provide integrated recreational and transportation
facilities at all army posts, camps, and stations.

1. Reference is made to letter AG 353.8 (5 Mar 43)OB-S-A-M, 10 March 1943, subject as above, in which it was directed that all personnel, regardless of race, would be afforded equal opportunity to enjoy recreational facilities on each post, camp, and station.

2. While in general the spirit of the above-mentioned letter has been observed, occasional reports indicate that practices exist on some installations that are not in harmony with its provisions.

3. *Exchanges.*—While exchanges and branch exchanges may be allocated to serve specific areas or units, no exchange will be designated for the exclusive use of any

---

[Memorandum, Maj. Gen. J. A. Ulio, the adjutant general, to commanding generals, 8 July 1944, subject: Recreational facilities, Modern Military Records Branch, National Archives, Washington, DC.]

particular race. Where such branch exchanges are established, personnel will not be restricted to the use of their area or unit exchange, but will be permitted to use any other exchange on the post, camp, or station.

4. *Transportation.*—Busses, trucks, or other transportation owned and operated either by the government or by a governmental instrumentality will be available to all military personnel regardless of race. Restricting personnel to certain sections of such transportation because of race will not be permitted either on or off a post, camp, or station, regardless of local civilian custom.

5. *Army Motion Picture Theaters.*—Army motion picture theaters may be allocated to serve certain areas or units but no theater or performance in any theater will be denied any group or individual because of race.

6. Effective compliance with War Department policies enunciated herein will be obtained through inspection by responsible commanders and inspectors general. Each inspector general will be directed that if, during a periodic inspection [of] a post, camp, or station, he discovers evidence of racial discrimination or direct or indirect violation of War Department policies on this subject, he will inform the commanding officer of the installation that such discrimination is contrary to War Department policy. If subsequent inspection of the installation indicates that proper remedial measures have not been taken, the commanding general of the service command will initiate action to ensure full compliance with the announced policy.

7. The commanding general, Army Air Forces [,] will bring the contents of this letter to the attention of each unit of his command which is authorized [by] an inspector general.

*Echoing General Marshall's contention that much of the racial
tension in the World War II army was connected with poor
leadership, the army staff launched a campaign to familiarize
its officers with the service's policy and programs, always tying
them to the principle of military efficiency.* Leadership and the
Negro Soldier *was a principal effort in this campaign. As an
extended treatment of the ideas expressed in an earlier army
pamphlet,* Command of Negro Troops, *the manual provided unit
commanders with a generally accurate and progressive statement of the contributions of black Americans to the defense
of their country and their current status in the army. The
foreword and a sampling of summaries suggest the tone of this
historic document.*

FOREWORD

War Department concern with the Negro is focused directly and solely on the
problem of the most effective military use of colored troops. It is essential that there be a
clear understanding that the army has no authority or intention to participate in social
reform as such but does view the problem as a matter of efficient troop utilization. With
an imposed ceiling on the maximum strength of the army it is the responsibility of all
officers to assure the most efficient use of the manpower assigned.

It is recognized that the proportions of Negro troops in some military activities will
be low, because Negro education and experience have been severely limited. The fact
that race prejudice does exist cannot, in the interests of efficient operation, be disregarded. Limited education and experience, however, can be offset in part by training,
and the restrictive effects of race prejudice may be reduced by a properly planned
informational and orientation program.

The issue is not whether the Negro will be used in the war; it is how effectively he
will be used. This question cannot be evaded. Furthermore, it cannot be met successfully
by uninformed judgments on the basis of civilian associations and personal views on the
subject. The problems involved are as technical as any other problem of personnel, and
can be solved only with the benefit of special study, full information, and a serious
interest in their resolution. . . .

CONCLUSIONS

Military Efficiency Requires Democratic Treatment for All
First of all, the officer must never forget that he is the leader of men who but a short
time ago were private citizens in a country which prides itself on its democracy and
individual liberty. . . .

Manpower Cannot Be Wasted
Second, as a matter of practical expediency, manpower problems are such that this
country cannot afford to waste any portion of it. . . .

[*Army Service Forces Manual M5: Leadership and the Negro Soldier*, October 1944, General
Reference Branch, Center of Military History, Washington, DC.]

Men Have Been Well Selected

In the third place, officers should have confidence that the men assigned to them have been selected with all possible care. . . .

Men Want to Serve Fully

Fourth, the records of Selective Service show negligible malingering and delinquency in responding to requests for personal information or to calls for service among Negro registrants. *This evidence of loyalty, supported by the record of voluntary enlistments and voluntary inductions, should leave no doubts in officers' minds concerning the willingness of Negroes to serve as soldiers.*[1] Indeed, in spite of continued complaints from the Negro public about the treatment of Negro soldiers and civilians both by the army and in civilian communities, there has been great pressure exerted by Negroes themselves to secure opportunities to participate more fully in all aspects of the military task, including combat. . . .

CONCLUSIONS FROM SCIENTIFIC INVESTIGATIONS

Studies and facts considered in this section point to the following conclusions:

(1) Competent scholars in the field of racial differences are almost unanimous in the opinion that race "superiority" and "inferiority" have not been demonstrated despite the existence of clearly defined and tested differences between individuals within every race.

(2) It is agreed also that most of the differences revealed by intelligence tests and other devices can be accounted for in terms of differences in opportunity and background. The important consideration at this point, then, is how to offer increased opportunities—both physical and cultural—to all handicapped groups, regardless of race, since these variables account in large part for poor performance and achievement in every group.

It is true that in certain areas Negroes show relative inferiority, but this is not necessarily inherent inferiority. There is always the deadening difference of inequality of background and opportunity. Moreover, although the intelligence and educational scores are lower for Negroes than for whites, there is a very large overlap in these scores; the test performance of many Negroes is equal or superior to that of many whites even under present conditions. The military potentialities of these Negroes should be utilized by the army just as in the case of white troops of similar ability. Special provisions should be made also to enable the lower-scoring group of Negroes to attain their full stature. These are considerations which should influence the development of army training programs. . . .

SUMMARY

While the effectiveness of any program designed to improve the civilian-soldier contacts and relationships in the camp community will rest in large measure on the initiative and imagination of civilian authorities, officers can do a great deal toward stimulating desirable relationships. Especially is this true where Negro soldiers are

---

[1]Emphasis in the original.

concerned. Based on the foregoing discussion, these are some positive steps that can be taken by those in command of Negro soldiers:

1. Determine what the prevailing community laws and customs are so far as recreation and public facilities are concerned.

2. Learn about the Negro population, its size, location and other characteristics. Check on the adequacy of the commercial, recreational and eating facilities.

3. Discuss the problems arising from the location of a contingent of Negro troops with the town officials and secure their cooperation. This includes the police officials, with whom mutual assistance must be arranged.

4. Meet with organizations of merchants and other civic organizations to secure their active participation in a program to make the Negro soldiers welcome. Be sure to include the editors of local newspapers among the people whose advice and cooperation you ask.

5. Seek out the outstanding persons, especially Negroes, in the community and determine what they can do through their organizations to help entertain the Negro soldier. Churches, schools, YMCAs, YWCAs, local war service commissions, and athletic clubs are often glad to help.

6. Get all the help you can from national agencies, particularly the USO, and the office of Community War Services. Their local representatives can often give valuable aid.

7. Tell the Negro soldier what steps have been taken to prepare the community for his coming and impress upon him his responsibility for good community relations. Lists of events and places open to him placed on company and day room bulletin boards will help.

8. Work out a fair distribution of the transportation facilities between the post and town with the bus officials.

9. Try to arrange for fair and adequate ticket-selling and other facilities in railroad stations for Negro soldiers.

10. See to it that the MPs are doing their work intelligently and effectively in full cooperation with the local authorities, fulfilling their obligation to protect the rights of all soldiers as well as to maintain law and order. Use Negro and white MPs if there are both Negro and white troops in camp.

11. Oversea duty requires an awareness that new problems of the Negro soldier's community activities and relationships inevitably arise in foreign countries, that although the officer's responsibilities and the basic principles of camp-community relations remain the same it is necessary to learn about local customs, traditions, and practices, and that extreme care must be taken to maintain respect for the American uniform whether worn by white or Negro soldiers.

*Exceptions to the army's strict segregation policy were rare
during the war, limited for the most part to hospitals, troopships,
and officer training schools. One further exception with
important repercussions for the future was the integration of
black infantry platoons into white companies during the last
months of the war in Europe. Needing more frontline combat
troops for the final assault on Germany, theater officials turned
to black volunteers. Some five thousand blacks offered to leave
the relative safety of the supply organizations, and eventually
more than two thousand joined the fighting. The original
announcement addressed directly to black units by Lt. Gen.
John C. H. Lee, although patronizing in tone, nevertheless
promised integrated combat duty. "It is planned to assign you
without regard to color or race to the units where assistance is
most needed and give you the opportunity of fighting shoulder to
shoulder to bring about victory." This notice was recalled and
revised by Gen. Dwight D. Eisenhower personally, and the
actual combat service was performed in all-black platoons.*

1. The supreme commander desires to destroy the enemy forces and end hostilities
in this theater without delay. Every available weapon at our disposal must be brought to
bear upon the enemy. To this end the theater commander has directed the communications zone commander to make the greatest possible use of limited-service men within
service units and to survey our entire organization in an effort to produce able-bodied
men for the front line. This process of selection has been going on for some time but it is
entirely possible that many men themselves, desiring to volunteer for frontline service,
may be able to point out methods in which they can be replaced in their present jobs.
Consequently, commanders of all grades will receive voluntary applications for transfer
to the infantry and forward them to higher authority with recommendations for appropriate type of replacement. *This opportunity to volunteer will be extended to all soldiers
without regard to color or race, but preference will normally be given to individuals
who have had some basic training in infantry.*[1] Normally, also, transfers will be limited
to the grade of private and private first class unless a noncommissioned officer requests a
reduction.

2. In the event that the number of suitable Negro volunteers exceeds the replacement needs of Negro combat units, these men will be suitably incorporated in other
organizations so that their service and their fighting spirit may be efficiently utilized.

3. This letter may be read confidentially to the troops and made available in
orderly rooms. Every assistance must be promptly given qualified men who volunteer for
this service.

[Memorandum, Lt. Gen. John C. H. Lee, commanding general, Communications Zone, ETO, for commanding general, Southern Line of Communications et al., 26 December 1944, subject: Volunteers for training
and assignment as reinforcement, Modern Military Records Branch, National Archives, Washington, DC.]

[1] Emphasis in the original.

*Despite the success of the integrated black platoons, attested to
by reports from the battlefield and attitudinal surveys of the
men involved, the chief of staff was hesitant about carrying the
experiment forward. Yet, significantly, General Marshall
wanted the experience gained on the battlefield considered by
the planners of the army's postwar policy.*

I agree that the practicability of integrating Negro elements into white units should be followed up. It is further agreed that the results of the survey of the Information and Education Division should not be released for publication at this time, since the conditions under which the platoons were organized and employed were most unusual.

The Special Planning Division is making an overall study of postwar utilization of Negro troops. The material being used as the basis for the study was obtained from the several combat theaters. It is estimated that conclusions and recommendations will be completed about 1 October. I recommend the attached report[1] be submitted to Special Planning Division for consideration in connection with the overall study.

[Memorandum, Gen. George C. Marshall for Mr. McCloy, 25 August 1945, Modern Military Records Branch, National Archives, Washington, DC.]

[1]Not included.

CHAPTER SIX
BLACKS IN THE NAVY, MARINE CORPS, AND COAST GUARD

The racial composition of the navy changed radically during World War II. From the small group, mostly stewards, on duty early in 1942, the number of blacks increased by V-J Day to 167 thousand, including seventy-three officers. Moreover, several of these officers and men were assigned to racially integrated organizations, and all training was being conducted in integrated classes.

The speed and extent of this dramatic change was a product of the navy's size and mission. Like the army, the navy was reacting to pressure from President Roosevelt, who was responding to the demands of black leaders deeply resentful of the navy's policy of recruiting a handful of blacks to function as stewards. Again like the army, the navy found that once it had to rely exclusively upon the draft for manpower, the percentage of blacks in its ranks increased rapidly. Initially, blacks were trained in segregated camps and assigned to racially exclusive units serving ashore. Echoing the army's creation of all-black combat divisions, the navy experimented with manning certain ships, among them the destroyer escort *Mason*, with black crews, thus sending at least a few blacks to sea. The experiment merely demonstrated the futility of creating all-black elements in the fleet.

Quite early in the war, the large, segregated units located ashore, such as ammunition depots and base companies, experienced increasing racial unrest that manifested itself in a number of violent incidents. Although the Bureau of Naval Personnel dispatched trained experts to warn local commanders of the connection between discrimination and racial conflicts, the navy had fallen victim to its policy of concentrating many thousands of black sailors, regardless of their demonstrated or potential skills, in a limited number of tedious jobs only remotely connected with fighting the war. Racial unrest in the shore establishment probably goaded James Forrestal into changing the policy toward blacks shortly after he became secretary of the navy in April 1944.

Forrestal obtained President Roosevelt's approval to assign black officers and men to fleet auxiliaries, in numbers not to exceed 10 percent of the crew. He also began recruiting black women as WAVES (members of the navy's women's auxiliary) and as nurses. At the insistence of WAVES officials, members of that organization trained and were assigned without regard to race. Forrestal accelerated the selection of black officers, a program begun at the urging of, among others, Adlai E. Stevenson, an assistant to Forrestal's predecessor. The first class of black officer candidates trained separately, but this form of segregation soon yielded before the demands of military efficiency. Forrestal pushed the integration of all naval training. Actually, integrated specialist training was already well underway, since the navy could not tolerate the inefficiency and expense of separate schools for the small number of black trainees involved. Before the war ended, even recruit training had been quietly integrated.

The use of the draft as a source of manpower forced the other components of the naval establishment, the Marine Corps and the wartime Coast Guard, to develop their own racial policies. In 1942, the Marine Corps, which had never enlisted Negroes, agreed to accept a small number of black inductees but organized them in segregated units much as the army was doing. The corps eventually recruited for wartime service more than nineteen thousand black marines.

The Coast Guard had accepted Negroes long before World War II, but most of these men had served at isolated lighthouses or remote lifesaving stations. A part of the navy during the war, the Coast Guard began to accept a proportionate share of black recruits. Once it became convinced that to concentrate black Coast Guardsmen in the shore establishment was inefficient, the service began assigning blacks to sea duty. Before reverting to Treasury Department control in 1945, the Coast Guard had developed perhaps the most advanced racial policy of the entire military establishment, with black officers commanding mixed crews and black enlisted men serving in a variety of specialties.

Assailed by black leaders and their allies, Sec. of the Navy
Frank Knox turned to the General Board, a group of senior
naval officers charged with offering advice on policy to the
secretary of the navy, for help in developing arguments for
refusing to enlist blacks in the general service of the navy.

17 September 1940

Memorandum for Captain Deyo:

Before the secretary left on his trip he asked that the board give him some reasons why colored persons should not be enlisted for general service. Here is what the board thinks of the subject.

W. R. Sexton

17 September 1940

Memorandum for the Secretary of the Navy

SUBJECT: Enlistment of colored persons in the US Navy.
Enclosure: Notes on same subject.

1. Colored men are enlisted only in the messman branch of the navy, and not for general service. Reasons for not enlisting colored men for general service include:
  (a) Experience of many years has shown clearly that colored men, if enlisted in any other branches than the messman branch and promoted to the position of petty officer, cannot maintain discipline among men of the white race over whom they may be placed by reason of their rating; as a result, teamwork, harmony and ship efficiency are seriously handicapped.
  (b) Each recruit is potentially a leading petty officer. It would be a waste of time and effort to recruit and train persons for general service, who by reason of their race and color could not properly and efficiently fill the higher ratings.
  (c) There are no separate units (such as submarines, destroyers, etc.) manned exclusively by colored personnel to which colored recruits could be assigned.

2. In making replies to suggestions that colored (Negro) citizens be enlisted for other than the messman branch, that is, for general service, it is recommended that such replies be substantially as follows:
  The question of enlisting men of other than the white race for general
  service in the navy has been under consideration for many years, and several
  experiments in this connection have been tried. Immediately after the World
  War, an attempt was made to man two ships entirely with men of the Filipino

---

[Memorandum, Adm. W. R. Sexton, chairman of the General Board for Captain Deyo, 17 September 1940, Operational Archives Branch, Naval Historical Center, Washington, DC.]

race, officered by white officers. This experiment proved a failure. Later an attempt was made to man one of the tugs in Samoa with men of the Samoan race. This likewise proved a failure. There is no reason to believe that such an experiment with men of the colored race would produce any different results.

An enlisted man in the navy is not enlisted for some special ship, but is subject to duty afloat or ashore in any naval activity. It would be impracticable to man any ship with certain men, whether white or colored, whose only assignment would be confined to that particular ship. The whole training and distribution system of the enlisted personnel of the navy makes it essential that men of any particular rating be available for any duty required of that rating for any ship or activity in the navy.

As you probably know, colored men are now enlisted in the navy for the messman branch, and in that branch they are given every opportunity for advancement to cooks and stewards, which, while not petty-officer ratings, receive the pay and allowances of such ratings. Experience of many years in the navy has shown clearly that men of the colored race, if enlisted in any other branch than the messman branch, and promoted to the position of petty officer, cannot maintain discipline among men of the white race over whom they may be placed by reason of their rating. As a result, teamwork, harmony, and ship efficiency are seriously handicapped. Obviously it would be a waste of time and effort to recruit and train persons for general service, who by reason of their race and color could not properly and efficiently fill the higher ratings.

The selection of men to man the navy is left to the discretion of the executive branch of the government. In the exercise of this discretion, the Navy Department endeavors to furnish naval vessels with crews consisting of men best qualified to meet the requirements of the special rating and branch to which they are assigned. This policy not only serves the best interests of the navy and country, but serves as well the best interests of the men themselves.

3. Certain notes are enclosed which may be of interest.

W. R. Sexton

Notes

1. The Congress has placed but few restrictions as to who may be enlisted in the navy; one of these relates to the minimum age at which a minor may be enlisted, with or without the consent of parents or guardians; another requires certain evidence as to date of birth of minors; and a third prohibits the enlistment of an insane or intoxicated person or of a deserter from the naval or military service of the United States. Otherwise, selection of men to man the navy is left to the discretion of the executive branch of the government, and the secretary of the navy establishes, from time to time, such standards, mental and physical, as may be deemed necessary.

2. All enlistments in the navy are for general service—that is, a man is not enlisted for some special ship or for some special service, but is subject to duty ashore or

afloat in *any*[1] naval activity. No promises are permitted to be made as to the future assignment or as to the future promotion of any recruit.

3. The navy accepted Negroes for general service for many years and until November 23, 1921, at which time all first enlistments in the navy were suspended. Prior to that date, most of the ships in the navy were coal burning, and most Negroes, other than messmen, were to be found as coal-passers and firemen. They were always something of a problem, and wherever possible were berthed, messed and stationed (in watches) together. Promotion into petty officer ratings was rare and confined almost entirely to the engineer ratings of watertender and oiler—with an occasional gunner's mate who was nearly always in charge of the armory, where he would be by himself. Experience indicated that to place Negro petty officers in charge of groups of white men was but to invite trouble, inimical to discipline and morale. In 1910, out of a total enlisted strength of 45,076, 3.4 percent or 1535 were Negroes, and in 1920, out of a total of 158,750, 2.8 percent or 3047 were Negroes.

4. Upon the resumption of enlisting recruits for general service, on May 16, 1922, only white men in the rating of apprentice seamen were accepted, and only Filipinos were enlisted for messman ratings. The enlistment of Filipinos was discontinued on January 1, 1931, and beginning January 1, 1933, enlistment of Negroes for messman ratings only was authorized. In 1930, the number of Negroes in service was 462 or 0.5 percent out of a total of 84,938, and in 1940, 4007 or 2.9 percent out of a total of 139,554.

5. During the past fifteen or twenty years, the navy has built up an excellent recruiting service. Recruiting officers take great care in the selection of recruits from the many applicants, looking particularly into the character, mental equipment and general aptitude of the men selected. Quotas are assigned to each recruiting center, and as a rule there is a waiting list of applicants. In the fiscal year ending June 30, 1940, some 178,001 men applied for enlistment, and only 38,783, or 21.8 percent, were accepted. The high quality of our enlisted men, which could be amply testified to by any officer, is the direct result of the careful, thorough manner in which this selective recruiting is conducted.

6. It is not possible to man any single vessel of the navy exclusively with Negro enlisted men. It may be stated as a fact that there are no Negroes in the service today who could fill the various petty-officer and nonrated billets required on a submarine, destroyer or larger vessel; the development of sufficient petty officers for a destroyer alone would take years of training and could only be accomplished by training them with white men, with resulting friction and decrease of discipline and morale. Further, the experiment has been tried of manning ships with men of the Filipino race, officered with white officers, and the experiment was a failure.

---

[1]Emphasis in the original.

*In the weeks following the Japanese attack on Pearl Harbor the
navy's refusal to accept blacks for duties other than messman
became increasingly unacceptable to President Roosevelt.
Knox's request that the General Board find places for 5,000
Negroes in the general service met with the usual arguments
against the use of black sailors. But if the board could turn
Secretary Knox down, it would meet its match in the president.*

I have had a memorandum from the president dealing again with the question of
enlistment of Negroes in the navy. In the president's reply, he asked me to return the
whole matter to the General Board for further study and report. It is his opinion that
there are additional tasks in the naval establishment to which we could probably assign
an additional number of enlisted men who are members of the Negro race.

The president is not satisfied with the alternative suggested by the recent decision
of the General Board, that Negroes, if enlisted in other than the messman branch, be
enlisted for general service. He thinks that some special assignments can be worked out
for Negro enlisted men which would not inject into the whole personnel of the navy the
race question.

_____

[Memorandum, Sec. of the Navy Frank Knox for Adm. W. R. Sexton, 13 February 1942, Operational
Archives Branch, Naval Historical Center, Washington, DC.]

●

*Under continued pressure from the president, the General Board
devised plans for the employment of black enlistees in the navy,
Marine Corps, and Coast Guard. It asked the secretary on
behalf of these services wide latitude in establishing racial
programs.*

1. Reference (a)[1] directed the General Board to give further consideration to the
subject of enlistment of men of the colored race in other than the messman branch, with
the object of determining to what additional tasks or special assignments in the naval
establishment enlisted men of the colored race may be assigned without injecting into the
whole personnel of the navy the race question. A further study of the subject is forwarded
herewith as Enclosure (A).[2]

2. The General Board fully recognizes and appreciates the social and economic
problems involved and has striven to reconcile these requirements with what it feels must
be paramount in any consideration, namely, the maintenance at the highest level of the
fighting efficiency of the navy.

3. In considering any program for the induction of Negroes into the naval service

_____

[Memorandum, Adm. W. R. Sexton, chairman of the General Board, to secretary of the navy,
20 March 1942, subject: Enlistment of men of the colored race in other than messman branch, Operational
Archives Branch, Naval Historical Center, Washington, DC.]

[1]Sec Nav Memo. (SC) P14-4/MM (08600A)/GEM dated 14 February 1942.

[2]General Board study of the enlistment of men of colored race in other than messman branch. [See
below p. 139.]

the problem of training these men becomes of paramount interest. The navy is making every effort to train the crews required to man the vessels of the rapidly expanding fleet. In order to provide petty officers for training stations and for nucleus crews for new construction, every combatant vessel of the fleet has been, and will continue to be, called upon to furnish petty officers which they can ill afford to lose if they are to maintain their battle efficiency and which they cannot replace except by the development of nonrated men in their own complements. In the face of such a vital wartime problem, which applies equally to the navy, Marine Corps and Coast Guard, the General Board feels impelled to express its conviction that to divert any part of the training effort to the development of Negro crews or Negro battalions would not produce a return in effective fighting units commensurate with the adverse effects on the training program and the efficiency of the fleet.

4. If it is determined by higher authority that social, economic and other considerations require the enlistment of men of the colored race in other than the messman branch, then the General Board considers that the organization of the colored units specified below would offer the least disadvantages and the least difficulty of accomplishment as a war measure:

(a) Service units throughout the naval shore establishment including shore activities of the Marine Corps and Coast Guard,

(b) Crews for yard craft and other small craft employed in naval district local defense forces,

(c) Shore-based units for other naval district local defense forces,

(d) Crews for selected cutters of the Coast Guard and employment of nonrated colored men in small number by the US Coast Guard Captains of the Port,

(e) Construction regiments, navy,

(f) Composite battalions, Marine Corps.

All of the above activities should be subject to current administrative arrangements by the proper agencies.

5. The General Board further believes that if a decision is made to proceed with this project, enlistments should be limited to the US Naval Reserve, the US Marine Corps Reserve, and the US Coast Guard Reserve. This would permit the enlistment of skilled men in petty-officer ratings for which qualified. It is recommended that wide latitude be granted the several administrative authorities as to rate of enlistment, method of recruiting, training and assignment to duty and that progressive experience determine the total number to be enlisted.

W. R. Sexton

ENCLOSURE (A)

II. *ASSUMPTIONS:*

1. That enlistment of men of the colored race for unrestricted service is considered by higher authority to be inadvisable.

2. That any practical plan, which would not inject into the whole personnel of the navy the race question, must provide for:

(a) Segregation of colored enlisted men insofar as quartering, messing and employment is concerned,

(b) Limitation of authority of colored petty officers to subordinates of their own race.

III. *GENERAL CONSIDERATIONS:*

1. Assuming that the enlistment of men of the colored race for unrestricted general service is inadvisable, the possible alternatives are as follows:

(a) Enlistment in selected ratings in designated branches,

(b) Enlistment in colored branches, to be established as such,

(c) Enlistment in colored units, to be established as such.

2. Pertinent considerations with regard to these three alternatives may be outlined as follows:

A. *Enlistment in selected ratings in designated branches:*

The several branches of Navy enlisted personnel are: (a) seaman branch, (b) artificer branch, (c) aviation branch, (d) special and commissary branch, (e) messman branch.

In each of these branches a definite precedence of ratings by classes is established by the Bureau of Navigation Manual, which precedence fixes the seniority with respect to responsibility and authority of each rating of that branch. Enlisted men are quartered, stationed and messed largely by rating and class groups. These men live, work, and eat together in a closeness of contact which has few parallels outside of the navy.

The Navy Regulations specify that all petty officers shall aid to the utmost of their ability in maintaining good order, discipline and all that concerns the efficiency of the command. To that end the Navy Regulations further provide that petty officers are always on duty and are vested with the necessary authority to report and arrest offenders.

It is manifest that a Negro, if inducted into any existing branch of the navy other than the messman branch, would work, eat, and sleep in the closest contact with his white shipmates, and in any but the lowest rating of the several classes would inevitably be in a position where he would exercise the authority with which all petty officers are clothed by the Navy Regulations.

There are many artisan ratings in the navy where the man is rated a petty officer largely because of his skill as a workman, rather than his ability as a leader. Therefore, upon cursory examinations, it might appear that ratings of this kind, of which carpenter's mate, metalsmith, painter, and shipfitter are examples, offer tasks to which we could properly assign an additional number of enlisted men of the Negro race. However, these artificers do not work alone but in groups where the senior petty officer is in charge. Moreover, on all ships the battle station of petty officers of these ratings is in the damage control party which includes men of many other ratings, thereby rendering segregation and limitation of authority impracticable. In action the survival of the ship may depend upon the leadership, initiative, self-reliance, resourcefulness or undirected prompt action on the part of any member of the damage control party.

Enlistment in selected ratings in designated branches would not provide the necessary segregation or limitation of authority which is necessary to prevent injecting into the whole personnel of the Navy the race question.

B. *Enlistment in Colored Branches, to be established as such.*

At the present time there are no colored branches other than the messman branch.

The establishment of other colored branches is subject to the following considerations:

(1) The *Seaman Branch* includes rated and nonrated men, distributed by divisions or departments as follows:

Boatswains mates	Deck divisions
Gunners mates	Deck divisions
Turret captains	Deck divisions
Torpedomen	Torpedo division
Quartermasters	Navigation Department
Signalmen	Communication Department
Fire controlmen	Gunnery Department
Coxswains	Deck divisions
Seamen	Deck divisions
Apprentice seamen	Deck divisions

(2) The *Artificer Branch* includes rated and nonrated men, distributed by divisions or departments as follows:

Machinists mates	Engine Division
Water tenders	Boiler Division
Electricians mates	Electrical Division
Radiomen	Radio Div. Comm. Dept.
Carpenters mates	C&R[3] Dept. Damage Control
Shipfitters	C&R Dept. Damage Control
Boilermakers	C&R Dept. Damage Control
Molders	C&R Dept. Damage Control
Patternmakers	C&R Dept. Damage Control
Printers	Communication Department
Painters	C&R Dept. Damage Control
Metalsmiths	C&R Dept. Damage Control
Firemen	Boiler Division

(3) The *Aviation Branch* includes rated men only, distributed by divisions or departments as follows:

Aviation machinists mates	
Aviation carpenters mates	
Aviation metalsmiths	Carriers: Aviation
Aerographers	Department.
Photographers	Other Vessels:
Aviation ordnancemen	Aviation Division.

(4) *Special and Commissary Branch* includes rated and nonrated men distributed by divisions or departments as follows:

Yeomen	All departments and divisions
Storekeepers	Supply Department

---

[3]Construction and Repair.

Musicians	Band
Buglers	Band & Marine Detachment
Ships cooks	Supply Department
Bakers	Supply Department
Pharmacists mates	Medical Department
Hospital apprentices	Medical Department

(5) The messman branch includes *nonrated men only*, distributed among the following officers messes:

Officers stewards, first, second and third class	Flag, Captain, Wardroom, Junior Officer and Warrant Officer messes.
Officers cooks, first, second and third class	
Mess attendants, first, second and third class	

These branches and ratings have been established as the result of long experience, and cover all requirements and adequately provide for the effective operation of naval vessels of all types and sizes. There appears to be no field in the organization of naval vessels for the establishment of additional branches and ratings solely for the accommodation of men of the colored race, therefore any colored man inducted into the naval service would necessarily have to be assigned to one of the rated or nonrated classes included in an existing branch.

It is evident from the above tabulation that, except in the messman branch and in the aviation branch, the various ratings and classes are so widely distributed throughout the ship or station that it would be impracticable to effect segregation in quartering, messing, and employment of colored ratings and also impracticable to effect the necessary limitation of authority of colored petty officers to men of their own race.

An all-colored aviation department in an aircraft carrier, resulting as it would in a major portion of the crew being composed of men of the colored race, would inject the race question to a marked degree. An all-colored aviation division in a battleship or cruiser, while constituting a unit of much smaller relative size, would nevertheless inject the race question to an equal degree. Segregation in quartering, messing and employment would be impracticable because of the necessity for frequent transfer of both flying and ground personnel between ship and ship, and ship and shore bases, and the relatively high rate of replacement of aviation personnel incident to war operations. Both in the case of the all-colored aviation department of the carrier and in the case of the all-colored aviation division of the battleship or cruiser, a limitation of the authority of colored petty officers to men of their own race would be impossible.

Enlistment for service in colored branch, to be established as such, would not provide the segregation or the limitation of authority which is necessary to prevent injecting into the whole personnel of the navy the race question. . . .

A complete all-colored crew for a specified naval auxiliary would solve the questions of segregation and limitation of authority but the organization and training of an efficient crew of men of the colored race, composed of all ratings up to and including the several classes of chief petty officer, would require a period of many years. An all-colored crew could not be organized and trained at a training station, and then assigned as a unit to take over and operate a naval auxiliary. Effective training could be gained only at sea, under the tutelage of experienced white officers and petty officers. This necessary training period at sea presents a serious problem with regard to segregation.

To maintain a colored crew of required ratings at full strength would necessitate the establishment and maintenance of a source of replacements. This would require the establishment of a colored training station ashore in which the Negro recruit would be given the fundamental training and processing necessary for all naval recruits preliminary to service afloat and also the establishment of trade schools for advanced training.

This project would involve an effort out of all proportion to the return in effective seagoing units which could be expected on the basis of the navy's actual experience with vessels manned by crews of other than the white race.

Colored crews for certain naval auxiliaries are considered to be impractical and highly undesirable, particularly as a wartime project. . . .

IV. *CONCLUSIONS:*

1. That, of the possible alternatives to enlistment of men of the colored race for general service, "Enlistment in selected ratings in designated branches" and "Enlistment in colored branches (to be established as such)" are both inadvisable.

2. That "Enlistment in colored units (to be established as such)" presents the only course which may be expected to approximate the segregation and the limitation of authority which is essential to preventing "injecting into the whole personnel of the navy the race question."

3. That the colored units, establishment of which would be practical and which would offer the least disadvantages and the least difficulty of accomplishment as a war measure, may be listed as follows:

    (a) Service units throughout the naval shore establishment including shore activities of the Marine Corps and the Coast Guard,

    (b) Crews for yard craft and other small craft employed in naval district local defense forces,

    (c) Shore based units for other naval district local defense activities,

    (d) Crews for selected cutters of the Coast Guard and employment of nonrated colored men in small numbers by the U.S. Coast Guard Captains of the Port,

    (e) Construction regiments, navy,

    (f) Composite battalions, Marine Corps.

4. That if men of the colored race are to be inducted into the services they should be enlisted in the US Naval Reserve, the US Marine Corps Reserve and the US Coast Guard Reserve. This would permit the enlistment of skilled men in ratings for which qualified.

The president reacted to the navy's proposed use of black
sailors.

I am interested in this second report of the General Board on the problem of Negroes in the navy.

The Ethiopian in the wood pile may be the last sentence of Section #5 in which it is recommended that wide latitude be given the several administrative authorities as to rate of enlistment, method of recruiting, training and assignment to duty and total number to be enlisted. I think that is a matter which should be determined by you and by me!

Please talk with me about this.

_____

[Memorandum, President Roosevelt for Secretary of the Navy Knox, 31 March 1942, Franklin D. Roosevelt Library, Hyde Park, NY.]

●

Secretary Knox approved plans drawn up by the Bureau of
Naval Personnel for the training of black sailors.

I approve of the suggestion contained in your memorandum of April 17,[1] namely that we train Negro recruits in the present training stations but in a way to accomplish segregation.

The plan you outline at Great Lakes is satisfactory. I looked over Camp Barry myself on Sunday and think you have just what you need for this purpose there. I personally believe that training station with a capacity of 2400 is probably all that you will need at the outset. If you need the additional unit, you can take it over. For the present, I think it well to keep the whole thing in one training station.

I also think it would be desirable to make some arrangement with the Hampton Institute for trade school facilities for the technical training of Negro recruits who have some civilian training along mechanical lines.

_____

[Memorandum, Sec. of the Navy Frank Knox for Rear Adm. Randall Jacobs, 21 April 1942, Navy and Old Army Branch, National Archives, Washington, DC.]
[1]Not included.

*Because it was ordered to rely almost exclusively on the
Selective Service System for its manpower, the navy was
concerned with the orderly training and limited employment
of black sailors planned by its General Board.*

I took up with the president today the matter of Negro selectees for the navy and explained to him that it was impossible for us to take any Negroes in excess of those set up in our quota for each month because of lack of facilities for training and because we lack opportunity to make use of their services without resorting to mixed crews, which is a policy contrary to the president's program.

The president approved my recommendation and instructed me to tell you to advise [Maj.] Gen. [Lewis B.] Hershey[1] for his guidance of this verbal order and I trust you will attend to this matter at once.

[Memorandum, Sec. of the Navy Frank Knox for Rear Adm. Randall Jacobs, 5 February 1943, Navy and Old Army Branch, National Archives, Washington, DC.]

[1]Director of Selective Service.

•

*Admiral Jacobs somewhat exceeded Secretary Knox's
instructions in stating that receiving blacks in excess of the
navy's monthly calls on the draft was "contrary to the
president's program."*

I am in receipt of a memorandum from the secretary of the navy wherein he advises me of a discussion with the president concerning the employment of Negroes in the navy.

The induction of Negroes in excess of the numbers requested in monthly calls will necessitate the resorting to mixed crews on vessels of the navy, which is a policy contrary to the president's program.

The secretary has been instructed by the president to tell me to advise you, for your guidance, of his verbal order.

The navy will, however, continue to employ Negroes to the capacity of the training facilities, which will be reflected in our monthly calls.

[Letter, Rear Adm. Randall Jacobs, chief of Bureau of Naval Personnel, to Maj. Gen. Lewis B. Hershey, director of Selective Service, 6 February 1943, Navy and Old Army Branch, National Archives, Washington, DC.]

The president demanded that the navy accept its share of
black draftees and urged that service to find more assignments
for black sailors.

I guess you were dreaming or maybe I was dreaming if Randall Jacobs is right in regard to what I am supposed to have said about employment of Negroes in the navy. If I did say that such employment should be stopped, I must have been talking in my sleep. Most decidedly we must continue the employment of Negroes in the navy, and I do not think it the least bit necessary to put mixed crews on the ships. I can find a thousand ways of employing them without doing so.

The point of the thing is this. There is going to be a great deal of feeling if the government in winning this war does not employ approximately 10 percent of Negroes— their actual percentage to the total population. The army is nearly up to this percentage but the navy is so far below it that it will be deeply criticized by anybody who wants to check into the details.

Perhaps a check by you showing exactly where all white enlisted men are serving and where all colored enlisted men are serving will show you the great number of places where colored men could serve, where they are not serving now—shore duty of all kinds, together with the handling of many kinds of yard craft.

You know the headache we have had about this and the reluctance of the navy to have any Negroes. You and I have had to veto that navy reluctance, and I think we have to do it again.

[Memorandum, President Roosevelt for Secretary of the Navy Knox, 22 February 1943, Franklin D. Roosevelt Library, Hyde Park, NY.]

●

The influx of black draftees placed severe stresses on the
Bureau of Naval Personnel's orderly plans for training and
assigning black sailors. Already, the increased numbers were
forcing a more careful check on the activities of local
commanders and a modification of the service's race policy.

1. For your information, Negroes are now being inducted into the naval service at a rate in excess of twelve thousand per month. By December 31, 1943, more than 107,000 Negroes will have been inducted into the navy. After training, they will be assigned as follows:

Stewards' Mates	26,578
Cooks and Bakers	12,084
Sea Bees[1]	17,000
Base Companies, SoPac[2]	5,000

[Memorandum, chief of the Bureau of Naval Personnel to all bureaus and offices, Navy Department et al., 12 July 1943, subject: The expanded use of Negroes, Navy and Old Army Branch, National Archives, Washington, DC.]

[1]Construction Battalions.
[2]South Pacific.

Base Companies at Boston, New York, Phila., Norfolk, New Orleans, San Francisco, and Seattle	2,000
Navy Yards and Stations	5,711
Air Stations	20,580 nonrated; 1,171 rated
Local Defense, District and Small Craft	4,239 nonrated; 3,477 rated
Net Depots & Defenses	977
Ammunition Depots	3,121
Section Bases	4,338 nonrated; 300 rated

2. Studies are now being made to determine the maximum numbers of the above which can be assigned for duty at specific activities under the above commands. In connection with this study, reference will be made to the recent report furnished by the addressees[3] which contains information on the numbers which can effectively be used. Before final determination has been made, a representative of the bureau will confer with personnel officers and with the commanding officers of the activities in question to make certain that the Negroes assigned will be used as planned, and that adequate housing, messing, and recreation facilities can be made available.

3. It is the policy of the bureau to assure:
   (a) That the class A school graduates are used in the work for which they are trained.
   (b) That Negroes are rated on the same basis as white personnel, and that the rated move upwards in the same manner as do white.
   (c) That wherever possible, and as soon as a sufficient number of trained Negroes make it possible, activities having large numbers of Negro personnel will become all-Negro, rated as well as nonrated.

4. It will be to the advantage of the commanding officers to encourage promotion of qualified Negro enlisted men as the bureau will continue to order white enlisted personnel, in all ratings, to sea, with the expectation that they will be replaced by Negroes.

5. It is recognized that many adjustments must be made in connection with this program and it is hoped that the addressees will make full recommendations in the premises from time to time.

> L. E. Denfeld
> The Assistant Chief of Naval Personnel

---

[3]All bureaus and offices, Navy Department; all sea frontier commands; commandants, all naval districts; commandant, Potomac River Naval Command; commandant, Severn River Naval Command; chief of Naval Air Operational Training Command; chief of Naval Air Technical Training Command; chief of Naval Air Intermediate Training Command; chief of Naval Air Primary Training Command.

Adlai E. Stevenson served as a special assistant to the secretary
of the navy during the war. Although others had proposed
the commissioning of blacks before him, Stevenson's
recommendation proved most fruitful.

I feel very emphatically that we should commission a few Negroes. We now have more than sixty thousand already in the navy and are accepting twelve thousand per month. Obviously this cannot go on indefinitely without making some officers or trying to explain why we don't. Moreover, there are twelve Negroes in the V-12 program and the first will be eligible for a commission in March, 1944.

Ultimately there will be Negro officers in the navy. It seems to me wise to do something about it now. After all, the training program has been in effect for a year and a half and one reason we have not had the best of the race is the suspicion of discrimination in the navy. In addition, the pressure will mount both among the Negroes and in the government as well. The Coast Guard has already commissioned two who qualified in all respects for their commissions.

I specifically recommend the following:

(1) Commission ten or twelve Negroes selected from top-notch civilians just as we procure white officers, and a few from the ranks. They should probably be assigned to training and administrative duties with the Negro program.

(2) Review the rating groups from which Negroes are excluded. Perhaps additional classes of service could profitably be made available to them.

I don't believe we can or should postpone commissioning some Negroes much longer. If and when it is done it should not be accompanied by any special publicity but rather treated as a matter of course. The news will get out soon enough.

[Memorandum, Adlai E. Stevenson for the secretary of the navy, 29 September 1943, Navy and Old Army Branch, National Archives, Washington, DC.]

*The first group of black officers was trained in segregated
classes at Great Lakes. The success of this group and a
second class of staff officers—chaplains, doctors, engineers,
and the like—as well as the pressing need to provide black
leadership for black units prompted the chief of the Bureau
of Naval Personnel to propose that more black officers be
commissioned from time to time. The obvious special expense
of training these small groups separately led, in the name of
military efficiency, to integrated training of all later black
officer candidates. A limited number of blacks were also
earning naval commissions through the navy's V-12 program
in various colleges throughout the country.*

1. Reference (a)[1] recommended the commissioning of twelve line officers and two officers for each of the staff corps.; reference (b)[2] authorized the commissioning of these twenty-two officers.

2. To date, this bureau has procured twelve line officers and two warrant boatswains. The initial quota of two officers for each of the five staff corps has not yet been filled.

3. Enclosure (1)[3] requests two chaplains, three dental officers, and three medical officers for duty in ComFourteen.[4]

4. In view of this request for Negro officers, it is recommended that authority be granted to commission line and staff officers from time to time to fill existing needs.

[Memorandum, Rear Adm. Randall Jacobs, chief of the Bureau of Naval Personnel, to Sec. of the Navy James V. Forrestal, 12 June 1944, subject: Procurement of Negro officers and warrants, Bureau of Naval Personnel Technical Library, Washington, DC.]

[1]BuPers Conf. ltr. Pers-1013-FB over QR/P14-2 dated 2 December 1943.
[2]SecNav Conf. memo (SC)P14-5 Serial 037000A dated 18 December 1943.
[3]Com14 restr. ltr. dated 2 May 1944 with CincPac&POA end-1 dated 16 May 1944. [Not included.]
[4]14th Naval District.

●

*Again, the expense of separate training facilities, in this case
the costly duplication of teachers and equipment needed to
train men in the navy's various specialist ratings, caused
the Bureau of Naval Personnel to integrate training classes.*

Action: All Ships and Stations

1. This letter is issued to clarify the policies of the Bureau of Naval Personnel with regard to the selection of applicants to fill advanced-school quotas by commands having jurisdiction over both white and Negro personnel.

[BuPers Circular Letter No. 194-44, 10 July 1944, Bureau of Naval Personnel Technical Library, Washington, DC.]

2. This bureau does not consider practical the establishment of separate facilities and quotas for those Negroes who qualify for advanced training under existing regulations and directives.

3. No discrimination as to race should be allowed to influence the nomination of candidates for advanced-school training. When Negro personnel are qualified under existing regulations and directives, they will be given the same consideration as white personnel and will be assigned to schools in the same manner and on the same basis.

●

The problems associated with large segregated units led the navy, as it had the army, to form a special group—in the case of the navy the Special Programs Unit in its personnel bureau—to advise commanders on ways to use black personnel efficiently and to reduce racial tensions. At first the unit's proposals made little headway in the bureau, but when James V. Forrestal became secretary at the death of Frank Knox in 1944 a new atmosphere swept through the department and many racial reforms were accepted. Long advocated by the Special Programs Unit, the enlistment and commissioning of black women quickly came about under Forrestal's leadership.

If and when Negro women are admitted to the Women's Reserve, it is proposed to adopt the following procedure:

First: Nominations of Negro women officers will be requested from a selected list of Negro and white men and women. To start the program not more than ten women will be appointed as officer candidates and will be sent for training to the Naval Reserve Midshipmen School (WR) at Northampton [Massachusetts]. They will assist in the subsequent planning and supervision of the program for Negro women which will be administered as an integral part of the Women's Reserve.

Second: For Negro enlisted women, recruit training will be conducted at the Recruit Training School (WR) the Bronx. It is planned to form a company of 240 Negro recruits to be housed together at the school but to share all facilities of the station with the other recruits. How many such companies will be trained will be determined by the needs of the service and the number of qualified applicants who are available.

Third: Specialized training will be conducted in existing facilities. An effort will be made to approximate for Negro women the ratio of rated to unrated women which applied to white recruits admitted at the same time.

Fourth: Negro women will be detailed wherever needed within the continental limits of the United States, preferably to stations where there are already Negro men.

[Memorandum, Sec. of the Navy James V. Forrestal for the president, 28 July 1944, Navy and Old Army Branch, National Archives, Washington, DC.]

Fifth: When government quarters are provided, they will not ordinarily be shared with white women but will be similar to those occupied by white women. Local conditions will determine whether or not the mess is shared by both races. On some stations Negro men and women will eat in their own mess halls. On other stations, they will share the mess with white personnel. In every case equal, if not identical, facilities will be provided for Negro and white personnel.

I propose to proceed with the above plan in the near future. I consider it advisable to start obtaining Negro WAVES[1] before we are forced to take them.

Your views would be appreciated.

---

[1]Women Accepted for Volunteer Emergency Service.

●

The White House seemed reluctant to order the enlistment of black women on the eve of a presidential election. When Republican spokesmen commented on the subject, however, the navy was quickly given permission to announce its enlistment plans. Thanks to the efforts of senior WAVES officials and the Special Programs Unit, the training of black WAVES proved more liberal in practice than anticipated in Forrestal's original proposal.

1. It is the established policy of the Navy Department, specifically approved by the secretary of the navy, that Negro women in the Women's Reserve shall be treated without discrimination.

2. It is anticipated that a very small number of Negro recruits will enter NTS,[1] the Bronx, on 28 December 1944. In view of this fact, there is no way in which these women can be housed, fed, or trained in a separate unit without obviously discriminating against them.

3. It is anticipated that the commanding officer, with the cooperation of his staff, can and will assimilate this small group of Negro WAVES into the training processes and living accommodations without making special or separate arrangements.

L. E. Denfeld
The Assistant Chief of Naval Personnel

[Memorandum, chief of the Bureau of Naval Personnel to commanding officer, NAVTRASCOL, the Bronx, New York, 8 December 1944, subject: Colored WAVES Recruits, Navy and Old Army Branch, National Archives, Washington, DC.]

[1]Naval Training Station.

As in the case of the army, the navy's leaders came to realize
that some of the rising racial tension in the service was
being caused by poor leadership.

Confidential

1. To obtain the best results in the utilization of Negro personnel, intelligent leadership, including active interest in the welfare of subordinates and realistically sympathetic understanding of the problems of Negro sailors, must be stressed.

2. In recognition of widespread uncertainties and misconceptions concerning the supervision of Negro personnel, the bureau has set up indoctrinal training programs to better prepare officers for this type of duty. The shore establishments have had the opportunity to send officers to this specialized training, and in addition the bureau has endeavored to assign officers with the desired background and training to activities having large numbers of Negroes. Indoctrinal training will be continued and is available to officers nominated by all interested commands.

3. Nevertheless, incidents have come to the attention of the bureau which indicate that in some cases officers assigned duties in connection with the supervision of Negro personnel, because of poor leadership ability, lack of understanding of the problems, or for other reasons, are not suited to this type of work. Continued wider participation of Negroes in naval activities, both ashore and afloat, makes it increasingly necessary that close attention be given to the type of supervision they have.

4. It is incumbent on, and expected of, each officer assigned to the command of Negro personnel that personal attitudes inimical to the best interests of the naval service be completely suppressed. However, it is recognized that certain officers will be temperamentally better suited for such command than others. Accordingly, it is directed that all commands give close attention to the proper selection of such officers, and to the constant review of their qualifications for this program.

[Memorandum, Rear Adm. Randall Jacobs, chief of Naval Personnel, to all ships and stations, 7 August 1944, subject: Administration of Negro personnel, Navy and Old Army Branch, National Archives, Washington, DC.]

●

Despite the steady barrage of complaints from the black
community concerning the image of stewards as servants
working in a racially separate branch, the navy continued
to push this service on black recruits.

Action: All Ships and Stations

1. In order to fill existing needs for personnel of the steward's branch, commanding officers are authorized to effect changes from general-service ratings not above

---

[BuPers Circular Letter No. 227-44, 12 August 1944, Bureau of Naval Personnel Technical Library, Washington, DC.]

pay grade four to steward's branch ratings of those Negro enlisted men who desire such change. Such change will be effected in the same pay grade in which the man is serving and provided the man is qualified for his new rating in accordance with the Bureau of Naval Personnel Manual.

2. It is believed that if commanding officers point out to this personnel the advantages of the steward's branch, such as more rapid advancement in rating, less strenuous work, better working hours, etc., there will be a substantial number requesting transfer. Care should be exercised, however, that only such personnel that commanding officers feel capable of performing the duties of steward's rating should be allowed to change.

3. Page nine of the service record will indicate in the handwriting of the person desirous of change, above his signature, the following statement: "I request that I be allowed to change from general service to the steward's branch." A copy of this page will be forwarded the bureau.

4. Commanding officers will retain on board all persons so changed, reporting them under the steward's branch heading on Form BNP 625. A program of instruction will be instituted for such personnel. A report will be submitted on the last day of each month indicating the number who have been transferred from general service to the steward's branch during the period.

●

The demand for a wider range of assignments for black sailors, emanating from the black community but also from the harried assignment branches of the Bureau of Naval Personnel where the increases in black draftees was causing a surplus of blacks in shore units, caused the navy to experiment with all-black crews for warships. One unanticipated lesson was learned from this experiment: because of the shortage of black specialists some white sailors had to be temporarily included in the crews, thus creating integrated crews which served efficiently and peacefully on warships.

1. As directed by you, plans have been completed for the manning of one DE[1] and one PC[2] with enlisted Negro personnel, to the extent that Negroes are qualified for the billets called for in the complements.

2. The DE, USS *Mason*, which will be commissioned 29 January, 1944 at Boston, will

---

[Memorandum, chief of Naval Personnel to commander in chief, US Fleet, 1 December 1943, subject: Plans for the assignment of Negro enlisted personnel to one DE and one PC, Navy and Old Army Branch, National Archives, Washington, DC.]

[1]Destroyer Escort.

[2]Patrol Craft.

have included in its enlisted complement 143 Negroes out of a total enlisted crew of 183 men.

3. The PC 1264, which will be commissioned 24 March, 1944 at New York, will have in its complement fifty Negroes out of a total enlisted crew of sixty-one men.

4. Methods of assembling and training Negro crews follow those used for whites as nearly as possible.

5. As soon as Negroes can be trained to take over the top ratings, which at first will be held by white petty officers, they will be moved into these positions until the ships are manned with an entirely Negro enlisted crew.

L. E. Denfeld
The Assistant Chief of Naval Personnel

●

*The concept of all-black crews proved impractical, and
Secretary Forrestal decided to press for the use of black sailors
on board fleet auxiliaries.*

Up to the present time, the majority of Negroes who have been assigned to general service in the navy have been employed in the shore establishments of the continental United States or at advanced bases. This is in accordance with the secretary of the navy's letter to you of 25 February 1943, which you approved.

In effecting economies in the use of manpower, military personnel in the shore establishment of the navy is being continuously reduced. A heavy concentration of Negroes in the shore establishment, and the continual increase in the use of members of the Women's Reserve tends to prevent that interchange of white personnel between combat areas and the United States, which is conducive to morale.

From a morale standpoint, the Negroes resent the fact that they are not assigned to general-service billets at sea, and white personnel resent the fact that Negroes have been given less hazardous assignments ashore.

In the interest of conservation of personnel, I plan to expand the use of Negro personnel by assigning them to general sea-duty billets. Initially, this program will be confined to the large auxiliaries and limited to not more than 10 percent of the ship's complement. If results show the practicability thereof, I plan to extend the use of Negroes, in small numbers, to other types of ships as necessity indicates.

Your approval is requested.

[Noted on the original: "OK / FDR"]

[Memorandum, Sec. of the Navy James Forrestal for the president, 20 May 1944, Navy and Old Army Branch, National Archives, Washington, DC.]

When the service of black sailors in a limited number
of fleet auxiliaries had proved successful, the navy
announced its decision to make such service standard practice.
At the same time the Bureau of Naval Personnel placed a
quota on the number of blacks that might serve on any one
vessel.

1. Negro personnel of all general-service rating groups are now eligible for assignment to duty on board all auxiliary vessels of the fleet.

2. Assignment of subject Negroes to these vessels will be made through routine administrative channels as they are available, and in no case will the number assigned to any individual ship exceed 10 percent of the enlisted complement, excluding the steward's branch.

3. The policy of this bureau is one of racial nondiscrimination.

[BuPers Circular Letter No. 105-45, 13 April 1945, Bureau of Naval Personnel Technical Library, Washington, DC.]

●

The assignment of a black officer to the Mason *marked the*
beginning of a program that in the next few months would
lead to the assignment of black officers to auxiliary vessels of the
fleet. These men would serve in completely integrated
circumstances and routinely command white enlisted men.

1. This bureau will, in the near future, assign a Negro officer to your command.[1] He will have completed training in the V-12 and V-7 officer training programs, as well as the basic course at Naval Training Center, Miami, Florida.

2. This bureau does not look for any untoward incidents as a result of this assignment. Negro officers have been assimilated in the past, both within and outside the continental limits, and have performed their duties satisfactorily with both white and Negro subordinates.

3. It is assumed that the commanding officer will take any action that may be necessary to ensure the indoctrination of the officers and men attached to his command. Policies and procedures for Negro officers are the same as for all officers of corresponding rank.

[Memorandum, Rear Adm. Randall Jacobs, chief of the Bureau of Naval Personnel, to commanding officer, USS *Mason*, 19 March 1945, subject: Negro officer—assignment of, Operational Archives, Naval Historical Center, Washington, DC.]

[1]Similar memos were sent to other auxiliary vessels, including the USS *Kaweah* and the USS *Laramie*.

*The move toward widespread integration of the general service
accelerated in the last months of the war. As usual the navy
justified this major change in its racial policy in the name
of military efficiency.*

1. In order to obtain the maximum utilization of naval training and housing facilities, the
policy of maintaining a special training program and camp at Great Lakes for Negro
general-service recruits will be discontinued on 1 July 1945. The method of effecting this
change at Naval Training Center, Great Lakes, is left to the discretion of that command.

2. Induction centers will be directed to assign Negroes to recruit training on the same
basis as white[s] and will therefore assign them to the nearest recruit training command
with the exception of those classified as illiterate, who are to be ordered to Naval
Training and Distribution Center, Camp Peary, Williamsburg, Virginia, for special
training.

3. Recruit training commands are directed to assimilate Negro and white enlisted
personnel alike.

[Memorandum, Rear Adm. Randall Jacobs, chief of the Bureau of Naval Personnel, to commandants,
all naval districts *et al.*, 11 June 1945, subject: Negro recruit training—discontinuance of special program and
camps for, Navy and Old Army Branch, National Archives, Washington, DC.]

●

*In response to the directions of the secretary of the navy
and the General Board, the Marine Corps devised a plan for
the recruitment of 1,200 black reservists in a way "to inject
the question of race into the Marine Corps as little as possible."
By this the corps meant as segregated as possible. To avoid
the large expense incurred in setting up a duplicate training
facility for marine specialists, the service sought to recruit
blacks who could, without training, move into many of the
specialist occupations—drivers, barbers, cooks, radio operators,
and the like—needed in any large combat unit. When this
proved impossible, other plans had to be considered.*

I. DISCUSSION:

1. Reference (a)[1] provided for enlisting 1200 colored troops for duty with the
Fifty-first Composite Defense Battalion. It provided that 900 would be enlisted prior to
1 August 1942, the remaining 300 to be enlisted in October 1942. Of the above, 647
have been enlisted and 428 of these have been called to duty, the remaining 219 are still

[Memorandum, director, Division of Plans and Policies, to commandant, 29 October 1942, subject:
Enlistment of colored personnel in the Marine Corps Reserve, Reference Section, Office of the Director of
Marine Corps History and Museums, Washington, DC.]

[1]Appr DP&P Memo #10568, dated 30 April 1942.

inactive. The Division of Recruiting states that the reason they have not procured the first 900 is due to the qualifications prescribed for the remainder. For a list of occupational specialists desired, see Enclosure (A).[2] It is doubtful if even white recruits could be procured with the qualifications listed in Enclosure (A).

2. To overcome the shortage of occupational specialists among white recruits, the Marine Corps has had to enlist men for general duty and send them to schools or training camps for special training in the occupation in which they were desired. It is believed that a modified form of this program should be followed for Negro recruits. That is, not send the Negro recruit to the specialist school, unless there is a colored school available, but send instructors to the Negro camp to conduct the special schools required.

3. It is believed that the above program should be expedited.

4. Attention is invited to enclosures to schools for colored personnel.

II. ACTION RECOMMENDED:

1. That the Division of Recruiting be authorized to procure 553 colored recruits (the balance unprocured of the 1200 originally provided for); said recruits to be qualified for general duty, and to include, insofar as practicable, the specialists desired. (ACTION: Division of Recruiting)

2. That these men be ordered to an inactive duty status until such time as facilities are available for their reception and training at The Training Center, New River, North Carolina. (ACTION: Division of Recruiting)

3. That 200 of these men be ordered monthly to active duty at The Training Center, New River, North Carolina. (ACTION: Division of Reserve; Division of Personnel; DP and P[3]—M-3 Section)

4. That provisions be made for training these colored troops as occupational specialists as required, this training to be conducted at their camp at New River, North Carolina, or at appropriate schools for colored service personnel. (ACTION: DP and P—M-3 Section)

III. CONCURRENCES:

1. The Division of Recruiting concurs.
2. The Division of Personnel concurs.
3. The Division of Reserve concurs.

K. E. Rockey

---

[2]List of Occupational Specialists for Composite Defense Battalions.
[3]Division of Plans and Policies.

The president's decision to make all the services use the draft
meant a large and unexpected increase in the number of
black marines. (More than 19,000 blacks would serve in the
Marine Corps during World War II.) The corps' personnel
planners were hard pressed to find places to use the black
recruits in a completely segregated service.

1. *Problem*:

Procuring, training and assigning to duty about one thousand Negroes per month; this to be accomplished in such manner as to introduce the racial question into the Marine Corps as little as possible; that is, insofar as possible, to keep colored personnel segregated from white personnel.

2. *Procuring*:

Call on Selective Service. *Note*[1]: From experience tables prepared by the army the Negroes procured through Selective Service will probably fall into intelligence groups as shown below. For ready comparison, the normal grouping of white personnel received through the draft is also shown:

	Class:	Negro Percent	White Percent
I	Superior	0.6	7.6
II	Above Average	5.0	29.2
III	Average	16.5	32.7
IV	Below Average	30.4	21.6
V	Inferior	47.5	8.9
		100.0	100.0

3. *Training*:

The most immediate problem to be solved is suitably isolated housing facilities for recruit training. It is estimated that if we receive 1000 Negroes per month, minimum requirements must be sufficient for housing 3000 recruits plus overhead. The next step to be solved would be facilities for specialized training. This could be done through contract with Negro civilian schools; through use of naval facilities, or by organizing our own training facilities.

4. *Duty Assignment:*

The following, listed in manner of preference, are submitted as the type of duty which can best be performed by colored personnel and at the same time disturb the Marine Corps as little as possible from mingling with Negroes:

    (a) Composite battalions (up to twelve hundred a year)
    (b) Messmen's branch (about thirty-five hundred)
    (c) Large Marine Corps bases for assignment to the following duties: (1)

[Memorandum, Division of Plans and Policies to director, Division of Plans and Policies, 26 December 1942, subject: Colored personnel, Reference Section, Office of the Director of Marine Corps History and Museums, Washington, DC.]

[1]Emphasis in the original.

messmen in large general messes; (2) chauffeurs; (3) messengers, post exchange clerks, and janitors; (4) maintenance and policing.

5. From the table shown in paragraph two above, we can expect very few men having sufficient intelligence to be of much use to combat organizations. It is proposed that whenever a Negro at any station is deemed sufficiently capable to be promoted to noncommissioned-officer rank, that he be transferred for duty with a composite battalion. This latter provision will largely tend to do away with the charge of race discrimination as every Negro is placed in position for advancement as rapidly as he can so qualify.

●

The Marine Corps commandant announced plans for the employment of the black draftees and offered his commanders some rather dubious advice on leading black units.

1. Approximately ten percent of all enlisted men inducted into the Marine Corps subsequent to 1 February 1943 will be Negroes. The assimilation of this number of Negroes will in time result in a wide dispersion of this personnel throughout the Marine Corps. With a view to assisting commanding officers in formulating plans and providing facilities for the reception and employment of colored personnel, the following information on the subject is furnished.

2. Present plans contemplate that initially colored personnel will be employed as follows:
Messman branch
>   Officers' messes (combat units)
>   General officers' quarters (public)
Organized combat units
>   Composite defense battalions, Fleet Marine Force
>   Separate infantry battalions, Fleet Marine Force
Depot companies (including Fleet Marine Force units)
Motor transport units (including Fleet Marine Force units)
Special detachments, Marine Corps activities in US
Guard detachments, US naval activities.

3. Colored personnel will be given their basic training at Camp Lejeune, New River, North Carolina. Training of messman branch personnel and organization training of colored Fleet Marine Force units will also be conducted at Camp Lejeune.

4. In plans for employment of Negroes, the aim will be to use the maximum practicable number in combat units. The bottleneck in forming and training combat units of colored personnel is the lack of noncommissioned officers. In view of the above, every

---

[Memorandum, commandant, US Marine Corps, to distribution list, 20 March 1943, subject: Colored personnel, Reference Section, Office of the Director of Marine Corps History and Museums, Washington, DC.]

effort will be made to locate Negroes having the requisite qualities of intelligence, education, and leadership to become noncommissioned officers. When once located they will be trained and promoted as rapidly as they can qualify for higher positions. Units being formed for duty with the Fleet Marine Force will, in all cases, have first call on Negro personnel of noncommissioned officer caliber.

5. Mixing of white and colored enlisted personnel within the same unit will be avoided, except as may be temporarily necessary in providing white noncommissioned officers. Plans should contemplate relief of these white noncommissioned officers as rapidly as colored noncommissioned officers can be qualified.

6. As indicated above, the use of colored personnel in guard detachments and marine barracks at naval shore activities is contemplated. In priority of selection of stations for assignment of Negroes, the Marine Corps will endeavor to conform to the action taken by the navy in their assignment of colored personnel to stations. To avoid mixed guards, colored personnel for this duty will be assigned initially to individual posts in sufficient numbers to relieve all white marines of the sixth and seventh pay grades, relieving personnel of other grades as rapidly as practicable.

7. The long experience of the army with regard to Negro military organizations indicates the importance of the following considerations:

(a) Successful units were commanded by excellent to superior white officers who were firm but sympathetic with their men, and who thoroughly knew their individual and racial characteristics and temperaments. These officers once assigned were not changed. The success of a Negro organization has depended largely on the personality of its commanding officers. It has taken this commander many months to gain their loyalty but once it is gained, they follow his leadership without question. Where one commander has been replaced by another officer of equal ability, it has taken the latter many months to gain their loyalty. In view of this characteristic, great care should be exercised in the initial choice of officers assigned to colored units, and, once assigned, every effort should be made to retain them in that organization.

(b) Successful organizations have had colored noncommissioned officers. In nearly all cases to intermingle colored and white enlisted personnel in the same organization has led to trouble and disorder.

(c) Everyone prefers employment on work for which he volunteers, but the Negro is even more influenced by this consideration than is the white. In view of this characteristic, the exigencies of the service permitting, they should be grouped and assigned the type of duty they prefer.

8. A study of the cause of most racial disturbances in military establishments has disclosed the following:

(a) *Lack of Discipline.*[1] It is seldom that well-disciplined Negro troops have been disorderly. It is not expected that the Marine Corps, if it maintains the same discipline among colored troops as for other marines, will have any trouble from this source.

(b) *Lack of Recreational Facilities.*[1] Recreational facilities for colored personnel at the post or station should equal in all respects that supplied for white marines. In most cases it is not the lack of recreational facilities at the post at which serving which is the

---

[1]Emphasis in the original.

main source of trouble, but the fact that the adjacent towns do not offer sufficient desirable recreational facilities for members of the colored race, with the result that they are, of necessity, driven to the place which they would not frequent of their own choice. Practically the only solution to this problem is through the local civilian officials. Every effort should be made to have the community concerned provide adequate recreational facilities. Lacking this cooperation, the only other method of preventing trouble is by extensive use of highly trained military police, both white and colored.

(c) *The Negro Press.*[1] Every possible step should be taken to prevent the publication of inflammatory articles by the Negro press. Such control is largely outside the province of the Marine Corps, but the Marine Corps can, by supplying the Negro press with suitable material for publication and offering them the cooperation of our Public Relations Division, properly encourage a better standard of articles on the Negro in the military service.

9. Colored personnel within the continental limits of the United States will be transferred only on orders of this headquarters; beyond the continental limits of the United States, they may be transferred in such manner as the corps, area, or force commander may direct.

10. Information relative to complements and dates of assignment will be furnished later.

H. Schmidt
Acting

DISTRIBUTION LIST:
   CG, 1st MarAmphCorps[2]
   CG, Defense Force, Samoan Group
   CG, MarForces, 14ND[3]
   CG, Dept of Pacific
   CG, FMF,[4] San Diego Area
   CG, MCR,[5] San Diego, Calif.
   CG, MB,[6] Quantico, Va.
   CG, Camp Lejeune, New River, N.C.
   CG, MB, Parris Island, S.C.

---

[1]Emphasis in the original.
[2]Commanding General, 1st Marine Amphibious Corps.
[3]Naval District.
[4]Fleet Marine Force.
[5]Marine Corps Recruit Depot.
[6]Marine Barracks.

The commandant issued basic instructions in regard to the
promotion and assignment of black marines.

1. Enclosure (A)[1] is forwarded for your information and guidance in connection with the handling of colored personnel.

2. The initial assignment of colored personnel to marine barracks and marine detachments at posts and stations within the continental limits of the United States will be in the rank of private first class and private.

3. While rapid promotion, when deserved, is necessary, it is essential that in no case shall there be colored noncommissioned officers senior to white men in the same unit, and desirable that few, if any, be of the same rank.

4. Subject to the above provision, promotion of colored personnel is authorized in the same manner as applicable to all marines. In case where, for example, a colored corporal is qualified for promotion to sergeant prior to the time all white corporals in the unit have been replaced by colored ones, recommendations will be made to this headquarters, and if the recommendation is approved, the man will be transferred to a post where his services can be utilized in the higher rank. The same procedure will be followed through all the ranks until only colored noncommissioned officers are employed in all colored units. The above does not apply to members of the steward's branch.

5. Beyond the continental limits of the United States, commanding officers will control promotions of colored personnel as necessary to carry out the spirit of the directive.

6. On all change sheets and strength reports, colored personnel will be shown separately. They will not be included in quotas for transfer unless transfer orders so state, except that beyond the continental limits of the United States they may be transferred in such manner as the corps, division, wing, area or force commander may direct.

7. Since the inclusion of colored personnel in Marine Corps organizations is a new departure, it is requested that commanding officers make a study of one situation as it exists from time to time and the problems involved, and make reports to the commandant, Marine Corps. This report should include the adaptation of the Negroes to military discipline and guard duty, their attitude towards other personnel, and vice versa, liberty facilities, recreation facilities, and any other matter that would be of interest to the commandant.

8. All marines are entitled to the same rights and privileges under Navy Regulations. The colored marines have been carefully trained and indoctrinated. They can be expected to conduct themselves with propriety and become a credit to the Marine Corps. All men must be made to understand that it is their duty to guide and assist these men to conduct themselves properly, and to set them an example in conduct and deportment.

[Commandant, US Marine Corps, Letter of Instruction No. 421, 14 May 1943, Reference Section, Office of the Director Marine Corps History and Museums, Washington, DC.]

[1]Copy of ltr CMC to distribution list, AO-3EO-kb, (0167743) dated 20 March 1943. [Not included.]

9. Commanding officers will see that all men are properly indoctrinated with the spirit of paragraph eight above, particularly when Negro troops are serving in the vicinity.

●

In many respects the Coast Guard's racial experiences during World War II paralleled those of the navy, although in this smaller service the presence of hundreds of black seamen often integrated in fact what was segregated in theory. While the navy experimented with all-black crews and eventually assigned blacks to fleet auxiliaries, the Coast Guard quietly integrated several ships. The guiding spirit behind this program was Lt. Comdr. Carlton Skinner who later testified concerning his experiences before a committee investigating the racial policies of the armed forces.

From the viewpoint of pure military or naval theory, it seemed clear that Negroes would have to be used for general duty at sea. I am not well versed in military theory but one of the major problems of a naval commander must be that of organizing the available personnel and available equipment so as to make the strongest and hardest hitting force possible. He cannot afford, whether from sentiment or prejudice, to use his men or equipment below the limits of their capacity. While the Negro group as a whole, due to various reasons of environment, nutrition, lack of schooling, etc. would not have the same capacity as the white group, individuals in it would be of far greater capacity than individuals in the white group.

While I was working this out in my mind, I had the interesting example before me on the cutter *Northland* of a Negro mess attendant who was a fine machinist. He had passed examinations for first class motor machinist's mate and was being used in the engine room, but we were unable to give him a machinist's mate rating because of the established policy of using Negroes only in the wardroom. We had at the same time, some white men in the deck force who never could qualify for petty officer ratings either on deck or in the engine room.

I carried this kind of logical development further to see what would happen when Negroes were assigned to general duty at sea. I concluded that the shock of the innovation, the experience of many officers at using Negroes in other than servant capacities, the probable suspicion on the part of many of the Negroes of the service's intentions, and prejudice on both sides would lead to many failures and disciplinary problems which would react against the development.

It seemed clear that the innovation should be made strictly in conformity with regular service requirements on a vessel on regular duty, but should be made with the help

[Testimony of Carlton Skinner before the President's Committee on Equality of Treatment and Opportunity in the Armed Services, 25 April 1949, Files of the President's Committee on Equality of Treatment and Opportunity in the Armed Services, Harry S Truman Library, Independence, MO.]

of a sympathetic commanding or executive officer, who would take the time and trouble to make it work and not report failure when the first problem developed.

I outlined all of this in a letter to the commandant of the Coast Guard and in the fall of 1943, he detached me from the shore duty I had had for the preceding six months and assigned me to the USS *IX 99*, a weather patrol ship, operating out of Boston.

The force commander for the weather patrol was very friendly and had already arrived at somewhat similar conclusions and begun replacing the deck force of the *IX 99* with colored seamen, fresh from boot camp.

I made one trip on the *IX 99* as a watch officer and upon our return to Boston, received orders to take command. She was a large vessel and carried a crew of 175 and 22 officers. I had command for approximately a year. She was then decommissioned for reasons of technical unsuitability—she was a German-built vessel and repair parts were difficult to obtain.

During the year, I operated with varying percentages of Negro crew up to about 65 percent and with from 2 to 4 Negro officers. We had no segregation or discrimination. White and colored slept in the same compartments and ate at the same mess tables. Colored officers and petty officers had white petty officers and seamen under them and vice versa. During that time we performed all our duty creditably, completed all assignments and, in our regular Atlantic Fleet inspection, on a comparative basis with other ships under the top command of Commander Destroyers Atlantic Fleet, were rated excellent or very good in every department. Also, during this period, the ship satisfactorily went through two complete Navy Board of Survey and Inspection inspections with a regular navy admiral and commodore as senior member each time. I think the captain[1] will bear me out there—that is not an easy thing to do.

Following decommission, I was sent to Miami for a training course and was then assigned to relieve command of an escort ship operating in the North Pacific. With two of the four colored officers and about thirty of the enlisted men from the *IX 99*, I was flown to Adak in the Aleutians and we reported aboard the USS *PF 5*. This vessel, with 12 officers and 200 men, remained on convoy duty along the Aleutian chain until nearly the end of the war, when it was one of a group lend-leased to Russia. Again, it performed all its duty creditably, survived all inspections and had no major problems. There was no segregation by compartments, departments or messes and white and colored performed the duties of their rates. More colored sailors were assigned and represented about 40 percent of the crew at the time of transfer. . . .

Since I was anxious to make these ships regular fleet units, undistinguishable from any other—though not undistinguished—I did not keep notes on the detailed development of the mixed-crew principle. I delegated responsibility to my executive and engineer officers and the other officers in accordance with Navy Regulations and made no effort to give any unusual treatment to anyone. The major policy that men were to be treated and used as sailors, not as colored or whites[,] was controlling and little else was needed. It is interesting that the naval system of interchangeability of personnel based on technical qualifications is very well adapted to the integration of a minority racial group.

By Navy Regulation and policy, a petty officer has certain authority over the unrated men, has certain responsibilities and is required to perform certain duties. Our

---

[1]Capt. Fred R. Stickney, representing the Navy Department.

operation insisted on this and if a colored sailor was in charge of a work detail he was responsible for getting the work done. If he was merely one of the working party, he had to carry his full share of the load. On this basis, men very soon became carpenter's mates or boatswain's mates or signalmen, not white or colored.

While we operated as regular fleet units, we were distinctive until the latter days of the war and there was always shoreside discussion. To some extent we were on trial and that meant that we had to be correct and proper and perform our duties smartly. Laxness or sloppiness or inefficiency in our unit would tend to be noticed slightly sooner than on another unit. Fortunately, since at no time did either crew become completely colored, we were not subjected to the kind of spotlight that several racial experiments in the armed services suffered.

My conclusions were:

1. Negro personnel should be used interchangeably with white in all general-duty positions. No position in a naval force should be barred to a Negro. Any other policy will weaken the service by preventing it from using its men to best advantage.

2. There should be no segregation aboard ship, in shore stations or in any working, messing, berthing, or training facility. Negro and white seamen should attend the same boot camps and the same training schools. This is economical because you don't need separate, expensive facilities; it is simpler to administer; and it leads to uniformity in training. Life in the compressed space available aboard ship is difficult enough to regulate without throwing in the added and artificial factor of segregated quarters or messes based on color.

3. Negro and white sailors should have equal opportunity for all advanced training. They should be admitted to service schools on the basis of ability and aptitude. There should be no quota assignments for training. This will make the best use of the available manpower. In the selection of Negroes as petty officers, I favor emphasis on rating them aboard ship. At present, the Negro in sea duty is roughly comparable to the recently commissioned reserve officer. He is new and relatively untried.

There are certain seagoing activities and practices which become instinctive when learned at sea and are, to some extent, the cachet of the sailorman—the evidence that he is an old salt not a boot. These cannot be learned at shore schools. As a newcomer to sea duty, the Negro will have more self-assurance if he instinctively uses the jargon of the sea, like port and starboard for left and right, ladder for stairway, and hatch for door and is familiar with the seagoing duties of his shipmates.

4. A quota system should be established requiring every ship or unit to have a certain percentage of Negroes, but not more than another percentage. I would suggest 5 to 25 percent as the limits, but would leave the exact limits to the service personnel office. . . .

CHAPTER SEVEN
PLANS FOR BLACKS IN THE POSTWAR
ARMED SERVICES

The armed forces and their critics in the black community shared both dissatisfaction with the role of black servicemen during World War II and determination to adopt new policies in the postwar era. This basic agreement aside, the two groups differed widely on what these new policies should be. The civil rights organizations demanded immediate integration and equal opportunity for blacks in the services, as a matter of justice. Military planners, concerned with military efficiency, as they interpreted it, favored some form of racial quota and limitations on the assignments available to blacks.

Whatever the outcome of this debate, one thing was certain: the armed forces could not resurrect their prewar practices. Three factors combined to ensure far-reaching change. One was the democratic feeling marshaled during the war against the Axis dictatorships, another the rising political strength of the black community, and the third a growing awareness within the services that postwar manpower needs would prove too great, and endure too long, to be supplied by calling upon just a part of the populace. A draft would be necessary, and any such system would have to function with a minimum of racial discrimination. Idealism, political expediency, and military realities thus combined to bring about change in the racial policies of the armed forces.

Before deciding upon any changes, the army and navy reviewed the status and record of wartime black personnel. The army conducted a worldwide survey of commanders whose views were summarized by the major army commands. With a few striking exceptions, these reports merely criticized black combat units, failing to perceive how racial discrimination affected the morale, efficiency, and performance of these battalions, regiments, and divisions.

The navy's study of wartime black activity followed a different course. Secretary Forrestal sent his friend Lester Granger on lengthy field trips throughout those commands where large numbers of black sailors had served. As one might expect from the executive secretary of the National Urban League, a civil rights organization, Granger tended to look beyond military accomplishments or failures, analyzing instead the impact of treatment received by wartime black sailors or marines and making detailed recommendations for changes in racial policy. Granger's insistence that segregation prevented the efficient use of manpower helped Forrestal devise a postwar program for the navy by reconciling the blacks' demand for justice with the concern of naval officers for effective performance throughout the fleet.

Meanwhile, the civil rights groups joined their allies and sympathizers in the press and Congress, celebrating the loyal, efficient, and at times heroic efforts of thousands of black servicemen in a variety of wartime duties. Like the army's studies, which overemphasized the failings of large black units, the propaganda directed against segregation proved equally unrealistic in its stress upon heroism.

Both services adopted new racial policies in 1946. Although substantially different in content, the directives proved remarkably similar in effect. As a result, postwar black servicemen remained few in number, restricted as to assignment, and most often segregated.

The army's new policy, set forth in War Department Circular 124, commonly called the Gillem Board report after the document from which it was derived, followed an exhaustive review by a group of senior officers headed by Lieut. Gen. Alvan C. Gillem. The circular sought the impossible—to preserve segregation while ensuring equal treatment for blacks in the army. Treating the black community as a statistical abstraction rather than blacks as individuals, it established as its goal an army 10 percent black, a figure roughly comparable to the percentage of blacks in the nation's population. Later criticized as a device to limit black participation, the quota represented a sincere effort by the Gillem Board, as well as the secretary of war and those staff officers who accepted the report, to guarantee that a representative number of blacks would be included in the postwar army. The new policy called for the assignment of black recruits to every branch of service, so that trained cadres would be available for any black units organized as a result of a future mobilization. It also provided in certain exceptional cases for racially integrated service. The handiwork of the Gillem Board would remain in effect for more than six years.

The navy's new policy, promulgated as Bureau of Naval Personnel Circular Letter 48–46, promised the impartial treatment of Negroes in an integrated service, but the actual lot of the black sailor was little better than that of his army counterpart. The circular letter did not apply to the Marine Corps, and the token number of black marines would continue to serve in segregated units. Unlike the army's more restrictive policy, the circular letter did not provide for a specific black quota, but on the other hand it did not offer Negroes training in a wide range of occupations. Consequently, a large majority of the small number of black sailors who remained beyond the postwar demobilization found themselves, as before the war, in a racially separate stewards' branch.

*Concerned with the status of black soldiers in the postwar army,
Truman K. Gibson, Jr., offered Assistant Secretary McCloy some
advice. Although he disavowed any desire to pressure the army in
the matter, Gibson made clear the political realities of the army's
situation.*

1. One of the matters I wanted to discuss with you on Friday was that of publicly announcing, as soon as practicable, that the War Department has undertaken an intensive and comprehensive study for the purpose of developing plans for the postwar utilization of Negro troops in the army; that this consideration will include all experiences gained during the present war and that the many issues with which the War Department has been confronted will be given full attention. This suggestion, of course, assumes favorable action by the advisory committee on your memorandum on this subject.

2. Similar announcements about other issues have been made in the past. Recently, the appointment of a General Staff committee to consider National Guard plans was announced by the secretary of war. The press is currently carrying stories on the recent War Department circular setting out the general principles of national military policy to govern preparation of postwar plans.

3. Such an announcement is vitally needed at this time. It would not, of course, be as dramatic as John P. Lewis' proposal for the announcement of a mixed unit, but it would still carry some degree of assurance to Negroes that the War Department is now planning so as to avoid many of the mistakes that were made both before and during this war, which in turn were repetitions of those made during the World War.

4. In this connection, I would like to remind you of Mr. Lewis' appraisal of current Negro attitudes. While the army has made rapid progress recently, still, it must be remembered that many of the incidents on which popular attitudes are based were responsible for the corrective action taken. Of even more importance is the fact that the treatment of Negroes in the army is one of the major issues among Negroes in the current political campaign, which fact has in effect, rightly or wrongly, transformed the army into sort of a whipping boy for both parties. While my appraisal of the role of the army is opinion, the basis is not speculation or rumor. I have at all times maintained close relationships with the editors of the major Negro papers in an effort to keep abreast of current attitudes. Recently, two of these editors have been named directors of Negro campaign publicity for the Republican and Democratic parties. I have talked with both of these men. In addition, I have spent most of my weekends this summer with a Republican national committeeman, who has no hesitance about expressing himself frankly to me. My former law partner is, as you probably know, the assistant chairman of the Democratic National Committee. In addition to those contracts [*sic*], I have made an effort during the summer to talk with as many Negroes as possible to sound out their attitudes toward the army. Incidentally, my appraisal of the situation has been corroborated by many recent articles, notably one that appeared in the July issue of *Harpers Magazine*.

[Memorandum, Truman K. Gibson, Jr., for Ass't Sec. of War John J. McCloy, 5 September 1944, subject: Public announcement of study of postwar utilization of Negro troops, Modern Military Records Branch, National Archives, Washington, DC.]

5. The army has certainly learned during the past four years that Negro opinion in this country cannot be disregarded and particularly at election time. Witness the presidential election of 1940. In October of that year the president announced (1) General Davis'[1] promotion; (2) appointment of a civilian aide[2] to the secretary of war; (3) the army's position with respect to the utilization of Negroes (subsequently circulated in the army as a statement of basic War Department policy); (4) the inclusion of Negroes in the Army Air Forces (though plans were not really commenced by the army until a year later and with two years elapsing before actual training was begun).

6. Some persons close to the president have already started working along this same line. It has been proposed that another Negro general be appointed and that certain other steps be taken in connection with the army. Again, this is not speculation on my part. In these circumstances, it seems to be a fair conclusion that the army has the choice of initiating some intelligence [*sic*] and constructive steps itself or of being forced again by pressures from outside sources.

7. Please understand that this frank appraisal is being sent you for your personal information. I have no desire to exert pressure on the army by pointing out facts of a political nature, however true and unpleasant they might be. I feel strongly that any step that would stand to interfere with an adequate consideration by the General Staff of all matters pertinent to the development of a proper and reasonable overall policy should be strenuously resisted. Particularly would I oppose any precipitate move that would smack of politics. Though I know it is not necessary, I want to assure you that I have no political interests one way or the other. If I had a major interest at the moment it would be to get out of my present position as rapidly as possible, having just about reached the limit of my ability to serve as a "middleman," absorbing gripes and complaints in person, by mail and telephone all day and most of the night. My concern is that the War Department adopt a decent and fair overall policy in order that the devastating effect of our tortuous experiences during the last few years be avoided in the future. I believe few officers in the army realize the effect on the spirits of Negro soldiers and civilians alike of the experiences during the last four years, while the many statements of policy were developed on a hit-and-run, trial-and-error basis. In this connection, I of course realize that great progress has been made. Equally as clear, however, it is that in no sense has this resulted from advance planning. The officers' promotion policy came after three-years' experience with bad policy and as a result of trouble and discontent. The decision to utilize Negro troops in combat came only after lengthy intradepartmental debates which are still all too familiar to you. Similarly could the entire list of other positive steps be run down.

8. Though we are in an exceedingly difficult and potentially dangerous situation at the present, I am not pessimistic about the future, particularly since a start has been made on the General Staff study. Since this is a frank and personal appraisal, I should like again to express my appreciation for your sympathetic interest and cooperation in matters involving Negroes. In closing, I again urge an early public statement, preferably in the secretary's press conference, setting forth in general terms the fact of the commencement of a study to develop plans for the postwar utilization of Negro troops.

---

[1] Brig. Gen. Benjamin O. Davis.

[2] Judge William H. Hastie.

Gibson recommends that in making its decisions about the postwar status of black soldiers the army should avoid an unquestioned acceptance of its racial traditions and seek a flexible policy with integration as its eventual goal.

I recently talked with General [Ray] Porter about the postwar Negro plan study. I outlined to him the same objections we had discussed. He agreed that the study outlined should be reexamined and plans to call in General [Frederick H.] Osborn and Dr. [Walter L.] Wright of the Historical Division, and others in the War Department for assistance in preparing additional materials. At his request and after an examination of all the available mobilization plans and studies about Negroes, I sent him the following memorandum:

1. Since the expansion that began in 1940, the army has been constantly faced with pressures for a change of its Negro policies. In response to these and because of the large number of Negroes inducted as a result of the nondiscriminatory proviso in the Selective Service Act of 1940, many changes have occurred. These changes have usually encountered stiff resistance in the army. This was true of the officer candidate training program, the utilization of Negro pilots in the Army Air Forces, and the statements of nondiscriminatory policies respecting the use of recreational facilities on posts, camps, and stations. Despite these changes, the basic policies of the army have remained essentially unchanged during the war. Nevertheless, although there has been no basic change in policy, there is growing doubt among representative army officers whether the army is making the most efficient use of the 10-12 percent of available manpower represented by Negroes. It is widely recognized that in a future emergency, this 10-12 percent might represent the margin necessary for military success.

2. Prior to 1940 there had been several studies into the performance of Negro troops that served as basis for the several statements and policies governing the employment of negro personnel in the army. . . .

3. The general conclusion that has resulted from these studies has been that the army should use Negro troops only in segregated units; that as few Negro organizations as possible should be established and that these should be noncombatant. The following consistently appeared in all plans prior to 1941: "The largest unit of any arm or service to be organized of Negro personnel is the regiment." (Memo, chief of staff, Subject: Employment of negro manpower, 3 June 1940, G-3, 6541-527.)

4. The basic approach that had been evolved was that change should occur only in the face of pressures. That this was an officially approved course, was recognized in a study which candidly admitted that a reappraisal of policies was necessary as the result of "continuous and increasing political and racial pressure for higher command and greater representation of the Negro in combat organizations." (Memo to chief of staff, subject: Employment of Negro manpower, 3 June 1940, G-3-6541-527.)

5. In my opinion, it is important that the current study avoid an unquestioning acceptance of the premises on which past policy was based and recognize that the nature

[Memorandum, Truman K. Gibson, Jr., for Ass't Sec. of War John J. McCloy, 8 August 1945, Modern Military Branch, National Archives, Washington, DC.]

of the racial problem before the army has materially changed since 1940. These changes are due to the differences in attitudes of drafted Negroes and those who have repeatedly volunteered for service in the old regular army; the advances in the level in Negro education since the last war when most of the present policies were determined; and the more vocal and organized opposition of Negro and liberal groups towards the War Department Negro policies. It is a safe assumption that Negroes will be included in relatively large numbers in the postwar army, whatever final type of organization is decided upon. In view of this, the current study should determine whether and to what extent the basic attitudes developed in the preceding studies and the policies resulting therefrom should be altered.

6. In connection with the consideration of necessary changes, I suggest an examination into the following:

(a) Inquire into the present policy of segregation. This is the basic problem before the War Department. As indicated above all of the preceding studies have proceeded on the assumption that segregation is necessary. Experiences during this war in army hospitals and officer candidate schools and with the integrated Negro platoons in Europe certainly raise questions about the continuance of this policy which should be inquired into. These experiences are, perhaps, too selective to afford clear answers, but, being the only army experiences with nonsegregation they should not be ignored. On the other hand, reports of the performance of large segregated organizations like the Ninety-second Division should also be carefully examined. Attention should be given in this connection to the effect of placing together in one organization large numbers of men whose AGCT[1] scores are low.

The latest available army-wide AGCT scores of whites and Negroes show the following percentage distribution:

Whites		Negroes	
I.	6.6	I.	.03
II.	29.1	II.	3.4
III.	32.6	III.	12.7
IV.	25.8	IV.	45.6
V.	5.9	V.	38.0

Following normal assignment methods, it is apparent that a minimum of 83 percent of men in classes IV and V will be concentrated in any segregated Negro combatant unit. Certainly the effects of such a concentration should be carefully considered along with reports of performance.

In examining the effects of the policy of segregation it is not enough to compare reports of the performance of Negro troops with those of whites. The reports must also be examined with the point of view of determining whether the performance of Negro troops would be improved or impaired by changing the policy of segregation. Every possible precaution must be utilized to avoid the error common to all previous studies of this problem, namely, that of ascribing failures of Negroes to racial characteristics without considering the possibilities that such failings as occur may be due to lack of

---

[1]Army General Classification Test.

educational, social and economic advantages which would affect other personnel in the same way under similar conditions, or the possibility that these failures may be due to defects in army policy.

(b) Investigate the navy's experience with its recently announced policy of integrating Negroes into all branches of the service on the basis of ability alone. It would be pertinent in this connection to inquire why this course is being pursued by the navy, as well as how it is working. The navy's decision in this connection represents a more profound change than any that has been adopted by the army, since it involves a clean break with prior naval policy and experience. Recently at a press conference in the office of the secretary of navy, a special assistant who had made a tour of naval installations was quoted by the press as having said "the navy is so far ahead of the army in its Negro policies that it isn't even funny."

(c) Collect all available evidence. In this process it should be constantly kept in mind that the army's experiences outside the area of existing segregation has been limited and that, therefore, the reports of the performance of Negro units will necessarily reflect judgment on the performance of Negro troops under the existing segregation policy. Only in very rare instances will those submitting reports be able to indicate the level which could have been achieved by the same troops had they been used as a small integrated minority in mixed units. This condition will not necessarily reflect a bias or prejudice on the part of those submitting reports. It would be difficult for anyone to conjecture about a condition so foreign to actual experience.

(d) Consider necessary policy changes on a long-term basis. It has been often stated that the army is considerably ahead of the majority of most parts of the country in its handling of Negroes. Unfortunately, this statement is often used as an excuse for not changing policies. Future policy should be predicated on an assumption that civilian attitudes will not remain static. The basic policy of the army should, therefore, not itself be static and restrictive, but should be so framed as to make further progress possible on a flexible basis and thus avoid the possibility of drastic changes imposed by legislation. This necessitates consideration of both short-term and long-term objectives. . . .

*In the last months of the war, the War Department Special Staff
solicited the views of the army's commanders on the performance
of black troops and their future place in the army. These
opinions were summarized by the major service components, the
Army Service Forces, Army Air Forces, and Army Ground
Forces. Although a curious amalgam of prejudicial sentiments
and professional judgments, these opinions and
recommendations would be a major influence on the army's
decisions on the use of black soldiers in the postwar period.*

SECTION I—GENERAL

2. *Scope:*

    a. In the preparation of this study it has been assumed that for political, socio-logical, or other reasons, Negro troops will participate in the postwar military establishment. Accordingly, the study is confined to the question of how best to train and utilize Negro troops in the postwar Army Service Forces. . . .

SECTION VI—RECOMMENDATIONS

    28. The recommendations below are an outgrowth of conclusions arrived at by the technical services and service commands, reviewed in the light of such theater reports as have been available up to this date. They do not reflect any position on the question of the native equality or inequality of the races, nor, do they present any position in the wisdom of segregation in the social sense. They seek to ensure most efficient training and utilization of Negro manpower in the postwar military establishment.

    29. It is recommended with respect to:

    a. *General Policies*
        (1) That the induction or enlistment of Negro personnel below the minimum specifications contained in then current regulations be prohibited.
        (2) That standards for the appointment of officers be adhered to without deviation for the sake of maintaining racial percentages.

    b. *Training*
        (1) That literacy training and training of grade V personnel be continued in order that the large percentage of Negro troops in these classes may be qualified for normal training programs.
        (2) That Negroes be trained in small units of company size.
        (3) Segregation of personnel into homogeneous elements during training be practiced.
        (4) That in all training installations white officers be assigned as trainers for all Negro soldiers until they are assigned to T/O[1] units.

    [*Army Service Forces Study Concerning Participation of Negro Troops in the Postwar Military Establishment*, enclosure in memorandum, Lt. Gen. Leroy Lutes, chief of staff, Army Service Forces, for director, Special Planning Division, War Department Special Staff, 1 October 1945, subject: Participation of Negro troops in the postwar military establishment, Modern Military Branch, National Archives, Washington, DC.]
    [1]Table of Organization.

(5) That noncommissioned officers be required to satisfactorily complete a leadership course before assignment to training organizations or T/O units.

(6) That Negro troops be provided with 33 to 50 percent additional training time above that required by similar white troops to accomplish desired objectives.

(7) That an overstrength of from 25 percent to 50 percent in the officer personnel be assigned to Negro T/O units and allotted to training units while training Negro individuals.

(8) That Negroes be trained for units which do not require technical skill, such as dump truck companies, port companies, quartermaster service companies, and other labor-type units.

(9) That Negroes be trained in such military occupational specialties as painters, cooks, bakers, orderlies, truck drivers, ammunition handlers, stevedores, freight handlers, and others of low-skilled requirements, and not be trained in such military occupational specialties as armorers, machinists, topographical specialists, and others of similar nature requiring high technical skills. (See Enclosure No. 1[2] for list of MOSs[3] in which Negroes have performed satisfactorily).

c. *Utilization*

(1) That Negroes be utilized in all major forces and that they perform their proportionate part of the complete program, including overseas and combat duty.

(2) That as a rule Negroes be not used in units where a maximum of responsibility is placed on the individual for the care, maintenance and operation of mechanical equipment.

(3) That extreme care be exercised in the selection of officers for duty with Negro troops.

(4) That white officers assigned to Negro troops be reassigned after a two-year tour of duty.

(5) That special care be exercised in the selection of Negro chaplains.

(6) That Negro T/O units of service type be limited to company size. This should not be interpreted to prohibit the utilization of such companies under appropriate battalion and group headquarters.

d. *Irritations and Disorders*

(1) That policies be adopted which will remove or lessen as far as possible the causes of racial irritations and disorders. . . . Attention in this connection is invited to the attached ASF[4] confidential letter, subject "Problems Relating to Negro Military Personnel," file SPX 291.2 (26 Jan 45) OB-S-SPDC, dated 30 January 1945, which suggests methods of dealing with racial problems; and to War Department Pamphlet 20-6, *Command of NegroTroops*, dated 29 February 1944. . . . Attention is also invited to ASF Manual M-5, *Leadership and the Negro Soldier.* . . .[5]

---

[2]Not included.

[3]Military Occupational Specialty.

[4]Army Service Forces. Attachment not included.

[5]See above p. 128.

The conclusions and recommendations of the air commanders
were collected and forwarded by the Air Staff.

4. Pursuant to the memorandum[1] referred to in paragraph three above there is transmitted herewith the study conducted by the Army Air Forces, conforming to the desired outline. The study indicates:

a. That the policies of the Army Air Forces conformed to War Department policies with respect to training and utilization of Negro troops.

b. That in training of personnel

Negroes were selected for specialist training on the same basis as white troops with the exception of aviation cadets who were accepted with a lower stanine (aptitude) score in order to secure sufficient candidates to meet Negro pilot requirements.

c. That in training of pilots, navigators and bombardiers

(1) More extensive screening was necessary to secure candidates for pilot training among Negroes than among whites.

(2) The training time required for Negro pilots was the same as for white pilots.

(3) The proficiency attained by graduates compared to whites.

(4) The elimination rate and accident rate was higher for Negroes than for whites.

d. That in combat (flying) units

(1) The training time for Negro units was considerably longer than for white units.

(2) The proficiency of Negro combat flying units was below that of white units.

(3) The intelligence and educational level of Negroes was decidedly below whites.

e. That in technical schools

(1) The training time in technical schools was the same for Negroes as for whites.

(2) The proficiency attained by Negro graduates compared to that of white.

f. That in on-the-job training

(1) The proficiency attained in on-the-job training by Negro specialists was below that of white.

(2) The training time in on-the-job training was longer in the case of Negroes.

g. That in combat support units

(1) The unit proficiency in training of Negro support units was below that in white units.

(2) The training time required for Negro support units was longer than for white units.

[AAF Summary Sheet for Special Planning Division, War Department Special Staff, 12 October 1945, subject: Participation of Negro troops in the postwar military establishment, Modern Military Branch, National Archives, Washington, DC.]

[1]Memorandum, director, Special Planning Division, to commanding general, Army Air Forces, 23 May 1945.

h. That in performance
    (1) The Negro combat flying units performed creditably—limited by lack of initiative on the part of Negro pilots and the unsatisfactory maintenance of aircraft.
    (2) The overseas performance of the Negro air service group was unsatisfactory.
    (3) The performance of personnel in combat support units was generally satisfactory although less than white. The degree of proficiency was limited by the shortcomings of Negro enlisted men, noncommissioned officers and privates. Negro officers were satisfactory but less proficient than white. There are exceptions of superior performance in practically all grades and MOSs.
    (4) The performance of combat support units was generally satisfactory except where the mission involved highly technical skills.
    (5) The performance of individuals in the ZI[2] in base units was generally satisfactory—some individuals performing very satisfactorily, satisfactorily, and unsatisfactorily in practically all functional fields.
i. That overseas there was very little disorder or irritation arising from racial conflicts, however in the ZI the following are the general reasons for irritation and disorder.
    (1) The unwillingness of the northern Negro to accept the restraints imposed upon him in southern civilian communities and his reaction to the social segregation which such restraint implies. The majority of complaints have emanated from northern Negroes or have been inspired by Negroes from northern cities.
    (2) The insistence of Negro officer personnel for a strict interpretation of paragraph nineteen of AR 210-10 relating to the common use of officers' clubs by both white and Negro officers.
    (3) The sense of Negro flyers that the exercise of command function is not an exclusive prerogative of the white officer and that equal opportunity for both command promotion should be vested in the Negro officer of demonstrated qualifications. . . .

ACTION RECOMMENDED

It is recommended that the recommendation in the attached study[3] be approved by the War Department. . . .

Summary [of attached memorandum]—The degree to which Negroes can be successfully employed in the postwar military establishment largely depends on the success of the army in maintaining at a minimum the feeling of discrimination and unfair treatment which basically are the causes for irritations and disorders. The importance of this problem must be recognized, for whether Universal Military Training is adopted as a peacetime measure or not, in the event of a future emergency the army will employ a

---

[2]Zone of the Interior.
[3]Memorandum, deputy chief of Air Staff for chief of staff.

large number of Negroes and their contribution in such an emergency will largely depend on the training, treatment and intelligent use of Negroes during the intervening years.

It is believed the recommendations made in this report lend themselves to minimize irritations and disorders in which the attitude of civilian population plays such an important part.

RECOMMENDATIONS

1. It is recommended that
a. The policy on training Negro troops in the Army Air Forces be
    (1) That Negro personnel and units be trained on the same basis and standards as white personnel and units.
    (2) That qualified Negroes be obtained for pilot training and technical specialists by the application of careful screening and selection.
b. The policy on utilization of Negroes be
    (1) That Negroes be utilized and assigned to jobs and units consistent with their qualifications and their ability to meet established training standards in the following manner:
    (a) In separate combat flying units to the maximum extent to which these units can be manned by qualified Negro personnel.
    (b) In separate service units to the extent necessary to support the Negro combat units.
    (c) In other separate established T/O units in which Negroes performed most satisfactorily in World War II (Avn. Squadron, QM Tank Company, Ordnance Co (Avn), Chemical Maintenance Company, Chemical Depot Company, Air Cargo Resupply Squadron, Engineer Units where the mission does not require a high degree of professional skill), and in such other units as their capabilities warrant.
    (d) In base units on jobs requiring the maximum utilization of their individual abilities.
    (e) To the maximum extent of their capability and availability as instructors for Negro units and for on-the-job training.
    (f) To command and administer Negro units to the maximum extent possible. Where there are not sufficient qualified Negro officers white officers who are thoroughly qualified by training or experience to handle Negro troops should be utilized until such time as they can be replaced with qualified Negro officers.
    (g) As to location
        1. Equal opportunity should be given Negro troops for overseas service in all locations except extremely cold climates.
        2. Negro units be assigned to localities where large civilian Negro population are located to afford adequate off-post recreation. It is desirable, where military requirements permit to avoid subjecting Negro soldiers to civil laws not compatible with those they are accustomed to.
    (h) As to size of units
        1. Combat and combat service support units should not exceed that of a group.

   2. Combat support units should not exceed that of a battalion.
   (i) War Department regulations be applicable to Negro personnel in the same manner as to white personnel and where disciplinary action is required, no favoritism or discrimination should be shown. It is essential that Negroes be treated and considered as individuals and not as a group.
   (j) That care be exercised not only in selection but also in training of noncommissioned and officer personnel assigned to Negro units. Alert, intelligent leadership whether Negro, white, or Negro and white, is one of the most important factors in maintaining the balance, proficiency and morale of Negro units as well as individuals.
   c. Policies with regard to segregation be
      (1) That segregation of Negroes into administrative units is desirable.
      (2) Segregation for recreation, messing, and social activities, on the post as well as off, be established in accordance with the customs prevailing within the surrounding civilian communities.
   d. That Negroes in the army as a whole be prorated among the three major forces in proportion to their respective sizes and in no case shall the number of Negroes in the Air Forces exceed 10 percent of the overall strength of the Air Forces.

●

The conclusions and recommendations of the ground
commanders were collected and forwarded by the commander
of the Army Ground Forces.

   3. Every effort was expended to approach the subject with an open mind in making this study constantly keeping in view the desirability and necessity for employing most effectively the large reservoir of manpower available in the Negro population of the United States. In approaching the problem of the utilization of the Negroes, certain considerations must be given to their present social status. After due consideration it is concluded that policies for their utilization must be based only upon the capabilities of the Negroes.

RECOMMENDATIONS

   1. That the conclusions reached in this study, as stated in Section III (Tab D),[1] be the basis for the formulation and implementation of policies for the future utilization of the Negro in the armed forces of the United States.

   2. That a policy be formulated at once on the future utilization of Negroes in *all the armed forces of the United States.*[2]

[Memorandum, Col. E. F. Olsen, ground adjutant general, for chief of staff, US Army, 28 November 1945, subject: Participation of Negro troops in the postwar military establishment, Modern Military Branch, National Archives, Washington, DC.]

[1]See below.
[2]Emphasis in the original.

3. That as soon as such a policy is formed, a War Department policy based thereon be formulated and that policy implemented by the major forces of the War Department.

Study on Participation of Negro Troops in the Postwar Military Establishment

SECTION I. GENERAL

2. Concepts

a. Before considering any recommendations for the utilization and participation of Negro troops in the postwar military establishment, it was necessary to make a thorough study of the reports from the commanders of the combat theaters and major forces. Furthermore, conclusions were not drawn until after careful examination of the historical records covering all previous wartime experiences was made. The result of such research established a common profile which lead to several clearly defined concepts, namely:

(1) That the promotion in the army of social aims which have not been attained in the country as a whole would materially impede the army in its effort to build promptly and efficiently a force capable of carrying out the security of the nation in the time of emergency.

(2) Reduced to the simplest terms there are two broad methods of employing Negroes in the postwar military establishment, or in the event of another national emergency. One is the assignment of individuals to units according to color; the other is the assignment of individuals without regard to color. By making concessions to both methods a third method is conceived whereby Negro units of an adaptable size may be attached to white units for training as well as utilization.

(3) The history of the Negro soldier, both in peace and wartime, indicates that his greatest concern is that of race. In many instances, they have put advantage to race before service to their country. This factor must be recognized and obliterated, to the extent that their country, of which they represent approximately 10 percent of the population, comes first above everything else, and that military considerations alone should govern in war.

(4) The intelligence and education of Negroes assigned to particular units should approach that of the whites in comparable units.

(5) That the acceptance of Negro manpower into the military service shall be based on the same physical and mental standards as applicable to other races, and then in numbers equal to the percentage of Negro personnel in the total population of the country. . . .

SECTION III. CONCLUSIONS

From the foregoing study the following conclusions are made:

1. That the conception that Negroes should serve in the military forces, or in particular parts of the military forces, or sustain battle losses in proportion to their population in the United States, may be desirable but is impracticable and should be

abandoned in the interest of a logical solution to the problem of the utilization of Negroes in the armed forces.

2. That the military manpower of the United States in time of emergency should be assigned to service under the Selective Service and other applicable laws without regard to race.

3. That those selected for service in the military forces should be assigned to duties in accordance with their potential capabilities.

4. That the same standards should apply to all in the utilization of the individuals of all racial groups in the military forces.

5. That the same standards should apply to the assignment, promotion, and the provision of living and recreational facilities, and for awards to individuals of all racial groups.

6. That where required standards of proficiency of individuals or units cannot be obtained in the normal allotted periods of training, additional instruction should be prescribed.

7. That special attention should be given to the methods of training and handling Negro units with a view to developing the most adaptable procedures and techniques.

8. That the opportunities for developing officers and noncommissioned officers, both in time of peace and war, be equally available to members of all races.

9. That, although Negroes and other enlisted men should not be mixed in the same company or detachment under present conditions, companies or battalions composed of Negro enlisted men should be employed alongside of other units in regimental or higher formations. In general Negroes should not be organized into units larger than battalions until their capabilities are further demonstrated.

10. That insofar as capable officers can be developed, the organizations composed of Negro enlisted men should be officered by members of that race.

11. That there should be included on the staff of each echelon which contains a unit or units made up of Negroes, officers of that race who can advise as to the problems of assignment and training involved.

12. That Negro units should be included in the regular army, National Guard, and organized reserves in all types of units which their capabilities permit.

13. That units composed of Negroes should be so stationed within the continental limits of the United States as to ensure that there will be adequate Negro population close by to provide the necessary social life for the troops and to ensure that other causes for racial friction in the locality will be at a minimum.

14. That a policy with regard to the utilization of Negroes should be formulated at once as applying to all the armed forces followed by the implementation of that policy within the several forces of the War Department.

15. That an effort should be made to improve relations with the press as regards the Negroes in the armed forces.

16. That the foregoing are applicable to both peace and wartime and to the UMT[3] program.

---

[3]Universal Military Training.

While the army sought the views of its commanders, the
secretary of the navy sent a personal representative to observe
racial conditions in his far-flung units. Lester Granger,
executive secretary of the National Urban League, travelled
extensively and submitted voluminous reports that were used by
the secretary and the Bureau of Naval Personnel in developing
the navy's postwar policy. Granger's investigative technique and
conclusions were described in the following statement to
the press.

At Pearl Harbor and thence forward, we followed the same procedure that had been followed in other tours made by Mr. Roper[1] and myself. We had called on the commanding officer of each activity and talked with him about his opinions and facts regarding the performance and morale of the Negro personnel, and the relationships between whites and Negroes. Then we would journey to the activities and talk with the men themselves away from the presence of any commissioned officers, white or colored, and so we had free play to get the off-the-record or on-the-record candid opinions of the Negro men in the navy as to the conditions under which they are serving and reactions thereto. Following these discussions, if we felt we picked up any information, we would return to the commanding officer at headquarters and talk with him about the conditions, opinions, and discoveries, and discussed them to see what additional information he had to give us and also to offer advice on the settlement of situations that we thought demanded his special attention.

We found three important results derived from that method of approach:

In the first place, the Negro personnel themselves were given an opportunity to place on record their own feelings about racial policies and their reactions, and that gave them, aside from the informational value, a chance to blow off steam and talk to people who are especially interested in their problems, the interested persons in the conditions under which they were living.

In the second place, the commanding officers were informed of situations of which they were not aware themselves, or were given a fresh point of view which they had previously lacked.

In the third place, we found that commissioned officers and Negro enlisted personnel together were helped by being made aware of more progressive developments that were taking place in other areas of naval activities. Sometimes an officer would feel

---

[Minutes of press conference held by Lester B. Granger, 1 November 1945, Navy and Old Army Branch, National Archives, Washington, DC.]
[1]Lt. R. P. Roper, USN.

he held all the wisdom and encompassed all the experience in the navy in his activity of command and, when he was told of what was being done successfully in other activities by other commanding officers, his eyes were opened.

We found on the whole—when I say "we," I think I am speaking for the whole group when I make these observations—that the morale and the performance of Negro enlisted personnel in the Pacific generally corresponds to that of whites. If you had to draw a graph curve to follow those of whites and one for Negroes, you would find they correspond very closely with the difference that the Negro curve would be a bit lower in the scale, and that's because the similar service conditions affect similarly both groups.

I should like to impress upon you that these men are living under terrific handicaps at the present time. Most of them have been overseas for long periods, for ten, twelve, eighteen and twenty-five months overseas; and, if any of you have not lived on a Pacific island for as long as a month, I recommend that to you as an experience calculated to increase your Christian virtues if there are any to be increased. There is a tendency to boredom and homesickness now that the war is over and there is no more of the excitement, of danger—imminent or potential—and then there are various irritating conditions that exist which the men themselves feel are needlessly endured. The result is that there is a tendency to magnify the existence of the actuality of these grievances or even to imagine their existence. Of course, that means that is merely a reflection of the homesickness and boredom and the isolation that the men are suffering.

In the case of Negro personnel, although these symptoms are pressing, they are all the stronger because of the frequent discouragement and resentment which Negroes feel over service conditions which they feel racially discriminatory and which frequently are racially discriminatory. I think it should be emphasized that the tendency of these men is not to direct their resentment against the navy [*sic*] service as a whole, but rather against the activity commands with which they are associated, and that to us emphasizes the need for very careful selection of the officers who are going to be in contact with and in command of Negro personnel.

We found several general situations in all of which charges of racial discrimination arose whether proven or not. One would be the several examples which we encountered of commanding officers who exhibited racial prejudice themselves which prevented impartial and effective administration in their command.

Again we observe base-wide or area conditions which were beyond the control of the commanding officers themselves, but which were prejudicial to the welfare of the units they headed. We also noted that there were several regulations established for the whole navy or branch of the navy which bore with special hardship upon Negro personnel because, in establishing and administering these regulations, not enough recognition was given to the relatively late admission of Negroes into general service, into new branches of the service.

Finally we found in at least two cases, the construction battalion—the CBs—and the Marine Corps, that initial absorption of Negro personnel seemed to be characterized by lack of good planning with regard to the realities of the Negroes' racial experience.

As we began to visit and categorize these various activities which we inspected, we found that the highest morale and the most praiseworthy performance was most apt to be found among the crews of the ships—the officers of ships' crews, the Negro members— and within air stations, air bases, and air fields. I would rank the ships' crews highest.

I am informed that there are more than 200 auxiliary ships in the navy now which have included Negroes in their crews up to at least a maximum of 10 percent of the total ship's crew, and we visited 3 of those ships—the *Arctic*, the *Bridge*, and the *Boreas*—all berthed at Pearl Harbor. With the exception of the *Boreas*, we found, upon talking with the skipper, the Negro crews, and some of the white crew members themselves, that careful pains had been taken by the commanding officers to avoid any racial differentiation in the assignment of quarters or duties, or promotional opportunities. The men were absorbed into the crew and handled just as any other members of a navy crew would be, and they had been chosen, these Negroes themselves, for superior qualifications. They were men with rates, men who had naval standards as quartermaster rates, as shipfitters, as carpenter's mates, machinist's mates, etc., and their experience, their training, and their background were apt to be more closely comparable to those of their white fellows, and to be true in a heterogeneous unselected mass of Negro personnel. So there was a minimum of difficulty involved in adjusting these men to their ships' duties and to their relationship with the white fellows.

I excepted the *Boreas* from the ships which I mentioned because we found that on that one ship there seemed to be an attempt to separate the Negro crew from the rest of the outfit.

THE PRESS: What kind of a ship was it?

MR. GRANGER: A refrigerator ship, loosely designated as an auxiliary vessel properly called a reefer.

I mentioned that, because of those three ships the *Boreas* was the only one that seemed to show any strain between the white and Negro crew. Even that strain was much less than the strained relations we found existing on shore activities. Just as in the case of the air fields, we found the same sort of approach.

The air field at the Naval Air Station at Kanohe, Oahu, on the Hawaiian Islands was almost a model of good race relations and wise officer leadership. Just as those were high on the scale of good morale, so were the base companies, the construction battalions, lowest on the scale. We visited a number of CB outfits called "CB Specials" because, instead of being regular construction battalions, were organized especially for stevedoring purposes. We visited eight of those, all CB Specials. We found one which stood up very high. The first two CB battalions on the Subic Island on Luzon in the Philippines had an excellent record in morale, fine officer-enlisted men relationships, and good relationships between white and Negro personnel. There were ten Negro chief petty officers in the outfit which is the highest number of Negro chiefs to be found in any navy activity that we visited.

In contrast with this good outfit, we found a number of CB Special outfits that were pretty low on the morale scale. We deemed that it was because they were badly conceived from the racial standpoint to begin with. There were whites and Negroes in the same companies. All of them included whites and Negroes, but they could not be called truly racially mixed outfits. All the whites were in the headquarters company, and all the stevedoring companies, the three other companies, were composed of Negroes with this exception, that there were few whites who were assigned to supervisory jobs as in the stevedoring outfits, which means in the long run, in the last analysis, you have a situation with all of the heavy laborious, what in civilian life was unskilled, work being done by Negroes, whereas the whites were confined to white-collar or skilled and supervisory jobs. It is an unfortunate duplication of the conditions we find in civilian life, and it gave plenty of fuel to the natural suspicion of Negroes in a racially segregated activity.

The base companies showed the same improper original organization. Base companies correspond to the stevedoring companies of the labor battalions in the army, and correspond on the mainland to the work at the ammunition depots—the loading and unloading of vessels, the handling of supplies.

At the beginning of the assignment of Negroes to the Pacific, these base companies were sent out without rated petty officers, a mass of 200 or 500 men shipped across the country and out to the Pacific under the command of one commissioned officer which meant they neither had Negro leadership included in the ranks, rated men, nor did they have any provision for the assignment of rates which meant they were a needless group in the real sense of the word. They were often not attached to regular outfits with the result that morale and performance were at a low level. There have been a good many steps taken to correct that situation within the last year. These companies have begun to be reorganized into what I call "Logistic Support Companies" where the rating structure is the same as in other outfits, giving qualified Negroes a chance to be promoted to petty-officer ratings and giving the men a chance to have the benefit of leadership of members of their own race.

I have described the best and the worst kinds of organizations that we found. Somewhere between the best and the worst would be the marine outfits. There are a number of Negro marine outfits in the Pacific. Two of them were trained for combat purposes, the Fifty-first and the Fifty-second Defense Battalions, antiaircraft outfits. Neither of these battalions had a chance to see service at the front. We found one on the island of Eniwetok, a little island a mile and a half long a quarter of a mile to a half mile wide, full of sand with exactly seventy-three palm trees on it—I counted them—and with the highest point above sea level less than 10 feet. On that island were six thousand men of whom about twelve or fourteen hundred were Negroes. We found race relations as such on an island in pretty good shape and an intelligent commanding officer doing all he could to make up for the physical and geographic inadequacy in the men's environment. We found the marine outfit there unhappy because they [sic] were stranded on a distant tiny island base, having been trained for combat and never had a chance to see it, and they felt they were among the war's neglected.

They found their first cousins on the island of Guam, the Fifty-second Battalion that had moved from base to base, hoping all the while to get into the war, and who were ordered to Okinawa only to have their orders countermanded because by that time the air attacks on Okinawa ceased and the high command deemed there were enough personnel on the island; so they were stuck on Guam and that naturally affected the morale of these men. But beyond that, we found a feeling among these men that the marine policy was not that of the whole navy, even as far from perfect as that whole navy setup is, that the Marine Corps was adhering to a policy of strict segregation and limited opportunity. We found disappointment among those men, that none of the men who had been produced from the ranks and sent to officer candidate school were given commissions. I was told that there were five officer candidates at the marine officer school, but none of the five succeeded in getting a commission. You can imagine the reaction of the men to that fact. Finally, their feeling of resentment was aggravated by the fact that a number had sought to reenlist, but were told that no orders had yet been received for the reenlistment of Negroes in the regular marines.

Just a few more words about the conditions under which these men are serving—I found, of course, intense desire on the part of everyone to whom I talked—white or

Negro—to get back home. Life on an island is tough. The recreational facilities are practically nonexistent. They are offset in recreational facilities established within the naval encampment, but ping pong tables, letter writing, radio programs, record playing, and even basketball and swimming have their limitations as leisure-time activities, leisure-time outlets, and sooner or later the men want to get out and get in touch with civilian population, to meet girls or women—it makes no difference. They want feminine companionship. In most cases, that simply isn't there. The native population is small and backward from the standpoint of our standards of civilization; and, of course, there is intense competition in most cases for the attentions of native women; but the supply of civilians is too small, and the standards of civilization are too different. With the exception of Honolulu and possibly Manila areas, there is no civilian contact for these men. In the first place, on those islands, the population is tired from having these long and intense concentrations of naval and military personnel; and, in the second place, the civilian populations are too small to carry the load of more soldiers and sailors on Oahu than civilians and they are sick to death of them as in the past four years as we can easily understand; and, in many cases, the enlisted servicemen are sick to death of the civilians. There is that constant irritating point at which both whites and Negroes are apt to come in contact with each other as they come in competition with each other for the admittedly inadequate sources of recreation, and so the men want to get out of it. They want to get home.

They are subject to tropical enervation. The constant living under hot climates, moist climates, with temperature of 80 [degrees] at night and 90 or 100 in the daytime, takes something out of the men. That has been another proposition that has given officers concern. Finally, men are worried at what is happening at home. I have gotten signs of intense interest among white and Negro personnel as to what plans are being made here at home for reversion to peacetime conditions. They are irritated at the slowness of Congress to get through certain legislation that is necessary to sound reconversion. They are angry over stories of conflict between labor and management. They are irritated over an apparent growing indifference of the civilian population to cleaning up the remainder of the war's responsibilities simply because the actual fighting is over. They are pretty discouraged in many cases about their chances for fair and fruitful reentrance into civilian life.

I found that our party gave some attention on Guam to the causes that led up to the racial difficulties of last December. Some of you may not know of these difficulties. During the fall months—late summer and fall months on the island of Guam there were increasing instances of fighting between Negro and white enlisted personnel, chiefly the Negro members of the depot outfits located in the naval barracks and the white members of the marine guards and other marine outfits. The fighting broke out sporadically. It first involved individuals, then involved small groups, and finally culminated in a demonstration on the day before Christmas and Christmas Day in 1944 when a number of Negroes were arrested in a governmental truck, in two trucks which they had commandeered evidently and armed with revolvers which were actually taken from the naval armory. They were going down to meet the whites whom they alleged had threatened to meet them in bloody combat. The Negroes were arrested and tried. Forty-five of them were convicted of rout and illegal possession of government property—rout being the charge of riot or exciting [sic] to riot or planning to riot. As a result, there has been a tremendous discussion of that trial and the fate of the forty-five Negroes who were convicted.

We had open to us the records of the court of inquiry which served as a grand jury within civilian life, and the court martial which was the actual trial. I did not inspect these records at length myself, but they were inspected by two members of my party, two capable Negro lawyers—I hope capable—they are supposed to be capable. I did not find they took exception to the technical conduct of the trial, but they shared my own conviction. In the first place, the court of inquiry showed the disposition to excuse the conflict by dismissing the conflict situations as being personal and unorganized and purely individual. As I have pointed out to the officers with whom I spoke out in Guam, any individual's conduct in the navy becomes official when it affects the welfare of his comrades in the navy service, and it is hard for me to understand why, merely because of racial instances, they became unimportant merely because they were individual, unorganized, and personal; and, secondly, that the constant repetition of these incidents showed a developing trend of strain, tension, and conflict which should have been acknowledged and corrected long before the December occurrences took place, and I have expressed that opinion to the secretary and expect to discuss it with him at a later date. That conflict is only typical of frequent hostilities that exist between Negroes and whites in the area of shore patrol responsibilities.

The absence of Negro members of the shore patrol on the bases we visited accentuated in the minds that here is a hostile, repressive force because Negroes as civilians have had experience in being involved with an all-white police force which was anti-Negro. The assumption that the police force will not accept a Negro as a member is emotionally misdirected in its attitude toward Negro offenders, those accused of offenses. Just the setup of all-white patrols sets up an atmosphere of friction and distrust that makes possible its extension into the conflict area. That's a problem which I discussed with commanding officers, and which has received their thoughtful attention. I can't guarantee what will happen in any of the situations that have been discussed, but I do know that, as we have come back and touched one or two of the spots which we visited on the way out, we found that many of our recommendations had been put into effect and that the colored men themselves with whom we talked have expressed appreciation of the value of our visit and the improved conditions; so that in summing up our feeling about this trip, I think I am safe in saying that all of our party feel that the navy's handling of Negro servicemen has greatly improved during the last three years, improved remarkably, and a glance at the records shows how rapid and great that progress has been.

At the beginning of 1942, Negroes were accepted into the navy only for steward service. Early in 1942, the department moved to open practically all branches of general service to them; but, still handicapped by errors, traditional errors, the department made two mistakes. One was the establishment of a separate training program at Camp Robert Small, and the other was the overwhelming concentration of Negroes in ordnance service which resulted in large numbers of Negroes being found in ammunition depots.

Some of the unhappy developments of 1943 and 1944 stimulated further creation and further impression of racial policies, until early in 1945 a program was announced and steps were taken to initiate a policy of admitting Negroes actually to all branches of service and to removing progressively any aggravated situations or discriminatory situations which interfered with, on the one hand, good morale among Negroes, and, on the other hand, efficient performance in the navy service. I found toward that eventual achievement that progress in the Pacific has lagged behind standards on the mainland.

There are fewer cases of exemplary leadership. There are more cases of inept, if not downright biased, leadership. On the whole, I feel that the Pacific experience is symptomatic of a greatly improving navy, and I feel that even the worst conditions in the Pacific are far better than many of the best general conditions which were experienced before 1945.

I feel that the most serious failures in the administration of racial policy has to do with the selection of officers who were to command Negro personnel. That selection process has not been sufficiently worked out. It has not been effectively worked out, and too often we have found officers in charge of outfits largely Negro who knew the surface of things, but deep down underneath were not prepared, not capable of handling Negro troops to the full extent of their ability and effectiveness.

We found also that the larger the concentration of Negro troops, the more apt we were to find conditions dangerous to morale and effective naval performance. We, in return, convinced the civilian members of our party that the final answer to a democratic and completely efficient navy is going to be found in the abolishment of all types of segregation, and the more that you tend to segregate, the more you tend to develop situations which kick back upon the navy itself. We are not theorizing in that respect because we have actually found by test that the most happy experience for Negroes and for whites, for commanding officers and for enlisted men is to be found in these activities where the proportion of Negroes is either less than or comparable to the proportion of the white population, and where the training of Negroes is comparable to the experience and training to their white associates. When these conditions have been satisfied, there has been practically no exhibitions of any special racial difficulties.

Our feeling is that it is time past, time for the abolition of any special approach to the service of Negroes in the navy. The Negro has made the best kind of serviceman, and the service becomes most efficient when approach to Negro service is placed on exactly the same level as approach to discipline and efficiency of any other naval personnel. That's our feeling. Those are our findings, and that's the formal report. . . .

●

The secretary of war organized a board of general officers under Lt. Gen. Alvan C. Gillem, Jr., to prepare a policy for the use of black "manpower potential" in the postwar period. The Gillem Board sat for many weeks, interviewing scores of witnesses and reviewing the mountain of reports and recommendations collected on the subject. Their conclusions, approved by the secretary of war and the chief of staff, formed the basis of the army's postwar policy, published in the form of WD Circular 124, that was to remain in force for some six years.

To effect the maximum efficient utilization of the authorized Negro manpower in the postwar period, the War Department has adopted the following policy:

[War Department Circular No. 124, "Utilization of Negro Manpower in the Postwar Army Policy," 27 April 1946, Modern Military Branch, National Archives, Washington, DC.]

Negro manpower in the postwar army will be utilized on a broader professional scale than has obtained heretofore. The development of leaders and specialists based on individual merit and ability, to meet effectively the requirements of an expanded-war army will be accomplished through the medium of installations and organizations. Groupings of Negro units with white units in composite organizations will be accepted policy.

IMPLEMENTATION OF POLICY

In order to develop the means required for maximum utilization of the authorized manpower of the nation in the event of a national emergency the following will obtain:

1. The troop basis for the postwar army will include Negro troops approximately in the 1:10 ratio of the Negro civilian population to the total population of the nation.

2. To meet the requirements of training and expansion, combat and service units will be organized and activated from the available Negro manpower. Employment will be in Negro regiments or groups, separate battalions or squadrons, and separate companies, troops or batteries, which will conform in general to other units of the postwar army. A proportionate number of these units will be organized as part of larger units. White officers assigned to Negro organizations will be replaced by Negro officers who prove qualified to fill the assignment. In addition, Negro manpower with special skills or qualifications will be employed as individuals in appropriate overhead and special units.

3. Additional officer supervision will be supplied to units which have a greater than normal percentage of personnel within the AGCT classification of IV and V.
50 percent or more class IV and V, 25 percent increase of officers.
70 percent or more class IV and V, 50 percent increase of officers.
Increased officer personnel will be of company grade.

4. The planning, promulgation, implementation, and revision of this policy will be coordinated by the assistant for planning and policy coordination, Office of the Assistant Chief of Staff, G-1, War Department General Staff.

5. Officers will be accepted in the regular army through the operation of the present integration policy without regard to race.

6. The present policy of according all officers, regardless of race, equal opportunities for appointment, advancement, professional improvement, promotion, and retention in all components of the army will be continued.

7. Negro reserve officers will be eligible for active duty training and service in accordance with any program established for other officers of like component and status. All officer requirements for expansion of the regular establishment as distinguished from the regular army and for replacement, regardless of race, will be procured in the existing manner from current sources; namely; ROTC honor students, Officer's Reserve Corps, direct appointments, graduates of officer candidate schools, regular army appointments from the Army of the United States and graduates of the United States Military Academy.

8. All enlisted men whether volunteers or selectees will be accorded the same processing through appropriate installations to ensure proper classification and assignment of individuals.

9. Surveys of manpower requirements conducted by the War Department will include recommendations covering the positions in each installation of the army which could be filled by Negro military personnel.

10. At posts, camps, and stations where both Negro and white troops are assigned for duty, the War Department policies regarding use of recreational facilities and membership in officers' clubs, messes or similar organizations as set forth in paragraph 19, AR 210-10, WD Memorandum 600-45, 14 June 1945, and WD letter, (AG 353.8 (5 July 44) OB-S-A-M) 8 July 1944, Recreational Facilities, will be continued in effect.

11. Considering essential military factors, Negro units will be stationed in localities and communities where attitudes are most favorable and in such strength as will not constitute an undue burden to the local civilian facilities.

12. Commanders of organizations, installations, and stations containing Negro personnel will be responsible for the execution of the War Department policy. Maximum latitude is authorized in the solution of purely local problems.

13. Commanders of all echelons of the army will ensure that all personnel under their command are thoroughly indoctrinated with the necessity for the unreserved acceptance of the provisions of the policy.

14. WD letter (AG 219.21 (10-9-40)M-A-M) 16 October 1940, War Department policy in regard to Negroes, is rescinded since the policy expressed therein has been amplified and superseded by the policy enunciated herewith.

15. The above stated policy is the direct result of the report made by a "Board of Officers on Utilization of Negro Officers in the Postwar Period," convened 4 October 1945 by the direction of secretary of war. The following approved board report is published for the information of all concerned:

Report of Board of Officers on Utilization of Negro Manpower in the Postwar Army

26 February 1946

I. PURPOSE

A. *Statement of the Problem:* The board was directed in a memorandum dated 4 October 1945 to prepare a broad policy for utilization of Negro manpower in the military establishment, including the development of means required in the event of a national emergency.

The proposed policy and means will cover:
1. Broadening the professional base of Negro personnel in the regular army.
2. Organization of Negro units.
3. Implementation and revision of policies by a staff group.
4. Induction and training of Negro personnel.

5. Indoctrination of all ranks throughout the service in the policy promulgated.

The plan proposed is based upon the lessons of experience and envisions maximum efficiency in the use of all authorized manpower in the event of another emergency straining every resource of the nation.

B. *Plan of Investigation:* The board has concerned itself with an examination of past and present War Department policies, their effectiveness during the period between World Wars and in World War II, and the advisability of continuing these policies during the postwar period. In the course of its proceedings, the board has obtained a free expression of the views of representative military and civilian leaders.

Essentially the problem has resolved itself into the following questions:

1. How shall Negro personnel be utilized in the army in the event of another national emergency?
2. What basis of Negro personnel is necessary in the postwar army in order to provide for rapid expansion in time of war?
3. What shall be the scope of the War Department General Staff and of subordinate commanders in implementing any policy adopted?
4. How shall authorized Negro personnel be selected, processed, trained and assigned?
5. Shall changes in policy be adopted and promulgated immediately?

II. FACTS BEARING ON THE PROBLEM

A. *GENERAL ASPECTS OF NEGRO MANPOWER POTENTIAL*

The United States of America has just successfully concluded a global war which strained her manpower, industry and material resources to the utmost. Every citizen of the democracy was called upon to exert the utmost effort as part of the national team. That every citizen did so, to the limit of his and her ability, is history.

The natural and artificial resources of any nation are dependent upon and reflect the vigor of her manpower. An intelligent patriotism is imperative, if the nation is to vindicate the past, maintain the present, and rise to its future destiny.

LESSONS GAINED FROM WORLD WAR II

Lessons of primary military interest gained from the experience of the last five years are:

That there is a limit to the amount of manpower available in the nation to form a modern military organization capable of prosecuting the major war;

That the manpower available, of itself, varies in quality.

The principle of economy of forces clearly indicates, therefore, that every effort must be expended to utilize efficiently every qualified available individual in a position in the military structure for which he is best suited. It follows logically that we must always strive for improvement in the quality of the whole.

THE NEGRO MANPOWER POTENTIAL

The Negro constitutes approximately 10 percent of the civilian population of the country and thus becomes no small part of the manpower reservoir available for use in time of peace or in the event of a national emergency.

An impartial review and analysis of the progress made by the Negro citizen between

World War I and World War II, particularly in the last five years, has led this board to the conclusion that comprehensive study involving the Negro manpower of the nation in the military establishment is timely.

The Negro is a bona fide citizen enjoying the privileges conferred by citizenship under the Constitution. By the same token, he must defend his country in time of national peril. Testimony presented to this board has indicated that the Negro is ready and eager to accept his full responsibility as a citizen.

It follows therefore:

That the Negro, desiring to accept his legal and moral responsibility as charged by the Constitution, should be given every opportunity and aid to prepare himself for effective military service in company with every other citizen who is called.

That those charged with the utilization of manpower in the military establishment have an equal legal and moral obligation under the Constitution to take all steps necessary to prepare the qualified manpower of the nation so that it will function efficiently and effectively under the stress of modern battle conditions.

ASSIGNMENT DIFFICULTIES IN WORLD WAR II

During the national emergency just concluded, approximately 949,000 Negroes, including reserves and volunteers, were selected for use in the army. These men were obtained from a reservoir of approximately 2,463,000 Negroes who registered for service. In the placement of the men who were accepted, the army encountered considerable difficulty. Leadership qualities had not been developed among the Negroes, due principally to environment and lack of opportunity. These factors had also affected his development in the various skills and crafts.

CORRECTIVE MEASURES

In the opinion of the board, many of these difficulties can be overcome by forward planning, and by the development of a broader base of trained personnel, both officer and enlisted, than that which existed prior to World War II. This nucleus can assimilate a much larger proportion of the available Negro manpower than was done heretofore.

EFFECTS OF THE WAR

No study would be complete that failed to evaluate the collateral education gained by every Negro man and woman during the war years. The imprints of travel, of bettered living and health conditions, plus the increased financial resources, have left a mental stamp which will persist and continue to become more articulate.

During the last few years, many of the concepts pertaining to the Negro have shown changing trends. They are pointing toward a more complete acceptance of the Negro in all the diversified fields of endeavor. This trend has been noticeable to a greater extent in the northern and western sections of the country. The Negro to a greater extent has been accepted in industry, and in administrative and scientific fields, both as individuals and groups, with good results. This acceptance has resulted in better wages which automatically raised his standard of living. Of more importance from a military viewpoint, however, are the opportunities which have been afforded the Negro to expand his knowledge of the trades and skills. The latter have a ready market in the intricacies of a modern military machine.

Many Negroes who, before the war, were laborers, are now craftsmen, capable in many instances of competing with the white man on an equal basis. This change in the industrial status has, further, allowed the Negro to give his children more and better education. In many colleges and universities of the north and west, the Negro student is accepted solely on the basis of his individual merit and ability. This rise in the technical and cultural level of the Negro has, in turn, given him a more articulate voice in government.

RELATED PERTINENT DATA

The Negroes' increasing capability for participation in society and government is evident from consideration of the facts below:

Growth in Educational Attainments

	All Negroes, World War I	Negroes of 12 Southern States, World War II	Other Negroes, World War II	Whites of US, World War II
1 to 8 years grade school	95%	64%	40%	26%
1 to 4 years high school	5	32	53	62
1 or more years of college	few	4	7	12

Rate of Negro Emigration from the South

	World War I	World War II
Ratio of Negroes who came from north of Mason-Dixon Line:	1 to 5	1 to 3

Increase in Negro Participation in Government

	1938	1944
Percent of all persons employed by federal government in Washington who were Negroes	8.4	19.2
Percent of above Negroes whose jobs were custodial	90	40

Increase in Industrial Experience

The great expansion of industry during the war gave the Negro greater opportunity to gain industrial experience than every before. The War Manpower Board reports that Negro participation in defense industries increased from 3 percent in 1942 to 8.3 percent in 1944, or over 100 percent. This increase in industrial experience is an important factor when considering manpower from the standpoint of national defense.

FACTORS AFFECTING FUTURE UTILIZATION

These three factors of education, craftsmanship, and governmental participation have enhanced the military value of the Negro. A broader selectivity is now available than was heretofore possible, with a resultant beneficial effect on military efficiency.

SCOPE AND NATURE OF POLICY

While the lessons learned from the service of the Negro in the war just concluded are still fresh in our minds, and while the people as a whole are still military minded, it is the considered opinion of this board that a progressive policy for greater utilization of the Negro manpower be formulated and implemented now, if the nation is to establish its military structure on the experiences of the past. The nation should not fail to use the assets developed through a closer relationship of the races during the years of war.

The policies prepared by the War Department should be progressively flexible. They should envision the continued mental and physical improvement of all citizens. They should be implemented *promptly*.[1] They *must*[1] be objective by nature. They must eliminate, at the earliest practicable moment, any special consideration based on race. They should point towards the immediate objective of an evaluation of the Negro on the basis of individual merit and ability. They should point towards a long-range objective which visualizes, over a period of time, a still greater utilization of this manpower potential in the military machine of the nation.

REQUIRED ACTION

Courageous leadership in implementing the program is imperative. All ranks must be imbued with the necessity for a straightforward, unequivocating attitude towards the maintenance and preservation of a forward-thinking policy.

B. *SUMMARY OF EVALUATION OF COMBAT PERFORMANCE—WORLD WAR II*

1. *General*

A careful analysis of the combat service performed by the Negro in World War II indicates clearly that: The participation of the Negro in World War II was in many instances creditable, and definitely contributed to the success attained by our military forces.

No analysis would be complete, however, that fails to evaluate the disadvantages under which the Negro entered the conflict and which militated against his success.

2. *Disadvantages Accrued to the Negro*

The records and testimony indicate that: (1) Although it was definitely known that the Negro manpower would amount to approximately 10 percent of the manpower available for war, plans were not prepared prior to World War II for mobilization and employment of major units of all arms. This resulted in some instances in a disproportionate allocation of lower bracket personnel to combat elements. (2) Likewise, no provisions were made initially for utilizing the Negro manpower in supporting-type combat units. These eventually embraced all categories. This latter condition apparently resulted from the pressure initiated by the Negroes themselves. (3) The initial lack of plans for the organization and utilization of the wide variety of combat units was reflected in frequent reorganization, regrouping, and shifting from one type of training to another. For example, some engineers and artillery were thus affected. (4) Evidence

---

[1]Emphasis in the original.

indicates that in some instances units were organized without definite T. of O. and E.[2] and without a general prescription as to the missions for which organized. This was an expediency to offset the lack of plans when manpower was suddenly made available in large numbers. (5) The above factors, when added to the definite lack of information as to ultimate time and place of assignment and mission to be assigned the various units, was undoubtedly confusing to the Negro mind and may have become a contributing cause for some of the reported failures in combat. (6) Official reports on Negro units do not reflect many factors which may have been contributing causes of the substandard performance in combat.

An overall far-reaching factor which affected adversely the efficiency of combat units of all types was the shortage of trained subordinate leaders. This shortage stemmed directly from limitations for which the army was only partially at fault. Environment and lack of administrative and educational advantages in prewar days greatly handicapped the Negro in the performance of his wartime duties.

3. Advantages Accrued to the Negro

Likewise in estimating the combat record of performance, careful scrutiny must be given to the advantages which accrued to the units from the Negro manpower and the resultant benefits derived therefrom. Consideration must be given to the facts that: (1) First-class equipment and material, and ample munitions for training purposes, were made available. (2) Favorable training areas and aids were placed at the disposal of commanders and in many cases, especially in combat units, normal training periods were extended to ensure adequately trained units. (3) Experienced white commanders were assigned to direct training and to lead the major elements into action. (4) The combat units were carefully staged into the theater of operations and all echelons of command were briefed meticulously prior to entry into action. (5) Reorganization and regrouping were practiced with the objective of enhancing the chances of success of the units involved.

4. Deductions of Facts

Certain facts were deduced from a careful check of the records and the testimony of commanders, observers and participants in the war just terminated, and arrived at after weighing the advantages and disadvantages previously outlined.

These are: (1) There is substantial evidence to indicate that the least proficient performance has been derived from combat units which were required to close with the enemy to accomplish a prescribed mission. (2) In general, relatively slight losses were experienced by Negro infantry units. (3) There was ample evidence to show that in certain instances small infantry composite units, Negro platoons in white companies when ably led were eminently successful even though relatively heavy casualties were suffered. (4) The board likewise was convinced from evidence that the Negro soldier will execute in satisfactory manner, combat duties in a supporting-type unit; for example, an artillery battalion. (5) Evidence definitely indicated that the largest use of Negro manpower was in the service-type units, and that in this field they demonstrated their highest degree of efficiency. However, some service units functioned directly in

---

[2]Table of Organization and Equipment.

support of combat units, being to all intents and purposes a part of them. Many of these elements performed most creditably.

5. *Summary*

From the evidence presented by the most experienced commanders, the board cannot fail to conclude that the results obtained by all units are in direct proportion to the leadership demonstrated. The failures of Negro units have in almost every case been attributed to the lack of leadership qualities of junior officers and noncommissioned officers. Leadership, therefore, must be stressed and the development of all attributes which contribute to this and must be the prime objective of those responsible for the training of the postwar army. In this endeavor, most benefit will be derived from the broader scope of activities which have been opened to the Negro during five years of war.

A corollary to this first objective is clearly defined, for it leads directly toward the second objective.

Infantry must be made more effective. When the quality of the close combat elements composed either wholly or in part from the Negro component is raised to the level desired and expected, the army of this nation will be immeasurably improved.

In implementing the recommended program, all types of Negro units should be included in the peacetime army. These units should eventually be officered by Negro officers. In organizing units, a preference should be given to combat-type units, especially infantry units, in which the Negro has demonstrated the least degree of efficiency. The training of these units should stress initiative and command ability on the part of the Negro soldier in order to improve his character and confidence, educate him to assume responsibility, raise his morale, and better prepare him to assume the duties of a combat soldier.

After weighing the evidence carefully and objectively, it seems evident that certain remedial action can and must be taken. By so doing, the War Department will enhance the military value of this potential and thereby increase the efficiency of the armed forces of the nation.

III. CONCLUSIONS

Having considered the factual and other official materials made available by the War Department and the oral testimony of over sixty military and civilian witnesses, this board has arrived unanimously at the following conclusions:

1. A comparison of the Selective Service Records in two wars indicates that the Negro manpower which may be expected to become available to the army in case of another national emergency will no doubt exceed that of World War II.

2. Considering the advances made by the Negro civilian during the period between World War I and World War II and the increase in numbers available for military service, it is concluded that adequate plans were not prepared for the ultimate utilization of this manpower.

3. The advancement of the Negro in education, skills and crafts and resultant economic betterment definitely indicate that if prompt and adequate steps are taken at

this time, a greater and more efficient use can be realized from this manpower in the military establishment of the future.

4. In the light of past experiences, it is believed that many of the difficulties and much of the confusion encountered in the placement of the Negro manpower during the Selective Service period of World War II could have been eliminated had War Department policies been fully implemented.

5. The experiences gained in the utilization of the Negro manpower in two major wars lead to the definite conclusion that if remedial action is taken by the War Department at this time, many of the apparent deficiencies of the Negro soldier can be eliminated and more efficient results derived from this manpower in the future.

6. Many of the deficiencies of leadership attributed to the Negro soldier in the past can be eliminated by creating in the postwar army, for purposes of expansion, a broader Negro base of both officers and enlisted men to assist in the training of the peacetime army and to provide cadres and leaders to meet more efficiently the requirements of the army in the event of a national emergency.

7. Creation of a broader Negro base in the postwar army logically includes organization of appropriate elements of any female component.

8. To ensure understanding and a basis for planning purposes there must be established a ratio of Negro to white manpower in the postwar army. This ratio, for the present, should be that which exists in the civil population.

9. In World War II some types of Negro units demonstrated greater proficiency than others. In general, service units have performed in a more satisfactory manner than combat units. Likewise, some units have consistently better combat records than others. In organizing or activating Negro units to create a broader base in the postwar army, it is concluded that combat units be stressed.

10. For efficient results, the implementation and progressive development of a general policy in preparation for full utilization of Negro manpower in a national emergency will require the closest cooperation and coordination with the War Department, between the War Department and field commanders, and between local commanders and local civil officials.

11. Creation of a War Department general staff group of selected officers, experienced in command, who can devote their time to problems involving minority racial elements in the military establishment is necessary to ensure adequate and continuous coordination and cooperation in implementing policy. Creation for the same purpose of a similar group on the staff of each major command is necessary.

12. The *War Department*[3] policy announced for the administration and utilization of minority groups in the *postwar army*[3] should be carefully coordinated with policies *of the sister*[3] services.

13. Testimony before this board has indicated that units composed largely of personnel classified in the two lowest grades on the AGCT scale require more officer

---

[3]Emphasis in the original.

supervision in training and in the field than units composed of personnel of normal distribution. It is concluded, therefore, that attachment of officers to units including abnormal proportions of personnel in grades IV and V on the AGCT scale is necessary when time is the critical factor, as it will be under war conditions or under a system of universal military training. This procedure is not necessary in the regular army in peacetime.

14. The training advantages accruing from a favorable climatic or terrain conditions should be evaluated against the factor of unfavorable community attitude with its resultant effect on both training and morale. Troop locations should be selected after a consideration of these opposing factors, due regard being given in all cases to the fact that small civilian communities are incapable of absorbing large numbers of military personnel regardless of race. Exceptions to this principle may be necessary in the event of universal military training, for general efficiency of the military establishment, or in the interest of national security.

15. Regardless of source or procurement and of racial antecedents all officers of all components of the army should be accorded equal rights and opportunities for advancement and professional improvement as prescribed by law and regulation; and all officers should be required to meet the same standard for appointment, promotion, and retention in all components of the army.

16. The sources of potential officer material can be extended and fostered through the medium of a more comprehensive ROTC and an army leadership school program.

17. Processing of all personnel entering the army, whether volunteers or selectees, through reception and training centers promote and maintain the efficiency of the army and will ensure proper assignment of individuals.

18. The high reenlistment rate of professional privates in Negro units has in the past denied entry into the service to much potential officer and noncommissioned officer material. Economy and efficiency demand that men of low intelligence and education who have proven incapable of developing into specialists or leaders be eliminated from the service at termination of the first enlistment. Any policy implemented should include all races.

19. There are many places in the framework of the overhead units at army installations where Negro personnel with special skills can be utilized to advantage as individuals. Periodic surveys of the installations are necessary to determine such positions.

20. Experiments and other experiences of World War II indicate clearly that the most successful employment of Negro units occurred when they were employed as units closely associated with white units on similar tasks, and a greater degree of success was obtained when small Negro organizations were so employed.

21. Experience, education and tolerance on the part of all personnel of the army will serve to rectify many of the difficulties inherent in a mixed or composite unit.

22. Present War Department policies pertaining to the administration of educational, recreational and messing facilities and of officers' clubs at posts, camps and

stations where racial minority elements are located are considered adequate for the present and should be continued in effect.

23. The adoption and promulgation without delay of a broad, comprehensive and progressive policy for the utilization of Negro manpower in the postwar army will stimulate the Negro's interest, eliminate some of the frustrations, improve morale, and facilitate the development of individual ability and leadership.

24. The adoption and promulgation of a policy for utilization of Negro manpower in the military establishment will not in itself achieve the desired result. Steps must be taken concurrently to inform and indoctrinate all ranks of the military establishment concerning the importance to the national security of the successful accomplishment of the program.

25. The approval and promulgation of a constructive and progressive policy involving the utilization of this manpower potential should be effected without delay. By such procedure the War Department will indicate clearly an endeavor to capitalize on and benefit from the lessons learned in the school of war.

26. Existing laws, regulations and official publications should be examined for determination of any conflict with the proposed policy envisaging a greater utilization of Negro manpower.

27. Publication of the approved policy by the War Department will facilitate an understanding attitude insofar as the press of the nation is concerned and thereby indicate that a progressive program aimed directly at the objective of more effective manpower utilization is being implemented.

IV. RECOMMENDATIONS

A. *Policy*

In order that authorized Negro manpower may be utilized with maximum efficiency during the postwar period, this board recommends that the War Department adopt, promulgate and implement the following policy:

To utilize the Negro manpower in the postwar army on a broader professional scale than has obtained heretofore, and through the medium of installations and organizations, to facilitate the development of leaders and specialists to meet effectively the requirements of an expanded war army.

B. *Implementation of Policy*

In order to develop the means required for maximum utilization of the authorized manpower of the nation in the event of a national emergency, it is further recommended:

1.a. That combat and service units be organized and activated from the Negro manpower available in the postwar army to meet the requirements of training and expansion and in addition qualified individuals be utilized in appropriate special and overhead units.

b. The proportion of Negro to white manpower as exists in the civil population be the accepted ratio for creating a troop basis in the postwar army.

2. That Negro units organized or activated for the postwar army conform in

general to other units of the postwar army but the maximum strength of type units should not exceed that of an infantry regiment or comparable organization.

3. That in the event of universal military training in peacetime additional officer supervision is supplied to units which have a greater than normal percentage of personnel falling into AGCT classifications IV and V.

4. That a staff group of selected officers whose background has included command of troops be formed within the G-1 division of the staffs of the War Department and each major command of the army to assist in the planning, promulgation, implementation and revision of policies affecting all racial minorities.

5. That there be accepted into the regular army an unspecified number of qualified Negro officers; that officers initially selected for appointment in the regular establishment be taken from those with experience in World War II: that all officers, regardless of race, be required to meet the same standard for appointment.

6. That all officers, regardless of race, be accorded equal rights and opportunities for advancement and professional improvement; and be required to meet the same standard for appointment, promotion and retention in all components of the army.

7. That Negro officers to meet requirements for expansion of the regular establishment and for replacements be procured from the following sources:
   (a) Reserve officers, including ROTC graduates, who shall be eligible for active duty training and service in accordance with any program established for officers of like component and status.
   (b) Candidates from the ranks.
   (c) Graduates of the United States Military Academy.
   (d) Other sources utilized by the army.

8. That all enlisted men, whether volunteers or selectees, be routed through reception and training centers, or other installations of a similar nature to ensure proper classification and assignment of individuals.

9. That reenlistment be denied to regular army soldiers who meet only the minimum standards.

10. That surveys of manpower requirements conducted by the War Department include recommendations covering the positions in each installations of the army which could be filled by Negro military personnel.

11. That groupings of Negro units with white units in composite organizations be continued in the postwar army as a policy.

12. The principle that Negro units of the postwar army be stationed in localities where community attitudes are most favorable and in such strength as will not constitute an undue burden to the local civilian population be adopted; exceptions to this principle to be premised on the basis of military necessity and in the interest of national security.

13. That at posts, camps and stations where both Negro and white soldiers are assigned for duty, the War Department policies regarding use of recreational facilities

and membership in officers' clubs, messes or similar social organizations be continued in effect.

14. That commanders of organizations, installations and stations containing Negro personnel be fully cognizant of their responsibilities in the execution of the overall War Department policy; and conversely that they be permitted maximum latitude in the solution of purely local problems.

15. That the War Department, concurrently with promulgation of the approved policy, take steps to ensure the indoctrination of all ranks throughout the service as to the necessity for an unreserved acceptance of the provisions of the policy.

16. That approval and promulgation of a policy for utilization of Negro manpower in the postwar army be accomplished with the least practicable delay.

17. That upon approval of this policy steps be initiated within the War Department to amend or rescind such laws and official publications as are in conflict therewith.

18. That the recommended policy as approved by the War Department, with reference to the utilization of the Negro manpower in the postwar army be unrestricted and made public.

Alvan C. Gillem, Jr.	Lewis A. Pick
Lt. Gen., US Army	Maj. Gen., US Army
Chairman	Member
Winslow C. Morse	Aln D. Warnock
Brig. Gen., US Army	Brig. Gen., US Army
Member	Recorder, without vote

APPENDIX

The Board of Officers, in a supplementary memorandum, approved the following statement with regard to the objectives of its report:

Objectives: The board visualizes at this time only two objectives:

The Initial Objectives: The utilization of the proportionate ratio of the manpower made available to the military establishment during the postwar period. The manpower potential to be organized and trained as indicated by pertinent recommendations.

The Ultimate Objective: The effective use of *all* manpower made available to the military establishment in the event of a major mobilization at some unknown date against an undetermined aggressor. The manpower to be utilized, in the event of another major war, in the army without regard to antecedents or race.

When, and if such a contingency arises, the manpower of the nation should be utilized in the best interests of the national security.

The board cannot, and does not, attempt to visualize at this time, intermediate objectives. Between the first and ultimate objective, timely phasing may be interjected and adjustments made in accordance with conditions which may obtain at this undetermined date.

(AG 291.2 (20 Apr 46))
By order of the secretary of war:

OFFICIAL: Dwight D. Eisenhower
Edward P. Witsell   Chief of Staff
Major General
The Adjutant General

●

*The navy announced its postwar policy that provided for the
integration of the general service.*

Action: All Ships and Stations

1. Reference (a)[1] provided for the assignment of Negro members of the commissary branch to all activities of the naval service. Reference (b)[2] made Negro personnel in all ratings eligible for assignment to duty aboard all auxiliary vessels of the fleet. Reference (c)[3] reemphasized the navy's policy of nondifferentiation because of race or color, in the administration of its personnel.

2. This letter supersedes references (a) and (b), which are hereby canceled. Effective immediately all restrictions governing the types of assignments for which Negro naval personnel are eligible are lifted. Henceforth they shall be eligible for all types of assignments in all ratings in all activities and all ships of the naval service.

3. Commanding officers will thoroughly familiarize themselves with reference (c) and will take necessary steps to assure that its provisions and intent are known and understood by officer and enlisted personnel under them.

4. In the utilization of housing, messing, and other facilities, no special or unusual provisions will be made for the accommodation of Negroes.

5. A redistribution of personnel by administrative commands is hereby directed so that by 1 October 1946 no ship or naval activity will have in excess of 10 percent Negro naval personnel. In view of current involvement with demobilization processes, the initiation of this program is left to the discretion of administrative commands.

6. The provisions of paragraph five above are not applicable to the assignment of enlisted personnel of duty at the Naval Academy in view of the requirements for steward's branch.

                                                              T. L. Sprague

---

[BuPers Circular Letter No. 48-46, "Negro Naval Personnel, Abolishment of All Restrictions Governing Types of Assignment for Which Eligible," 27 February 1946, Technical Library, Bureau of Naval Personnel, Washington, DC.]

[1] BuPers Circ. Ltr. 72-44, not included.
[2] BuPers Circ. Ltr. 105-45, not included.
[3] Alnav 423-45, not included.

*Although the Marine Corps was part of the naval establishment,
its personnel decisions were not subject to the dictates of the
Bureau of Naval Personnel, and BuPers Letter 48-46 did not
apply to it. In developing an independent postwar race policy,
the corps hoped to retain the army's segregation system without
committing itself to a specific numerical quota or any notion of
"separate but equal" service.*

I. PROBLEMS:

1. It is proposed herein to present to the commandant the entire picture of the postwar Negro situation as it pertains to the Marine Corps in particular, and to the service in general, in order to provide a foundation for the rendition of answers to the following questions:

(a) Should separate Negro units be maintained in the postwar Marine Corps, or should Negroes be assimilated into white units and all marines, irrespective of race or color, be assigned alike?

(b) What is the total number of Negro marines that the Marine Corps can absorb and utilize in the postwar organization?

II. DISCUSSION:

1. In October 1945, by reference (a)[1], the commandant approved a plan for the demobilization of Negro marines from a war strength of approximately 17,135, to a proposed peace strength of 2800 based on the following postwar requirements:

Navy and Marine Corps activities in US	414
Aviation (US and FMF)	290[2]
FMF (Ground)	1847
Nonavailable	249
	2800

2. By the contents of reference (b)[3], all commanding officers having Negroes under their command, were informed that the various directives concerning enlistments, reenlistments, etc., in the regular Marine Corps (i.e., Letters of Instruction No. 1187 and No. 1194) were not intended to restrict enlistment of Negro marines, except as to the strength of the force presently authorized for peacetime operation. Further, this directive authorized the enlistment in the regular establishment of Negro marines and Negroes honorably discharged from the Marine Corps as a result of adjusted service rating credits, within certain quota assignments of the total authorized of 2800. As a result of this authority, there are now a total of 542 regular Negro marines.

3. As noted above, all tentative plans which have been made so far concerning the

---

[Memorandum, director, Division of Plans and Policies, for commandant of the Marine Corps, 13 May 1946, subject: Negro personnel in the postwar Marine Corps, Reference Section, Office of the Director of Marine Corps History and Museums, Washington, DC.]

[1]Conf. Memo DP&P (O1A28945), to CMC, dated 15 October 1945.

[2]All steward's branch personnel. [Footnote in the original.]

[3]Ltr. CMC, MC-588721, to Distr. List, dated 11 December 1945.

status of Negro personnel in the postwar Marine Corps, have been founded on an estimate that there are requirements for about 2800. Further, all such plans made have been based on the practice adopted when Negroes were first taken into the Marine Corps, that separate Negro units will be maintained.

4. Brief summaries of army and navy thought and policy on the subject of Negroes in the respective peacetime services, are contained in the following paragraphs:

(a) *Navy*—The policy of the Navy Department regarding racial minorities is contained in reference (c).[4] This states that in the administration of naval personnel, no discrimination shall be made because of race or color, and, further, that in their attitude and day-to-day conduct of affairs, naval officers and enlisted men shall adhere rigidly and impartially to Navy Regulations, in which no distinction is made between individuals wearing the naval uniform or the uniform of any of the armed services of the United States because of race or color. Reference (d)[5] announces the abolishment of all restrictions governing types of assignment for which Negro naval personnel are eligible, and provides that, henceforth, Negro personnel are eligible for all types of assignments in all ratings in all activities and all ships of the naval service. Reference (d) provides that in the utilization of housing, messing, and other facilities, no special or unusual provisions will be made for the accommodation of Negroes. In addition, the navy has directed a redistribution of personnel by administrative commands so that by 1 October 1946, no ship or naval activity will have in excess of 10 percent Negro naval personnel.

(b) *Army*—The War Department recently has appointed a board of four general officers to investigate war plans for the use of Negro personnel in the army. The board recommended the retention of distinct Negro units but provided, however, for the organization of Negro troops into units no larger than an infantry regiment or a comparable organization. Specifically, the new army policy, as a result of the recommendations of the board, provides for the creation of all types of Negro units, both combat and service, on the 1:10 proportion of Negro to white civilians. Further, in the postwar army, Negro units will be stationed in localities where community attitudes are most favorable and in such strength as will not constitute an undue burden on the local civilian population. The board noted that experiences in World War II have proven that the most successful employment of Negro units occurred when they were employed as units closely associated with white units on similar tasks, and, further, that the results obtained by all Negro units was in direct proportion to the leadership demonstrated. In addition, the board reported that the creation of a broader Negro policy in the postwar army logically includes the organization of appropriate elements of any female component.

5. It is considered that there are two courses of action which the Marine Corps might take at this time regarding Negroes in the peacetime organization:

(a) Negroes may be taken into the regular Marine Corps, subject to limitations on the total number required, and their services utilized in separate Negro units as well as in the stewards' branch.

(b) Negroes may be taken into the Marine Corps on the 1:10 proportion of Negro to white civilians, or on the basis of some other proportion, and assigned to white units.

---

[4]ALNAV 423-45.

[5]BuPers Circ ltr. No. 48-46, dated 27 February 1946.

6. It appears that the Negro question is a national issue which grows more controversial yet is more evaded as time goes by. During the past war the services were forced to bear the responsibilities of the problem, the solutions of which were often intended more to appease the Negro press and other "interested" agencies than to satisfy their own needs. It is true that a solution to the issue was, and is, to entirely eliminate any racial discriminations within the services, and to remove such practices as separate Negro units, ceilings on the number of Negroes in the respective services, etc., but it certainly appears that until the matter is settled on the higher level, the services are not required to go further than that which is already custom. It is noted that the navy is still setting a ceiling of 10 percent of its strength as Negro—it is not simply taking in 437,000 personnel.[6] The army continues to believe that the maintenance of separate Negro units best suits its needs and also is enlisting Negroes only up to 10 percent of its postwar strength. As far as the Marine Corps is concerned, it merely is submitted as a fact that the maintenance of separate Negro units has been a satisfactory procedure for solving the Negro problem and, consequently, does not appear to dictate the need for such a radical trend as complete racial nondistinction. It is proposed, therefore, that the policy of supporting separate units for the assignment of Negro marines, be continued in the peacetime Marine Corps, and that the total number of Negroes in the Marine Corps be based on an established quota.

7. However, until the policy of maintenance of Negro units in the peacetime Marine Corps has been approved by the commandant, it is considered inappropriate that such a quota for Negro personnel be established. This is substantiated by the fact that it now appears that the tentative quota which has been the basis of all planning to date, that of 2800, as well as the distribution within that figure, does not necessarily reflect the requirements as now known. Further, were the commandant to favor the assimilation of Negroes in white units, there would appear to be no necessity for a quota, as such, but merely the establishment of a percentage of the total authorized enlisted strength to be colored. Therefore, it is proposed to submit no recommended quota at this time; rather, to call for intermediate plans to be made by the appropriate agencies at Headquarters Marine Corps who will submit, for review and consolidation by this division, the maximum number of Negro marines, not to exceed 10 percent of the total authorized, that can be utilized in each of the following categories, under the existing policy of separate Negro units:
(a) Fleet Marine Force—Ground
(b) Fleet Marine Force—Aviation
(c) Marine detachments afloat
(d) Marine activities at naval shore establishments
(e) Marine activities at naval air stations and training bases
(f) Marine security forces outside US
(g) Training activities (less avn)
(h) Logistic establishments
(i) Aviation shore establishments

---

[6]Correction on the document. Originally the clause read "it is not simply taking in 437,000 'warm bodies.'"

III. ACTION RECOMMENDED:

1. That the policy of maintaining separate Negro units in the Marine Corps be continued.

2. That upon approval of paragraph III, 1, above, recommendations be submitted by the action agencies indicated in the subparagraphs below, to the Division of Plans and Policies, concerning the maximum number of Negroes, not to exceed 10 percent of the total authorized, that can be utilized in the various designated categories of the peacetime Marine Corps; and that, upon receipt of the above recommendations, a study be prepared establishing a quota for Negro marines. (ACTION: DP&P—G-1 Section.)

    (a) Fleet Marine Force—Ground (Action: DP&P,[7] G-3 and G-4 Sections)
    (b) Fleet Marine Force—Aviation (Action: DivAvn[8])
    (c) Marine detachments afloat (Action: DP&P, G-1 Section)
    (d) Marine activities at naval shore establishments (Action: DP&P, G-1 Section)
    (e) Marine activities at naval air stations and training bases (Action: DivAvn)
    (f) Marine security forces outside US (Action: DP&P, G-1 Section)
    (g) Training activities (less Avn) (Action: DP&P, G-3 Section)
    (h) Logistic establishments (Action: QM[9] Dept)
    (i) Aviation shore establishments (Action: DivAvn)

IV. CONCURRENCES:

1. The director of personnel concurs.
2. The director of aviation concurs.

                                                             G. C. Thomas

---

[7]Director, Plans and Policies.
[8]Director of Aviation.
[9]Quartermaster.

CHAPTER EIGHT
SEGREGATION UNDER SIEGE

All the services interpreted their racial policies to impose segregation on the great majority of black personnel after World War II. The navy channeled its black enlistees into the stewards' branch. The larger army and air force assigned most Negroes to segregated units that theoretically provided unlimited opportunities and training but, in fact, offered very few positions that required unusual skills or specialized training. The Marine Corps not only reduced its black strength to mere token representation but also abolished all black combat units. All the remaining Negro marines were then reassigned to service or guard detachments.

The services justified segregation, inherently unequal and unjust in terms of treatment and opportunity, in the name of military efficiency. Basing their policies on the myth of racial inferiority, military leaders argued that the fewer the number of black servicemen, the less the armed forces would be burdened by the inept and unteachable. Carrying the argument beyond efficiency, they insisted that segregation benefited these blacks by sparing them the humiliation and resentment that would result inevitably from competition with whites.

Such was the theory. In actual practice, military efficiency suffered precisely because the services were trying to maintain segregation, which wasted manpower. To complicate the situation, the services tried at the same time to honor the promise of better opportunities for the black soldier or sailor. The attempt failed on all counts. On the one hand, many of the separate black units served no purpose except to provide a place to assign blacks. On the other, it proved impossible to achieve any semblance of equal opportunity within segregated units, and planners quickly gave up the struggle. In the end, a limited number of Negroes served in a restricted number of mostly segregated occupations. Consequently, a major aim of peacetime service—the training of cadres for the kind of mobilization believed necessary for another war—was frustrated.

Presidential politics forced a resolution of the problem. The continuing protests of the increasingly powerful civil rights organizations were of pressing concern to the first secretary of defense, James Forrestal, who took charge of the newly combined military establishment in 1947. Forrestal was working for gradual improvement in the lot of black servicemen, but he moved too slowly to satisfy the nation's black leaders. Their demands for integrated and unlimited service were backed by black votes and increasing black political awareness and were beginning to receive a sympathetic hearing within the

Truman administration. In contrast, many of the Defense Department's military and civilian officials clung to traditions and prejudices that caused them to resist change in racial policies. In the end, Forrestal's philosophy of gradual change proved inadequate, and the president felt compelled to intervene. On 26 July 1948, Mr. Truman issued his historic order requiring equality of treatment and opportunity for all servicemen, an order that he later admitted meant racial integration.

*Because of high recruitment and low discharge rates among
black soldiers, the number of blacks in the army rose rapidly in
1946. The effect of this rapid rise was especially noticeable in
the black units serving in the occupation forces in Germany and
Japan. In these units, inequities in assignments and promotions,
frequent discrimination in housing and recreational facilities,
and problems of crime and punishment—all problems
associated with the army's segregation policy—were painfully
evident. Among the numerous official and private investigations
of racial conditions in these units was one conducted by Frank
L. Stanley, president, Dowdal H. Davis, Jr., vice-president, and
William O. Walker, past president, of the Negro Newspaper
Publishers Association. The secretary of war thus received a
perceptive critique from a group of black reporters.*

American forces in the ETO[1] and MTO[2] are handicapped by redeployment and deactivation. Many of the younger soldiers now in Europe failed to receive basic training in America. Several units are without full complement or officer strength. PWs and German civilians are performing work that entails trust and confidence because of the obvious shortage of troops necessary to fulfill the duties of the Army of Occupation. Inexperienced and youthful noncoms are shouldering important responsibilities in some instances while certain basic officers, such as a chaplain, are not to be found in certain companies. We found one company with only 1 commissioned officer, while another in the same area numbered twenty-one in strength, seven officers and fourteen enlisted men.

There are no mixed units. Neither were any Negro infantry units found. Although we saw many WACs, none were Negro. The 761st Tank Battalion and 30th Field Artillery were recommended to us by the War Department as crack outfits for observation. Upon arrival in Germany, we were informed that these units were in the process of deactivation. This illustrates one of the foremost problems—deactivation of combat units and their absorption into quartermaster or general service. While such procedure may be necessitated by the general need for experienced men, it is a demoralizing force. For example, the 761st, possessors of one of the best records in the whole army, was designated for occupational duty. With this announcement, many reportedly reenlisted last fall. However, according to reports, the 761st since V-E Day has done nothing of an occupational nature except guarding an enemy chemical warfare dump for a very short period. In like manner, officers of combat units like the Ninety-second Division have been transferred to general service.

Aside from Gen. Mark W. Clark (Vienna) and Gen. John C. H. Lee (Caserta), we were unable to find any officers with official knowledge of the Gillem Report, despite its adoption as the new army policy on March 1, 1946. Obviously, the War Department has not channelled this report to our overseas commands.

[*Report of the Negro Newspaper Publishers Association to the Honorable Secretary of War, Judge Robert P. Patterson, on Troops and Conditions in Europe*, 18 July 1946, Modern Military Branch, National Archives, Washington, DC.]

[1]European Theater of Operations.

[2]Mediterranean Theater of Operations.

Until this report is implemented overseas, as well as at home, we can expect low morals [*sic*] and continued discrimination. The present status of 514th QM Battalion is an excellent illustration. This group is composed of twelve white officers and twenty-eight Negro enlisted men. There are four battalions, two white and two Negro, making up forty-nine companies of which twenty-seven are Negro. The crux of this situation is that some top officers do not want Negroes controlling the activities of white companies and they want the 514th deactivated, transferring the Negro officers to the 513th at Bremerhaven. According to the records, the 514th are high-type soldiers without a single case of VD, or courts martial since last September. In addition, both commanding officers, Colonels Haynes and Printup are openly protesting this move. This is the nearest approach we found in all Europe to integration and democracy. Despite the change in policy promised by the War Department, the 514th is designated for the scrap heap.

Similarly, in the 838th Av. Eng. Btn., at Marcianise, Italy, we found several companies ranging in strength from two hundred to four hundred men with only one commissioned officer for each company. Two of these companies are commanded by air corps officers with no previous troop command experience. The total Negro officer strength in the 838th is a provost marshall [*sic*], adjutant, special service officer, chief warrant officer, a junior warrant officer, and one company commander. This battalion has low morale, high VD, and below average billets. These poor records are blamed on inadequate Negro officer personnel.

We cannot urge you too strongly, Mr. Secretary, to effect the policy of integration promised in the Gillem Report. The very people whom the Army of Occupation seeks to democratize are aware of the army's policy of separation of Negro and white, and they, both our allies and the natives of occupied countries, question us strongly for seeking to teach what we fail to practice, both at home and abroad. We feel that the War Department has its greatest opportunity to develop an integrated army now. A large number of our top officers in Europe are southerners, and many of them without official knowledge of the Gillem Report, indicated a willingness to give Negroes a fair chance in integrated units and commands. Another favorable factor is that we found practically no discrimination of Negro soldiers by the civilians in any of the countries visited. Generally Negro soldiers are accepted on character and conduct just as the white soldiers are. There are instances of discrimination of a fear type resulting from the hate propaganda spread by Americans themselves.

We can do much toward establishing democracy overseas by thoroughly educating our armed forces on the real meaning and spirit of democracy and further by showing people everywhere that we *can*[3] and *will*[3] practice it.

We found no mixed socials. The Red Cross Clubs with all-white workers do not discriminate generally, but Negroes cannot dance in them. However, there were excellent clubs for Negro troops under able leadership.

There appeared to be no friction between Negro and white soldiers despite their failure to socialize together, and the usual competition for women that exists among all men. On the whole, the billets, mess, recreation, morale and health conditions ran the scale without regard to color. Wherever we found capable, intelligent and impartial leadership, conditions and soldiers under this type of command were generally good.

---

[3]Emphasis in the original.

Invariably, those units with the poorest records and billeted in the worst areas had very poor and indifferent leadership. The conduct of the Negro soldier was no better or worse than that of the white soldier. Bad conduct is consistently reflected in leadership, poor camp locations, inadequate recreation, low classifications and hostile military police. On the question of MPs, we received numerous complaints about their persistent efforts to discourage associations with the white population, particularly women. Strong-arm methods are employed at the mere sight of a Negro soldier and a white girl, regardless of her character. The natives reflect seriously on this racial distinction in our army. Actual testimony freely given to us by many civilians reveals their unwillingness to discriminate. In Mannheim, Germany, Naples and Leghorn, Italy, we recommended to the executive officers the use of integrated MP units of Negro and white soldiers. This, we believe, is the only sound solution.

On the matter of housing, there were several bad posts, while others were good. In some instances, billets had to be provided from bombed buildings which are greatly in need of repair. Others are located in isolated wooded areas with men living under substandard conditions regardless of the fact that no warfare is being conducted by us at present. Chief examples of extremely poor housing were: (1) 838th Av. Eng. Btn. (Marcianise, Italy); (2) 110th Port Battalion, (Leghorn, Italy); and (3) 837th Eng. Av. Btn. (Istres, France). The very worst of the lot is the 837th. Conditions here were terrible. The countryside is arrid [sic], rocky and most undesirable. Barracks are ill-kempt and the camp's whole appearance is depressing. Here we saw the worst guard-house of all. It was a barbed-wire enclosure located in the hot sun with no shelter of any sort, except one small latrine, and pup tents, which the men were forced to sleep in. We witnessed no such similar guardhouse in any of the German prisoner of war camps visited. The commanding officer, Lt. Col. John E. Minahan, seemed absolutely uncon-cerned about the camp's appearance, troop morale or anything else.

Further, on the matter of location of Negro troops and type of work performed, they were conspicuously absent from the ETO headquarters, Frankfurt. If they were sta-tioned near, they had no official duties in Frankfurt. Not a single Negro officer appeared to be on the staff of Gen. Joseph T. McNarney. In like manner, we found no Negroes in military government. Especially did we look for them in the key cities of the American occupied zone. What few Negro troops there were in Berlin, (3416th QM Trk. Co., and 3233rd QM Service Co.) were scheduled to be moved out. Similarly, in Nurnberg at the trials, not a black face was in evidence. It appears that we could at least have integrated MP units guarding these war criminals, if this thing called democracy is to take real root over there. Negro troops should be a part of every garrison of American soldiers in every European center.

The high rate of VD among American troops is alarming. There is visual evidence of the army's continuous fight to stamp out this monster. The general carelessness on the part of our GIs, especially when drunk, is terrible; coupled with this is the obvious indifference of the civilians. The military government's efforts to aid in civilian VD treatment by supplying penicillin is commendable. Troop VD records seemingly were high or low in direct proportion to the interest of executive officers. It is our opinion that we could make faster progress in the VD fight if more officers would assume personal responsibility. . . .

It appears necessary, however, for the army to review the racial attitudes of all officers assigned to command Negro troops in order to determine fitness. The Negro is an

American citizen and an integral part of the army. Therefore, greater selectivity should be used in accepting enlistees in order to reduce the preponderance of lowly classified men presently in fours and fives.[4] Moreover, special efforts should be made to train more Negro officers at West Point with a view toward integrated staffs. Greater emphasis should be placed also on the training of these troops particularly for overseas duty. . . .

RECOMMENDATIONS

1. Immediate implementation of the Gillem Report to the extent of mixed units and commands.

2. Thorough orientation of all troops and officers on proper racial attitudes and the art of getting along with troops of a different race in the same army.

3. Elimination of inequitable billets, recreational facilities, disciplinary measures and post assignments based solely on race.

5. [sic] Integration of Negro personnel into military government along all levels.

6. Station and utilize Negro troops, preferably integratedly, in key occupied centers, such as Frankfurt, Berlin, Nurnberg and Munich.

7. Continued campaign against VD by quartering soldiers under governable conditions, by requiring civilian examinations, and by instituting a vigorous ban against excessive drinking and drunkenness.

8. Integration of Negroes into all MP and SP units dealing with Negro and white soldiers in an effort to reduce racial friction and to further prevent usurpation of authority.

9. Removal of PWs from positions of trust and confidence; assignment of American troops to duties they are especially qualified for without regard to color.

10. Greater educational training of enlistees, before overseas duty, to materially reduce low classifications and to improve the lot.

---

[4]Classes IV and V, AGCT.

*The army found it impossible to carry out the provisions of the
Gillem Board policy. A key provision of the new policy, for
example, called for the integration of black and white units
into progressively smaller composite units. Yet the army staff
found it impossible to arrange for the assignment of a black
battalion to a white combat division.*

1. Reference War Department Circular 124, 27 April 1946.

2. Referenced circular includes the promulgation of the grouping of Negro units with white units to a single larger organization as a War Department policy.

3. It is understood informally that the 555th Parachute Battalion is presently assigned at Fort Benning and is attached to the 82d Airborne Division for administration and training.

4. In order to expedite the formation of mixed white and Negro type units, your comment is requested on the feasibility of and recommendations for accomplishing the assignment of the 555th Parachute Battalion to the 82d Airborne Division in lieu of one of the white battalions presently assigned, and at the same time authorizing the remaining white parachute battalions to carry a temporary overstrength in personnel in order that by reason of this action no white personnel must be transferred from the division. Correct Table of Organization and Equipment strength for the division must be attained by normal attrition at the earliest practicable date.

[Disposition Form, Brig. Gen. G. L. Eberle, assistant chief of staff, G-3, for commanding general, Army Ground Forces, 3 June 1946, subject: Formation of composite white-Negro units, Modern Military Branch, National Archives, Washington, DC.]

●

*The commander of a major element of the army forces offered
his interpretation of the army's new race policy in arguing
against the formation of composite units.*

1. Reference is made to attached Disposition Form, WDGCT 291.21 (30 Apr 46), 3 June 1946, subject as above.[1]

2. The 555th Parachute Infantry Battalion[2] is presently stationed at Fort Bragg, North Carolina, and is attached to the 82d Airborne Division.

3. It is the understanding of this headquarters that the formation of white-Negro units is to follow two concepts:

[Memorandum, commanding general, Army Ground Forces, for chief of staff, 21 June 1946, subject: Formation of composite white-Negro units, Modern Military Records Branch, National Archives, Washington, DC.]

[1]Formation of composite white-Negro units.

[2]Negro enlisted personnel. [Footnote in the original.]

a. The formation of composite white and Negro units by attaching a separate Negro company and a separate white company to a battalion headquarters (and separate battalions to group headquarters, etc) and,

b. The formation of organic white and Negro units by assigning a Negro company as an organic part of a table of organization white battalion thus replacing an organic white company (and similarly for battalions in regiments, etc).

4. It is recognized that the policies enunciated in Circular 124, War Department, 1946, are designed for the postwar army, and therefore implementation must be progressive over a period of time. Implementation has been initiated in forming composite units according to the concept of paragraph 3a. above, and the current status of the 555th Parachute Infantry Battalion is consistent with that concept.

5. The assignment of the 555th Parachute Infantry Battalion as an organic part of the 82d Airborne Division, thereby replacing one of the white battalions of the division, is not considered feasible at this time for the reasons stated below.

a. The concept of paragraph 3b., above, is considered to be a part of the longer range implementation of Circular 124, and subject to considerable study.

b. The 555th Parachute Infantry Battalion has never been up to strength due to lack of volunteers, thus the potential power of the division would be reduced.

c. The effect on the combat efficiency of the division must be studied to determine the results of placing in combat a parachute regiment composed of two white battalions and one Negro battalion.

d. Study must be given to the desirability of having a Negro battalion assume the history of a white battalion by replacing it as an organic part of the division.

For the commanding general:

G. W. Zeller
Capt., AGD
Asst. Ground Adj. Gen.

●

The army ground forces commander found reasons to reject the army staff proposal to give the Eighty-second Airborne Division an extra battalion.

1. Reference is made to memorandum, subject: "Formation of composite white-Negro units," dated 21 June 1946.

2. The War Department recognizes the nonfeasibility of replacing one of the organic battalions of the 82d Airborne Division by the 555th Parachute Infantry Battalion.

3. Your comments and recommendations are requested on the feasibility of

[Disposition Form, Lt. Gen. C. P. Hall, director of organization and training to commanding general, Army Ground Forces, 24 July 1946, subject: Formation of composite white-Negro units, and comment no. 2, dated 1 August 1946, same subject, Modern Military Records Branch, National Archives, Washington, DC.]

providing a special T/O&E for the Eighty-second Airborne Division, thereby authorizing an additional battalion above the present authorized divisional strength. The 555th Parachute Battalion could then be assigned to the 82d Airborne Division without eliminating one of the white battalions. This assignment would add impetus to the training of the 555th Battalion, provide more and better Negro parachute recruits and implement the policies prescribed in War Department Circular 124.

COMMENT NO. 2[1]

TO: Director of Orgn & Tng, WDGS FROM: CG, AGF DATE: 1 Aug 1946

1. This headquarters is unalterably opposed to the publication of special tables of organization and equipment unless such special tables are required in carrying out the combat mission of the unit concerned.

2. The inclusion of a separate infantry battalion in a division is unsound from a tactical and organizational viewpoint.

3. It is undesirable to have divisions organized differently solely for the purpose of assigning a Negro unit to one division.

4. It is most doubtful that assignment of the 555th Parachute Infantry Battalion to the 82d Airborne Division would improve the training or any other element of the battalion beyond the results obtained by the battalion's current attachment to the division.

For the commanding general:

G. W. Zeller
Capt. AGD
Asst. Ground Adj. Gen.

---

[1]Memorandum, from commanding general, Army Ground Forces, to director of organization and training, 1 August 1946.

●

The director of the Organization and Training Division explains why the black parachute battalion will have to remain "attached" rather than "assigned" to the famous Eighty-second Airborne Division.

3. Discussion:

a. The present mission of the Eighty-second Airborne Division necessitates the maintenance of the highest degree of training possible.

b. The 555th Parachute Battalion is presently attached to the 82d Airborne Division for administration and training. The battalion is not up to full strength of qualified

---

[Memorandum, Lt. Gen. C. P. Hall, director of organization and training, for Sec. of War Robert P. Patterson, 19 September 1946, subject: Request for memorandum, Modern Military Records Branch, National Archives, Washington, DC.]

parachutists. However, a large number of personnel have been entered into training in an attempt to bring the unit up to full strength of qualified parachutists.

c. Reference Army Ground Forces' comment in paragraph 5d (Tab C),[1] it is not the intention of the War Department to authorize units to assume either the numbered designation or history of other units in the event of replacement.

d. The utilization of Negro manpower in separate battalions, such as the 555th Parachute Battalion, is in accord with the intent of War Department Circular 124, dated 27 April 1946.

4. In view of the foregoing discussion, the present attachment of the 555th Parachute Battalion to the 82d Airborne Division was not changed.

---

[1]See above, p. 214.

●

Marcus H. Ray succeeded Truman Gibson as the civilian aide to the secretary of war. His report to the secretary on conditions he encountered during a tour of installations in Europe clearly illustrated the failure of the army to carry out some of the provisions of its postwar race policy.

DISCUSSION:

a. It was felt that the reassignment of qualified Negro personnel from units or organizations where they are now sorely needed, to overhead installations would work a hardship upon the base units without ensuring a compensating increase in the efficiency of the overhead installations.

The assignment of carefully selected Negro personnel to overhead installations offers an immediate opportunity for overt implementation of the current War Department policy. This would build morale among Negro personnel, stimulate the development of individual ability, and gain public support for the plan of releasing substandard men, while concurrently making full use of the available skills of high-grade enlistees. With the out phasing of Negro units in the theater currently set up, there will be surplus personnel from among whom representative individuals may be selected.

b. Since the work of the occupying force is mainly administration and supply and there are no combat units per se, excepting the constabulary, Negro combat units have been deactivated or converted to service-type organizations.

I do not believe the Negro soldiers are being given the opportunity to put their service-developed skills to work. There are no Negro units in the theater engaged in other than service-type work with the exception of four AGF[1] bands. Many men with good records and possessing measurable skills are assigned without reference to these skills to

---

[Memorandum, Sec. of War Robert P. Patterson for deputy chief of staff, 7 January 1947, Modern Military Records Branch, National Archives, Washington, DC.]

[1]Army Ground Forces.

organizations which by reason of their missions could not profitably use them, for example, radio technicians, armorers, and motor maintenance men.

c. Because of the racial ideologies of the German people, it was thought inexpedient to assign Negro personnel to the constabulary as this assignment would require supervision and police control over German nationals.

To accept the racial prejudices of the German people as a reason for the nonutilization of the American soldier who happens to be nonwhite is to negate the very ideals we have made a part of our reeducation program in Germany. In talking with representative German nationals, such as the burgomeisters and police representatives, I found no carry-over of Nazi racial ideologies directed against the American Negro soldier. The expected ideological difficulties in the use of Negro troops in Germany have not materialized. In those areas, for example, Graffenwohr, where only Negro soldiers are located, the German youth program is progressing as well under the direction of colored soldiers as in other parts of Germany where only white troops are stationed.

d. It was determined that the assignment of Negro military police would increase morale and remove some of the problems in the control of Negro personnel. General McNarney has directed that two units of military police, composed of Negro personnel, be organized and trained.

e. There were reported incidents of friction between white and Negro soldiers during the off-duty hours. A physical separation of the installations housing white and black troops was initiated as an answer to these incidents of friction.

The Army Information and Education Division has prepared an orientation program to aid in overcoming such difficulties. As pointed out in the Gillem Report, the adoption and promulgation of a policy for the utilization of Negro manpower in the military establishment will not in itself achieve the desired result. Steps must be taken concurrently to inform and indoctrinate all ranks of the military establishment concerning the importance to the national security of the successful accomplishment of this program. I noted a general reluctance to accept realistically the fact that racial prejudice was existent and a part of the problem. Any plan to overcome these conflicts between white and colored soldiers which did not first attempt to educate above the prejudices would, I believe, fall short of the target.

f. The Palm Garden Red Cross Club, located within the military compound at Frankfurt, had refused Negroes admittance. The adverse morale effect of this, especially upon the one Negro unit (427th ASF[2] band) assigned and quartered within the compound, was immediate. This situation was corrected when brought to General McNarney's attention.

g. The venereal disease and crime rates of the Negro soldiers as compared with the rates of the white soldiers fall into the pattern of the AGCT[3] results wherein the percentages are as follows:

	I	II	III	IV	V
White	6.1%	29.3%	32.5%	29.5%	5.5%
Negro	0.3%	3.6	13.3	47.6	35.2

---

[2] Army Service Forces.
[3] Army General Classification Test.

During 1 January through 31 August 1946, the average theater strength was: 351,602 white and 51,082 Negro.

The major crime rate per 1,000 military population was: 3.17 white and 7.4 Negro. Venereal cases per 1,000 military population were: 179 white and 898 Negro.

The high venereal disease incidence and high court martial rates are in direct proportion to the high percentage of class IVs and Vs. It was agreed that the release of substandard men of proven nonadaptability as provided by War Department Circular 241, CS, would make for an immediate reduction of these figures.

2. There was a general lack of military smartness in the enlisted personnel seen in the European Theater which may have been indicative of a mental attitude not proper for the job at hand. An item which loomed was the poor appearance and lack of proper maintenance of the vehicles used by the US Army Forces. I believe the condition of the transportation tends adversely to affect army prestige among German nationals.

3. Negro War Department civilian employees were in many cases not being utilized in the skills for which originally recruited by Overseas Placement, Washington, DC. The public conduct of many civilian employees, both white and colored, did not tend to increase the prestige of the United States. I saw examples of riotousness and public drunkenness, the identity of the persons concerned being determined by the uniform authorized for civilian employees.

4. The interest shown in War Department Circular 241, CS, which allows the release of those enlisted men who cannot be economically trained or who are incapable of serving in the army in a desirable manner, points to an early reduction in the number of substandard men. It is noted though, that 30 percent of the cases actioned are recommended for blue discharges (discharge without honor). This type of discharge denies veterans' rights under the GI Bill. I do not believe the use of the blue discharge to be in the spirit of the circular. This circular was the answer to the effort to rid the army of unprofitable personnel by reducing in numbers from the lower-intelligence end of the measuring scale. The original enlistment of men with AGCT scores of less than 70 is chargeable to the army and not to the men concerned.

From the date 10 August 1946 to 21 November 1946, USFET[4] reports the following actions under War Department Circular 241:

Type of Discharge	White	Blue	Total
Whites	1958	521	2479
Negroes	1593	1027	2620

In some cases the releases are accompanied by ceremonies which are a further indication of a misunderstanding of the spirit of the circular. As an example, excerpts are reproduced from such an order:

---

[4]United States Forces European Theater.

HEADQUARTERS
476th QUARTERMASTER GROUP (TC)
APO 168   US ARMY

AG 220.801   *26 October 1946*
SUBJECT: Undesirable Personnel
TO: All Unit Commanders

1. This headquarters is in receipt of orders directing return of EM listed below to the United States for discharge under the provisions of AR 615-368 and AR 615-369.

2. It is directed that each commander will read this letter and names of EM ordered discharged at a company formation called for this purpose.

3. Unit commanders will stress the fact that these men are being eliminated from the army because of their own misconduct and that men separated in this way are forever barred from the military or naval service of their country.

4. The following named EM have been ordered to return to the ZI[5] for discharge this date: . . .

5. The general conduct of troops in USFET, although below the standard of the war army, was not unsatisfactory. A larger proportion of Negro soldiers were creating disciplinary problems, but this I attribute to the higher percentage of substandard men, devoid of motivation. The overall conduct of the majority of Negro troops closely paralleled that of the white component.

6. In the Mediterranean Theater of Operations, conferences were held with Lieutenant General [John C. H.] Lee, Major General [Lawrence C.] Jaynes, Brigadier General [Kenneth T.] Blood, and commanding officers of all Negro organizations. The utilization of the Negro was measured by his capabilities. There were assignments to headquarters and overhead installations, including the assignment of a Negro officer to the war crime[s] trials as a member of the staff of prosecutors. One of the most highly rated military police units is the Ninetieth MP Company, officered and personneled by Negroes. The general state of morale, discipline, and training is high. A selected company of Negro soldiers is assigned to duty as guards for the US embassy at Rome. Circular 124, CS, on utilization of Negro manpower in the postwar army, has been made the basis for Negro troop usage. Army supported recreational facilities are open to all military personnel without regard to race or color. The release of unprofitable personnel is being processed by careful screening at the company level.

7. In Austria, a conference was held with Gen. Mark Clark and members of his staff. There were no Negro troops currently stationed in Austria, but orders have since been issued moving a railroad car company of selected Negro personnel to Vienna. The planned utilization of the Negro personnel is in keeping with current policy. The general appearance of US military personnel was excellent with an apparent high state of discipline and morale.

---

[5]Zone of the Interior.

8. The Swiss leave center at Mulhouse is well organized and prepared to handle at least twice the present load. In Switzerland, representative citizens, including the president of the Swiss Hotel Association, were pleased with the conduct of American soldiers while on tour. I feel that the wholesome moral atmosphere in Switzerland is offering a solution to the leave interests of our military personnel in the European area.

RECOMMENDATIONS:

1. That there be a restatement to the army of the objectives of the War Department policy on utilization of Negro manpower in the postwar army.   O&T[6]

2. That a Negro combat unit be organized and assigned to duty as a component of an organization of the constabulary of USFET.   O&T
P&O[7]

3. That there be a review of policies now in effect in USFET on discharges allowed under Circular 241, CS, with a view toward a reduction in the number of blue discharges.   P&A[8]

4. That selected qualified Negro personnel currently assigned USFET be integrated in overhead installations as individuals.   P&A
P&O

5. That a qualified representative of Overseas Placement, Washington, DC confer with its representatives in USFET on recruitment and assignment practices to ensure an understanding of War Department policies.   CPD of
OSW[9]

6. That increased emphasis be placed upon Army Information and Education efforts to combat racial misunderstandings by an additional allotment of time for such orientation.   I&E

Marcus H. Ray
Civilian Aide to the
Secretary of War

---

[6]Organization and Training.
[7]Plans and Operations.
[8]Personnel and Administration.
[9]Office of the Secretary of War.

Another important provision of the army's race policy called for the use of additional officers in some black units. Yet based on a study of black units stationed in the United States (the so-called ZI), the army staff discovered just how many such extra officers would be needed. These recommendations were never carried out.

DISCUSSION

1. Reference is made to paragraph three, WD Circular 124.

   3. Additional officer supervision will be supplied to units which have a greater than normal percentage of personnel within the AGCT classification of IV and V.

   50 percent or more Class IV and V, 25 percent increase of officers.

   70 percent or more Class IV and V, 50 percent increase of officers.

   Increased officer personnel will be of company grade.

2. Reference is made to paragraph two, WD Circular 124.

   2. . . . White officers assigned to Negro organizations will be replaced by Negro officers who prove qualified to fill the assignment.

3. This branch recently directed TAG[1] to make a special study of Negro T/O&E units in the ZI to determine the extent to which the officer assignment thereto complies with paragraphs two and three of WD Circular 124 cited above. (D/F to TAG, file CSGPA 291.2 [11 Jun 47], subject: "Implementation of WD Cir 124," dated 8 Dec 47). In compliance TAG has furnished the attached report (TAB A).[2] This report provides basic information on some 78 of the 100 Negro T/O&E units in the ZI covering:

   a. The AGCT composition of the troops assigned to each such unit.

   b. The T/O&E authorized officer strength of each such unit.

   c. The additional officer strength called for by paragraph three, WD Circular 124 based upon the AGCT composition of the Negro troops assigned to the unit in question.

   d. The actual officer assigned strength of that unit as of reporting date.

   1. From these reports it appears that paragraph three, WD Circular 124, covering officer strength needs considerable implementation. These facts appear to be substantiated.

   a. Total T/O&E authorized officer strength for Negro units 656

   b. Total officer assigned strength for seventy-eight Negro units 584

   c. Total officer *shortage*[3] without any implementation of paragraph three,

WD Circular 124 in 78 Negro units 72

[Memorandum, Maj. J. F. Leiblich et al., for General Paul, 29 April 1948, subject: Assignment of officers to Negro T/O&E units in compliance with WD Circular 124, 1946, Modern Military Records Branch, National Archives, Washington, DC.]

[1] The Adjutant General.

[2] Not included.

[3] Emphasis in the original.

d. Total additional officers authorized by paragraph three, WD Circular 124, based upon the AGCT composition of assigned troops in seventy-eight Negro units 187

e. Total officer shortage if paragraph three, WD Circular 124 were completely implemented for seventy-eight Negro units 259

2. The figures set forth above deal in total officer strengths without regard for the officers' individual race. If paragraph three, WD Circular 124 rests on the theory that management of low-mental-capacity Negro troops requires an increased officer strength for each unit, it is certainly vital that full officer complements under normal T/O&E authorization be provided without delay and the shortage of seventy-two officers below T/O&E authorization be remedied immediately.

3. From this report it further appears that paragraph two, WD Circular 124 (replacement of white officers) needs considerable implementation. These facts appear to be substantiated.

a. Total number of officers assigned to seventy-eight Negro units 584

b. Total number of Negro officers assigned to seventy-eight Negro units 179

c. Additional Negro officers who should be assigned to comply with paragraph two, WD Circular 124, replacing white with Negro officers 65

d. Assuming that the additional total officers required to bring the seventy-eight Negro T/O&E units to T/O&E officer-authorized strength were all Negro, these additional Negro officers would be required 72

e. Total Negro officers required for seventy-eight Negro units at T/O&E officer strength under paragraph two, WD Circular 124 77

f. Assuming that the additional total officers required to bring seventy-eight Negro units to the extra officer strength authorized under paragraph three, WD Circular 124, were all to be Negro, an additional Negro officer strength would be required, amounting to 187

g. Total Negro officers required for seventy-eight Negro units if both paragraph two, WD Circular 124, calling for replacement of white officers and paragraph three, WD Circular 124, calling for additional officers were implemented 100 percent 664

4. The 664 additional Negro officers required to meet paragraph two and three, WD Circular 124, would increase the Negro officer percentage from 1.200 percent to 2.052 percent of the total authorized officer strength and from 1.256 percent to 2.149 percent of the total actual officer strength.

RECOMMENDATIONS

1. The following recommendations are made concerning the implementation of paragraph two and three, WD Circular 124:

a. That the seventy-two-officer shortage under T/O&E authorized strength for the seventy-eight Negro units be immediately remedied by the assignment to those units of the missing seventy-two officers. Before paragraph three is implemented by adding extra officers, all Negro units should be brought to full T/O&E officer strength. Special requisitions for specific MOS[4] by unit should be requested immediately. The specific units and their station location which the report showed to be below T/O&E authorized strength are listed in Tab B.[5]

b. That 112 additional officers be assigned to these Negro T/O&E units under the provisions of paragraph three, WD Circular 124, to units with AGCT composition of 70 percent or more in grades IV and V. (AGCT below 80.) These specific units, their station location and number of officers required are listed in Tab C.[5] It is recommended that an immediate special requisition be requested for the specific MOS required for the officers in question.

c. That when a and b above have been accomplished, that the seventy-five additional officers be assigned to units whose AGCT composition is between 50 percent and 70 percent in grades IV and V. These units, their station location, and numbers of officers required are listed in Tab D.[5]

d. That implementation of paragraph two, WD Circular 124 on the replacement of white with Negro officers be accomplished in these priorities consistent with the available supply of suitable Negro officers:

(1) The replacement of any white officers now assigned to one of these Negro units by a Negro officer whenever one of these white officers is reassigned.

(2) The assignment of the seventy-two officers under paragraph a above.

(3) The assignment of the 112 officers under paragraph b above.

(4) The assignment of the seventy-five officers under paragraph c above.

e. That an immediate study be made of the possible procurement of *additional*[6] Negro officers to accomplish the conversion called for by paragraph two, WD Circular 124. This study should include reserve officers eligible for recall to extended active duty, participants in and graduates of senior ROTC units, individuals undergoing competitive tours, officer candidate school and distinguished military graduates. It must be recognized that within the army today there are only 757 Negro officers available (exclusive of those assigned to T/O&E units covered in this memorandum) to supply the 665 required for seventy-eight Negro ZI units alone. Many of these 757 Negro officers are already assigned to Negro T/O&E units overseas. It is not recommended that we consider as a remedy for the 665 shortage, any mass reassignment from bulk to T/O&E organizations.

2. That a special enlisted procurement and assignment project be developed by this branch to remedy the sorry condition of the units listed in Tab C, 70 percent of whose troops fall in AGCT grades of IV and V.

3. That when reports are received from the unreported twenty-three ZI T/O&E units, that they be similarly analyzed and reported upon to this division.

---

[4]Military Occupational Specialty.

[5]Not included.

[6]Emphasis in the original.

4. That each overseas theater be required to obtain and submit similar reports on its own Negro T/O&E units so that the worldwide picture can be obtained.

J. F. Lieblich   C. G. Dunn
Major, GSC[7]   Lt. Colonel, GSC

A. T. McAnsh   J. J. O'Hare
Colonel, GSC   Brigadier General, GSC
Ch/C&S Br.   Chief, MPMG

---

[7]General Staff Corps.

●

James C. Evans, Marcus Ray's successor as civilian aide, won from Sec. of the Army Kenneth Royall approval to drop racial quotas on army calls for draftees. As Evans suggested, the army staff planned to preserve the quota on black soldiers by regulating the number of blacks attempting to enlist. The decision to stop using draft quotas would become important in the Korean War era.

1. It is urged that the secretary of the army take the initiative in abolishing the earlier procedure of requisitioning quotas of selectees from Selective Service by race. As indicated in conference with the secretary today, only favorable developments are to be anticipated from such a significant decision.

2. Statistically, it may be pointed out that if selectees are called by their date of birth, the authorized one-in-ten racial ratio would hold since this ratio is predicated upon the one-in-ten ratio in the population.

3. It may be expected that a larger proportion of white selectees will be exempted, while a large proportion of Negro selectees will be rejected for deficiencies. These factors would tend to keep the one-in-ten ratio in balance. Any unbalance could be corrected by controls over voluntary enlistments.

4. Approval by the secretary of this recommendation, which I understand is not without prior contemplation, will carry significant implications throughout the armed forces and beyond.

[Memorandum, James C. Evans, civilian aide to the secretary of the army, for the secretary of the army, 22 June 1948, subject: Selective Service quotas and race, Modern Military Records Branch, National Archives, Washington, DC.]

*Reacting to the army staff's concern that the number of black
soldiers would be allowed to exceed the 10 percent quota, the
chief of staff obtained the secretary of the army's approval for
the continued restriction of black enlistments.*

The attached summary of statements on the question of removing restrictions on
Negro enlistments, and the conclusions thereon, was presented to the secretary who
concurs in our recommendation that we continue the Gillem Board policy and not open
up unlimited Negro enlistments for a period of four weeks or longer. We will continue
our present policy.

ONB

SUMMARY

6 August 1948

1. Present Negro strength of the Department of the Army is 62,000 which
includes personnel in ARWAF[1] and in the pipeline. This strength represents 12 percent
of the army strength which is above the level established by the Gillem Board.

2. The induction policy of nonracial discrimination will obviously ensure at least
10 percent of inductees will be Negro.

3. The training divisions are above their capacity now. A high volunteer enlistment rate is expected to continue. These volunteers plus those inducted will continue to
fill these divisions to or beyond their capacity.

4. Ten to fifteen thousand Negro enlistments could be consummated in any four-
week period if restrictions were removed.

5. It is not feasible to send Negroes direct[ly] to units as these units are not
equipped to process, classify, equip, and give basic training.

6. The army is popular with Negroes as evidenced by the Negro strength, in spite
of quotas and AGCT limitations. The 10 percent policy is understood by all. Segregation after enlistment is the crux of the problem.

CONCLUSIONS

7. White enlistments would necessarily have to be curtailed to handle this Negro
load.

8. The long range effect of unrestricted Negro enlistments could produce a
disproportionately large pool of career Negro soldiers which would unbalance the
composition and effectiveness of the army.

[Memorandum, ONB (General Omar N. Bradley, chief of staff of the army), for Lt. Gen. W. S. Paul,
9 August 1948, Modern Military Records Branch, National Archives, Washington, DC.]

[1]Army personnel still assigned to units in the new air force.

RECOMMENDATIONS

9. Recommend the Department of the Army continue the Gillem Board Policy and maintain a Negro strength of 10 percent by continuing the present quota system.

> W. S. Paul
> Lieutenant General, GSC
> Director of Personnel and Administration

●

*The navy was also experiencing difficulty in carrying out
the provisions of its new racial policy. Specifically,
problems associated with the status of black stewards, the
small percentage of black sailors in the general service,
and the lack of black officers continued to remind the
reformers that the navy was failing to live up to the promise
of its integration policy. Lt. Dennis D. Nelson, one of the
few black officers to remain on duty after the war, was
especially concerned with the status of the stewards,
always a sore point with black leaders.*

In view of public attitudes, the large proportion of Negroes in the stewards' branch of the navy, the need for improving their morale and efficiency in the service, the following recommendations are made.

It is agreed that all branches of the naval service are necessary in its conduct and maintenance, and from the lowest echelon upward all phases of the service should be conducted, supervised and maintained with efficiency and dignity. The stewards' branch—a branch of the service less technical in nature than any of the others—still requires skill and training. The navy should do all possible to provide constant and adequate leadership and supervision of these men, and to dignify as far as possible their lesser though important tasks.

The general type of Negroes selected for the stewards' branch has done little to stimulate the Negro's interest in naval service, and for the most part the laxity in training, supervision in duty and their off-duty conduct and activities has lessened to a marked degree the respect that the Negro public should hold for the service.

It is a well-known fact that for the most part the men of the stewards' branch have been most limited in educational and vocational backgrounds, and that this part of the service because of its limitation has attracted a proportionally large percentage of substandard and underprivileged individuals. Because of the navy's policy in making this branch a separate division of labor limited to minority groups (Filipinos and Negroes) the Negro public openly resented and opposed the navy.

[Memorandum, Lt. Dennis D. Nelson to Rear Adm. R. F. Hickey, deputy director, Office of Public Relations, 26 March 1948, subject: Problems of the stewards' branch, Navy and Old Army Branch, National Archives, Washington, DC.]

The navy should supervise and train men of the stewards' branch with greater care. The fact that they are the principle [sic] handlers of food requires a better health program (the high V.D. rate jeopardizes the health of the entire crew); they are often the custodians of personal gear of officers and crew.

There are too numerous instances where stewards are ill-supervised—no officers to whom they are directly responsible—and their own unit leadership is totally based on seniority rather than capable leadership.

There are innumerable instances of conflict and difficulties that beset stewards in their relations to the outfit to which they are assigned and much can be done to eradicate them, and to raise the dignity of the branch and the morale of its members.

To eliminate some of the prevailing conditions and hostile attitudes within the service as far as the stewards' branch is concerned, to raise the morale of men both in and out of the division, the following suggestions are proposed:

a. Eliminate the stewards' branch as a separate division of labor. It is suggested that any person or persons capable of performing steward's duties or needed in such categories be so employed regardless of race and be rated according to duties performed as in other branches of the service.

b. Provide adequate and permanent officer supervision of stewards in all units, and capable and responsible PO[1] leadership.

c. Develop capable PO leadership throughout the stewards' branch—and leadership qualities become one of the considerations for ratings, as well as proficiency and good conduct, and provide adequate training for their work.

d. Make possible a bonafide CPO[2] rate for stewards as in all other branches of the service with similar emoluments, privileges and responsibilities accorded.

e. Provide full CPO ratings for stewards, and this be given on the basis of experience and proficiency—and such chiefs be accorded the rights and privileges of CPOs of other branches of the service.

f. Discontinue the use of CPO uniforms for stewards below the rate of CPO.

g. Improve the working uniform of stewards for convenience and appearance—giving them instead a seaman's "look" as other crewmen and eliminate the ill-fitting and shabby outfits used. (The present white coats are most impractical from the point of view of appearance, laundrying and general care.)

h. Provide better-planned considerations for liberties and leaves, so that there will be fewer conflicts and inconsistencies that tend to lower the morale of the men concerned.

i. Care should be taken to make no obvious racial distinctions in segregation of quartering, messing, etc., in keeping with the navy's overall policy of integration.

j. Refrain from the use of "Boy" in addressing stewards. This has been a constant practice in the service and is most objectionable, is in bad taste,

---

[1]Petty Officer.
[2]Chief Petty Officer.

    shows undue familiarity and pins on a badge of inferiority, adding little to the dignity and pride of adults.

  k. An overall indoctrination of all personnel throughout the naval establishment of the policy of integration—from the recruit training level up. This training of a nucleus of navy personnel—in peacetime and while the organization is most highly selective in its personnel—would offset many personnel difficulties during periods when the service must be rapidly increased.

  l. It is suggested that a committee be formed to work out the details of the above program, and the resulting study and recommendations be made to cognizant bureaus. Such a committee might also include Mr. Lester Granger and Mr. James Evans who have knowledge of these problems and have worked on similar problems of the other services.

    It has been most apparent from former navy men who have served in the navy in the capacity of stewards, and civilians and members of the press having contact with them, that the service has been quite unsatisfactory where the stewards' branch is concerned, and complain bitterly because of the above-mentioned ills. This situation prevailing in the light of present and future manpower needs will prove detrimental to the navy in its efforts to procure the best prepared and efficient men for the service.

    The army and air force have developed programs and plans to dignify the uniform and the job performed by their personnel regardless of job levels and types through *Army Talk* #172, "Why a Uniform?" The efforts to develop pride in self and in the services will doubtless pay increased dividends in work performed and in the increased morale of their personnel. There are numerous group and individual problems to be solved in the stewards' branch, and it is conceivable that many of the individual problems can and will be eliminated by prompt attention to those that affect the group.

    Consideration must be given to the fact that the armed forces are growing concerns, the enlargement of which only multiplies the existing problems. This added to the growing attitudes of young educated Negroes against any form of military service in the face of the resistance of the nation to civil rights, and the resulting lack of patriotism in "What the hell are we fighting for" and "To risk life and limb—for what?"—makes this problem one of vital importance where the navy is concerned. Possible solutions require no change in policy and would not require considerable study and effort to improve the situation.

    The president is aware of this growing animosity of the Negro public to military service—and this has been indicated quite recently at a White House conference as indicated by the attached newsclipping.[3]

    It is apparent, of course, that the stewards themselves are not blameless, and that they are able to hide away many of their own inadequacies behind existing conditions in the service. The improvement of regulations pertaining to stewards would eliminate the basic problems—and the stewards' branch would gain the dignity and importance needed in their work—and would develop personal pride in themselves as well as in the service.

---

[3]Not included.

*Elevated to the role of advisor in the new office of secretary of
defense, Evans traded on his friendship with the first secretary of
the air force, W. Stuart Symington, to make some key
recommendations on the employment of blacks.*

1. *Introduction.* In view of the projected expansion of the air force, and for other reasons, it seems well to treat further some current aspects of service by the Negro in the air force.

2. *Lockbourne.* Lockbourne Air Force Base, as the air base for Negro airmen, should be deemphasized. The Negro units now concentrated there should be decentralized. Transfer, reassignment and diffusion, whether by individuals or by small units (as was earlier contemplated in the Gillem Board Report) should be upon the basis of technical specialty and proficiency, primarily, and not upon the basis of race primarily, as in the past.

3. *Colonel Davis and staff.* Colonel B. O. Davis, Jr. should be placed in position to accept the opportunity to attend the Command and Staff School at the Air University without further postponement. This or other opportunity for diverse experience and training appears long overdue for Colonel Davis, the ranking Negro in the air force. The same applies to a number of others who, like him, have been considered indispensable in racially aligned services and duty, in view of the small number of qualified leaders that it has been possible to develop from the late beginning of the Negro in the air force.

4. *Assignment opportunities.* Versatility and proficiency are augmented by variety of training, experience, and opportunity. Debilities and deficiencies accrue inevitably from the situation in which one officer, Colonel Davis, has always been in command of practically all Negro rated officers in the air force; and, conversely, all the Negro rated officers in the air force have been practically always under the command of one officer, namely, Colonel Davis. Again, it is not reasonable to conclude that all Negro airmen may be most effectively utilized as fighter pilots alone, nor ground troops mainly in Squadron "F" labor units.

It is believed that a parallel situation will not be found in the services; and that racial alignment as the sole basis is not sufficient explanation for this situation, nor does it provide adequate justification for the resultant losses in air potential.

5. *CO Replacement.* It is contemplated that the transfer of Colonel Davis at the present time would necessitate the assignment of a base commander and a wing commander not of the Negro race. There should be no hesitancy in proceeding in this direction if an assignment is made on the basis of qualifications. No Negro officer having yet had time and opportunity to acquire the requisite qualification, no direct alternative exists; and no difficulty should be experienced in clearly stating the position and the action taken in view thereof.

6. *Recommendations.* Accordingly, it is recommended that immediate consideration be given to:

[Memorandum, James C. Evans, advisor to the secretary of defense, for secretary of the air force, 7 June 1948, subject: Negro air units, US Air Force Files, Washington National Records Center, Suitland, MD.]

A. Proceeding with the decentralization of the Negro airmen now concentrated at Lockbourne Air Force Base;

B. Providing opportunity for Colonel Davis to move on to other duties and training opportunities;

C. Carefully selecting commanding officer and staff personnel qualified to handle the proposed operation both from the Lockbourne Air Force Base end, and at the air installations to which transfer of Negro individuals and units would be made.

7. *Background.* The contents of this memorandum represent conclusions from studies of this subject within and without the department by military and civilian leaders, Negro and otherwise, and are believed to be in conformity with clear directives received from above and currently in effect.

●

The commandant of the Marine Corps established a quota of
2302 black marines and approved a plan for their distribution
in the corps.

1. By approval of reference (a)[1], the commandant authorized the recruiting of 1120 Negro marines from civilian sources, at a rate not to exceed 200 per month. As of 17 October 1946, a total of 971 Negroes had been recruited from these sources, and statistics indicate that during the past two months the major portion of Negro entries in the regular Marine Corps were obtained from these first enlistments.

2. Reference (b)[2] called for the enlistment of twenty-five Negroes, in addition to the September quota, who had backgrounds which would qualify them for cook or steward ratings and who would volunteer to enlist with the intention of selecting the stewards' branch upon completion of recruit training. Further, reference (a) provided for the enlistment of forty out of each subsequent monthly quota of Negro first enlistments, who would qualify under these same stipulations.

3. Reference (c)[3], which is now being routed for concurrence before submission to the commandant, contains a survey of the postwar requirements, based on billets, of Negro marines, and contains the recommendation that such requirements be established initially as 2302 (including 302 stewards'-branch personnel). This survey incorporates all recommendations submitted by cognizant agencies at this headquarters and is derived from the following distribution:

[Memorandum, director, Division of Plans and Policies, for commandant, 23 October 1946, subject: Enlistment of Negroes, Reference Section, Office of the Director of Marine Corps History and Museums, Washington, DC.]

[1] Memo, DP&P, AO-1-apc, to CMC, dated 3 May 1946.

[2] Memo, DP&P, AO-1-msk, to CMC, dated 30 September 1946.

[3] Conf. Memo, DP&P (O1A26846) to CMC, dated 20 September 1946, as modified by (O1A29046) dated 18 October 1946.

Fleet Marine Force, ground	941
Fleet Marine Force, aviation	111
Marine activities at naval shore establishment	315
Marine security forces outside US	664
Training activities	55
Miscellaneous	55
Nonavailable	161
Total	2302

4. Recruiting reports as of 17 October 1946, indicate that a total of 2139 Negroes have enlisted in the regular Marine Corps, including first enlistments and reenlistments. Applying a normal attrition factor to this figure, plus an additional factor based on reports from Camp Lejeune that it has been necessary to weed-out many unsuitable recruits, it is estimated that, as of the same date, there were approximately 1935 regular Negro marines.

5. An analysis of recruiting statistics shows that, since July 1946, an average total of 140 Negroes enter the regular Marine Corps every ten days. This average in all probability will be substantially reduced because of the fact that two-year enlistments are no longer available. However, it appears safe to assume that a ten-day average of ninety Negro enlistments will be maintained.

6. From the foregoing, it appears that the proposed postwar requirement of 2302 will be met on or about 30 November 1946, providing the present practice of accepting first enlistments is not necessarily stopped upon the attainment of the full quota of 1120 Negroes from civilian sources.

7. It is proposed, in this connection, that Negro enlistments and reenlistments be continued, irrespective of the 1120 total quota for first enlistments, at the present rate of 200 per month for first enlistments (including 40 for eventual assignment to the stewards' branch), until 30 November 1946.

8. It is considered necessary also to establish recruiting quotas for the maintenance of the postwar Negro requirements after those requirements are initially reached on 30 November 1946. Based on normal attrition factors, a monthly quota of about fifteen would be sufficient to maintain the Negro component at authorized strength. However, another factor to be considered is the great number of two-year enlistments (estimated to be about 66 percent of the total Negro enlisted) which will be affected by the program of accelerated attrition. It is believed that a total monthly quota of fifty Negro first enlistments and reenlistments for the next six months is required for the initial maintenance of the postwar Negro strength.

9. ACTION RECOMMENDED:
(a) That Negro enlistments and reenlistments be continued at the present rate of 200 first enlistments (including 40 for the stewards' branch) and unlimited reenlistments, per month, until 30 November 1946, and that the existing ceiling of 1120 total Negro first enlistments be revoked. (ACTION: Div Rctg).
(b) That, commencing in December 1946, and continuing for six months, a total

of fifty Negroes be enlisted per month, including first enlistments and reenlistments. (ACTION: Div Rctg).

(c) That the problem of Negro enlistments be restudied prior to 1 June 1947. (ACTION: DP&P, G-1).

G. C. Thomas

●

As late as November 1949, more than a year after Pres. Harry Truman called for new racial policies in the services, the Marine Corps was finding it necessary to form new segregated units to create assignments for its black personnel, now numbering only 1104 men.

1. Reference (a)[1] recommended that upon reorganization of the Fleet Marine Force under the "K" series tables of organization, certain units be designated for the assignment of colored marines. Subsequent to approval of reference (a) changes were made in organization under the "K" series which changed the strength or eliminated units previously approved for the assignment of colored marines.

2. The actual strength of ground duty personnel, colored, has averaged 1104 since January, 1949. Allowing an eight percent nonavailable factor, approximately two hundred additional billets are now required.

3. Units now designated for assignment of general duty colored personnel are:

(a) Security and Supporting Establishments:

MB, NAD[2], Earle, NJ	120
MB, NAD, Ft. Mifflin, Philadelphia, Pa.	41
MB, NAD, Oahu	170
MB, Camp Lejeune, NC (Montford Point Camp Security Gd)	50
MCRD[3], Parris Island, SC	6
	387

(b) Fleet Marine Forces:

Depot Platoon, Support Company, 1st CSG[4]	32
Truck Company, 2d CSG, Service Command, FMF	63
Support Company, 1st Service Bn, 1st MarDiv	150
Support Company, 2d Service Bn, 2d MarDiv	150
Maintenance Platoon, 2d Service Bn, 2d MarDiv	30
	425
Total	812

[Memorandum, director, Division of Plans and Policies, for commandant, USMC, 14 November 1949, subject: Designation of units for assignment of Negro marines, Reference Section, Office of the Director, Marine Corps History and Museums, Washington, DC.]

[1] DP&P Study #88-49 approved 29Jul49.

[2] Naval Ammunition Depot.

[3] Marine Corps Recruit Depot.

[4] Combat Service Group.

4. It is proposed to designate the following additional units for assignment of Negro marines:

Support Company, 1st CSG, Service Command (74)	
(Includes depot platoon previously approved for such assignment)	42
Depot Platoon, Support Company, 2d CSG	47
Security Division, Operations Group Barstow	
Daggett	57
Yermo	69
Total	215

5. RECOMMENDATION:

That the units listed in paragraph four above be designated, as required, for assignment of colored personnel.

(ACTION: PersDept).

W. F. Coleman
Acting.

●

Opposition to segregation in the armed forces continued to mount in the postwar years. Not all of this opposition came from the black community. The recommendations of the president's own Committee on Civil Rights carried particular weight in an election year when the interests of minority voters was of great concern to the incumbent. The president did not submit the committee's recommendations to Congress, preferring to act on them himself.

All of the armed forces have recently adopted policies which set as explicit objectives the achievement of equality of opportunity. The War Department has declared that it "intends to continue its efforts to make the best possible use of available personnel resources in the postwar army and in any future emergency, without distinction as to race, religion, color or other nonmilitary considerations." The Navy Department, speaking for both the navy and Marine Corps, has stated that

No distinction is made between individuals wearing a naval uniform because of race or color. The navy accepts no theory of racial differences in inborn ability, but expects that every man wearing its uniform be trained and used in accordance with his maximum individual capacity determined on the basis of individual performance.

The Coast Guard has stressed "the importance of selecting men for what they are, for what they are capable of doing, and insisting on good conduct, good behavior, and good

---

[*To Secure These Rights: The Report of the President's Committee on Civil Rights,* 1947, Library of Congress, Washington, DC.]

qualities of leadership for all hands. . . . As a matter of policy Negro recruits receive the same consideration as all others."

However, despite the lessons of the war and the recent announcement of these policies, the records of the military forces disclose many areas in which there is a great need for further remedial action. Although generally speaking, the basis of recruitment has been somewhat broadened, Negroes, for example, are faced by an absolute bar against enlistment in any branch of the Marine Corps other than the steward's branch, and the army cleaves to a ceiling for Negro personnel of about 10 percent of the total strength of the service.

There are no official discriminatory requirements for entrance into the navy and the Coast Guard, but the fact that Negroes constitute a disproportionately small part of the total strength of each of these branches of service (4.4 and 4.2 percent, respectively) may indicate the existence of discrimination in recruiting practices.

Within the services, studies made within the last year disclose that actual experience has been out of keeping with the declarations of policy on discrimination. In the army, less than one Negro in seventy is commissioned, while there is one white officer for approximately every seven white enlisted men. In the navy, there are only 2 Negro officers in a ratio of less than 1:10,000 Negro enlisted men; there are 58,571 white officers, or 1 for every 7 enlisted whites. The Marine Corps has 7,798 officers, none of whom is a Negro, though there are 2,190 Negro enlisted men. Out of 2,981 Coast Guard officers, 1 is a Negro; there are 910 Negro enlisted men. The ratio of white Coast Guard commissioned to enlisted personnel is approximately 1:6.

Similarly, in the enlisted grades, there is an exceedingly high concentration of Negroes in the lowest ratings, particularly in the navy, Marine Corps, and Coast Guard. Almost 80 percent of the Negro sailors are serving as cooks, stewards, and steward's mates; less than 2 percent of the whites are assigned to duty in the same capacity. Almost 15 percent of all white enlisted marines are in the three highest grades; less than 2½ percent of the Negro marines fall in the same category. The disparities in the Coast Guard are similarly great. The difference in the army is somewhat smaller, but still significant: Less than 9 percent of the Negro personnel are in the first three grades, while almost 16 percent of the whites hold these ranks.

Many factors other than discrimination contribute to this result. However, it is clear that discrimination is one of the major elements which keeps the services from attaining the objectives which they have set for themselves.

The admission of minorities to the service academies and other service schools is another area in which the armed forces have enjoyed relatively little success in their efforts to eliminate discrimination. With regard to schools within the services, the disparities indicate that selection for advanced training is doubtless often made on a color basis. As for the service academies, in the course of the last seventy-five years the Military Academy at West Point admitted a total of only thirty-seven Negro cadets, while the Naval Academy at Annapolis admitted only six. The Coast Guard Academy, while it selects applicants on the basis of open, competitive examinations without regard to color, has no knowledge of any Negro ever having been accepted. The absence of Negroes from the service academies is unfortunate because it means that our officers are trained in an undemocratic environment and are denied the opportunity to learn at an early stage in their service careers that men of different races can work and fight together harmoniously.

State authorities promulgate the regulations concerning enlistment of Negroes and the formation of Negro units in the National Guard. Most states do not have Negro units; of those that do, all but three require segregation by regulation. Of thirty-four states answering an inquiry made by the President's Advisory Commission on Universal Training, only two permit the integration of Negroes with white units. The commission, commenting on discrimination, observed that it

> *considers harmful the policies of the states that exclude Negroes from their National Guard units. The civilian components should be expanded to include all segments of our population without segregation or discrimination. Total defense requires the participation of all citizens in our defense forces.*

Looking to the future, the commission also found that some of the present practices of the armed forces would negate many of the benefits of the proposed universal training program. Speaking of this program, it said:

> *. . . it must provide equality of privilege and opportunity for all those upon whom this obligation rests. Neither in the training itself, nor in the organization of any phase of this program, should there be discrimination for or against any person or group because of his race, class, national origin, or religion. Segregation or special privilege in any form should have no place in the program. To permit them would nullify the important living lesson in citizenship which such training can give. Nothing could be more tragic for the future attitude of our people, and for the unity of our nation, than a program in which our Federal government forced our young manhood to live for a period of time in an atmosphere which emphasized or bred class or racial differences.*

When an individual enters the service of the country, he necessarily surrenders some of the rights and privileges which inhere in American citizenship. The government in return undertakes to protect his integrity as an individual and the dignity of his profession. He is entitled to enjoy the respect which should be shown the uniform of the armed services of the United States by all persons. Unfortunately, however, the uniform is not always accorded the esteem it warrants. Some of our servicemen are all too often treated with rudeness and discourtesy by civil authorities and the public. There are numerous instances in which they have been forced to move to segregated cars on public carriers. They have been denied access to places of public accommodation and recreation. When they attempt to assert their rights, they are sometimes met with threats and even outright attack. Federal officials find they have no present authority to intervene directly to protect men in uniform against such abuses.

The record is not without its brighter side. A start has been made toward eliminating differentials in opportunity and treatment of minorities in the armed forces. The army is making experimental use of small all-Negro units as organic parts of large white organizations. Significantly, of the thirty-seven Negroes admitted to the Academy at West Point since 1870, twenty-one were accepted in the last ten years. In 1947, five Negroes were accepted, the largest enrollment of Negro cadets for a single year in the last seventy-five years. The navy has adopted a policy of nonsegregation and has officially opened all branches to all personnel. The Coast Guard has abandoned, as a matter of policy, the restriction of Negro guardsmen to duty as cooks, stewards, and bakers. Training courses, indoctrination programs, pamphlets, and films have been provided for officers and enlisted men in the army and navy to promote understanding between groups and to facilitate the use of minority personnel.

But the evidence leaves no doubt that we have a long way to go. The armed forces, in actual practice, still maintain many barriers to equal treatment for all their members. In many cases, state and local agencies and private persons disregard the dignity of the uniform. There is much that remains to be done, much that can be done at once. Morally, the failure to act is indefensible. Practically, it costs lives and money in the inefficient use of human resources. Perhaps most important of all, we are not making use of one of the most effective techniques for educating the public to the practicability of American ideals as a way of life. During the last war we and our allies, with varying but undeniable success, found that the military services can be used to educate citizens on a broad range of social and political problems. The war experience brought to our attention a laboratory in which we may prove that the majority and minorities of our population can train and work and fight side by side in cooperation and harmony. We should not hesitate to take full advantage of this opportunity.

The enactment by Congress of legislation, followed by appropriate administrative action, to end immediately all discrimination and segregation based on race, color, creed, or national origin, in the organization and activities of all branches of the armed services.

The injustice of calling men to fight for freedom while subjecting them to humiliating discrimination within the fighting forces is at once apparent. Furthermore, by preventing entire groups from making their maximum contribution to the national defense, we weaken our defense to that extent and impose heavier burdens on the remainder of the population.

Legislation and regulations should expressly ban discrimination and segregation in the recruitment, assignment, and training of all personnel in all types of military duty. Mess halls, quarters, recreational facilities and post exchanges should be nonsegregated. Commissions and promotions should be awarded on considerations of merit only. Selection of students for the Military, Naval, and Coast Guard academies and all other service schools should be governed by standards from which considerations of race, color, creed, or national origin are conspicuously absent. The National Guard, reserve units, and any universal military training program should all be administered in accordance with these same standards.

The committee believes that the recent unification of the armed forces provides a timely opportunity for the revision of present policy and practice. A strong enunciation of future policy should be made condemning discrimination and segregation within the armed services.

The enactment by Congress of legislation providing that no member of the armed forces shall be subject to discrimination of any kind by any public authority or place of public accommodation, recreation, transportation, or other service or business.

The government of a nation has an obligation to protect the dignity of the uniform of its armed services. The esteem of the government itself is impaired when affronts to its armed forces are tolerated. The government also has a responsibility for the well-being of those who surrender some of the privileges of citizenship to serve in the defense establishments.

The most notorious opposition to continued segregation in the
armed forces came from the well-known black labor leader,
A. Philip Randolph. Reaction to his testimony before the Senate
Armed Services Committee on the 1948 draft bill revealed
strong sentiment existing among young blacks for a boycott
of the segregated services.

There can be no doubt of my facts. Quite bluntly, Chrm. Walter G. Andrews of the House Armed Services Committee told a delegation from this organization that the War Department plans segregated white and Negro battalions if Congress passes a draft law.

The Newark *Evening News* of March 26, 1948, confirmed this in a Washington dispatch based on official memoranda sent from Secretary Forrestal's office to the House Armed Services Committee. Nine days ago when we called this to the attention of the commander in chief in a White House conference, he indicated that he was aware of these plans for Jim Crow battalions. This despite his civil rights message to Congress.

We have released all of this damaging information to the daily press, the leaders of both parties in Congress, and to supposedly liberal organizations. But we, a relative handful of exceptions, we have found our white "friends" silent, indifferent, even hostile. . . .

With this background, gentlemen, I reported last week to President Truman that Negroes are in no mood to shoulder a gun for democracy abroad so long as they are denied democracy here at home.

In particular, they resent the idea of fighting or being drafted into another Jim Crow army. I passed this information on to Mr. Truman not as a threat, but rather as a frank, factual survey of Negro opinion.

Today I should like to make clear to the Senate Armed Services Committee and through you, to Congress and the American people that passage now of a Jim Crow draft may only result in a mass civil disobedience movement along the lines of the magnificent struggles of the people of India against British imperialism.

I must emphasize that the current agitation for civil rights is no longer a mere expression of hope on the part of Negroes. On the one hand, it is a positive, resolute out-reading [*sic*] for full manhood. On the other hand, it is an equally determined will to stop acquiescing in anything less. Negroes demand full, unqualified, first-class citizenship.

In resorting to the principles and direct-action techniques of Gandhi, whose death was publicly mourned by many members of Congress and President Truman, Negroes will be serving a higher law than any passed by a national legislature in an era which racism spells our doom.

They will be serving a law higher than any decree of the Supreme Court which in the famous Winfred Lynn case evaded ruling on the flagrantly illegal segregation practiced under the wartime Selective Service Act. In refusing to accept compulsory military segregation, Negro youth will be serving their fellow men throughout the world.

I feel qualified to make this claim because of a recent survey of American psychologists, sociologists, and anthropologists. The survey revealed an overwhelming belief among these experts that enforced segregation on racial or religious lines has

[U.S., Congress, Senate, Committee on Armed Services, *Universal Military Training*, 80th Cong., 1st sess., 1948.]

serious and detrimental psychological effects both on the segregated groups and on those enforcing segregation.

Experts from the South, I should like to point out, gentlemen, were as positive as those from other sections of the country as to the harmful effects of segregation. The views of these social scientists were based on scientific research and their own professional experience.

So long as the armed services propose to enforce such universally harmful segregation not only here at home but also overseas, Negro youth have a moral obligation not to lend themselves as worldwide carriers of an evil and hellish doctrine. . . .

While I cannot with absolute certainty claim results at this hour, I personally will advise Negroes to refuse to fight as slaves for a democracy they cannot possess and cannot enjoy.

Let me add that I am speaking only for myself, not even for the Committee Against Jim Crow in Military Service and Training, since I am not sure that all its members would follow my position. But Negro leaders in close touch with GI grievances would feel derelict in their duty if they did not support such a justified civil disobedience movement, especially those of us whose age would protect us from being drafted. Any other course would be a betrayal of those who place their trust in us. I personally pledge myself to openly counsel, aid, and abet youth, both white and Negro, to quarantine any Jim Crow conscription system, whether it bear the label of universal military training or selective service.

I shall tell youth of all races not to be tricked by any euphonious election-year registration for a draft. This evasion, which the newspapers increasingly discuss as a convenient way out for Congress, would merely presage a synthetic "crisis" immediately after November 2d when all talk of equality and civil rights would be branded unpatriotic while the induction machinery would move into high gear. On previous occasions I have seen the "national emergency" psychology mow down legitimate Negro demands.

From coast to coast in my travels I shall call upon all Negro veterans to join this civil-disobedience movement and to recruit their younger brothers in an organized refusal to register and be drafted.

Many veterans, bitter over army Jim Crow, have indicated that they will act spontaneously in this fashion, regardless of any organized movement. "Never again," they say with finality.

I shall appeal to the thousands of white youth in schools and colleges who are today vigorously shedding the prejudices of their parents and professors. I shall urge them to demonstrate their solidarity with Negro youth by ignoring the entire registration and induction machinery.

And finally I shall appeal to Negro parents to lend their moral support to their sons, to stand behind them as they march with heads high to federal prisons as a telling demonstration to the world that Negroes have reached the limit of human endurance, that, in the words of the spiritual, we will be buried in our graves before we will be slaves.

May I, in conclusion, Mr. Chairman, point out that political maneuvers have made this drastic program our last resort. Your party, the party of Lincoln, solemnly pledged in its 1944 platform a full-fledged congressional investigation of injustices to Negro soldiers. Instead of that long overdue probe, the Senate Armed Services Committee on this very day is finally hearing testimony from two or three Negro veterans for a period of twenty minutes each. The House Armed Services Committee and Chairman Andrews went one step further and arrogantly refused to hear any at all.

Since we cannot obtain an adequate congressional forum for our grievances, we have no other recourse but to tell our story to the peoples of the world by organized direct action. I do not believe that even a wartime censorship wall could be high enough to conceal news of a civil disobedience program.

If we cannot win your support for your own party commitments, if we cannot ring a bell in you by appealing to human decency, we shall command your respect and the respect of the world by our united refusal to cooperate with tyrannical injustice. . . .

We shall wage a relentless warfare against Jim Crow without hate or revenge for the moral and spiritual progress and safety of our country, world peace, and freedom.

Finally let me say that Negroes are just sick and tired of being pushed around and we just do not propose to take it, and we do not care what happens.

●

With opposition to the services' racial policies mounting,
Pres. Harry S Truman issued his historic document declaring
that there should be equality of treatment and opportunity for
all persons in the armed services without regard to race, color,
religion, or national origin.

EXECUTIVE ORDER 9981
ESTABLISHING THE PRESIDENT'S COMMITTEE ON
EQUALITY OF TREATMENT AND OPPORTUNITY IN
THE ARMED SERVICES

WHEREAS it is essential that there be maintained in the armed services of the United States the highest standards of democracy, with equality of treatment and opportunity for all those who serve in our country's defense:

NOW, THEREFORE, by virtue of the authority vested in me as president of the United States, by the Constitution and the statutes of the United States, and as commander in chief of the armed services, it is hereby ordered as follows:

1. It is hereby declared to be the policy of the president that there shall be equality of treatment and opportunity for all persons in the armed services without regard to race, color, religion or national origin. This policy shall be put into effect as rapidly as possible, having due regard to the time required to effectuate any necessary changes without impairing efficiency or morale.

2. There shall be created in the national military establishment an advisory committee to be known as the President's Committee on Equality of Treatment and Opportunity in the Armed Services, which shall be composed of seven members to be designated by the president.

[Executive Order 9981, 26 July 1948, Harry S Truman Library, Independence, MO.]

3. The committee is authorized on behalf of the president to examine into the rules, procedures and practices of the armed services in order to determine in what respect such rules, procedures and practices may be altered or improved with a view to carrying out the policy of this order. The committee shall confer and advise with the secretary of defense, the secretary of the army, the secretary of the navy, and the secretary of the air force, and shall make such recommendations to the president and to said secretaries as in the judgment of the committee will effectuate the policy hereof.

4. All executive departments and agencies of the federal government are authorized and directed to cooperate with the committee in its work, and to furnish the committee such information or the services of such persons as the committee may require in the performance of its duties.

5. When requested by the committee to do so, persons in the armed services or in any of the executive departments and agencies of the federal government shall testify before the committee and shall make available for the use of the committee such documents and other information as the committee may require.

6. The committee shall continue to exist until such time as the president shall terminate its existence by executive order.

●

Questioned by a reporter concerning the expression "equality of treatment and opportunity," the president admitted that he meant integration.

4. Question: Mr. President, to go back to the first question, does your advocacy of equality of treatment and opportunity in the armed forces envision eventually the end of segregation?

The president: Yes.

[President's News Conference of 29 July 1948, *Public Papers of the Presidents, 1948*, Government Printing Office, Washington, DC.]

*In an attempt to soften the opposition to the services' racial
policies, Sec. of Defense James V. Forrestal had called a
national defense conference on Negro affairs to meet at the
Pentagon on 26 April 1948. Here, under the chairmanship of
Forrestal's friend and ally from his navy days, Lester Granger,
a group of distinguished black leaders were given the opportunity
to question defense officials about the current status and future
opportunities for blacks in the armed forces. Expecting some
support for his policies of gradual reform, Forrestal heard
only demands for total, immediate integration of servicemen.
Although none of these leaders would espouse the extreme
position of A. Philip Randolph, they nevertheless made clear
their total opposition to Forrestal's racial policies. Their final
report was prepared in the wake of the Truman order with the
coming presidential investigation of the services in mind.*

Dear Secretary Forrestal:

Approximately four months have passed since a group of Negro conferees met at
your invitation in Washington on April 26th to discuss the racial policies of the United
States military establishment. The meeting ended in a fashion that was probably as
disappointing to the heads of the military establishment as it was to the conferees
themselves. The conference group's unanimous opinion stated to the secretary of
defense and later to the press was that neither that group nor any other representative
Negro leadership could give advice to the defense officials of our country under
conditions that implied condoning of racial segregation or any other form of racial
discrimination. . . .

[The] secretary was made aware in emphatic terms that no member of the
conference group would for one moment agree that segregation is necessary or justifiable
as a policy; and that no member would agree to advise with the Office of Defense to the
end of perpetuating and improving the administration of a segregated form of service. It
was declared that the conferees were unanimous in *desiring to end, and not perpetuate,*[1]
racial segregation in all phases of national life. Their availability as future advisors,
whether as individuals or as a group, was dependent upon assurance that their services
would be directed toward the elimination of racial segregation and other forms of
discrimination.

This moral position assumed by the conferees has been justified by subsequent
developments. It was our insistence that the president of the United States had an
obligation derived from the Constitution itself and from the specific responsibility of his
office to move with courage and practical wisdom toward elimination of discrimination,
including segregation, from all areas of the military establishment. The president's
executive order on the subject, already referred to, constitutes a heartening first step in
this direction. Recommendations of the committee which the president will appoint and
the action taken by the Office of Defense upon those recommendations may well
constitute the second and decisive step.

[Letter, Lester Granger to Sec. of Defense James V. Forrestal, 26 August 1948, Modern Military
Records Branch, National Archives, Washington, DC.]

[1]Emphasis in the original.

In his action the president has the unqualified approval not merely of 15 million Negro Americans, but also that of millions of other citizens of various races and faiths; for thoughtful and liberty-loving citizens are now thoroughly aware that racial segregation in our armed forces injures the morale of those directly affected, impairs the efficiency of our national defense, and harms the reputation of our nation in the world at large precisely because racial segregation is so sharply at variance with the intent and the ideals of democracy. The steps which have already been taken in the more forward-looking service branches, and the success which has thus far attended such efforts furnish conclusive proof that the goal is attainable in other branches, and the success which has thus far attended such efforts furnish conclusive proof that the goal is attainable in other branches if sufficient wisdom and courage are displayed by official leadership.

It is as unwise as it is unsound to cite the resistance of military leadership against basic changes in policy as sufficient cause for delaying immediate and effective action. This would imply that basic citizenship policies are controlled by military instead of civilian leadership, and such an implication must never be accepted by a peace-loving democratic people. It is true that changes in basic attitudes cannot be accomplished by miraculous overnight conversion of the public, but this is all the more reason for moving immediately with a program of indoctrination, education, discipline and progressive demonstration in order to speed final definitive action.

Even without introduction of the president's executive order the army is obligated by its adoption of the original Gillem Board report to implement it under its broadest rather than its narrowest construction. It is our understanding that the broad construction provided for a scientifically experimental program including the development, not simply of Negro company units integrated with white units in battalions and regiments, but also company and platoon units wherein Negroes and whites are trained, fed and housed together with absolutely no racial separation. If such projects had been initiated, the army would by now have acquired a fund of information similar to that acquired by the navy, as it progressed from a few all-Negro-manned vessels, to a 10 percent distribution of Negro personnel among a limited number of ships, to the present unsegregated assignment of Negro personnel in all ships of the service. In fact, the army has some store of experience built up by its own policy in training and assigning Negro specialists and in certain activities of the Army Air Forces.

In conclusion, it should be stated that the Washington conference on April 26th was undoubtedly a helpful experience for the conferees present, as well as for the Office of Defense, if it is regarded as exploratory in nature. The conferees had an opportunity to learn at firsthand of actual conditions and attitudes prevailing within the military establishment and to acquaint the military leadership with the thinking of representative Negroes on the subject of racial policy. It was made clear that there could be no meeting of minds between representative Negro leadership and their government, except on the basis of agreement that racial segregation in the armed forces is intolerable to the people of a free country.

With such agreement, the conferees[2] reaffirm their readiness and availability to offer practical suggestions as to how segregation can be eliminated and the safety of our country be advanced rather than imperiled.

---

[2]The committee was composed of: Sadie T. M. Alexander, John W. Davis, Truman K. Gibson, J. W. Gregg, Charles Houston, John H. Johnson, Mordecai Johnson, P. B. Young, Ira F. Lewis, Benjamin E. Mays, Loren Miller, Hobson E. Reynolds, Channing H. Tobias, George L. P. Weaver, Roy Wilkins, and Lester B. Granger (chairman).

CHAPTER NINE
THE FAHY COMMITTEE

President Truman appointed a committee, chaired by Charles Fahy, to determine how best to carry out the newly announced policy of equal treatment and opportunity. Working with the armed services and the secretary of defense, this group was enjoined to oversee the development of programs embodying the spirit of Executive Order 9981, which forbade racial discrimination in the armed forces. The committee used two techniques in hammering out a new definition of equal treatment and opportunity. Besides conducting public hearings, designed to elicit testimony that established the status of Negroes in the services and identified the policies responsible for their condition, Fahy and his colleagues held sustained private negotiations with defense officials. These various sessions convinced Fahy and his colleagues that the only just course for a democratic society was to purge its armed forces of racial quotas and racial segregation, taking a first step toward creation of a military establishment in which ability, rather than race, determined advancement.

Turning the services' old arguments against those who had invoked them, the Fahy Committee demonstrated conclusively that segregation and other forms of discrimination resulted in armed forces that were inherently inefficient. The validity of this argument was finally accepted even by those who had formerly resisted its conclusions. Fahy and his fellow committee members thus permanently altered the structure of race relations within the services.

The committee's relationship with the military establishment was uneven. The group had hoped to work closely with the secretary of defense in designing and enforcing the new policy that President Truman had directed. Both James Forrestal and Louis Johnson, who succeeded Forrestal in March 1949, retained an active interest in the subject but responded differently to institutional pressures. Forrestal recognized the committee's right to review and approve the programs being fashioned by the services. Secretary Johnson tried to curb the committee's power during the lengthy negotiations that brought about the army's racial policy. Fahy, however, appealed to the White House and the president upheld his group's right of review.

The first plan accepted by both the committee and the secretary of defense was that submitted by the air force. This newest of the services proposed a gradual integration of its all-black flying units, though not necessarily all other units manned exclusively by Negroes, and abolition of the racial quota.

243

The navy shared the air force view that segregation was inefficient, but circumstances delayed action. The existence of a separate stewards' branch, the paucity of black officers and seamen, and a continued lack of confidence among Negroes in the navy's good intentions stalled the formulation of a plan acceptable to the committee and the secretary of defense. Finally, at the committee's suggestion, the navy agreed that chief stewards would hold the rank of petty officers and that a special effort would be made to enroll more blacks in the naval service, in general, and in officer training programs, in particular.

The months of painstaking negotiation with the army provided the central drama of the committee's existence. The major points of contention centered around the committee's demand that the army abandon its racial quota and provide Negroes with equal access to military schooling and equal opportunity for all the various military assignments. Fahy and the others believed that if these provisions went into effect simultaneously, the integration of the army, even though somewhat drawn out, would be assured. The army eventually agreed to these demands, but not before it received the president's promise to reimpose racial quotas in case of "a disproportionate balance of racial strengths."

The president adjourned the Fahy group, after approving all these agreements executed by the committee and the secretary of defense with the services, declaring that the armed forces would be allowed to carry out their programs without outside supervision.

The president's meeting with members of the committee and
Pentagon officials launched the most exhaustive study of race
and the armed forces ever carried out by the federal government.
It is interesting to note that Secretary of the Air Force Symington,
perhaps carried away by the occasion, promised changes in
air force policy exceeding by far the modest program planned by
the Air Staff.

[The first meeting of the President's Committee on Equality of Treatment and Opportunity in the Armed Services, was held at 12:15 P.M., 12 January 1949, in the Cabinet Room of the White House, with President Truman presiding.]

President Truman: Well, gentlemen, I issued an executive order, last spring, or fall—I forget the date of it—on the better treatment—not "fair" treatment but "equal" treatment in the government service for everybody, regardless of his race or creed or color, and it's slowly and gradually taking hold. And I have asked you gentlemen to serve on this commission in an effort to expedite the thing in the government service so that you can actually carry out the spirit, as well as the letter, of the order. And I hope you will make a survey of the situation, not only in the military services, but in all the branches of the federal government, and then inform me of anything that's lacking, and make any suggestions that you deem necessary for the improvement of the situation.

I appreciate the fact that you're willing to serve on this commission—committee, whatever you want to call it—and I'm satisfied that with this sort of a setup we can get the thing working as it should work.

The navy's made some progress; army, of course, has made great progress. I don't know about the air force.

Secretary Forrestal: The air force has come along—what they have in mind, Mr. President, is a very progressive—

President Truman: I want this rounded out a little bit. I want the Department of the Interior, the Commerce Department, the Treasury Department, interviewed on the subject why you are in existence, and let's make it a government proposition, as well as an armed services. Of course, as commander in chief, I can issue orders to the armed services, and, if there is some legal approach in all the rest of the branches of the government, we might as well make a complete program out of it while we are at it, and not limit it to just one branch of the government. That's what I have in mind all the way down the line.

Not only that, I think that we've got to go further—not at this time, but later—and see that the state and local governments carry out the spirit of the laws which we hope to get on the books down here during this session of Congress.

If anybody's got any suggestions to make to me on the subject, I'd be glad to listen to them.

Secretary Forrestal: Charlie.

Mr. Fahy: Mr. President, may I say, as the chairman of the committee, we appreciate this opportunity to meet with you when we are really getting down to work,.

["First Meeting of the President's Committee on Equality of Treatment and Opportunity in the Armed Services," 12 January 1949, *Records of the President's Committee on Equality of Treatment and Opportunity in the Armed Services*, Harry S Truman Library, Independence, MO.]

and Secretary Forrestal and Secretaries Royall, Sullivan, and Symington.[1] We'll push along now and do the best we can. We are very grateful to you for this little meeting and encouragement to us and outline of what you expect. We will plug along and come back to you with the best results that we can and do the best we can.

President Truman: That's what I look for and I want it done in such a way that it is not a publicity stunt. I want concrete results—that's what I'm after—not publicity on it. I want the job done and I want to get it done in a way so everybody will be happy to cooperate to get it done. Unless it is necessary to knock somebody's ears down, I don't want to have to do that, but, if it becomes necessary, it can be done. But that's about all I've got to tell you.

Mr. Granger: May I ask you a question, Mr. President? Is there any thought in your mind as to the length of the life of this group?

President Truman: Well, I had hoped that you would be ready to come back to me with some concrete proposition not later than the first of June, and then, if it is necessary to continue, why, we can go on from there, in order to give you plenty of time. I'd like to have the outline of the situation before the Congress adjourns in case we need to ask for any legal amendments to the law because, in that hearing, at that time, we will endeavor to pass the civil rights program as outlined in my message on the subject in the last Congress. I hope to get some concrete results of that in the Eighty-first Congress.

Secretary Symington: As long as you mentioned the air force, sir, I just want to report to you that our plan is to completely eliminate segregation in the air force. For example, we have a fine group of colored boys. Our plan is to take those boys, break up that fine group, and put them with the other units themselves and go right down the line all through these subdivisions 100 percent.

President Truman: That's all right.

(To Mr. Dawson)[2] Don, I think I notice one more "club" standing out there.

Mr. Dawson: They're here, all right!

[The photographers then entered and took photographs of the group.]

President Truman: It's been a pleasure, gentlemen. Thank you all very much.

[The meeting was then adjourned at 12:25 P.M.]

---

[1]Kenneth C. Royall, secretary of the army; John L. Sullivan, secretary of the navy; and W. Stuart Symington, secretary of the air force.

[2]Donald Dawson, administrative assistant to the president.

What Sec. of Defense Louis A. Johnson intended as a general interpretation of the Truman order for his subordinates in the services became a serious attempt to initiate a racial reform independent of the White House and the Fahy Committee. The key statement in this public announcement was that the services were to devise specific programs which would be reviewed by the secretary's Personnel Policy Board. With this instruction, Johnson thrust himself into the center of the fight over equal treatment and opportunity.

1. a. It is the policy of the national military establishment that there shall be equality of treatment and opportunity for all persons in the armed services without regard to race, color, religion, or national origin.

b. To assist in achieving uniform application of this policy, the following supplemental policies are announced:

(1) To meet the requirements of the services for qualified individuals, all personnel will be considered on the basis of individual merit and ability and must qualify according to the prescribed standards for enlistment, attendance at schools, promotion, assignment to specific duties, etc.

(2) All individuals, regardless of race, will be accorded equal opportunity for appointment, advancement, professional improvement, promotion and retention in their respective components of the national military establishment.

(3) Some units may continue to be manned with Negro personnel; however, all Negroes will not necessarily be assigned to Negro units. Qualified Negro personnel shall be assigned to fill any type of position vacancy in organizations or overhead installations without regard to race.

2. Each department is directed to examine its present practices and determine what forward steps can and should be made in the light of this policy and in view of Executive Order 9981, dated July 26, 1948, which directs that this policy shall be put into effect as rapidly as possible with due regard to the time required to effectuate any necessary changes without impairing efficiency or morale.

3. Following the completion of this study, each department shall state, in writing, its own detailed implementation of the general policy stated herein and such supplemental policies as may be determined by each service to meet its own specific needs. These statements shall be submitted to the chairman of the Personnel Policy Board, Office of the Secretary of Defense, not later than 1 May 1949.

[Memorandum, Sec. of Defense Louis Johnson for the secretary of the army et al., 6 April 1949, Modern Military Records Branch, National Archives, Washington, DC.]

*After discussion and some minor amendment in the Fahy
Committee and the Personnel Policy Board, the air force plan
to integrate elements of the service was approved by Secretary of
Defense Johnson. The plan, with an implementing letter from
the chief of staff, was promulgated to the air commanders on
11 May 1949.*

Confidential

April 30, 1949

MEMORANDUM FOR THE CHAIRMAN, PERSONNEL POLICY BOARD, OFFICE OF THE SECRETARY OF DEFENSE

Reference is made to the recent memorandum from the secretary of defense, which directs each department of the national military establishment to examine current personnel policies to determine what forward steps can and should be made in the light of the policy enunciated therein and in view of Executive Order 9981.

The Department of the Air Force has completed such a study and has determined certain supplemental policies to meet the specific needs of the air force.

In implementation, it is planned that the all-Negro 332d Fighter Wing at Lockbourne will be inactivated and the personnel redistributed throughout the air force worldwide.

Concurrently, qualified Negro personnel in other air force units will be afforded the opportunity to attend service schools or transfer to traditionally white units in accordance with the requirements of the air force and the qualifications of the individuals.

It is contemplated that, for the present, certain Negro service-type units will continue to exist since they are efficiently performing a necessary air force function. Individuals in those units, however, may qualify for assignment to any air force activity, and may attend technical or other service schools which will enhance their qualifications without regard to the previous limitations imposed by Negro units and Negro vacancies.

With the adoption of this policy, the principle of Negro quotas to maintain Negro units must, of necessity, be discarded because racial quotas are not consistent with free competition on the basis of merit and ability.

Drafts of proposed air force directives have previously been furnished to the Fahy Committee and to the chairman of the Personnel Policy Board, Office of the Secretary of Defense. Upon the advice of the chairman of the Personnel Policy Board, par. 4c(4) of the confidential letter to the commanding generals, major commands (Subject: Implementation of Air Force Letter 35—) has been revised with regard to key personnel in Negro units. This subparagraph now states that "If they are in key positions and are required for the successful functioning of the unit, they will be considered and handled in exactly the same manner as other-than-Negro personnel in similar circumstances."

[Attachments to memorandum, Ass't. Sec. of the Air Force Eugene M. Zuckert for Sec. of the Air Force W. Stuart Symington, 29 April 1949, subject: Department of the Air Force implementation of the Department of Defense policy of equality of treatment and opportunity in the armed services, US Air Force Files, Washington National Records Center, Suitland, MD.]

Drafts of proposed air force policy statement and implementing directives are attached.

W. Stuart Symington

FIRST ENCLOSURE

11 May 1949

SUBJECT: Implementation of AF Letter 35–3
TO: Commanding Generals, Major Commands

1. The general plan of implementation of AF Letter 35–3 is contained herein for the information and guidance of all concerned.

2. The elimination of special consideration on the basis of race is an essential element of equality of treatment and opportunity. Therefore, Negro personnel may be assigned to any position vacancy for schools which will enhance their qualifications and value to the air force, based upon the merit and ability of the individuals concerned and without reference to "Negro quotas" or "Negro vacancies."

3. The implementation of AF Letter 35–3 can best be accomplished through the careful selection and assignment of skilled and qualified Negro personnel to appropriate duties in air force units and overhead installations. It has been proven in both the navy and the Coast Guard, and on a smaller scale by our own experience in the Air Training Command, that well-qualified Negro individuals can be absorbed into white organizations without insurmountable social or morale problems arising as a result of such assignment.

4. The plan of implementation of AF Letter 35 [–3] is substantially as follows:

a. The commanding general, Continental Air Command, will establish at Lockbourne Air Force Base a board of officers for the purpose of examining the qualifications of all air force personnel at Lockbourne and making recommendations as to the subsequent assignment of those individuals. Continental Air Command will report to this headquarters the name, rank, and serial number, MOS,[1] and recommended assignment of those individuals as they are examined. Individuals who are eligible for separation from the service under current directives will be separated. Individuals who require and are qualified for further training will, as training facilities permit, be provided with appropriate training.

b. This headquarters will assign to the major commands, by MOS and in accordance with existing vacancies, those Negro individuals who are reported as fully qualified in their MOS.

c. Each major command will assign these Negro personnel to organizations and duties in accordance with their qualifications and as indicated in paragraph three above. In addition, each major command will carefully screen its Negro personnel who are enlisted or commissioned in the air force:

> (1) Individuals who are presently assigned to a unit which is manned by Negroes, but who are demonstrating their qualifications by actually performing duties in a competent manner with a white organization should be

---

[1]Military Occupational Specialty.

transferred to the organization with which they are performing their duties.

(2) Individuals who are assigned to and who are performing duties in organizations manned by Negroes but who possess the necessary skills and qualifications for assignment to a white unit, should be assigned to appropriate vacancies within the command or reported to this headquarters as available for reassignment.

(3) Individuals who are qualified for and desire attendance at service schools will be handled in exactly the same manner as other-than-Negro personnel of similar qualifications.

(4) Individuals who are qualified under (1), (2), or (3) above may be retained in all-Negro organizations if they so desire. If they are in key positions and are required for the successful functioning of the unit, they will be considered and handled in exactly the same manner as other-than-Negro personnel in similar circumstances.

d. It is desired by this headquarters that the screening and reassignment of Negro personnel as outlined above be started without delay and that the full implementation of the policies contained in AF Letter 35–3 be generally accomplished by 31 December 1949.

5. The provisions of AF Letter 35–3 do not apply to army units or army personnel on duty with the air force.

6. The president's executive order outlining the national policy on this subject is apended (sic) hereto for your further information. It is essential that the provisions of AF Letter 35–3 and the detailed instructions herein be placed in effect gradually, smoothly, and without friction or incident. Prompt and appropriate disciplinary action will be taken where necessary to prevent friction or incidents. Commanders at each echelon will give their personal attention to the proper implementation of this policy.

By command of the chief of staff:

11 May 1949

Draft
Air Force Letter
No. 35–3

SUBJECT: USAF Personnel Policies
TO: Commanding Generals and Commanding Officers, all USAF Activities

1. It is the policy of the United States Air Force that there shall be equality of treatment and opportunity for all persons in the air force without regard to race, color, religion or national origin.

2. To ensure uniform application of this policy, the following supplemental policies are announced:

a. There will be no strength quotas of minority groups in the air force troop basis.

b. Some units will continue to be manned with Negro personnel; however, all Negroes will not necessarily be assigned to Negro units. Qualified Negro personnel may be assigned to fill any position vacancy in any air force organization or overhead installation without regard to race.

c. To meet the requirements of the air force for qualified individuals, all air force personnel will be considered on the basis of individual merit and ability and must qualify according to the prescribed standards for enlistment, attendance at schools, promotion, assignment to specific duties, etc.

d. All individuals, regardless of race, will be accorded equal opportunity for appointment, advancement, professional improvement, promotion and retention in all components of the Air Force of the United States.

e. Officers will be accepted into the regular air force through the operation of existing programs and in accordance with their qualifications without regard to race.

f. All enlisted personnel will be accorded identical processing through appropriate installations to ensure proper classification and assignment of individuals.

g. Directives pertaining to the release of personnel from the services shall be applied equally without reference to race.

3. The planning, promulgation and revision of this policy will be coordinated by the director of personnel planning, Office of the Deputy Chief of Staff, Personnel, Headquarters USAF.

4. Commanding officers are hereby directly charged with the responsibility for implementation of the above policy.

5. Commanders of all echelons of the air force will ensure that all personnel in their command are thoroughly indoctrinated with the necessity for the unreserved acceptance of the provisions of this policy.

6. Army units and individuals with the air force will continue to be governed by the policies promulgated by the army.

7. All prior policy statements with regard to Negro personnel which are contrary to the above are hereby rescinded and superseded by the policy enunciated herewith.

By order of the secretary of the air force:

Hoyt S. Vandenberg
Chief of Staff, United States Air Force

On 11 May 1949, the secretary of defense rejected the proposed race reforms of the navy and army and called on them to plan "specific additional actions" to accelerate their rate of progress toward the goals announced in the Truman order. The navy's second submission was approved by Secretary Johnson with the blessings of the Fahy Committee, and new directives concerning the status of blacks in the navy were promulgated in a series of "Alnavs" and BuPers Circulars.

1. Reference is made to your memorandum of 11 May 1949 on the subject of equality of treatment and opportunity in the armed forces. The Navy Department has reexamined the current situation and proposes to take the following specific additional action:

(a) Promulgate a statement of the Navy Department's policy regarding minority races. Copy of proposed directive attached.

(b) Augment efforts to obtain Negroes to enlist in the navy by (1) the assignment of Negro petty officers to duty in the Navy Recruiting Service, (2) ordering to active duty volunteer qualified Negro reserve officers to assist in the recruitment of Negroes, and (3) slant recruiting advertisements, posters, films, and pamphlets to attract Negroes to the navy by use of photographs showing whites and Negroes working together in the naval service.

(c) Exert greater effort to attract qualified Negro students to participate in the NROTC program. Special efforts were made last fall to attract Negro high-school students to participate in the program. The results will not be known until after the beginning of the academic year in 1949. It is believed they were not as good as expected. More vigorous efforts will be made this next year.

(d) Promulgate a directive to ensure that all members of the stewards' branch who are in all respects qualified are given an opportunity to change their rate to another rating branch.

(e) Change the status of chief stewards to that of chief petty officers.

(f) The Marine Corps will disestablish the present separate Negro recruit training facility and integrate the training of Negro recruits with that of whites.

2. The Navy Department proposes to undertake immediately a study to determine in what categories personnel with an applicant qualification test score of less than 45 can be employed without detriment to the service.

Dan A. Kimball
Acting Secretary of the Navy

[Memorandum, Acting Sec. of the Navy Dan A. Kimball for the secretary of defense, 23 May 1949, subject: Equality of treatment and opportunity in the armed forces, Modern Military Records Branch, National Archives, Washington, DC.]

49–447—POLICY REGARDING MINORITY RACES
23 June 1949

Action: all ships and stations

1. Reference (a)[1] is canceled and superseded by this letter.

2. It is the policy of the Navy Department that there shall be equality of treatment and opportunity for all persons in the navy and Marine Corps without regard to race, color, religion, or national origin.

3. In their attitude and day-to-day conduct of affairs, officers and enlisted personnel of the navy and Marine Corps shall adhere rigidly and impartially to the Navy Regulations, in which no distinction is made between individuals wearing the uniform of these services.

4. All personnel will be enlisted or appointed, trained, advanced or promoted, assigned duty, and administered in all respects without regard to race, color, religion, or national origin.

5. In the utilization of housing, messing, berthing, and other facilities, no special or unusual provisions will be made for the accommodation of any minority race.

Francis P. Matthews
Secretary of the Navy

CIRCULAR LETTER NO. 115–49

25 July 1949

Action: all ships and stations

1. In accordance with a recent directive of the secretary of the navy, chief stewards are hereafter to be considered as chief petty officers and will be accorded the prerogatives of that status as prescribed by US Naval Regulations and Bureau of Naval Personnel Manual. They shall take precedence immediately following chief dental technicians.

2. Appropriate changes to reference (a)[2] will be promulgated.

T. L. Sprague
Bureau of Personnel

CIRCULAR LETTER NO. 141–49

30 August 1949

Action: all ships and stations

1. Effective 1 January 1950, stewards, first-, second-, and third-class, will be considered petty officers of their appropriate pay grade and will be accorded the

---

[1]Alnav 423–45.
[2]BuPers Manual (1948).

prerogatives of that status as prescribed by US Navy Regulations and Bureau of Naval Personnel Manual. They shall take precedence immediately after dental technician, first-, second-, and third-class, respectively.

2. The secretary of the navy has authorized a change, effective on the above date, in the uniform prescribed for stewards, first-, second-, and third-class, which will require them to wear the same type of uniform as is prescribed for other petty officers. More detailed information concerning the uniform change will be published at a later date. In the meantime, commanding officers are requested to advise stewards, first-, second-, and third-class, under their commands of this prospective change in order that they may anticipate their needs in regard to uniforms.

3. Appropriate changes to Bureau of Naval Personnel Manual will be promulgated.

T. L. Sprague
Bureau of Personnel

●

As its investigations progressed, the Fahy Committee came to understand that the key to its arguments with the army's segregationists was the question of military efficiency. In its second report to the president, the group outlined its minimum demands.

As the committee proceeded with its examination into the personnel practices of the services, it became apparent that the question of equality of treatment and opportunity, in addition to the moral principle involved, is inextricably bound up with the problem of the most efficient use of manpower. As war becomes more technical and the machinery of war more mechanical, it makes greater, rather than less, demand upon the nation's available manpower. This demand is not alone for greater numbers of men, but for men with a wider range of ability and skill. Consequently, the nation cannot afford to use its military personnel below their full capacities, or fail to train adequately all men regardless of race.

The committee believes the available military manpower will not be used at maximum efficiency unless all men and women in uniform are given an equal opportunity to discover and exploit their capabilities. This interdependence of the objectives of equal opportunity and military efficiency the committee has kept constantly in mind as it has formulated its recommendations. . . .

THE ARMY

The recommendations which the president's committee is presently making for army action in order to advance toward equality of treatment and opportunity and achieve more efficient utilization of manpower are as follows:

[President's Committee on Equality of Treatment and Opportunity in the Armed Services, *Second Interim Report*, 27 July 1949, Harry S Truman Library, Independence, MO.]

I. Classification—Military Occupational Specialties

A. All military occupational specialties (MOS) should be open to qualified personnel.

B. Every person processed at a training division should receive his appropriate military occupational specialties solely and strictly on the basis of classification procedures, without regard to race or the requirements of racial units.

Purpose and justification. At the present time all MOS are theoretically open to all qualified personnel in the army. Actually, many MOS are closed to Negroes because the range of Negro Table of Organization and Equipment (T/O&E) units do not require as many MOS as does the range of white T/O&E units. The above recommendation is designed to make all MOS open to qualified men regardless of race or possible utilization in racial units.

II. Assignment to Army Schools from Training Divisions

A. The present racial quotas for selection for army schools from the replacement stream (training divisions) should be abolished.

B. Personnel should be assigned to schools from the replacement stream solely on the basis of qualification and aptitude without regard to race or possible utilization in racial units.

Purpose and justification. At the present time there are no racial qualifications for those army-school courses to which qualified recruits are sent after basic training. However, the army sets racial quotas for these courses. The army defends the racial quotas on the ground that it cannot school Negroes beyond the requirements of Negro T/O&E units and racially mixed overhead installations. But since Negro units do not require all the specialties represented in white units, and since the use of Negroes in overhead installations is dependent upon the local commander, the army's present policy actually denies to qualified Negroes the opportunity to attend many army-school courses. For example, there are currently 106 courses for recruits from the training divisions. Of these, only 21, or 19.8 percent, are open to Negroes. The remainder of the courses have no Negro quotas, and consequently qualified Negroes are not permitted to attend them, even if the army is below authorized strength in those special skills.

It is the intent of the above recommendation that qualified men from the replacement stream should be assigned to army-school courses without regard to race or possible utilization in racial units. The committee does not believe it can recommend less than this in the light of the policy enunciated by the president.

III. Assignment and Utilization of Replacement Stream Students

All replacement stream students, upon completion of their courses in army schools, should be assigned to units or overhead installations, and utilized by local commanders, without regard to race or vacancies in racial units.

Purpose and justification. The committee believes that, having given a man special training, the army should use that man in his specialty, wherever it needs that specialty, without regard to race. The army is below authorized strength in many MOS in white units. Yet, under its present policy, it cannot use available, qualified Negro specialists to bring those deficient MOS up to strength.

At the present time a local commander has the authority to use a man in a duty MOS different from his assigned MOS. He also has the authority to readjust or redesignate MOS. The committee is conscious that flexibility in administration and command requires that the commander have this authority. At the same time the committee believes it is essential that commanders use the men assigned to them with full regard to their MOS, and especially that specialists upon completion of school training should be utilized in their specialty without regard to race or vacancies in racial units.

IV. Assignment to Army Schools of Personnel from Major Commands

A. Personnel assigned to major commands should be detached for army-school training solely on the basis of qualification, without regard to race or possible utilization in racial units.

B. Negro quotas in major commands for school selection of assigned personnel should be abolished.

C. Major commands should not impose racial quotas in the distribution of their overall school quotas within their command.

D. Negroes, currently assigned to major commands, who possess the minimum qualification for army schools and who wish to attend an army school, should be reclassified; and those who are qualified in their primary or secondary MOS should be sent to an appropriate school as soon as possible, but in any event within forty-eight months, to the extent required to meet the army's overall needs in the particular MOS concerned.

Purpose and justification. While all courses are theoretically open to qualified Negroes in army commands, actually the limitations of Negro T/O&E units prevent qualified Negroes from attending many courses. Commanders do not request schooling for Negroes, even if qualified, unless they can use these trained Negroes in racial units or overhead installations. Qualified Negroes in major commands, who desire and have not been able to go to school, should have the opportunity to do so, if there is need for their specialties, in order that the army should not lose any potential skills. It is intended that this provision shall be administered consistently with the similar opportunities accorded qualified white personnel, and not to the exclusion of the latter. Because the facilities of the army schools are limited, this recommendation should be effected gradually over the next four years.

V. Assignment and Utilization of Personnel from Major Commands upon Completion of School Courses

All personnel detached from major commands for schooling, upon completion of their courses, should be assigned and utilized without regard to race or vacancies in racial units.

Purpose and justification. See III above.

VI. Personal Preference in the Assignment of Men in Grades 4–7

So long as there continues to be predominantly racial units in the peacetime army, the committee suggests that the army may wish to give consideration to permitting an enlisted man in the four lowest grades, subject to the approval of his commander, to remain in a unit predominantly composed of personnel of his own race, if he so requests.

The committee would limit this suggestion to the peacetime army, since the "ultimate objective" of the Gillem Board was the "effective use of *all* manpower made available to the military establishment in the event of a major mobilization . . . without regard to antecedents or race."

The committee would not suggest that officers and noncommissioned officers in the first three grades should have such choice. These officers and noncommissioned officers receive their promotions on a worldwide basis; they have applied for and accepted promotions, and their responsibilities to the service should include unquestioning acceptance of assignment.

VII. Abolition of the Racial Quota and Establishment of a Quota on the Basis of the General Classification Test

A. The racial quota, recommended by the Gillem Board and established as army policy and practice in War Department Circular No. 124, which sets a troop basis of nine whites for one Negro, should be abolished.

B. For the purpose of procurement through voluntary enlistment, the army should institute a quota system based upon the General Classification Test, the quota for each grade in the GCT to be determined by ascertaining the existing GCT distribution in relation to normal distribution in the army during the operation of Selective Service in World War II. These quotas would have to be adjusted to the fact that the army does not now accept voluntary enlistments of men below GCT 80. Overages in each of the top three GCT categories would be applied against the next category below.

In support of the quota system, the army argues that it is necessary in order to prevent Negroes from enlisting in the army in numbers disproportionate to their percentage of the civilian population. Since the army enlists men at GCT 80—in contrast to the mental qualification of 90 for navy and air force enlistment—the army contends that, without a racial quota, it would have no way of controlling the enlistment of Negroes, most of whom fall in the lower GCT classifications.

The numbers of Negroes in the army which would result from the abolition of the quota is impossible to predict, as it would depend upon a number of variable factors. In any event, the committee believes the solution to this problem is the substitution of a quota system based on the distribution of personnel in GCT grades as revealed by experience in World War II. By such a quota system the army could at once ensure itself of not getting too many low-score recruits, whether white or Negro.

In order to control the number in GCT Grade IV, reenlistment of men in this category would have to be controlled. Therefore the committee would suggest that:

> 1. A man in GCT Grade IV, completing his first term of enlistment and scoring below 80 in Aptitude Area I test, should not be allowed to reenlist.
> 2. A man with more than one term of enlistment who is in GCT Grade IV and scoring below 80 in Aptitude Area I test, be not allowed to reenlist except upon waiver by the adjutant general in the interest of army efficiency.

There is good precedent for such a policy in the Gillem Board Report which animadverted upon the practice of allowing low-score men to reenlist for repeated terms.

VIII. Equalization of Mental Qualifications for All Three Services

There should be parity of mental qualifications for enlistment in all three services, and the navy and air force should accept low-score personnel according to their ability to use them; provided, that final decision on this recommendation may await completion of the job analysis to be conducted by the national military establishment in the next year.

Purpose and justification. There is a long-standing dispute between the army on one hand and the navy and the air force on the other, over the question of whether there should be parity of mental standards for enlistment and induction in all three services.

The army has had to drop its entrance qualifications to GCT 80 in order to get enlistments. The navy and air force have been able to keep up to strength with an enlistment standard of GCT 90. Moreover, the army is required to take men at 70 under Selective Service. The air force and navy are under no such legal compulsion.

The army argues that the navy and air force skim the cream of the manpower pool. Therefore, the army wants a parity of entrance scores for all three services under both Selective Service and voluntary enlistment. Furthermore, it wants all inductees and enlistees allocated by mental grade to each service in proportion of the authorized strength of each service to the overall strength of the three services.

The navy and air force reply that they should not be obliged to accept enlistees at GCT 80, when they can get men at GCT 90. They contend, further, that their services, being more technical than the army, require men of higher mental qualifications.

The Department of the Army has stated to the committee that if there were parity of entrance qualifications, it could abandon the racial quota.

A year ago the secretary of defense ruled that when all services were dependent upon induction, there should be parity of mental standards. Under voluntary enlistment, however, he ruled that there need not be common mental qualifications.

The committee is convinced there is some justice in the army complaint that the unequal standards for enlistment operates to the disadvantage of the army. It does not agree, however, that low-score men should be allocated to the services on such an arbitrary basis as the proportion of each service to the overall military strength.

The committee believes the question of parity of mental standards for enlistment and the equitable division of low-score men between the services may be much clarified by the job analysis which will be undertaken during the next year in all three services. . . .

Eager to be through with the lengthening controversy between the army and the Fahy Committee, Secretary Johnson hastily approved a new army proposal that, while promising some improvement in the status of black soldiers, would have retained segregation. The committee took the matter to the president and not so subtly offered to make its disagreement with the army public. The president sided with his committee, and with this exchange the secretary of defense retired from the picture, leaving the committee and the army to thrash out their differences with the White House looking on.

MEMORANDUM FOR THE PRESIDENT

Attached is a brief Further Interim Report from your committee regarding the recent army announcement of its new racial program. Though the new program is a step forward, its effectiveness is seriously impaired by the failure to provide that, after the men have acquired their military occupational specialties and have completed their school courses, they shall be assigned according to their qualifications and without regard to race or color. The committee therefore has come to the conclusion, as a result of its studies, that the army should supplement its new program to cover definitely this problem of assignment. The adoption of the assignment policy which we have urged means the beginning of integration by a slow and practical process and provides for a better army.

The question remains as to how the matter should now be handled. We suggest, for your consideration, the following:

1. That the president ask Secretary Johnson to straighten the matter out by a supplementary statement. This statement, the committee believes, should have committee approval before issuance.

2. That the committee release to the press a statement of its recommendations to the army, in substance as set forth in the accompanying report.

3. That the committee resume discussions with the army. If this course is adopted, however, the president may wish to advise the secretary of defense that the committee's recommendations conform to the requirements of Executive Order 9981.

> Charles Fahy
> Chairman
> For the Committee

FURTHER INTERIM REPORT TO THE PRESIDENT

A further Interim Report is made to the president at this time because of the announcement September 30, 1949, of approval by Sec. of Defense Louis Johnson of a program proposed by the Department of the Army to give greater assurance of equality

---

[Memorandum, Charles Fahy for the president, 11 October 1949, with attached Interim Report and presidential comment, Harry S Truman Library, Independence, MO.]

of treatment and opportunity to army personnel. Approval had been previously given by the secretary of defense to policies of the air force (May 11, 1949) and the navy (June 7, 1949), both of which services met standards of policy deemed satisfactory by the committee. The policy of the army remained a matter of active consideration and discussion between the army and the committee.

At a meeting of the committee on October 5, 1949, we considered, among other matters, the announcement of September 30, 1949, regarding the army program. We respectfully comment on that program as follows:

1. We approve the provisions which open military occupational specialties (MOS) to qualified personnel without regard to race, which abolish the present Negro quotas for selection to attend army schools and which require that such selection will be made from the best qualified personnel without regard to race or color. These provisions conform with recommendations made to the army by the committee. This policy must apply to all personnel, including personnel already assigned to units as well as new enlistments.

Furthermore, it is the committee's intention that additional Negro units will not be formed in order to create spaces to absorb Negro personnel who receive schooling and acquire technical occupational specialties as a result of the army's removing racial restrictions on MOS and service schools.

2. We also approve the statement of policy regarding promotions, providing for open competition on army-wide examinations against a single standard and without regard to race or color. This conforms with present practice.

3. We also approve the provisions that ROTC students attending summer training camps as members of school units to which they are regularly assigned will be trained with those units without regard to race or color.

4. The benefit of the new policy of opening military occupational specialties (MOS) to all personnel without regard to race or color and abolishing the present Negro quotas for army schools (points one and two of the army program) will be largely nullified by the failure of the program to provide that personnel, to whom these opportunities will be accorded, will be assigned without regard to race or color. Unless assignments are so made, and are not restricted as at present to Negro and overhead units, the principle of equality of treatment and opportunity is not carried forward and the manpower of the army is not utilized to the best advantage. The committee is convinced that this further logical step is required to effectuate the president's Executive Order 9981 and the statement of the secretary of defense of April 6, 1949, in endorsement of the president's order. Furthermore, failure to do so would create a differential between the racial policies of the three services—a differential at variance with the president's expressed intention and the concept of a unified national defense program.

5. There remains for further consideration the recommendation which the committee has made to the army for the abolition of the 10 percent racial quota. We will continue our discussion on this point with the determination to reach a satisfactory solution.

6. We note that in the announcement of September 30, 1949, Sec. [of the Army

Gordon] Gray refers to a new reenlistment policy under which the army limits reenlistments to those who during their first regular enlistment qualify for promotion to private first class, if unmarried, and to corporal, if married, and that all personnel are eligible to win these promotions. The secretary states that this policy is expected to produce greater economy and efficiency by gradually eliminating those who fail to demonstrate the capacity to advance; and that its progressive application will assure continuing opportunities to highly qualified individuals, both Negroes and others, to enlist. This policy is consistent with suggestions made by the committee.

Charles Fahy
Chairman
For the Committee

[Noted on the original: "Harry[1]—Read this and then take up with Johnson. HST"]

---

[1]Maj. Gen. Harry H. Vaughan, military aide to the president.

●

The Fahy Committee never demanded the immediate and total integration of the army. It reasoned that, if all Negroes were assigned freely to jobs for which they were eligible by training and aptitude in any unit where such jobs existed, the goal of equal treatment and opportunity would eventually be achieved. On 16 January 1950, the army and the committee reached agreement on the first of the major issues separating them. The army issued orders that qualified black soldiers would be eligible for jobs in any unit.

1. *Policy.* The policy of the Department of the Army is that there shall be equality of treatment and opportunity for all persons in the army without regard to race, color, religion, or national origin. All manpower will be utilized to obtain maximum efficiency in the army.

2. *Responsibility.*

a. Commanders of all echelons of the army will ensure that all personnel under their command are thoroughly oriented in the necessity for the unreserved acceptance of the provisions of these policies.

b. Commanders of organizations or installations containing Negro personnel will be responsible for the execution of these policies.

c. The planning, promulgation, implementation, and revision of these policies will be coordinated by the director of Personnel and Administration, General Staff, United States Army.

[US Army Special Regulations No. 600-629-1, 16 January 1950, "Utilization of Negro Manpower in the Army," Modern Military Records Branch, National Archives, Washington, DC.]

3. *Periodic Review of Utilization of Negro Manpower.* A board of senior army officers will be convened from time to time to determine current progress under the policies and implementation prescribed herein and to reexamine and revise the fundamental policies for the utilization of Negro manpower.

4. *Enlisted Personnel Processing.* All enlisted personnel without regard to race or color will be accorded the same reception processing through appropriate installations to ensure proper initial classification.

5. *Army School Training.* Army school quotas for replacement-stream personnel, and requests for and issuance of school quotas for assigned enlisted personnel will make no reference to race or color. Selection of personnel to attend army schools will be made without regard to race or color. Graduates of army schools will be used in positions where their school-acquired skill may be utilized in accord with personnel management regulations equally applicable to all enlisted personnel.

6. *Eligibility for Military Occupational Specialties.* Military occupational specialties will be open to qualified enlisted personnel without regard to race or color. Utilization of Negro personnel in military occupational specialties will be in accord with personnel management regulations equally applicable to all enlisted personnel.

7. *Enlisted Promotions.* The promotion system of the enlisted career guidance program will be administered on an equal merit basis so that all promotions will be obtained by open competition, on examinations uniform throughout the army, against a single standard, without regard to race or color.

8. *Officer Personnel Management.*
a. Officers will be procured for the regular army and for the Officers Reserve Corps without regard to race or color.
b. All officers, regardless of race or color, will be afforded equal opportunities for advancement, professional improvement, extended active duty, active-duty training, promotion, and retention in the army.

9. *ROTC Students at Summer Training Camps.* ROTC students attending summer training camps as members of school units to which they are regularly assigned will remain together and be trained together without regard to race or color.

10. *Utilization and Assignment.*
a. In furtherance of the policy of the president as expressed in Executive Order 9981, dated July 26, 1948, that there shall be equality of treatment and opportunity for all persons in the armed services without regard to race, color, religion or national origin, it is the objective of the Department of the Army that Negro manpower possessing appropriate skills and qualifications will be utilized in accordance with such skills and qualifications, and will be assigned to any T/D[1] or T/O&E unit without regard to race or color.
b. In consonance with the foregoing, and as additional steps towards its attainment:
(1) The Department of the Army will publish periodically to major commanders a

---

[1]Table of Distribution.

list of the critical specialties in which vacancies exist within the army. The first such list is being published concurrently herewith in DA AGO letter dated 16 Jan 1950. Major commanders concerned will assign Negro personnel who possess any of such critical specialties to any T/D or T/O&E unit in their areas having such critical specialist vacancies, without regard to race or color.

(2) In addition to the provisions of subparagraph (1) above, to fill other vacancies requiring special skills, qualified Negro specialists may be assigned to any appropriate unit by order of the major commander concerned.

●

The White House staff began to show increasing interest in the progress of the committee's negotiations with the army on the remaining issue between them: the 10 percent racial quota.

Charles Fahy and the secretary of the army have had a friendly and encouraging talk on the Fahy Committee's remaining recommendation—the substitution of an achievement quota for the present racial quota.

The attached graph[1] illustrates the real problem of bringing about equality of treatment and opportunity in the army; that is, the great difference between Negro and white soldiers in education and resulting mental achievement. The steps the army has already taken will help to equalize opportunity, without interfering with efficiency or morale. But for these steps to have a significant effect, it is necessary to have men in the army who can take the best advantage of them. A proposal is now being circulated to the members of the Fahy Committee, and will shortly be presented to Secretary Gray, which will improve the quality of the army by raising the level of its Negro recruits.

It will also remove the racial quota, which has been subject to heavy criticism, and which has restricted the enlistment of high-grade Negroes without preventing the enlistment of low-grade men.

The substance of the committee proposal is:

1. To require all recruits, both white and Negro, to score at least 90 on the GCT test.

2. To take steps making it difficult for soldiers, both white and Negro, now in the army, to reenlist if they are perennial low-score men, or are otherwise inept. The army already has this proposal under consideration.

3. Simultaneously with these two steps, to eliminate the present racial quota of one Negro for every nine whites.

This proposal seems fair and sensible; and is gradual in that Negro units would gradually disappear, but would not be abolished overnight.

The question has been raised as to what proportion of the army would be Negro

---

[Memorandum, David K. Niles for the president, 7 February 1950, Harry S Truman Library, Independence, MO.]

[1]Not included.

under this procedure. Only time will tell. Estimates vary greatly. My own guess is that there will be substantially less Negroes in the army, but they will more nearly approach the whites in capability, so that the personnel management problem will be much simpler and more satisfactory to everyone.

Judging by World War II figures, only 16.6 percent of all Negro men of military age will score 90 or better on the GCT test. Hence, with a cutoff score of 90, this percentage (16.6 percent) would be the maximum of Negroes enlisting in the army, if every Negro of military age entered the service, and none selected navy or air force. The true number, of course, would be much smaller than this, since some men are disqualified by health, others are gainfully occupied; still others are students, and of those who volunteer, some elect navy or air force. The number might even approach the percentage of Negroes over GCT 90, which is only 2.8 percent of all men scoring 90 or better.

These are the approximate ranges, I should think, to the percentage of Negroes in the army under the Fahy proposal. The actual percentage would tend toward one or the other of these possibilities, depending on how many low-score men the army permits to reenlist.

If the proportion of Negroes becomes unwieldy, or is so small as to be unfair, the procedures can easily be revised by adjusting the GCT score minimum up or down from 90. Properly combined with procedures for preventing the reenlistment of inept men, both Negro and white, the substitution of an achievement quota would have the effect of correcting an imbalance in the army, under which any true equality of opportunity is impossible. The navy and air force have already discovered this fact, have substituted a GCT quota for a racial quota, and are very pleased with the results.

●

The secretary of the army agreed to drop the racial quota, but not without a significant condition that he communicated to the president.

You will recall my statement to you that I would give continued study to the feasibility of utilizing some other system for regulating army enlistments than the present controls based on racial quotas. In pursuance of this continuing study, I have now determined to make a trial run of a new system for regulating enlistments into the army. This new system will continue to control the total number of individuals enlisted each month at the number required to man the army at its authorized strength. It will, however, open up all enlistments within this overall number to any applicant, without regard to his race or color, meeting a single set of mental, physical, psychiatric, and moral enlistment standards.

If, as a result of a fair trial of this new system, there ensues a disproportionate balance of racial strengths in the army, it is my understanding that I have your authority to return to a system which will, in effect, control enlistments by race.

[Noted on the original: "APPROVED HARRY S TRUMAN"]

[Letter, Sec. of the Army Gordon Gray to the president, 1 March 1950, Official File, Harry S Truman Library, Independence, MO.]

Armed with the president's permission to reinstate the quota
"if there ensued a disproportionate balance of racial strengths
in the army," Secretary Gray prepared specific plans for
dropping restrictions on the enlistment of blacks in the army.

Responsive to your request (communicated by Mr. David K. Niles) I am summarizing both the method and the timing which is to be involved in lifting racial enlistment quotas by the army, pursuant to the policy and plan which I recently discussed with you.

The army computes in advance the number of recruits it will require for each succeeding month and issues monthly recruiting targets. Beginning with the month of April the practice of issuing separate recruiting targets for whites and Negroes will be suspended and enlistments in the army, within the monthly recruiting target, will be opened to all qualified individuals without regard to race or color. This will apply equally to both males and WACS.

Instructions fixing the April recruiting target under this new policy will be issued to army field agencies 27 March.

With the concurrence of the Fahy committee, no advance public statement will be released and the action will be handled in a routine manner. It is probable, following the receipt by army field agencies of these instructions, that press inquiries will be stimulated. If so, I will merely acknowledge after the fact that army enlistments within the monthly enlistment ceiling have been opened to all qualified persons without regard to race or color.

[Memorandum, Sec. of the Army Gordon Gray for the president, 24 March 1950, subject: Discontinuance of racial enlistment quotas, General Archives Branch, Washington Records Center, Suitland, MD.]

•

I appreciated your memorandum in regard to discontinuance of racial enlistment quotas.

I am sure that everything will work out as it should.

[Memorandum from the president to the secretary of the army, 27 March 1950, Harry S Truman Library, Independence, MO.]

•

The Army Staff announced the end of racial quotas to its
commanders.

Effective with the month of April all enlistments in the army within overall recruiting quotas will be open to qualified applicants without regard to race or color.

[Message, Department of the Army, G-1, to chief of Army Field Forces and army commanders, 27 March 1950, Modern Military Records Branch, National Archives, Washington, DC.]

*The Fahy Committee issued a final report that described in
detail its negotiations with the services and the reasons for
its actions.*

I. TOWARD THE GOAL: A SUMMARY OF PROGRESS

Executive Order 9981, issued on July 26, 1948, declared it to be "the policy of the president that there shall be equality of treatment and opportunity for all persons in the armed services without regard to race, color, religion or national origin."

"This policy," the president directed, "shall be put into effect as rapidly as possible, having due regard to the time required to effectuate any necessary changes without impairing efficiency or morale."

By the same order the president announced there would be created in the national military establishment a committee of seven members with authority "to examine into the rules, procedures and practices of the armed services" in order to determine what changes were necessary to carry out the president's policy.

In discharging its duties, the committee was directed by the president to confer and advise with the secretary of defense and the secretaries of the three services, and finally to make recommendations to the president and the aforementioned secretaries.

The Committee Interprets Its Mission

At the outset of its deliberations the committee was agreed that the problem with which it was charged was not merely one of simple justice. In addition to the factor of equality of treatment and opportunity was the factor of military efficiency, the making of a better armed service.

In the committee's view the task could not be accomplished solely on the basis of information gathered in formal testimony, though such testimony must be a necessary step in the committee's inquiry. The president had directed the committee to examine into the procedures and practices of the three services. Such an examination, the committee decided, required three lines of inquiry, each one of which would provide a check upon the other two.

First, it was necessary for the committee to have a comprehensive understanding of the whole field of personnel policy and administration in the three services, including recruitment, basic training, technical training, assignment, promotion, and the so-called career guidance programs. Without such information the committee did not feel competent to judge (a) whether the services were denying opportunity to any of their personnel solely on account of race and (b) whether their racial policies and practices promoted or reduced military efficiency.

Second, the committee needed to make a study of the historical experience of the three services with racial groups, for it was on the basis of this experience that the services largely explained and rationalized their present policies and practices.

Third, the committee wished to supplement its technical and historical studies with field trips so that it would have firsthand information.

One other problem concerned the committee. This was how best to secure the

[*Freedom to Serve: Equality of Treatment and Opportunity in the Armed Services*, Modern Military Records Branch, National Archives, Washington, DC.]

endorsement by the armed services of those measures which, in the committee's judgment, might be needed to effect the president's policy. The committee believed that progress could be made most readily by a presentation of the facts, by suggestions for corrective measures, and by convincing the services of the reasonableness and effectiveness of its recommendations. The services, though subject to civilian control, are old institutions with long-established customs and habits. The committee believed that reforms would be more readily accepted and make headway faster if they represented decisions mutually agreed upon. Imposed decisions can be enforced by discipline but joint decisions engage the loyalty of those who have concerted them.

Therefore the committee decided that it would confer with the services at each step of the way, confident that its recommendations would win support as the services became convinced they were sound in principle and would improve the efficiency of the military establishment. If this could be accomplished, the committee contemplated that its recommendations would be implemented concurrently with their acceptance, and that a report to the president would then represent not a future objective but a program in being. This plan of work had the president's approval.

The Course of the Inquiry

At the beginning of its inquiry the committee heard testimony from sixty-seven witnesses, including the secretaries and assistant secretaries of the army, navy, and air force, as well as the army chief of staff; the deputy chief of naval operations for personnel, the air force director of personnel planning, the army director of personnel and administration; a former assistant secretary of war who headed the Special Troop Policies Committee in World War II; the chairman of the board of general officers that in 1945 formulated a new army racial policy; civilian personnel experts from the three services; and individuals and representatives of civilian organizations concerned with minority group interests.

The testimony of these witnesses, totaling 1,025 pages, has been bound and indexed. Copies are being deposited with the secretary of defense, the secretaries of the army, navy, and air force, the general staffs of the army and air force, the Bureau of Personnel of the Navy, the Library of Congress, and the Archives.

Through the cooperation of the Navy Bureau of Personnel, the Office of the Director of Personnel Planning in the air force, the Army General Staff Divisions of Personnel and Administration and Organization and Training, the Personnel Research and Procedures Branch of the Army Adjutant General's Office and the Historical Records Section of the Army, the committee has been able to secure a comprehensive understanding of the personnel policies and operations of the three services and a thorough knowledge of the policies governing minority groups.

These agencies made freely available to the committee and its staff all the historical and technical information necessary to the committee's study, and representatives of the services were always available to the committee for guidance and consultation. The day-to-day conferences and collaboration of the committee's staff and the technical experts of the services greatly facilitated the work of the committee.

Finally, the committee and its staff made field investigations covering eight navy ships and stations, seven air force bases, and ten army posts. In addition the committee itself has held more than forty meetings.

The scope of the executive order required that there be equality of treatment and opportunity for all persons in the armed services without regard to race, color, religion, or national origin. Members of various minority groups have asserted the existence of discrimination on these grounds, but no evidence was presented to the committee and no specific facts were found indicating formally defined service policies denying equality of treatment and opportunity except with respect to Negroes. In their case practices resulting in inequality of treatment and opportunity had the sanction of official policy and were embodied in regulations.

The committee felt, therefore, that its examination should leave room for gathering facts and developing conclusions affecting all minorities, but that it should proceed with the material on hand concerning the specific status of Negroes in the services. Once this racial factor should be satisfactorily disposed of, the committee believed, a formula would be evolved applicable to all minorities. For this reason specific mention is limited throughout the report to recommendations and changes affecting Negroes.

There follows a summary account of the extent to which the president's executive order presently is being implemented, with an indication of the policy changes that have been put into effect by the services since the order was issued in July 1948.

The Navy

All jobs and ratings in the naval general service now are open to all enlisted men without regard to race or color. Negroes are currently serving in every job classification in general service.

All courses in navy technical schools are open to qualified personnel without regard to race or color and without racial quotas. Negroes are attending the most advanced technical schools and are serving in their ratings both in the fleet and at shore installations.

Negroes in general service are completely integrated with whites in basic training, technical schools, on the job, in messes and sleeping quarters, ashore and afloat.

Chief, first-, second-, and third-class stewards now have the rate of chief, first-, second-, and third-class petty officers. (Policy change adopted June 7, 1949.)

Stewards who qualify for general ratings now can transfer to general service.

The Marine Corps, which as a part of the navy is subject to navy policy, has abolished its segregated Negro training units. (Policy change adopted June 7, 1949.) Marine Corps training is now integrated, although some Negro marines are still assigned to separate units after basic training. In this respect the effectuation of navy policy in the Marine Corps is yet to be completed.

The Air Force

The air force announced its new racial policy on May 11, 1949. As a result of this policy, the all-Negro 332d Fighter Wing at Lockbourne Field, Ohio, has been broken up, and its personnel either sent to school for further training, transferred to white units in other commands, or separated under current regulations.

A majority of other Negro units has also been abolished. As of January 31, 1950, only 59 Negro units remained, and 1,301 units were racially integrated, as compared with 106 Negro units and only 167 mixed units on June 1, 1949, when the air force policy went into effect.

Approximately 74 percent of the 25,000 Negroes in the air force on January 31, 1950, were serving in integrated units; and 26 percent still were serving in Negro units. This integration process is continuing.

All air force jobs and schools are open to qualified personnel without racial restriction or quotas. Six percent of the total personnel attending technical training schools in January 1950 were Negro.

Negroes serving in mixed units and attending service schools are integrated with whites in living conditions.

The Army

All army jobs now are open to Negroes. (Policy change adopted September 30, 1949.)

All army-school courses are open to Negroes without restriction or quota. (Policy change adopted September 30, 1949.)

For the first time Negroes no longer are limited in assignment to Negro and overhead (housekeeping) units, but are to be assigned according to their qualifications to any unit, including formerly white units. (Policy change adopted January 16, 1950.)

Negroes serving in mixed units will be integrated on the job, in barracks and messes. (Policy change adopted January 16, 1950.)

The 10 percent limitation on Negro strength in the army has been abolished, and there no longer are Negro quotas for enlistment. (Policy change adopted March 27, 1950.)

The succeeding chapters contain a more detailed account of the committee's recommendations to the services and the extent to which the president's policy is being implemented.

II. TWO BASIC QUESTIONS

Two principal questions have engaged the attention of military planning staffs whenever they have considered the question of Negro utilization:

1. Do Negroes have the mental and technical qualifications to be used in the full range of military jobs?

2. Shall Negroes be utilized only in Negro units?

Until quite recently all three services had invariably taken the position that (1) Negroes do not have the education and skills to perform efficiently in the more technical military occupations, and (2) Negroes must be utilized, with few exceptions, in segregated units. The basis for this position may be briefly summarized as follows:

1. Tests conducted by the military disclosed that the level of ability and technical skill of Negroes as a group is considerably below that of whites as a group. The services realized that Negroes as a group have not enjoyed comparable educational advantages with whites, and have not had the same opportunity to learn skilled trades. But the services contended that, regardless of the causes of this differential in group ability and skill, they were confronted with a fact which bears upon military utilization, and in the

interest of military efficiency they must recognize this fact. Therefore, it was maintained, Negroes could not be employed over the same range of military jobs as whites; they must be utilized in a limited number of jobs, the majority of them unskilled or semiskilled.

2. As for the question of racial segregation, the military services argued that they must be guided by precedent and custom. The services must keep abreast of civilian sentiment and practice; at the same time they must take care not to get ahead of the country. To do so might create difficulties which would be reflected in morale and military efficiency. Expediency then, and not racial prejudice, imposes on the military a policy of limiting the assignment of Negroes to Negro units.

Meeting the military on its own premise and considering these questions strictly from the viewpoint of military efficiency, the committee had serious doubts as to the reasoning by which the military had traditionally arrived at its policies of limited utilization and racial segregation. To begin with, however, the committee's skepticism was based on reason rather than on direct observation.

The committee, conscious of the handicaps under which many Negroes live and their lack of full educational advantages, did not question the contention that the Negro population as a whole did not parallel the white population as a whole in technical skills or education. This was confirmed by tests administered to all personnel in two world wars. For example, 67.8 percent of the 8,720,764 white enlisted males tested by the army from March 1941 through May 1946, scored 90 and above in the General Classification Test.[1] Of the 1,036,819 enlisted male Negroes tested, only 16.6 percent scored 90 and above. Again, 14.4 percent of the whites tested were below 70, as against 51.6 percent Negroes below 70.

The disproportion in the GCT spread for white and Negro elements in the peacetime army is not so great, partly because of more selective recruiting and partly because of a higher rate of separation for inability to absorb instruction. Even so, 38 percent of the Negroes in the army, as of March 31, 1949, were 90 and above, as contrasted with 67.2 percent of the whites 90 and above.

The committee did not dispute this situation. What the committee questioned were the conclusions which some military officials drew from it. Conceding the differential in skill and ability between the white and Negro elements in the services, did this group difference justify denying to the individual Negro—solely on the ground of race—the opportunity to qualify for, and serve in, any job whatsoever? To put racial restrictions upon job opportunities seemed to the committee to ignore completely the essential factor of individual differences. And insofar as a service refused to a single Negro the technical training and job for which he was qualified, by just so much did the service waste potential skills and impair its own effectiveness. Quite apart from the question of equal opportunity, the committee did not believe the country or the military services could afford this human wastage.

Furthermore, in considering the question of the Negro unit, it seemed to the committee that segregation merely aggravated this waste and multiplied the inefficiency. Because of the group differential in skill and education, it seemed obvious that Negro units could not be created which would perform the complete range of functions required in white units, and Negro units therefore could not provide the opportunity for the same

---

[1]The General Classification Test was designed to reflect readiness to absorb military training. [Footnote in the original.]

diversity of individual skills as white units. Yet a policy of segregation made mandatory the assignment of highly qualified Negroes to racial units where there might be no opening for their skills. At the same time that segregation deprived the skilled Negro of equal opportunity and deprived the service of his talent, it also magnified the inefficiency of the unskilled majority by concentrating them in separate units.

There still remained the question—and it was a question which had been raised whenever the services had considered proposals for widening the opportunities for qualified Negroes—whether, on balance, it were not better to suffer the loss of some individual skills through segregation than encounter difficulty through assigning whites and Negroes to the same unit. Would not the possible loss in efficiency which might result from impaired morale in mixed units (so went the hypothetical question) outweigh the actual loss in efficiency which resulted from racial restrictions upon employment and assignment?

As the committee sought an answer to these questions in the historical record and current practice of the services, the experience of the navy furnished the committee with valuable guidance.

III. THE NAVY

Two Assumptions Are Put to the Test and Two New Policies Are Adopted

It is the policy of the Navy Department that there shall be equality of treatment for all persons in the navy and Marine Corps without regard to race, color, religion, or national origin.

In their attitude and day-to-day conduct of affairs, officers and enlisted personnel of the navy and Marine Corps shall adhere rigidly and impartially to the Navy Regulations, in which no distinction is made between individuals wearing the uniform of these services.

All personnel will be enlisted or appointed, trained, advanced or promoted, assigned duty and administered in all respects without regard to race, color, religion, or national origin.

In the utilization of housing, messing, berthing and other facilities, no special or unusual provisions will be made for the accommodation of any minority race.

Secretary of the Navy
7 June 1949

Throughout American history until the end of World War I, the navy had enlisted Negroes for general service, and Negro sailors had served and fought with credit throughout the fleet. After the First World War, however, the navy halted Negro enlistments; and when they were opened again in 1932, Negroes were recruited only for service in the messman's branch.

This was the situation at the beginning of World War II and it continued until six months after Pearl Harbor. The Selective Service Act of 1940 provided that "in the selection and training of men under this Act, and in the interpretation and execution of the provisions of this Act, there shall be no discrimination against any person on account of race or color." This provision had no immediate effect in opening up general service ratings to Negroes, however, because the navy continued to rely on voluntary recruiting until February 1943.

Consequently the navy continued its peacetime policy of restricting Negroes to the messman's branch on the ground that "the enlistment of Negroes (other than as mess attendants) leads to disruptive and undermining conditions." In response to public inquiries, the navy issued a statement explaining that:

the policy of not enlisting men of the colored race for any branch of the naval service but the messman's branch was adopted to meet the best interests of general ship efficiency. . . . This policy not only serves the best interests of the navy and the country, but serves as well the best interests of [Negroes] themselves.

After Pearl Harbor, however, the navy was subjected to considerable pressure from Negro organizations to expand its utilization of Negroes. The navy at first continued to insist on the exclusion of Negroes from general service, arguing that Negroes were not as adaptable or efficient as whites, and that segregation on shipboard was not feasible. After several exchanges of memoranda, the president finally wrote to the secretary of the navy that the matter "should be determined by you and me." Consequently on April 7, 1942, the navy announced that effective June 1 Negroes would be enlisted for general service as well as mess attendants. But these volunteers, the navy made clear, would receive basic and advanced training in segregated camps and schools, would be utilized in segregated units, and would be limited in assignment to shore installations and harbor craft. Negroes in general-service ratings would not be billeted in seagoing vessels, but would be used principally in construction battalions under the Bureau of Yards and Docks, in supply depots, ordnance stations, and yard (harbor) craft.

In February 1943, as the result of a presidential directive, the navy finally began to receive its manpower through Selective Service, and at the same time the War Manpower Commission insisted that the navy accept Negroes proportionately with the other services. The navy's monthly quota of Negroes mounted quickly from 2,700 to 5,000 then to 7,350 and finally to 12,000. As the influx of Negro selectees increased, the navy soon discovered that it could not find employment for all of them in shore installations and harbor craft. It also discovered that while the majority of the Negroes received through Selective Service was best fitted for unskilled and semiskilled labor, there was a large number possessing technical skills which could not be put to use so long as navy policy prevented the assignment of Negroes to the fleet. At the same time, considerable resentment began to be manifested among Negroes because of the concentration of Negro sailors in ordnance battalions, ammunition depots, and construction units.

Partly in response to this public agitation and partly because of its own concern over the waste of manpower, the navy sought a solution that would make it possible to prevent the waste without actually assigning Negroes to white crews in the fleet, which it still feared would cause friction and affect ship efficiency. In late 1943, it manned a destroyer escort and a patrol craft with predominantly Negro crews under white officers. This experiment was only partly successful, and even if it had been entirely successful, it obviously offered no solution to the problem, for Negroes were not available to man segregated cruisers and carriers.

Nine months later, in August 1944, the navy tried another and more practical experiment, assigning Negroes to twenty-five auxiliary ships of the fleet. These Negroes were integrated completely with white crews, but no ship was assigned more than 10 percent Negroes in its enlisted complement.

From the experiment with the two segregated ships the navy had satisfied itself that Negroes could be utilized aboard seagoing vessels in a far greater variety of skills than had been supposed. And from the experiment of assigning Negroes to twenty-five auxiliary vessels the navy learned that Negroes could be placed in white crews without trouble. Having learned these two lessons, the navy in April 1945 announced that henceforth Negro personnel would be eligible for service in all auxiliary fleet vessels, though the 10 percent quota for each ship would still be observed.

Concurrently with the change of policy on fleet assignment for Negro general ratings, the navy issued a "Guide to the Command of Negro Naval Personnel," in which it stated that "the navy accepts no theories of racial differences in inborn ability, but expects that every man wearing its uniform be trained and used in accordance with his maximum individual capacity determined on the basis of individual performance."

Meanwhile, in July 1944, the navy had abandoned its segregated advanced training schools for Negroes at Camp Robert Smalls and at Hampton Institute, declaring that it did not "consider practical the establishment of separate facilities and quotas for Negroes who qualify for advanced training." Boot training remained segregated, however, until July 1945, when the separate training camp at Great Lakes was abolished, and Negro trainees were assigned to the same companies, barracks, and messes as whites.

In December 1945, the secretary of the navy issued a directive to all ships and stations—Alnav 423–45—stating that:

In the administration of naval personnel no differentiation shall be made because of race or color. This applies also to authorized personnel of all the armed forces of this country aboard navy ships or at navy stations and activities.

And finally on February 27, 1946, the navy took the inevitable step of opening up general service assignments without any restriction. In Circular Letter 48–46, the navy ordered that—

Effective immediately all restrictions governing types of assignments for which Negro naval personnel are eligible are hereby lifted. Henceforth, they shall be eligible for all types of assignments in all ratings in all activities and all ships of the naval service....

In the utilization of housing, messing and other facilities, no special or unusual provisions will be made for the accommodation of Negroes.

The Committee Looks at the Navy

The committee was satisfied that in 1949 the stated navy policy on utilization of Negro enlisted personnel was, on the whole, a good one. The navy promised to Negroes in general service full equality of treatment and opportunity. Had this policy been conscientiously carried out?

The records of the Bureau of Personnel show that Negroes are presently serving aboard ship and at shore installations in every general-service rating. They are not yet, however, represented in top grades within every rating. This does not at this time indicate inequality of treatment, the committee is convinced, because considerable time is required to achieve the grade of chief or first-class petty officer, and the navy policy is comparatively recent. Furthermore, to achieve advanced grades in the more technical ratings, an enlisted man must spend long periods at service schools.

Since the end of the war a gradual shift has been taking place in the proportion of Negroes in general service and the messman's branch. At the end of 1945, slightly over 5 percent of the Negroes in the navy were in general ratings and almost 95 percent in the messman's branch. At the present time 42.6 percent are in general service and 57.4 percent in the messman's branch. Within the near future the number of Negroes in general service will probably exceed those in the messman's branch, since the navy after the war had a surplus of mess attendants and is no longer recruiting them.

Visits by the committee and its staff to ships, schools, and naval installations confirmed the Bureau of Personnel figures.

At Newport, RI, base of Destroyers Atlantic Fleet, the committee found Negroes with general ratings serving in destroyer crews in a wide variety of jobs.

At the New London, Conn., base of Submarines Atlantic Fleet, Negro submariners were in the crews of submarines, serving not only as messmen but in general service as torpedoman, boatswain's mate, electrician's mate, radioman, sonarman, etc. Negroes were likewise attending the submariner's school in New London.

At the naval air base at Quonset, RI, Negro mechanics were servicing planes; and aboard the Essex class carriers, USS *Leyte* and USS *Kearsarge*, which happened to be docked at Quonset at the time of the committee's visit, Negroes were working throughout the ships, in the engine and boiler rooms, as crane operators, on the plane elevators, as quartermasters and boatswain's mates, and in many other capacities.

In boot camp at the Naval Training Station, Great Lakes, Ill., the committee saw Negro trainees being processed with whites on their arrival and assigned to the same companies. In the six technical training schools at Great Lakes—electronics technician, machinist's mate, electrician's mate, fire controlman, engineman, and journalist— Negroes were represented in every course except journalist. In the difficult electronics technician school, a forty-eight-week course requiring a qualifying GCT score of 130 (as contrasted with 110 for wartime officer candidate school), there were five Negro students.

The unvarying attitude of naval officers interviewed on the committee's trips was that they were interested solely in the maintenance of training standards and in job performance. If the individual Negro, like the individual white, met the standards and mastered his job, then he had a career in the navy.

Wherever the committee or its staff went in its investigation of navy practice, it found Negroes in general service—although in relatively small numbers—working, messing, and berthing side by side with whites, ashore and afloat.

Had the navy experienced any difficulty as the result of its policy of assigning men solely on the basis of individual ability and the needs of the service? The committee was particularly anxious to get a full and candid reply to this question, for until the navy had finally made the decision to assign Negroes to ships, it had firmly resisted any proposal to expand Negro utilization beyond the steward's branch on the ground that the intimate associations of ship life precluded any mixing of the races. Integration in general service, the navy had maintained, would not be in "the best interests of general ship efficiency."

The committee asked this question not only of commanding officers but also of petty officers and lower grades, both white and Negro. All of those questioned replied that there had been no racial friction. White and Negro sailors at times exchanged words and blows—as did white seamen among themselves—but these were flareups between individuals. There had been no racial animosity. So far as the committee could discover, what a sailor asked of his shipmate was that he do his job and not be a troublemaker.

The evidence on this question was reassuring, for it seemed to confirm a theory which the committee had held but which could be put to the proof only by field observation, namely, that respect created between individuals through competence on the job—the value which the workman sets upon workmanship—would translate itself over a period of time into personal respect and would facilitate the accommodation of the two races in their daily life, and thus act to break down artificial barriers.

The thing that most impressed the committee about the navy's experience was that in the relatively short space of five years the navy had moved from a policy of complete exclusion of Negroes from general service to a policy of complete integration in general service. In this about-face, the navy had not been primarily motivated by moral considerations or by a desire to equalize treatment and opportunity. Undoubtedly public opinion had been a factor in this reversal of policy, but chiefly the navy had been influenced by considerations of military efficiency and the need to economize human resources. Equality of treatment and opportunity, the navy had discovered, was a necessary and inevitable condition and byproduct of a sound policy of manpower utilization.

The navy had defended the nonutilization of Negroes in general service by citing the lower level of Negro skills and by appealing to the necessity of maintaining ship efficiency and ship morale. It had discovered that, as individuals, Negroes could be trained and utilized in as wide a range of skills as whites, and that failure to use them as individuals resulted in a waste of manpower which neither the navy nor the country could afford. Still driven by the imperative need for skilled men, the navy had put Negro ratings aboard ship and found that no trouble resulted. In defense of its new policy the navy now cites the skills of its Negro manpower and ship efficiency.

The Committee Makes Recommendations to the Navy

Although the committee found little to criticize in the new policy of the navy with respect to training and assignment, it was concerned that the opportunities which the navy offered had not attracted a larger number of Negroes to enlist for general service.

As of January 1, 1950—the date of the latest complete figures—the Negro enlisted strength was 15,747 out of a total of 330,098, or 4.7 percent. Of this total Negro enlisted strength 6,647 were in general ratings and 9,110 in the messman's branch. The percentage of Negroes in general ratings was exactly 2 percent.

The relatively small percentage of Negroes in general service could be partly attributed, the committee believed, to a long memory of the navy's earlier restrictive policy and to a general unawareness among Negroes that this policy had been discarded. Since the impression seemed to prevail that the navy lagged behind the other two services, the committee believed the navy should correct this impression.

The committee was also dissatisfied with the small number of Negro officers in the navy. During the war the navy had been slow to open its officer candidate school to Negroes. In 1942 two Negroes entered Harvard Medical School under the navy's officer training program. A year later the navy opened its V–12 program to Negroes; but since very few Negro students were enrolled in colleges offering V–12 training, only a small number of Negroes were in a position to take advantage of the program. Finally, in February 1944, the navy selected twenty-two Negro candidates for commissions in the Naval Reserve. Of these, twelve were finally selected for line officers and given the rank of ensign; ten were appointed staff officers with the rank of ensign or lieutenant junior grade and assigned to the chaplain, dental, medical, civil engineer, and supply corps.

By the end of the war the V–12 program had raised the number of Negro officers to fifty-eight. A few of these saw service on small craft or auxiliary ships, but for the most part they were assigned to recruit training and to technical training schools as instructors. Late in the war some of them were detailed to supply units in the Pacific where they commanded stevedore outfits.

After VJ-day, almost all the Negro officers, convinced by their wartime experience that the navy offered them no future, applied for demobilization and discharge. When the committee began its work early in 1949, there were only four Negro officers on active duty. On January 1, 1950, there were seventeen Negro officers on active duty, including two WAVE officers. Of these, eight were regular officers, and nine were reserve.

The two principal sources of naval officers at the present time are the Naval Academy and the Naval Reserve Officers Training Corps—the so-called Holloway program. When the Holloway program is fully operative, the navy will subsidize in part the college education of 15,000 students each year in 55 colleges and universities. There are presently two Negroes at Annapolis, and nine Negroes in the Holloway program. There are also twelve Negro college students taking summer training in the Reserve Officers Corps.

Although the competition for the Holloway scholarships is rigorous, the committee felt the small number of Negroes participating in its benefits was due partly to ignorance of the program among Negro students and partly, perhaps, to a suspicion that the navy, on the basis of its grudging and negligible commissioning of Negroes in World War II, did not welcome Negro officers. The committee again thought the navy should make quite clear that there were no racial restrictions upon Holloway scholarships and no racial bars to a navy commission, except to the extent that Negroes winning a Holloway scholarship are automatically limited in their selection of a school to those Holloway colleges which admit Negroes.

While the committee was satisfied that Negroes in general service enjoyed equal treatment and opportunity, it did find evidence of discrimination against Negroes in the steward's branch. Chief stewards in the navy, it learned, received the pay and the perquisites, but not the grade, of chief petty officer. The same was true of first-, second-, and third-class stewards.

In the hope of increasing the number of Negroes in general service and the Holloway program, and to correct the inequality in the steward's branch, the committee recommended in May 1949, that—

1. The navy, in its recruiting literature and press releases, make evident its policy of utilizing qualified Negroes in all general-service ratings on the same basis as white personnel.

2. A number of Negro reserve officers be recalled to active duty to serve in the recruiting program.

3. The navy take positive steps to inform Negro high school and college students of the Holloway program.

4. Chief stewards receive the grade of chief petty officer.[2]

On June 7, 1949, the Navy accepted all of the committee's recommendations. Five Negro reserve officers were selected to return to active duty in the recruiting service. In its recruiting matter and press releases the navy has taken pains to show Negro enlisted men working and living with whites in boot camp, technical schools, and aboard ship. Representatives of several Negro newspapers were in the press delegation on a European cruise of the USS *Missouri* in the summer of 1949, and filed stories and pictures to their papers on the job assignments and living conditions of Negro sailors aboard.

In the fall of 1949 Negro officers visited schools in Washington, DC, and sixteen southern cities to interest Negro students in the Holloway program.

In July 1949, the navy issued an order giving chief stewards the grade of chief petty officer, and a month later announced that, effective January 1, 1950, first-, second-, and third-class stewards would become first-, second-, and third-class petty officers.

In addition, the navy also announced in June that stewards would have the privilege, if qualified, of transferring to other ratings.

On its own initiative the navy abolished segregation in the Marine Corps during basic training. After basic training, however, some Negro marines are assigned to Negro units, and in this respect the Marine Corps has not yet fully carried out navy policy.

It is too early to judge the success of the measures undertaken to increase the number of Negroes in general service and in the Holloway program. Although the navy has given considerable publicity to the opportunities which general service offers to the qualified Negro, two factors have militated against an increase in the Negro strength in general ratings. First, recruiting quotas have been so drastically reduced in recent months that the number of Negro enlistments has not affected the percentage of Negroes in general ratings. Second, the rejection rate of Negro applicants has been much higher than that of whites. The navy's mental enlistment standard is currently at 90, and the percentage of Negroes above this level—16 percent against 67 percent for whites—is reflected in the enlistment figures. Furthermore, the small enlistment quotas have resulted in a waiting list which allows the navy to meet its monthly requirements from applicants on the list with the highest qualifications.

The navy's efforts to increase the number of Negroes in the Holloway program have also had disappointing results thus far. The reason for this seems to be twofold—the quality of education which Negroes in some parts of the country have received and the stiff competition which even the well-educated Negro applicant must meet. Although 2,700 Negroes in the 17 southern cities visited by navy representatives last fall filled out applications to take the preliminary examination, only 250 actually took the test. Of these 250, only 2 passed the examination and 1 of these later failed the physical examination because of poor eyesight.

Until Negroes receive more appointments to Annapolis, and until they can compete with greater success for Holloway scholarships, it is unlikely that the number of Negro officers will be much increased.

---

[2]Another recommendation, submitted to all three services, proposed that the services adopt equal enlistment standards. This recommendation was made conditional on a study by the Department of Defense to determine the jobs in each service which could be filled by men in the lowest category acceptable to all three services. This study has not been completed. [Footnote in the original.]

While the number of Negro officers and the percentage of Negroes in general service leave much to be desired, numbers alone, the committee is convinced, are not a reliable index of equal opportunity. So long as Negroes have a full and equal chance to enlist in general service and to qualify for NROTC scholarships, the situation with respect to numbers should improve as educational opportunities and facilities are made accessible to them.

IV. THE AIR FORCE

The President's Policy Is Put Into Effect and the Results Are Examined

It is the policy of the United States Air Force that there shall be equality of treatment and opportunity for all persons in the air force without regard to race, color, religion, or national origin. . . .

There will be no strength quotas of minority groups in the air force troop basis. . . .

Qualified Negro personnel may be assigned to fill any position vacancy in any air force organization or overhead installation without regard to race. . . .

All air force personnel will be considered on the basis of individual merit and ability and must qualify according to prescribed standards for enlistment, attendance at schools, promotion, assignment to specific duties, etc.

All individuals, regardless of race, will be accorded equal opportunity for appointment, advancement, professional improvement, promotion and retention in all components of the Air Force of the United States.

Air Force Letter
11 May 1949

The experience of the navy seemed to the committee to answer rather conclusively the two basic questions which had always been raised about the utilization of Negro personnel: Can Negroes be effectively employed in as wide a range of skills as white? Can the races be integrated on the job, in barracks and messes, without impairing morale and service efficiency? The navy had found that unless Negroes were trained and utilized according to their individual capacities, wastage of manpower resulted, and that this wastage was made inevitable by segregation. The navy had also found that Negro and white sailors would work together, eat at the same messes and sleep in the same quarters without trouble.

Confronted by the navy experience, some military officials maintained that it did not provide a reliable basis for generalization because of the relatively small number of Negroes involved. If, these officials suggested, Negroes had comprised 7 to 10 percent of the men in general service rather than 2 percent, the navy experience might have been quite different.

The committee was skeptical of this argument, but it could not gainsay it without concrete evidence to the contrary. The experience of the air force has supplied that evidence.

Air Force Racial Policy in World War II

During World War II the racial policy of the air force was that of the parent army—a 10 percent restriction on Negro enlisted strength, utilization in segregated units, and greatly limited job opportunities.

These policies were rigidly adhered to. By VJ-day there were approximately 140,000 Negroes in the air force—roughly 8 percent of total strength—and virtually all of them were in racial units. Except for the all-Negro 99th Fighter Squadron, the 332d Fighter Group, and the 477th Bombardment Group,[3] Negroes in the air force were concentrated for the most part in air cargo resupply squadrons, MP companies, ordnance ammunition companies, aviation engineer battalions, signal construction battalions, quartermaster truck companies, airdrome defense battalions, air base security battalions, and medical detachments. That is, Negroes had been used chiefly in service capacities and for heavy-duty work, regardless of their individual skills and aptitudes. The only notable exceptions to this rule, involving relatively few men, were the ground crews and administrative personnel attached to the three Negro flying units.

By the end of the war many high-ranking officers in the air force were convinced that the concentration of almost all Negroes in a relatively narrow range of duties had deprived the service generally of many skills which were lost by reason of segregation. The air force also discovered that the malassignment which resulted from segregation cut two ways. It not only condemned men of superior skill to jobs where their abilities were wasted; it also forced the placement of men of insufficient skill in positions for which they were not equipped. Any standardized military unit—whether manned by whites or Negroes—provides for so many officers and so many enlisted men of specified skills, depending on the function and mission of the unit. In a white unit, the only job qualification is ability. In a racial unit there is the additional qualification of color. If a first-rate Negro officer or specialist cannot be found for the job, then it must be filled by a second-, third-, or fourth-rate man, for the table of organization and equipment requires that the job be filled and racial policy insists it be filled by a Negro. The reverse side of the segregation coin was brought home to the air force most sharply when it formed the 477th Bombardment Group fairly late in the war. Since most of the more highly qualified Negroes were already in the services, the air force, in order to man the group, had to accept many men who did not come close to meeting air force standards.

In the two years following the war a number of memoranda were prepared by air force staff agencies, recommending that Negro airmen, like white, be used solely on the basis of their individual qualifications, and that no air force jobs carry a color bar. But these same memoranda were equally insistent that segregation must be maintained because of social custom and the possibility of difficulty if Negro and white airmen were placed in the same unit.

The authors of these memoranda had clearly recognized the waste of skilled Negro manpower. They had not yet arrived at a point where they saw that this waste could not be repaired within a framework of segregation.

---

[3]The 99th Fighter Squadron and the 332d Fighter Group saw service in the Mediterranean Theater. The 477th Bombardment Squadron had just completed training as the war ended. [Footnote in the original.]

The Air Force Adopts a New Policy

The air force remained impaled on the points of this dilemma until the president issued Executive Order 9981 in July 1948. Spurred by this order, the air force set to work to evolve a policy which would simultaneously improve the efficiency of the service and extend equality of treatment and opportunity to all personnel. By November 1948 it had framed such a policy and forwarded it to the secretary of defense, together with a detailed program for effectuating the policy within a year's time.

The new policy called for—

1. The abandonment of all racial quotas for enlistment and selection for service schools.

2. The opening of all occupational specialties to qualified personnel on the basis of ability without racial restriction.

3. The placing of enlistment, school attendance, assignment to duty and promotion on a basis of individual merit and ability according to prescribed standards.

Some Negro units, the air force stated, would be continued; but Negroes would not be restricted in assignment, nor necessarily assigned, to Negro units.

Apparently anticipating that this departure would be viewed with apprehension by some officers, Air Force Headquarters added as a note of reassurance:

> It has been proven in both the navy and the Coast Guard, and on a smaller scale by our own experience in the Air Training Command, that well-qualified Negro individuals can be absorbed into white organizations without insurmountable social or morale problems arising as a result of such assignment. Experience by sister services further indicates that a relatively small percentage of Negroes will be able to attain required standards in free competition with all other air force personnel.

The air force warned commanders that:

> care should be taken to ensure that a reasonably small number of Negro personnel is assigned to any individual white organization; in no case will the Negro enlisted strength of the organization exceed 10 percent of the total enlisted strength of the organization without prior approval of this headquarters. This limitation will not apply to student populations . . .

To effect this policy, the air force proposed to take the following steps:

1. A board of officers appointed by the Continental Air Command would screen the personnel at the all-Negro Lockbourne Air Base in Ohio, home of the 332d Fighter Wing. As a result of this screening, those men eligible for separation under current policies applicable to all personnel would be separated. All others would, according to their individual qualifications, be assigned to flying or technical schools for further training, or transferred to positions in other commands.

2. Further, each major command would screen its own Negro personnel for assignment according to the following rules:

a. Negroes currently assigned to Negro units but actually working with white organizations would be transferred to the organization with which they were performing their duties.

b. Negroes assigned to and working with Negro units, but possessing the skills and qualifications for assignment to white units, would be reassigned to vacancies in white organizations.

c. Negroes qualified for school training and desiring to attend school would be sent to technical schools for which they were qualified.

d. A Negro could be retained in a Negro unit if (1) he so desired, (2) he was in a key position and necessary to the successful functioning of the unit, (3) he was considered best suited for assignment in a Negro unit by his commander.

This policy and program, which had been formulated in response to the president's executive order, the air force laid before the president's committee at its first meeting in January 1949. The committee thought the proposals represented a great advance over existing policy. It had, nevertheless, serious reservations about two provisions in the new program—the 10 percent limitation upon Negro strength in any one unit, and the discretion left to commanders to determine whether individual Negroes were best suited for assignment to racial units. Consequently the committee decided to suspend judgment on the air force proposals until it had had an opportunity to make further studies of all three services.

On April 6, 1949, the secretary of defense released a memorandum which he had sent to the three service secretaries. In this memorandum he reiterated the president's policy on equality of treatment and opportunity and asked the services to prepare a program to carry out the executive order.

In reply to this memorandum the air force resubmitted its earlier proposals in essentially their original form. There were, however, significant omissions. In the first place, the air force had eliminated the 10 percent limitation upon Negroes in any one unit. Second, commanders were no longer empowered to decide whether individual Negroes were best fitted for Negro units. Finally, the air force had deleted its earlier estimate that "a relatively small percentage of Negroes will be able to attain required standards in free competition with all other air force personnel," and also its previous warning to commanders that Negroes must "be spread evenly through air force units" with only "a reasonably small number" in any white organization.

The changes in policy and language disposed of the committee's objections to the original draft, and the committee decided to await the results of this program before making any further recommendations to the air force. Meanwhile, the air force had reduced its estimate of the time required to effectuate the plan from one year to six months.

The Committee Looks at the Air Force

The air force began implementing its new program on June 1, 1949. During the ensuing months the committee did not inquire into the progress the air force was making, but voluntarily the air force submitted periodic reports on what it soon came to call its "integration program." At the end of November, exactly six months after orders had gone to field commanders, Air Force Headquarters notified the committee it was prepared for a thorough field investigation of the results of its new policy.

In the middle of January 1950, the staff of the committee made an investigation of seven air force bases. These were the Headquarters Base, Bolling Field, Washington, DC; Maxwell Air Force Base, the location of the Air War College and Air Command and Staff School, Montgomery, Ala.; Davis-Monthan Air Force Base in the Strategic Air Command, Tucson, Ariz.; Lackland Air Force Base, the basic training station at San Antonio, Tex.; Williams Air Force Base, Chandler, Ariz., a jet flying school;

Keesler Air Force Base, Biloxi, Miss., a technical training school in radar operations; and Scott Air Force Base, East St. Louis, Ill., a technical training school in radio repair and maintenance. The last four bases are all under the Training Command.

On this trip the committee's staff found only one segregated unit. At six of the bases visited, the so-called Air Base Service Squadrons—all-Negro units whose personnel worked with whites in various post housekeeping duties but returned to separate quarters for eating, sleeping, and recreation—had been broken up. The Negroes in these units had been screened, as directed by Air Force Headquarters, and those qualified for school training had been sent to school. Those not qualified for school training had been retained in their present jobs but transferred to white units. Those eligible for discharge under current regulations applying to all personnel had been separated. Whether retained in their present duties, sent to school, or transferred to other commands, they were now mixed with white airmen at work, in the classroom, and in barracks and messes.

At the basic training center at Lackland Field, Tex., Negro trainees upon their arrival were processed with white trainees, and assigned to the same flights and squadrons. Each flight of sixty trainees was in the immediate command of a flight chief and assistant flight chief, both noncommissioned officers. There were Negro flight chiefs and assistant flight chiefs at Lackland in charge of mixed flights. There were, as well, Negro instructors in some of the courses, and Negro counsellors advising trainees in the selection of their career jobs.

The same situation was observed in the technical schools in the Training Command. At Keesler Air Force Base in Biloxi, which trains officers and enlisted men in the operation of electronics and weather equipment, Negro students—officers and enlisted men—formed 7 percent of the total student population, and Negro enlisted men represented 7.7 percent of the total enlisted students.

At Scott Air Force Base, East St. Louis, which trains communications officers and radio repairmen, Negro students comprised slightly over 9 percent of the total enlisted school population.

At Williams Air Force Base, Chandler, Ariz., where jet pilots receive their training, there were three Negro officers instructing in jet fighters; two Negroes in training to be instructors in jets; and two Negro cadets receiving instruction.

At Davis-Monthan Air Force Base in Tucson, Negro mechanics were working on the line and in the hangars, servicing and repairing B–50 and B–29 bombers.

At Bolling Field, Washington, DC, the nonoperating base of the Headquarters Command, Negroes were working in maintenance and supply, refueling squadrons, motor vehicle squadron, air police, medical detachments, radio repair and food service. Prior to the integration program, the only Negroes at the Headquarters Base had been orderlies.

The Evolving Pattern Under the Air Force Policy

The new air force policy had said nothing about recreational facilities. These matters were left largely to the discretion and judgment of the individual commanding officer. The disposition of most commanding officers was not to impose a rigid pattern, but to keep the situation fluid and let relationships evolve according to the wishes of the men. The effect of this hands-off policy has been a steady movement in the direction of shared facilities. This apparently is not a conscious or calculated movement, but a natural development of daily contact at work, in school, in barracks and dining halls. Here again, mutual respect engendered on the job on in school seemed to translate itself into friendly association.

Almost without exception the commanders interviewed by the committee's staff stated that they had put the new policy into effect with some misgivings. They did not for a moment question the accuracy of headquarters opinion that "the traditional utilization of Negro manpower primarily in Negro units has contained certain elements of waste and efficiency [sic]." But they doubted whether, in open competition with whites, many Negroes would be able to qualify for technical positions, and they questioned whether the gain in manpower utilization would be worth the trouble they expected from assigning Negroes to white units.

Without exception commanding officers reported that their fears had not been borne out by events. A far larger proportion of Negroes than expected had demonstrated their capacity to compete with whites on an equal basis, to absorb highly technical school training, and to perform creditably in their subsequent assignments. Evidence of this ability to compete was supplied by the technical schools in the training command. In the six air force technical schools, Negro enlisted students, in December 1949, comprised 6.5 percent of total enlisted enrollment, as compared to the overall Negro enlisted strength of 7.2 percent. In some schools the percentage of Negro students exceeded the percentage of enlisted Negroes in the air force—an indication of the present quality of Negro enlistees.

The extent of malassignment under segregation is indicated by the results of the screening of Negro personnel ordered by Air Force Headquarters. At eight bases screened by personnel experts from Lackland Field, it was found that anywhere from 12 to 37 percent of the Negro airmen at these bases were qualified for further technical school training. With the abandonment of segregation these Negroes could be sent to school and then assigned to jobs in white units for which they were qualified.

Furthermore, commanders testified that racial incidents had diminished, rather than increased, since the new policy had gone into effect. With all schools and jobs open on a basis of merit, officers were no longer plagued with complaints of discrimination. Some officers who candidly stated their personal preference for the old ways nevertheless volunteered that the new program benefited the service and caused less trouble.

The Question of Numbers

The opinion had been expressed that the navy's policy of equal treatment and opportunity in general service was possible because Negroes represented only 2 percent of general ratings. The air force experience seemed to the committee effectively to contradict this argument.

On January 31, 1950, there were 25,702 Negroes in the air force—25,351 enlisted men and 351 officers. The percentage of Negro enlisted men was 7.2 percent; the percentage of Negro officers 0.6 percent.

A breakdown of Negro assignment by unit showed—

Negroes still in predominantly Negro units 6,773
Negroes in mixed units 11,611
Negroes in pipeline 7,318
                                                               25,702

Pipeline includes men in basic training, technical, and flying schools, and en route to new assignments. With few exceptions, the Negroes in pipeline are integrated with whites. The overall percentage of Negroes integrated during the first 8 months of the air force program was approximately 74 percent.[4] The number of integrated units totaled 1,301; the number of predominantly Negro units remaining was 59. In June 1949, when the new policy went into effect, there were 106 Negro units, and only 167 mixed units.

Within the Training Command, Negroes represented 0.9 percent of total personnel currently taking flight training; and 6 percent of total personnel in technical training schools. In basic training during January 1950, the Negro percentage was 8.8. In officer candidate training 3 percent of the candidates were Negro.

Conclusions

The following conclusions were borne out by the experience of the navy and air force:

1. The range of individual Negro abilities is much wider than the services had assumed prior to the opening of all jobs in the navy and air force.

2. Given sufficiently high enlistment standards, it does not follow that only a "relatively small percentage" of Negroes will be able to meet the competition of whites.

3. The services cannot afford to waste these potential Negro skills.

4. There will be wastage and malassignment of manpower under segregation because there is no assurance that individual Negro skills can be, or will be, utilized in racial units.

5. Integration of the two races at work, in school, and in living quarters did not present insurmountable difficulties. As a matter of fact, integration in two of the services had brought a decrease in racial friction.

6. The enlisted men were far more ready for integration than the officers had believed.

7. The attitude of command was a substantial factor in the success of the racial policies of the air force and the navy.

V. THE ARMY

Four Steps Forward

The policy of the Department of the Army is that there shall be equality of treatment and opportunity for all persons in the army without regard to race, color, religion, or national origin. All manpower will be utilized to obtain maximum efficiency in the army.

Army school quotas . . . will make no reference to race or color. Selection of personnel to attend army schools will be made without regard to race or color. . . .

Military occupational specialties will be open to qualified enlisted personnel without regard to race or color. . . .

In furtherance of the policy of the president . . . it is the objective of the

---

[4]It should be noted that of the 6,773 Negroes still in Negro units 2,369 were in army units assigned to the air force, to which the integration policy did not apply. Furthermore, there were 1,770 whites in the predominantly Negro units. [Footnote in the original.]

Department of the Army that Negro manpower possessing appropriate skills and qualifications will be utilized in accordance with such skills and qualifications, and will be assigned to any T/D [overhead] or T/O&E [organized] unit without regard to race or color.

SR 600–629–1
16 January 1950

Effective with the month of April all enlistments in the army within overall recruiting quotas will be open to qualified applicants without regard to race or color.

Staff Message to Army Commands
27 March 1950

There have been Negro units in the regular army ever since 1866 when Congress by statute established two infantry and two cavalry regiments of colored soldiers. In World War I Negroes served in a variety of supply and supporting units, principally in supply trains and in port, engineer, and pioneer troop battalions, and also in two combat divisions, both of which saw duty in France. The Ninety-second Division fought as a unit; the four regiments of the Ninety-third Division were separately brigaded with French divisions.

Although Negro combat outfits fought well in World War I and received several unit citations from the American and French governments, the performance of the Negro regiments was not uniform. After the war, studies by the army were critical of the organization and training of the Negro combat divisions. The Negro divisional regiments had not been trained together prior to embarkation, and divisional artillery did not complete its training until after it reached France. The nucleus of some of the regiments was National Guard units which were relatively well-trained and proficient; other regiments, composed largely of illiterate and unskilled recruits, were not effective. As a result the combat efficiency of the Negro regiments varied, and every study of Negro manpower utilization which was conducted by the Army War College between wars recommended that the army never again form Negro units of divisional size. Despite these recommendations and contrary to the assurance which the army gave to Selective Service that Negro divisions would not be formed, the Ninety-second and Ninety-third Divisions were reactivated in World War II.

The Army's Traditional Negro Troop Policy

Traditionally, two views have influenced army thinking on the utilization of Negro troops. First, that Negro troops must be used in separate units. Second, that Negro troop strength must not exceed the Negro proportion in the civilian population. In all mobilization plans between wars, the use of Negro soldiers was premised on these two principles.

On October 9, 1940, the White House released a statement which had been prepared by the War Department, declaring that—

It is the policy of the War Department that the services of Negroes will be utilized on a fair and equitable basis. In line with this policy provision will be made as follows:

1. The strength of the Negro personnel of the Army of the United States will be maintained on the general basis of the proportion of the Negro population of the country. . . .

7. The policy of the War Department is not to intermingle colored and white enlisted personnel in the same regimental organizations. This policy has been proven satisfactory over a long period of years and to make changes would produce situations destructive to morale and detrimental to the preparations for national defense. . . .

If military efficiency is taken as a criterion, the statement that the army's policy of segregation had "proven satisfactory over a long period of years" was not one which could be documented by the files in the Army's Historical Records Section, nor by the studies prepared by the Army War College. If the historical records established anything, they proved conclusively that the army had not received maximum efficient utilization from its segregated units and had experienced endless trouble. The War College studies, while rarely recommending the abandonment of segregation, made the same conclusions inescapable.

Furthermore, opinion among general officers did not uniformly support the army's traditional policy. As early as 1922, a distinguished general, a southerner, warned the army that the employment of Negro troops in large separate units wasted manpower and fomented trouble. Racial friction, this general declared, most frequently developed not between individuals but between groups, and he advised the army to intersperse Negro soldiers one or two to a squad. In this general's opinion, the internal esprit which inevitably developed in a small group of men engaged in the same task would assure the Negro of acceptance and protect him against discrimination. The result would be more effective utilization of Negro manpower, less trouble and better morale. The same counsel was offered to the army by another general officer at the beginning of World War II.

Most of the difficulties which the army had experienced in World War I were repeated and multiplied in World War II. By the spring of 1945, the assistant secretary of war heading the Special Troop Policies Committee, which had been created to deal with the mounting problems connected with Negro troops, came to the conclusion that, whatever arguments might be adduced in support of the army's racial policy, military efficiency and high morale were not among them. The assistant secretary urged the army to conduct a thorough staff and field study of the results of its racial policy and to revise that policy on the basis of past experience.

As a result of reports by field commanders throughout the war and the exhaustive study undertaken in response to the recommendation of the Special Troop Policies Committee, the army had also come to the conclusion by the fall of 1945 that its policy over a long period of years had not proved satisfactory and that changes must be made in the utilization of Negro troops in the postwar army.

Therefore, in October 1945, the army convened a special board of general officers, known as the Gillem Board, and charged it with submitting recommendations to the secretary of war and the chief of staff.

The Gillem Board

The Gillem Board sat for three and a half months. At the conclusion of its studies the board was possessed of two unshakeable convictions. First, that Negroes had made immense strides in education and industrial skill over the past twenty years; and, second, that the army had not taken sufficient account of this progress.

On these two facts the Gillem Board based its conclusions and recommendations. And in so doing, it rejected the counsel of several high-ranking officers who maintained that Negro soldiers had proved most effective in such jobs as truck driver and heavy construction worker, and should therefore be concentrated in the Engineer Corps and supply services.

The Gillem Board was firmly convinced that the army must expand, and not further contract, the jobs in which Negroes could serve. "Many Negroes," it declared, "who, before the war, were laborers, are now craftsmen, capable in many instances of competing with the white man on an equal basis." Therefore, "the principle of economy of forces clearly indicates . . . that every effort must be expended to utilize efficiently every qualified individual in a position in the military structure for which he is best suited."

But here the Gillem Board was confronted by a dilemma. How was this principle of economy of forces to be applied to Negro troops? Clearly there were only two courses open to the army if it were to "utilize efficiently every qualified individual in a position in the military structure for which he is best suited."

The army could treat the Negro soldier like any other individual, assigning him solely on the basis of ability and army need without any attempt at segregation because of race or color. Or the army could attempt to create a separate Negro army which would have the same variety of units and require the same range of skills as the white army.

The Gillem Board decided on the second alternative. It decided that segregation must be maintained; and therefore, if the Negro soldier were to be used according to his individual capacity, Negro units must be created which would conform in general to white units.

Having made this basic decision to segregate the Negro soldier and make him the subject of special treatment, the Gillem Board was compelled to make several consequent recommendations. In the first place, it was doubtful whether the army could actually form from the 10 percent Negro component the same variety of units as could be formed from the 90 percent white component, especially since the abilities and skills of the Negro soldiers, as a group, did not parallel those of the white soldiers as a group. Therefore, the Gillem Board proposed that individually qualified Negroes be assigned freely to overhead units as well as to regularly organized Negro units. An overhead unit is a post housekeeping detail which performs the duties connected with the administration of an army base. Negroes assigned to overhead units, the Gillem Board planned, would work with whites on a "duty interspersal" basis, but would have their own segregated messes, barracks and dayrooms. By opening up overhead installations to Negroes, the board hoped to provide job opportunities for those whose skills might not be used in regular Negro units.

In the second place, if the Negro soldier were to be considered a special case, then it was necessary that some agency be charged with looking after his welfare. The Gillem Board, therefore, recommended that a staff group be formed in the General Staff Division of Personnel and Administration and in the staff of each major command to plan, implement and revise policies affecting racial minorities. The board further recommended that the army periodically conduct manpower studies to determine the positions in each army installation which could be filled by Negro personnel.

The Gillem Board not only accepted the old premise that segregation is necessary;

it also reconfirmed the principle that Negro strength must be proportionate to the civilian population. But there was an inconsistency involved in this decision, and the Gillem Board was aware of it. While the Negro strength was at 10 percent, the army suspended original Negro enlistments. At the same time, it continued to reenlist Negroes. A large number of the Negro reenlistments were "professional privates"—men of low GCT score and little technical skill who had stayed in the army after the war and who were of limited value to a peacetime training army. How could a Negro with superior qualifications get into the army if the Negro quota were largely preempted by professional privates? And how could the army create new Negro units offering a wider range of skills if it did not have the Negroes with the necessary qualifications to man the units and if its reenlistment policy made it impossible to secure them?

To meet this difficulty the Gillem Board proposed that the army deny reenlistment to regular army soldiers, Negroes and whites alike, who met only the minimum enlistment standards. The Gillem Board hoped by this device to create room within the 10 percent quota for highly qualified Negroes who would have the skills required for the new units which were to be formed. It also hoped by the elimination of the professional private, both white and Negro, to improve the caliber of the peacetime training army.

Finally, the Gillem Board tacitly recognized the fact that segregation, in itself, undoubtedly had an effect on the efficiency and morale of Negro combat units. In the winter of 1945, some twenty-five hundred Negro soldiers from the supply services had answered a call for volunteers for frontline duty. These Negro volunteers had been formed into platoons and assigned to white companies. The combat performance of these platoons had effectively established the feasibility of integration at this level without difficulty.[5] The board acknowledged the success of this experiment in its conclusions:

> *Experiments and other experience of World War II indicate clearly that the most successful employment of Negro units occurred when they were employed as units closely associated with white units on similar tasks, and a greater degree of success was obtained when small Negro organizations were so employed.*

Consequently, the board recommended that "experimental groupings of Negro units with white units in composite organizations be continued in the postwar army as a policy," and that the ultimate objective of army policy be "the effective use of *all* manpower made available to the military establishment in the event of a major mobilization at some unknown date against an undetermined aggressor . . . without regard to antecedents or race."

These, then, were the six principal recommendations of the Gillem Board:

1. Negro units in the postwar army should in general conform to white units.

2. Qualified Negroes should be used in overhead units.

3. A staff group in Army Headquarters and in every major command should be created to supervise racial policy and practice.

4. Periodic surveys of manpower should be made to determine positions that Negroes could fill.

5. Reenlistment should be denied to the professional private.

---

[5]The report of the President's Committee on Civil Rights—*To Secure These Rights*—reproduces in large part the results of a survey among white soldiers following this experiment. Three out of four white soldiers said their attitude toward Negroes had changed after serving beside them in combat. The army, feeling that this experiment was not representative and fearing possible unfortunate repercussions, decided against publishing the results of the survey during the war. [Footnote in the original.]

6. There should be experimental groupings of Negro and white units.

If these key recommendations were adopted, the Gillem Board believed, the army would benefit by increased efficiency and the Negro soldier by fuller opportunity. But, the board admonished,

Courageous leadership in implementing the program is imperative. All ranks must be imbued with the necessity for a straightforward, unequivocating attitude toward the maintenance and preservation of a forward-thinking policy. Vacillation or weak implementation of a strong policy will adversely affect the army. The policy which is advocated is consistent with the democratic ideals upon which the nation and its representative army are based.

The Committee Looks at the Army

On the basis of its historical researches, the president's committee agreed essentially with the Gillem Board's assessment of the army's use of Negro manpower in World War II. The army, it was true, had underestimated the progress which the Negro had made in education and technical skill, and as a consequence had not realized the potential of its Negro manpower. The committee agreed that the army must henceforth utilize effectively every individual in the position for which he was best fitted.

The committee doubted, however, whether the recommendations of the Gillem Board were capable of achieving the board's objective. In the first place, and considering the problem purely in the abstract without any evidence of what the Gillem Board program had accomplished over three years, the committee questioned whether it were possible to equalize the job opportunities of white and Negro soldiers merely by creating new Negro units and by opening up overhead installations to Negroes.

In the second place, the committee doubted that the Gillem Board had sufficiently considered whether segregation must not by its very nature defeat the board's objective. Segregation, the committee was convinced, forced inefficiency in two ways. By requiring skilled Negroes to serve in racial units, the army lost skills which could find no place in Negro organizations. On the other hand, by concentrating large numbers of unskilled Negroes in combat units, it multiplied inefficiency. For example, the army had discovered in World War II that the combat effectiveness of white units was dangerously weakened when more than 5 to 10 percent of their men were in grade V, the lowest classification. Yet the army had sent Negro units into battle with 49 percent of the men in grade V, and 80–90 percent in grades IV and V. White combat units, on the other hand, averaged about 5 percent in grade V and 32 percent in grades IV and V.

Finally, the committee could find no justification for continuing the 10 percent quota system when the army's declared objective was the utilization of every qualified individual according to his ability. In this context, the policy of limiting Negro strength to the civilian proportion was irrelevant and arbitrary. The only relevant consideration was not whether the Negro strength was 10 percent or 12 percent, or even only 7 percent, but whether the Negroes in the army, given equal opportunity, met army standards and qualified for their jobs in competition with all other personnel. If as individuals they could satisfy the army's standards and meet the competition, then they should have the jobs; if they could not qualify or stand up against competition, then they should not have the jobs. But they should not be in the service simply because the army had a policy of maintaining an arbitrary 10 percent Negro strength.

In short, it seemed to the committee that the Gillem Board sought equal treatment and efficient utilization of manpower within a framework that foredoomed the realization of either.

These, however, were judgments that needed to be tested. What had actually been accomplished during the three years the Gillem Board's policies had been operative?[6]

With respect to the Gillem Board's recommendation to create Negro units conforming generally to white units, the army had in three years converted nineteen units from white to Negro designation. Of these nineteen units, five were divisional battalions; the remainder were nondivisional units, of which two were of battalion size, and the rest companies. Most of these units—four were artillery, one infantry, the rest heavy construction and service units—were of a type in which Negroes were already serving. Consequently while the conversion of the nineteen units from white to Negro increased the number of jobs, it did not much expand the types of jobs available to Negroes.

Despite some initial opposition to making Negro units organic parts of larger white organizations, the army had made progress in grouping white and Negro units together in composite organizations. This process had generally stopped, however, with the assignment of Negro battalions to white regiments, although there were several instances of Negro companies serving in white battalions.

The only really significant advance which resulted from the Gillem Board recommendations was made in utilizing Negroes in overhead installations. A survey taken in 1947, a year after the Gillem policy went into effect, showed that, army-wide, Negroes formed 13 percent of overhead employment. However, the pattern was far from uniform, some commands employing as much as 30 percent Negroes in overhead, and others employing a few or none at all. Moreover, although the picture looked good in total numbers, closer inspection showed that the majority of Negroes in overhead units were employed in a relatively few occupations—truck driver, cook, baker, duty soldier (manual laborer), and clerk typist. For example, of the 879 Negroes employed in overhead in the Third Army at the time of the 1947 survey, 597 were employed as cook, military policeman, duty soldier, duty noncommissioned officer, and truck driver.

Two years later in May 1949, the committee found much the same situation in a visit to Fort Knox. In one army service unit, forming the station overhead complement for Headquarters Section at Fort Knox, there were 666 whites and 165 Negroes, or over 19 percent Negroes—a very good numerical showing. But cooks, food service apprentices, MPs, firemen, duty soldiers, fire fighters, and truck drivers accounted for 109 of the 165 Negro positions. Moreover, in the army service unit serving as overhead for the headquarters company of the Armored School at Fort Knox, there were 155 whites in overhead and no Negroes. And in the division overhead for the Third Armored Division at Fort Knox, there were 1,200 whites and only 26 Negroes—most of them bandsmen and clerk typists.

The Gillem Board proposal to use Negroes in overhead units had doubtless widened somewhat the range of jobs available to Negroes in the army; yet when the committee in 1949 examined the whole field of army occupations, it found a large number of jobs which were still closed to Negroes.

---

[6]The army had not approved the board's recommendations on reenlistment and special staff groups. It did approve the recommendation on periodic surveys of jobs to be filled by Negroes, but these surveys were never made. [Footnote in the original.]

For example, as of August 1949, the army had 490 active occupational specialties. In 198 of these specialties, there were no authorizations at all for Negroes.

There were 245 specialties with authorizations for 10 or more whites and authorizations for 10 or less Negroes.

In 91 specialties there were authorizations for 10 or less Negroes and for 100 or more whites.

There were 144 specialties with authorizations for 10 or more whites and no authorizations for Negroes.

These figures give some idea of the failure of segregated and overhead units to furnish vacancies for skilled Negroes.

What made this situation even less defensible in the committee's view was the fact that the army was seriously understrength in a great many of the specialties which had no Negro authorizations. A representative sample of ten specialties taken from the records of February 1949 will give some idea of the denial of opportunity and potential waste of manpower resulting from segregation.

Occupational specialty	Number of men short	Negro authorization
Telephone operator	75	0
Portable power generator repairman	66	0
Shop maintenance mechanic	53	2
Radio repairman single channel	79	0
Transmitter attendant, fixed station	143	0
Telephone and telegraph repairman	79	0
Artillery mechanic AA minor maintenance	79	0
Repeaterman	528	4
Pharmacist	188	3
Welder armor plate	89	7

The areas in which this denial of opportunity was particularly noticeable were signal corps, ordnance, transportation, medical and finance.

A consequence of the denial of job opportunity was an equally serious deprivation of opportunity to attend army schools. The army assigned spaces in its schools on a racial basis, according to the requirements of white and Negro organizations. When the committee in the spring of 1949 examined the quotas for the technical school courses which were open to recruits at the completion of basic training, it found there were Negro quotas for only 21 of the 106 courses currently offered. That is, Negroes, even if qualified, were denied training at that time in 81 percent of the courses. The school spaces reserved for whites totaled 1,741; the spaces allotted Negroes were 82, or 4.4 percent of the total. A comparable situation existed with respect to quotas for school courses open to men already assigned to units. In only a relatively few specialties were Negroes detached from their units for school training, because their units had no call for the advanced skills which they would have learned.

It was this situation with respect to jobs and schools, which was revealed first by examination of army personnel records and then confirmed by field visits, that brought sharply to the committee's attention the interrelationship of segregation, unequal opportunity, and inefficient use of manpower. Negro units could not offer as wide a range of jobs as white units. Because the jobs were not available in segregated units, Negroes were often not given the military occupational specialty (MOS) for which they were qualified. Because they were not given the oppportunity to qualify for the jobs, they did not receive school training in these specialties. The end result was not only unequal opportunity for the Negro but a poorer, less efficient army.

Turning to the question of the 10 percent racial quota, the committee found an equally disturbing situation. From April through November 1949, the army closed down original Negro enlistments because the racial quota was full. Yet throughout this period it continued to reenlist men—both white and Negro—who were far below the current enlistment standard. As of March 31, 1949, almost 7 percent of white enlisted men in the army—37,708—and 15.6 percent of Negro enlisted men—10,840—were below 70 in the General Classification Test. Yet these men could, and many of them did, reenlist in the ensuing months when the army enlistment standard varied from 90 to 80 on the General Classification Test. In fact, 18.8 percent of white reenlistments and 41 percent of Negro reenlistments from March through June 1949 had GCT scores below 80.

This meant, so far as the Negro was concerned, that during the eight months when the quota was filled, the army would refuse to enlist a highly qualified Negro who scored in grade I but would reenlist a Negro professional private who fell in the lower range of grade IV or even in grade V.

Only two conclusions could be drawn from three years of experience with the Gillem Board policy, based upon the continuation of segregation and the quota system. First, the individual skilled Negro was not getting equal opportunity at army jobs and army schools; second, he was unlikely to get it while the army limited his assignment to Negro and overhead units and could refuse him enlistment under the quota system.

The Committee's Recommendations to the Army

With this situation in mind, the president's committee submitted to the army in May 1949, a four-point plan to achieve the president's objective:

1. Open up all army jobs to qualified personnel without regard to race or color.
2. Open up all army schools to qualified personnel without regard to race or color.
3. Rescind the policy restricting Negro assignments to racial units and overhead installations, and assign all army personnel according to individual ability and army need.
4. Abolish the racial quota.

When the secretary of the army had acquainted himself with the facts that lay behind the committee's recommendations on army jobs and schools, he recognized that changes were necessary to afford equal opportunity; and on September 30, 1949, he issued a new policy, opening all jobs to qualified personnel regardless of race and abolishing all racial quotas for school attendance.

The Negro soldier could not fully benefit by these two steps, however, unless the army also revised its policy on the assignment of Negroes. This was a much more thorny question for the army than it had been for the navy or the air force. After the war the navy had discharged most of the personnel in its segregated ordnance and construction companies. Thus, when it decided to admit Negroes into general service in the peacetime navy, it began virtually from scratch. There were no Negro units to disband, and the new Negro personnel enlisted met the relatively high peacetime standards.

The air force, it is true, had a large number of Negro units when it decided to integrate its Negro personnel. But many of these Negroes were already working with whites on the job, and after screening it was relatively easy to transfer to white units those Negroes who could continue in their present duties, and to send to school those who were qualified for further training.

The Negro enlisted strength in the army, on the other hand, constituted between 9 and 10 percent of total enlisted personnel. Many of these Negroes were in combat and combat support units. Some of these units were attached or assigned to larger white organizations which formed part of the immediate striking force. This complicated the problem, and the committee did not feel that it could reasonably recommend that all these Negro units be broken up all at once.

Therefore, the committee and the army, in consultation, worked out a policy and procedure on assignment which took account of the number of men involved and the time required to screen, train and reassign them.

On January 16, 1950, as a result of such consultation and joint effort, the army issued a policy statement declaring that—

In furtherance of the policy of the president as expressed in Executive Order 9981, dated July 26, 1948, that there shall be equality of treatment and opportunity for all persons in the armed services without regard to race, color, religion or national origin, it is the objective of the Department of the Army that Negro manpower possessing appropriate skills and qualifications will be utilized in accordance with such skills and qualifications, and will be assigned to any T/D [overhead] or T/O&E [regularly constituted] unit without regard to race or color.

In effectuation of this policy, the army announced it would take two steps immediately. First, it would publish periodically a list of critical specialties in which vacancies existed, and direct commanders to assign qualified Negroes to any unit requiring such specialties. Second, it would permit commanders to fill any other vacancies in white units with Negroes possessing appropriate skills. Concurrently with the release of this policy, the army published a first list of forty critical specialties.

There remained the question of the quota, and on March 27, 1950, the army announced to all commands that "effective with the month of April all enlistments in the army within overall recruiting quotas will be open to qualified applicants without regard to race or color."

With the army's announcement of the abolition of the racial quota, the committee's four principal recommendations to the army, essential to carrying out the president's policy, had been accepted.

As this report is submitted it is too early to appraise the effect of the army's new policy. However, the committee firmly believes that as the army carries out the committee's recommendations which it has adopted, then within a relatively short time Negro soldiers will enjoy complete equality of treatment and opportunity in the army.

VI. CONCLUSION

Whatsoever things are true . . . whatsoever things are just.

—St. Paul

The president's committee, as previously stated, began its task convinced that the problem confronting it could not be resolved by appealing to moral justice or democratic ideals alone. Military officials did not deny the claim of these ideals; they asserted, however, that in discharging their duty they must maintain military efficiency. The committee on its part did not deny the claim of military efficiency; but it believed the assumption that equality of treatment and opportunity would impair efficiency was of doubtful validity. The committee found, in fact, that inequality had contributed to inefficiency.

As a result of its examination into the rules, procedures, and practices of the armed services, both past and present, the committee is convinced that a policy of equality of treatment and opportunity will make for a better army, navy, and air force. It is right and just. It will strengthen the nation.

The integrity of the individual, his equal worth in the sight of God, his equal protection under law, his equal rights and obligations of citizenship and his equal opportunity to make just and constructive use of his endowment—these are the very foundation of the American system of values. The president's committee throughout its deliberations shaped its course consistently with these principles.

CHAPTER TEN
INTEGRATION

The actual integration of military units took place with surprising tranquility and comparative speed, considering the controversy that had surrounded the question of segregation in the armed forces. Even using the Department of Defense's exacting definition of integration—that is, a unit was considered segregated if more than 49 percent of its members were black— fewer than 5 years would elapse between the breakup of the racially segregated air force unit at Lockbourne Air Force Base, Ohio, and the announcement that the last all-black army unit had passed into history.

All the services had precedents to guide them through this peaceful change. The navy had integrated its general service, and all the services had ended segregation in their basic training centers. Officer training had been integrated throughout much of World War II. Even the army, the most steadfast defender of the old ways, was assigning some replacements without regard to race and had, by 1951, unofficially integrated hundreds of training and combat units in this fashion.

The air force made the promptest response to President Truman's integration order. Sec. W. Stuart Symington and Eugene Zuckert, his assistant secretary, reviewed the Air Staff plan for integrating the 332d Fighter Wing at Lockbourne and certain other black units. With the blessing of the secretary of defense and the Fahy Committee, Symington and Zuckert announced their service's approach on 11 May 1949. The number of all-black units began declining almost immediately. Although senior air force officials had anticipated rapid progress, the virtual elimination of segregation within the next year seemed to take them by surprise. Successful integration of the one fighter wing exerted an irresistible pressure on the service to continue the effort. A noticeable increase in the efficient use of manpower and the peaceful acceptance of integration within the air force were the determining factors in the decision to integrate completely.

The navy needed only to extend an existing racial policy throughout the service, rather than to adopt a radical new program, because a substantial minority of its black personnel already were serving in integrated units. In December 1949, Dan A. Kimball, the undersecretary of the navy, announced a series of reforms "to erase the distrust of the Negro public resulting from past discriminatory practices." Surprisingly, the navy's problems with segregation, brushed over so lightly by the Fahy Committee, resisted solution. As late as 1952, the stewards' branch remained 65 percent black and 35 percent Oriental. Black enlistment remained disappointingly slow. The navy had been the first to announce a policy of racial integration, but, ironically, it found itself suffering in comparison to the rapid progress of the other services in the early 1950s.

The Marine Corps contributed to the navy's image problem. The corps, the most segregated of services, yielded grudgingly to the pressure exerted by the Fahy Committee. The manpower needs of the Korean War, however, changed that attitude. Desperate to obtain trained men for its combat divisions, the Marine Corps dropped all racial barriers. In December 1951, the commandant issued an integration decree putting an end to the practice of creating units specifically for blacks.

The army remained generally segregated in 1951, despite the concessions won from the Defense Department by the Fahy Committee. As the Korean War entered its second year, segregation fell victim to the needs of combat. Although large numbers of blacks were available for the Far East theater, the army's segregation policy earmarked them for black units, and very few black combat units served in the Eighth Army in Korea. Again, a military manpower crisis forced open greater opportunities for blacks. In the summer of 1951, General Matthew B. Ridgway, the Far East commander, asked the army for permission to assign black riflemen to white infantry units, a practice that had been underway unofficially for several months. Only after a team of social scientists had studied this form of integration, and the president had granted approval, did the army chief of staff order the phased but complete racial integration of the Far East Command. So fundamental a change could not be limited to one theater by an army that routinely transferred men from one continent to another. The swift and quietly successful integration in Korea prompted the Department of the Army to undertake similar action in other overseas commands and finally in the United States.

The realization of Mr. Truman's goal of equal treatment and opportunity for blacks definitely could not be achieved merely by the integration of the active forces. Both the Eisenhower and Kennedy administrations wrestled with the complex and closely related problems of providing equality for black servicemen both at duty stations and in nearby communities, where segregation remained common. The two administrations found themselves trapped between the reluctance of military leaders to intervene in what traditionally were purely civilian concerns and the rising expectations of the emerging civil rights movement.

The civil rights movement sparked renewed debate over the military's racial policies. Despite a dramatic intensification of effort to eliminate discrimination in the armed forces, Robert S. McNamara, President Kennedy's secretary of defense, continued to limit his actions to matters that the preceding administration had considered within the province of the Defense Department. Ominously, charges of discrimination within the integrated services, rare since the early 1950s, began to reappear. This rising tide of complaints coincided with an attempt by the Kennedy administration to seize the initiative in civil rights, despite a lack of congressional support. In the end, these circumstances resulted in a new definition of equal treatment and opportunity that profoundly affected the armed forces.

*The air force performed a startling transformation during the
first year under its new racial policy. Col. Jack Marr, who
prepared this often-quoted summary of the service's integration
program, was responsible for the initial integration plan
submitted by the air force to the secretary of defense and the
Fahy Committee.*

9. The air force policy was published in Air Force Letter 35–3, 11 May 1949, and in addition to the basic policy "that there shall be equality of treatment and opportunity for all persons in the air force without regard to race, color, religion or national origin," certain supplemental policies were also expressed. The principal points of these were:

a. Racial quotas for enlistment, schools, assignments and other purposes would be abandoned.

b. All occupational specialties would be open to qualified individuals regardless of race.

c. Enlistment, attendance at schools, assignment to duties and promotion would be on the basis of individual merit and ability and according to prescribed standards.

d. Some Negro units would be maintained, since they were efficiently performing necessary air force functions, but Negroes would not be restricted to assignment in Negro units and could be assigned to any organization.

10. In implementation of the above, the 332d Fighter Wing was inactivated and its personnel were distributed throughout the air force worldwide in accordance with the qualifications of the individuals and the needs of the service. The qualifications of the personnel concerned were evaluated by a board of officers representing Air Force Headquarters, Continental Air Command, Air Training Command and the 332d Fighter Wing assisted by a team of classification specialists furnished by the Air Training Command. This screening started on 17 May 1949 and was completed, except for personnel who were absent on temporary duty, on 2 June 1949.

11. The reaction of Lockbourne personnel to the integration policy varied from individual to individual. There is definite evidence, however, that there was one faction which viewed the integration policy with extreme suspicion and distaste. A few hysterical letters and stories in the Negro press originated within this group. It is believed, however, that the majority of the individuals of the 332d Fighter Wing welcomed the opportunity to compete on an equal basis with all other air force personnel and accepted the air force policy optimistically. . . .

12. At the same time that the detailed processing of personnel of the 332d Fighter Wing was taking place, the commanders of all major commands of the air force were directed to screen and reassign their Negro personnel in accordance with the new policy. In this connection it should not be overlooked that the air force had also acquired experience in on-the-job integration of Negro personnel in considerable numbers. There were, at many air force bases, Negro units known as base service squadrons whose

[Report, Col. Jack Marr, Office of the Deputy Chief of Staff, Personnel, "A Report on the First Year of Implementation of Current Policies Regarding Negro Personnel," 9 July 1950, Modern Military Records Branch, National Archives, Washington, DC.]

members were assigned to various duties throughout the base. Many of these personnel were regularly asigned to duty with white units and were under the jurisdiction of the base service squadron in an administrative sense only. Since these personnel were demonstrating their ability to work side by side with white personnel and to perform competently the duties to which they were assigned, the commanders were directed to transfer these individuals to the units with which they were performing duty. Except for their own squadron overhead, some base service squadrons literally disappeared when these transfers were effected. Negroes in units other than base service squadrons were screened and reassigned, where appropriate, in accordance with their qualifications and the needs of the service.

13. Along with the announcement of the new policy the commander of each major command was further directed to give close personal attention to the implementation of the policy and to report any racial incidents or difficulties which could be attributed to the new policy. It was the desire of Air Force Headquarters to spot any undesirable trends or patterns quickly in order that prompt and effective action could be taken to keep the implementation running as smoothly as possible.

14. Without exception the incidents reported by the various commanders were inconsequential and, surprisingly enough, there were reported more incidents of white personnel attempting to introduce their colored companions into white theaters or eating places in southern communities than incidents of resentment of the presence of Negro personnel in the white units.

15. The air force had expected that the initial implementation would be accompanied by a certain amount of testing of the policy by both white and colored personnel. A typical occurrence of this nature involved a transient Negro corporal who stopped off at an air base in the South and went to the post exchange barber shop for a haircut. Since this was his first Negro customer, the civilian barber was of the opinion that he should not cut the hair and referred the airman to the post exchange officer. The post exchange officer was not in his office at the moment so the airman returned to the barber shop and insisted upon his haircut. Hasty words were followed by an exchange of blows. At another base a white airman decided that Negro airmen should sleep in a certain section of the barracks and attempted to carry out his decision. In each of these cases appropriate disciplinary action was taken. In addition to this type of occurrence there were cases of small groups of white airmen in southern towns going into soda fountains and ordering refreshments for themselves and a friend who would be along later. After the group was served they would signal to their colored friend to join them. These occurrences were not serious and no fights or riots were started although it is reported that one white airman was fined twenty-five dollars by the civil authorities for attempting to take his colored friend into a movie. In each case the commanders concerned cautioned their personnel against such actions, and there were no recurrences. While these events were typical of the small number of incidents that were reported to Air Force Headquarters, there is no doubt that the policy was generally accepted throughout the air force without difficulty. There were a few requests for transfer, usually on the part of the parents of white personnel who did not want their boys to serve in the same unit with Negroes. It appears, however, that the parents were considerably more concerned than the airmen themselves. While of no particular consequence, it is interesting to note

that there was also one Negro mother who objected to her son serving with white boys. In addition, there were a few airmen who stated that they would not reenlist because of the policy. Whether or not the air force actually lost anyone for this reason is not known.

16. Air Force Headquarters had expected that the implementation of this policy might proceed more rapidly in some areas then in others, and had assumed that racial incidents or friction might occur according to a geographical pattern. This was found to be in error, and the pattern which appeared in the first few months of implementation was a command pattern. In other words, some commands undertook to integrate with greater speed than others. After a few months even the most cautious of the commands became aware of the outstanding success of the policy in other commands, so that at the end of the year the basic pattern was one of surprisingly successful air force-wide integration in air force units.

17. Air Force Letter 35–3 specified that the policy contained therein applied only to the air force and that personnel in army (SCARWAF[1]) units on duty with the air force would continue to be governed by army policy. Since the army did not announce its integration policy until 16 January 1950[,] there are substantial numbers of individuals included in the following statistics who could not be integrated because of their assignment to army units on duty with the air force.

18. The rate at which the integration proceeded is indicated in the following statistics which are generally self-explanatory. Since units are not designated racially by the air force, Negro units, for the purpose of statistical reports on this subject, are arbitrarily defined as being units manned predominantly with Negro personnel. Practically all of these units are actually integrated in that there are both white and Negro personnel assigned, but in the interest of realism any unit which is manned over 50 percent with Negro personnel is, for this purpose, indicated as a Negro unit:

Month	Number of Negro Units	Number of White Units Containing Negroes
June 1949	106	167
July	89	350
Aug	86	711
Sep	91	863
Oct	88	1031
Nov	75	1158
Dec	67	1253
Jan 1950	59	1301
Feb	36	1399
Mar	26	1476
Apr	24	1515
May	24	1506

19. While the foregoing figures refer to the number of units involved in the redistribution of Negro personnel, the following figures indicate the number of personnel

---

[1]Composed of army personnel serving with the air force.

involved. It should be noted that students are included in the column headed "Pipeline," therefore any evaluation of the number of Negroes integrated should include the figures in this column, as well as the column headed "Negroes Assigned to White Units."

Month	Negroes Asgnd to Negro Units	Pipeline (Includes Students)	Negroes Asgnd to White Units
Jul 1949	14,609	4,724	2,645
Aug	11,921	6,749	5,228
Sep	11,521	6,160	7,130
Oct	9,522	7,198	8,782
Nov	8,038	7,229	10,414
Dec	7,402	7,033	11,456
Jan 1950	6,773	7,318	11,611
Feb	5,511	6,735	13,919
Mar	5,023	6,490	14,448
Apr	4,728	5,871	14,922
May	4,675	5,928	15,105

20. Under the Gillem Board policies monthly recruiting quotas were subdivided into white and Negro quotas, but with the adoption of the air force policy the separate recruiting quotas were discarded. It was not known whether recruiting on this basis would result in an increase or decrease of Negro recruits, nor was it of more than academic interest since all personnel were required to meet the same minimum standards of qualification. It is a fact, however, that there was an appreciable surge of Negro recruits during the early months of the new policy. This is not believed to be really related to the policy, however, because of an extremely abnormal recruiting condition which existed for a substantial portion of the period of this report. The army's Negro strength quota was filled and no Negroes were being accepted for initial enlistment in the army. As a result of this, many Negroes voluntarily enlisted in the air force although they had originally appeared at the joint army and air force recruiting stations with the intention of enlisting in the army. In addition, it appears that there may have been a small backlog of Negroes who had desired to enlist in the air force during previous months but who had reported to the recruiting station each month after the monthly quota had been filled. At any rate, the overall effect of recruiting without a Negro quota was negligible, and the Negro enlisted strength of the air force has been running between 7.1 and 7.2 percent of the total enlisted strength for the past several months.

21. In connection with recruiting, there is evidence of a certain amount of testing of the absence of racial restrictions by colored reporters who presumably felt that they would have the basis for a good story if they were rejected for enlistment in the air force. A recently published article of this type which has come to our attention concerns a Negro who was rejected for pilot training and whose civil rights were allegedly violated thereby. The fact that the individual did not meet the required physical standards for pilot training, and had been so informed, was of no consequence to the author of the article who concluded his story with the assertion that "there are hundreds and maybe thousands . . . who are denied admittance in the Air Corps [sic] on nonregulation but convenient excuses . . ."

22. Announcement and implementation of the policy also brought a small amount of correspondence from people who seemingly make a profession of being white or colored. The views expressed were generally fanciful and completely disregarded the efficient utilization of human resources as a necessary element of effective air power.

23. The following strength figures are included principally to round out the statistical picture. During the period of this report the command strength of the air force varied up and down a few thousand on either side of 415,000. While these figures show no appreciable change in Negro strength, this fact may in itself be reassuring to the factions who had voiced suspicion that the integration policy was an insidious way of either getting more Negroes into the service or keeping them out.

Month	Negro Officers (Incl SCARWAF)	Negro Enlisted (Incl SCARWAF)
Jun 1949	319 (47)	21,782 (2,196)
Jul	311 (30)	21,667 (2,175)
Aug	330 (32)	23,568 (2,275)
Sep	344 (29)	24,467 (2,462)
Oct	347 (20)	25,155 (2,826)
Nov	357 (19)	25,394 (2,930)
Dec	368 (18)	25,523 (3,072)
Jan 1950	351 (17)	25,351 (3,038)
Feb	344 (16)	25,484 (2,878)
Mar	343 (15)	25,390 (2,751)
Apr	336 (13)	25,185 (2,708)
May	341 (8)	25,367 (2,611)

26. In summary, it is the policy of the air force to utilize its personnel in accordance with their skills and abilities and the needs of the service rather than color. Our experience clearly indicates that this policy is in the interests of economy and effective air power as well as being in compliance with the directives of the president and the secretary of defense. The implementation of this policy within the air force has been extremely gratifying. It would appear at this time that the problems that have been mentally associated with the "mixing" of white and Negro personnel in the air force are largely imaginary. Racial feelings, racial incidents, charges of discrimination, and the problems of procurement, training, assignment and utilization which were associated with racially designated units have been reduced by an appreciable degree or eliminated entirely. That the application of the policy has been successful is clearly indicated in *Freedom to Serve* (the report to the president of the President's Committee on Equality of Treatment and Opportunity), the confidential reports of the major commanders which are on file in Air Force Headquarters and the numerous news and editorial comments on the subject which have been published during the past year.

*Responding to pressures exerted by the secretary of the navy and
the Fahy Committee, the Marine Corps ordered the integration
of some black specialists in white units.*

1. The following is Marine Corps policy regarding Negro marines:

(a) All previous statements of policy relating to Negro marines are revoked. (This revokes previous directives concerning mixed units.)

(b) Organizations of platoon strength or larger composed entirely of Negro enlisted personnel will continue and in the future will be designated, where appropriate, in both regular and reserve components. (Such designation may be made by this headquarters or by commanders of major regular or reserve units.)

(c) Individual Negro marines will be assigned in accordance with MOS[1] to vacancies in any unit where their services can be effectively utilized.

(d) In the organized reserve, authority for acceptance or rejection of an individual shall be vested in the commanding officer of each unit. For assignment to the organized Marine Corps Reserve, acceptance or rejection of an applicant shall be dependent entirely upon mental, moral and physical qualification and the existence of a vacancy wherein the applicant's services can be effectively utilized, without regard to race, color, religion or national origin.

By command of Gen. C. B. Cates

S. L. Howard
Major General, US Marine Corps
Acting Chief of Staff

[Marine Corps Memorandum No. 119–49, 18 November 1949, subject: Policy regarding Negro marines, Reference Section, Office of the Director of Marine Corps History and Museums, Washington, DC.]

[1]Military Occupational Specialty.

●

*After reviewing the programs set up to increase the number of
blacks in the navy, the orders issued to regularize the status of
chief stewards, and the studies instituted to find jobs for lower-
scoring enlistees, the undersecretary of the navy concluded that
the navy's major problem was one of image.*

2. It is considered that the navy's program to ensure equality of treatment is sound and that the necessary tools for carrying it out are available in the form of directives, orders, etc. There remains the continuing problem of educating personnel, both naval and civilian, to the fact that the navy is sincere in its policy. Great progress has been made in the education but it will require considerable time to eliminate completely racial differences within the navy and to erase the distrust of the Negro public resulting from

---

[Memorandum, Undersec. of the Navy Dan A. Kimball for chairman, Personnel Policy Board, 22 December 1949, subject: Implementation of Executive Order 9981, Modern Military Records Branch, National Archives, Washington, DC.]

past discriminating practices. Many Negro civilians continue to believe that Negroes are employed only in the stewards' branch. Releases to the Negro press by representatives aboard the USS *Missouri* on its recent trip to Europe emphasized the employment of Negroes in all ratings and did much to dispell [*sic*] this illusion. There is reason to believe that the final report of the President's Committee on Equality of Opportunity and Treatment in the Armed Services will show the vast improvement made by the navy in this regard. The attachments[1] hereto are pertinent.

3. In regard to comments or recommendations which may assist the navy and the Personnel Policy Board, it is submitted that no additional measures are necessary other than to continue implementation of existing directives. The results attained during a comparatively brief period indicate forcibly that racial tolerance is spreading and it is only a question of time until it will no longer present a problem within the navy.

---

[1]Not included.

•

*After years of almost total opposition to the concept, the Marine
Corps announced integration of the service. This decision was
reached not so much because the president ordered it or because
the black community demanded it, but because its units on the
Korean battlefield were desperate for men. Once accomplished
in Korea, integration was required everywhere in the corps to
provide for the orderly transfer of personnel.*

1. Reference (a)[1] is hereby revoked and superseded by this memorandum.

2. The following is the Marine Corps policy regarding Negro marines:
   (a) Individual Negro marines will be assigned in accordance with MOS to vacancies in any unit where their services can be effectively utilized.
   (b) In the organized reserve, authority for acceptance or rejection of an individual shall be vested in the commanding officer of each unit. For assignment to the organized Marine Corps Reserve, acceptance or rejection of an applicant shall be dependent entirely upon mental, moral and physical qualifications and the existence of a vacancy wherein the applicant's service can be effectively utilized.
   By command of Gen. C. B. Cates

M. H. Silverthorn
Lieutenant General, US Marine Corps
Chief of Staff

[Marine Corps Memorandum No. 109–51, 13 December 1951, subject: Policy regarding Negro marines, Reference Section, Office of the Director of Marine Corps History and Museums, Washington, DC.]
[1]Marine Corps Memorandum No. 119-49, see above.

*Complaints, especially concerning the racial composition of
the stewards' branch, continued to pour into the navy. Lester
Granger in particular was critical of the fact that the branch
remained exclusively nonwhite some five years after the Truman
order. In response the chief of naval personnel appointed a
committee to reexamine the navy's policy of separate messmen
service. As a result of the committee's findings and his
discussions with Granger, Vice Adm. J. L. Holloway outlined a
series of reforms. The reference to Maxwell Rabb[1] suggests that
the Eisenhower administration had taken an interest in the
outcome of the navy's reforms.*

1. Mr. Granger's luncheon visit with you is Thursday, 3 September. I hope you will
have opportunity to read this memorandum and attachments and discuss with me late in
the afternoon, Wednesday, the 2nd. Parenthetically, I note that Mr. Max Rabb's office is
calling Mr. Granger's office on Wednesday, the 2nd, expressing the hope that Mr.
Granger will drop by the White House after Mr. Granger's luncheon with you on
Thursday.

2. Enclosure (1)[2] is a rough draft of a letter for your consideration to be sent Mr.
Granger after his luncheon with you.

3. Since your visit with the three officers recalled to active duty to review the integration program in the navy, we have proceeded as follows:
       (a) Formed an ad hoc committee, headed by Rear Admiral Arnold, deputy
chief of naval personnel, and composed of senior and experienced officers in the
Bureau of Naval Personnel, together with a capable and senior officer from the
Bureau of Supplies and Accounts, to consider factors pertaining to the steward
group rating which will lead to further progress in eliminating points of friction. I
look to this committee for specific and constructive recommendations concerning
tangible administrative measures.
       (b) I have had the recruiting inspectors from the New England and mid-
Atlantic areas come into Washington, and have obtained their comment and
recommendation relative to recruiting some white personnel in the stewards'
branch. Both of the recruiting inspectors and my director of the Recruiting Division
recommend, with which I concur, against any method of recruitment of white
personnel which is not completely open and aboveboard. By improper procedures
is meant such a measure as offering higher places on our waiting lists to escape the
draft, if a white man should volunteer for the stewards' branch.
       The inspectors agreed that in areas where industrial integration has been
accomplished, as in the Detroit, Los Angeles and Buffalo areas, such may offer
possibilities in across-the-board recruiting. I am pursuing this matter further and

---

[Memorandum with second enclosure, Vice Adm. J. L. Holloway, chief of the Bureau of Naval
Personnel, for the secretary of the navy, 1 September 1953, subject: Mr. Granger's visit and related matters,
Navy and Old Army Branch, National Archives, Washington, DC.]

[1]Secretary to the cabinet.

[2]Not included.

have ordered the inspectors of the Great Lakes and west coast areas into the bureau for further discussion.

We must continue to emphasize that only those who so volunteer should enter the stewards' branch. We now, and will continue, to present the whole navy program in our recruiting talks. However, a skillful handling in the actual recruiting petty-officer level, may bring results in recruiting white personnel in areas referred to above. We are handling this matter verbally.

(c) I am considering ceasing for the time being at least separate initial recruitment in the stewards' branch except for the recruitment in the Philippines for which there are both commitments and pressing needs. Under these circumstances, I would enlist *all*[3] in the continental United States as seamen recruits, and assign to Stewardsman School, on a voluntary basis only *after*[3] completion of recruit training.

4. On receipt of the report of the ad hoc committee, referred to above, I intend to take definite administrative action. The administrative measures initiated must be well conceived, progressive rather than in toto, and we will give careful attention to future distribution in the fleet in well calculated proportions to selected commands, where the highest order of administrative leadership is ensured.

5. I shall keep you fully informed at all times in the premises.

6. I am attaching, as Enclosure (2), a copy of the report made to me by Commander [Durward] Gilmore and his group.

> Very respectfully,
> J. L. Holloway, Jr.
> Vice Admiral, US Navy
> Chief of Naval Personnel

ENCLOSURE TWO

31 August 1953

Vice Adm. J. L. Holloway, Jr., USN
Chief of Bureau of Naval Personnel
Navy Department
Washington 25, DC

Dear Admiral Holloway:

Pursuant to your letter of instructions dated 13 August 1953, we submit herewith our report concerning the status of integration of Negro military personnel.

To us it appears the navy has a sound and practical policy concerning minority groups, and that the policy is being carried out in spirit.

We feel the navy has made excellent progress in its continuing efforts to more

---

[3]Emphasis in the original.

efficiently utilize Negro personnel. Integration has been the means, and good public relations has been the result.

Considering the complete reversal of policy since the beginning of World War II, and being familiar with the growing pains that accompanied the evolution that brought about the current policy, considering the good results, and hoping for a continuation thereof in the future, we would be remiss if we did not mention the quality of leadership that led to these fine conditions we find in the navy today.

This complete reversal of policy resulting in the pleasant racial relations and effective utilization of Negro naval personnel could not have been accomplished without the open-minded and intelligent approach on the part of such people as Secretary Forrestal, his very effective aide, Capt. R. N. McFarlane, Mr. Lester B. Granger, executive director of the National Urban League as civilian advisory to Mr. Forrestal, Admiral Hillenkoetter, the then director of Planning Division of BuPers, and yourself as the then director of training in BuPers.

We feel it would be expedient at this time to give particular attention to the stewards' branch. The segregation in that branch is a sore spot with the Negroes, and is our weakest position from the standpoint of public relations. We recommend the following:

1. Abolish segregation in the stewards' branch and the separate recruiting for that branch.

2. Change the insignia from the crescent to some other. Negro people dislike being associated with menial tasks. They feel that serving in the stewards' branch is a menial task and that the crescent brands them as servants. The psychological effect of giving them another insignia should be helpful to morale.

3. Consider the possibility of consolidating the stewards' branch with the commissary branch.

As for the future, we recommend that the same type of open-minded, intelligent handling of this ever-continuing problem be assured. A slip could bring about the "making a mountain out of a molehill." Good public relations is a necessity. Frankly, since they are still available and possess all of the knowledge of the background, ability and integrity that could be hoped for, we would like to see Mr. Granger reinstated as civilian advisor to the secretary and Captain McFarlane back as an aide to the secretary. We feel certain that between these two men they would chart the best course for the navy and the very best of conditions would result. . . .

On 30 November 1949 Sec. of the Army Gordon Gray appointed
a board of general officers "to determine current programs under
existing policies governing the utilization of Negro manpower
in the army and to reexamine and review these policies in light
of changing conditions and experiences." Under the
chairmanship of Lt. Gen. Stephen J. Chamberlin, this group
consulted scores of witnesses and thousands of documents only
to conclude, in spite of the Truman order and the Fahy
Committee's findings, that the army should retain segregated
units and a quota on black enlistments. The board's report
represents the last official defense of segregation in the service.

d. Negro Units.

(1) Current practice in the army is to employ Negro regiments, battalions and companies in combat divisions, battalions in white regiments, and separate battalions, companies and detachments. Much testimony was heard from commanders concerning the performance of Negro units and the advisability of modifying this practice.

(2) It was obvious that large Negro units had not done well and that the greatest degree of success in combat was achieved when Negroes were used in small units in close proximity to white troops. Inference might be drawn that greater combat effectiveness might be attained by amalgamation of Negro and white soldiers in the same units. Such a solution, however, has many serious objections.

(a) Amalgamation would place the Negro in a competitive field he is not prepared to face, would deny opportunity and retard development of Negro manpower.

(b) There would be widespread resentment on the part of most white soldiers with a consequent destruction of combat effectiveness.

(c) It would place Negro officers and noncommissioned officers in command of white troops, a position which only the exceptional Negro could successfully fill.

(3) The objection to the Negro unit, namely that it includes an unduly high proportion of individuals with low GCT scores, is a minor one compared to the advantages of such an organization. This objection, too, can be overcome by raising the GCT level, by careful selection of officers and noncommissioned officers, by more and repetitive training, and by developing pride in the individual and in the organization.

(4) The fundamental decision as between the amalgamated and the Negro unit must be based on the combat effectiveness of the army as a whole, and not on the exploitation of all Negro manpower. The best evidence as to how maximum effectiveness can be achieved is found in the opinions of war-tested combat leaders who testified before this board. Almost without exception they vigorously opposed

[Memorandum, Lt. Gen. Stephen J. Chamberlin et al., to secretary of the army, 9 February 1950, subject: Report of board of officers on utilization of Negro manpower in the army, Modern Military Records Branch, National Archives, Washington, DC.]

amalgamation and strongly urged the retention of the Negro unit. This board concurs.

e. Size of Negro Unit.

(1) The majority of the commanders consulted expressed serious doubt as to the effectiveness in combat of the Negro unit of regimental size as a part of a division. They agreed, however, that such a unit should be retained in the army chiefly as a training base for Negro soldiers. They likewise agreed that the battalion is the most desirable size unit for incorporation in larger units. . . .

7. RECOMMENDATIONS:

a. The policies established by War Department Circular 124 (1946) as amended, and Army Regulations 210–10 and letter AGO 8 July 1944, pertaining to recreation, wherein not in conflict with recent changes of policy continue in effect.

b. That the 10 percent limitation on Negro manpower in the army be continued and that Negro units be continued.

c. That effort be continued to improve the standards of enlisted men in the army and that steps be taken to raise the Negro GCT level to that of whites, even if in the process the number of Negro soldiers should fall below 10 percent of the total.

d. That efforts be continued to perfect plans for the full utilization of Negro manpower for mobilization and war.

e. That no further changes be made in Department of the Army policies in the utilization of Negro manpower pending evaluation of experiences gained from the policies announced in Special Regulations 600–629–1, Department of the Army, 16 January 1950.

f. That a special group in the Department of the Army be established to keep under continuous study the problem of the efficient employment of Negro troops, and to assist in the planning, promulgation and revision of current policies.

> Stephen J. Chamberlin
> Lieutenant General, United States Army
> President
>
> Withers A. Burress
> Major General, United States Army
>
> John M. Devine
> Major General, United States Army
>
> M. Van Voorst
> Colonel, GSC
> Recorder without vote.

For some months, army commanders in Korea had been unofficially assigning their excess black replacement troops to their seriously undermanned white combat units. A similar unofficial integration was occurring in the basic training regiments in the United States where the segregation of draftees proved too inefficient and time-consuming. In May 1951, the Far East commander, Gen. Matthew B. Ridgway, formally requested that units in his command be integrated. As a start, he wanted the Twenty-fourth Infantry Regiment, his major black unit, broken up and its members distributed throughout the white units in his command.

SUMMARY

1. Commander in chief, Far East has requested authority to transfer the Twenty-fourth Infantry (Negro) to the zone of interior at zero strength and to activate another Regiment as an organic element of the Twenty-fifth Infantry Division (Tab A).[1]

2. CINCFE also proposes to integrate Negro personnel into all units on an army-wide percentage basis, which is approximately 12 percent for combat units. This would include the Fortieth and Forty-fifth Infantry Division. (Tab D)[2]

3. The former statutory requirement that two Negro infantry regiments and two Negro cavalry regiments remain active has been repealed (Sec. 401, AOA 1950).

4. Current policy precludes inactivation of a Negro unit concurrently with the activation of a similar white unit at the same station.

5. The best units available for activation and assignment to the Twenty-fifth Infantry Division are the Thirty-seventh, Fifty-second, Fifty-fourth and Fifty-fifth Infantry Regiments. Of these, the Thirty-seventh is the oldest (1916).

6. CINCFE was informed on 17 May 51 that restrictions contained in JCS 90000 continue to apply to the Fortieth and Forty-fifth Infantry Divisions pending further instructions (Tab C).[1] ACofS,[3] G-1 believes these restrictions should be removed to permit complete implementation of CINCFE plan (Part 2, Tab B).[1] ACofS, G-3 is preparing recommendations for JCS which will, when approved, remove these restrictions.

7. No valid objection to CINCFE proposal to integrate Negroes into all units is apparent except for the restrictions on the Fortieth and Forty-fifth Infantry Divisions.

[Disposition Form, Lt. Gen. Edward H. Brooks, assistant chief of staff, G-1, for chief of staff, 23 May 1951, subject: Utilization of Negro manpower, General Archives Branch, Washington National Records Center, Suitland, MD.]

[1]Not included.

[2]See below.

[3]Assistant Chief of Staff.

RECOMMENDATIONS

That the attached draft message to CINCFE be approved (Tab D).

DRAFT

"SIGHT—PRIORITY" message to CINCFE

This message in two parts.

Part 1. There is no legal objection to conversion Twenty-fourth Infantry in accordance with Part I your message C 62612. Consider this plan preferable to replacing Twenty-fourth Infantry.

However, if you still desire to replace the Twenty-fourth Infantry, authority will be granted to inactivate the Twenty-fourth Infantry and concurrently to activate the Thirty-seventh Infantry with the provision that the Twenty-fourth Infantry (inactive) remain in your command. Please advise.

Part 2. Department of Army approves integration of Negro personnel in all units under your command. However, integration of Negroes into units of Fortieth and Forty-fifth Infantry Divisions will not be effected until further instructions are received by you from Department of Army.

●

The Army Staff responded to the pressures of the battlefield and
approved Ridgway's request to integrate his command, after
clearing its decision with the secretary of the army,
congressional leaders, and the president.

For Ridgway from CSUSA[1] signed Haislip.[2]

Part 1. There is no legal objection to conversion of Twenty-fourth Infantry in accordance with part 1 your C 62612. Consider this plan preferable to replacing Twenty-fourth Infantry.

Part 2. Your recommendations re integration of Negro personnel in FECOM[3] is approved for planning purposes only. No implementing action as far as the Twenty-fourth Infantry Regiment, Fortieth and Forty-fifth Divisions are concerned will be taken pending further instructions from this headquarters. You will be advised when decision is reached.

[Message, chief of staff (Collins) to CINCFE (Ridgway), 28 May 1951, General Archives Branch, Washington National Records Center, Suitland, MD.]

[1] Chief of Staff, United States Army.

[2] General Wade H. Haislip, vice chief of staff.

[3] Far East Command.

*The chief of staff ordered the integration of the Far East
Command along the lines proposed by General Ridgway. The
Fourteenth Infantry would replace the Twenty-fourth Infantry
in the allied lines. The ratio of integrated black soldiers was
not to exceed 12 percent of all the men in the combat units.*

Part 1. No objection to using not to exceed 12 percent for all combat type units instead
of 10 percent infantry and 12 percent other combat [units].

Part 2. Effective 1 August '51, Fourteenth Infantry is transferred less personnel and
equipment from Camp Carson Colorado (Fourteenth Infantry less First Battalion) and
Fort Benning Georgia (First Battalion Fourteenth Infantry) to your command, relieved
from current assignment, and assigned as an organic element to Twenty-fifth Infantry
Division. As early as practical thereafter inactivate Twenty-fourth Infantry and concurrently reorganize Fourteenth Infantry under T/O&E 7–11N, 15 November '40, Circular
10–51, with authorized strength of 153 officers, 26 warrant officers, and 3483 enlisted
men. Department of Army confirmation letter follows.

Part 3. Desire you proceed with integration plan on the foregoing basis. It is believed
here that plan should receive minimum publicity until Twenty-fourth Infantry is inactivated at which time statement should be released. Public relations aspects are under
study here. Proposed statement will be prepared here and forwarded for your comments.

> A. C. McAuliffe
> Major General, GSC
> Assistant Chief of Staff, G-1

[Message, chief of staff (Collins) for General Ridgway, 17 July 1951, General Archives Branch, Washington National Records Center, Suitland, MD.]

●

*The successful integration of army units in the Far East caused
the Army Staff to consider initiating the process in its other
worldwide units. Its immediate concern centered around the
vast European Command with its large number of overstrength
black units. The continued segregation of this command
threatened to frustrate the normal day-to-day transfer of men
from the training centers at home and from the units in the Far
East where the percentage of black combat soldiers was
exceeding the guidelines established by the chief of staff.*

Personal for Handy from CSUSA signed Taylor.[1]

Would appreciate receiving soonest EUCOM[2] plan for racial integration in
combat units as discussed with you by Gen. [J. Lawton] Collins during recent visit.

[Message, chief of staff (Collins) to commander in chief, European Command (Handy), 4 December 1951, General Archives Branch, Washington National Records Center, Suitland, MD.]

[1]Lt. Gen. Maxwell D. Taylor, assistant chief of staff, G-3, operations.

[2]European Command.

*The Army Staff was unsatisfied with the integration plan
submitted by Gen. Thomas Handy, and the chief of staff
demanded that his commander in Europe make several specific
changes. Although the staff had assumed that integration
would be limited for some time to the army's overseas units
and the training centers, it had become clear by January 1952
that the complete integration of the army was about to begin.*

SUMMARY

1. In a letter to the chief of staff (Tab B, Ltr to CofS),[1] subject as above,[2] dated 14 December 1951, the European Command submits a study and plan for integrating white and Negro personnel in combat units.

2. The essential elements of the plan are:

    a. Approximately 10 percent Negroes will be included in white combat units.

    b. Certain Negro combat units will be inactivated.

    c. Integration will proceed on a unit-by-unit basis and will be accomplished over a period of approximately six months.

    d. Screening boards will be constituted to test and evaluate the fitness of Negro officers and noncommissioned officers (E–7, E–6 and E–5) for retention in a combat unit. Successful examinees will be integrated as individuals in existing or newly activated combat units.

    e. Individual Negroes not approved by the screening boards will be assigned to fill existing vacancies in EUCOM service units or reported to the Department of the Army for reassignment.

    f. All Negro enlisted personnel below the grade E–5 in Negro combat units will be integrated in white combat units without board examination.

    g. There is a need for publicity regarding the discontinuance of Negro combat units.

3. The EUCOM plan as it relates to combat units is generally congruent with a G–1 proposal for army-wide integration which is being concurrently submitted by summary sheet to the chief of staff for approval. However, the following discrepancies are noted:

    a. The proposal to select Negro personnel for assignment to integrated combat units through the operation of screening boards established for this specific purpose is neither equitable nor appropriate and would be the source of many legitimate complaints of discrimination. It is believed that all Negro enlisted personnel in existing combat units, regardless of grade, should be assigned initially

[Disposition Form, Lt. Gen. A. C. McAuliffe, assistant chief of staff, G-1, for chief of staff, 24 January 1952, subject: Racial integration in combat units, General Archives Branch, Washington National Records Center, Suitland, MD.]

[1]Not included.

[2]Racial integration in combat units.

to integrated combat units without preliminary board-screening procedures.

b. Consideration should be given to the inactivation of Negro units rendered surplus to command needs through reassignment of personnel. However, it is believed that, in most instances, the necessary changes can be effected through redesignation and removal of the racial-identifying symbol. When the command indicates that an appropriate percentage of white personnel has been assigned to Negro units, G–1 will take necessary action to delete the racial designation of the units.

c. It is not believed that the inactivation of Negro units as a consequence of integration will create adverse reaction either within the army or elsewhere. Integration should proceed routinely without press publicity.

4. The attached letter for signature of the chief of staff (Tab A, ltr for sig CofS)[3] approves the EUCOM plan except the use of screening boards to determine the fitness of Negro personnel for retention in combat units and the publicity release. It further indicates the need for plans to accomplish progressive integration in Negro service units, and refers to the more comprehensive provisions of the army-wide integration plan, a copy of which is enclosed.

RECOMMENDATIONS

1. That the proposed plan of EUCOM be approved with the following modifications:

a. The plan be extended to include service units in conformance with the concurrent army-wide integration plan.

b. The use of screening boards be eliminated.

c. The special publicity plans be eliminated.

2. That the attached draft of letter (Tab A, ltr for sig CofS) to CINCEUR[4] for signature of the chief of staff be approved.

LETTER OF THE CHIEF OF STAFF

General Thomas T. Handy   February 15, 1952
Commander in chief, European Command
APO 403, c/o Postmaster
New York, New York

Dear Tom:

Your plan for the integration of white and Negro personnel in combat units is in general agreement with our present thinking on integration. I am afraid, however, that I cannot accept your proposal to establish "screening boards" to test and evaluate the fitness of Negro officers and certain noncommissioned officers for retention in combat units.

I realize the need for assuring continued effectiveness of integrated units, however,

---

[3] See below.
[4] Commander in Chief, Europe.

the appearance of selected Negroes before boards prior to integration will undoubtedly be the source of many legitimate complaints of discrimination. It does not appear that such a screening will assure effective operation of integration since the bulk of Negroes in combat units will be assigned without selectivity. It is therefore believed that all Negro enlisted personnel in existing combat units, regardless of grade, should be assigned initially to integrated units without preliminary board-screening procedures. It is expected thereafter that standards for retention in combat assignment will be equally applicable to all members of a unit regardless of race.

The inactivation of Negro units actually rendered surplus to the needs of the command through the reassignment of personnel will be approved upon request. However, it is believed that, in most instances, the necessary changes can be effected through the redesignation of units and the removal of racial identifying symbols. The inactivation of units solely because of their Negro history is not contemplated.

Your plan should be extended to include integration in service units. Implementation should be either current with or following integration in combat units, at your discretion, and over whatever period of time it may require. In this regard your six-month target date for combat integration may reasonably be extended to one year, if required. Service unit integration may require one to two years for completion.

In regard to the plan for special publicity, I do not believe that adverse reaction will result from the inactivation of certain Negro units as a consequence of integration. Furthermore, special publicity regarding integration or inactivation of units may invite rather than preclude criticism. Accordingly, the program of integration should proceed as quietly and as routinely as possible without fanfare or publicity of our seeking.

With the exceptions and modifications noted above your plan for integration in combat units is approved.

Faithfully yours,
Joe

●

Sec. of Defense Charles E. Wilson announced that the last
segregated unit, i.e., one with black personnel numbering
49 percent or more of its total strength, had been eliminated.

Continued progress has also been made in carrying out the full integration of Negro personnel in the armed forces. The program advanced more rapidly than was considered possible at an earlier date and without untoward incidents. All-Negro units were abolished by the services ahead of the original deadline of June 30, 1954. In addition, racial quotas have been eliminated, and the utilization of Negro personnel is now based solely on individual merit and proficiency. All service schools and training programs are open without racial restrictions. The armed forces also provided, within their own spheres, notable examples of racial integration in housing, transportation, schooling, recreation, and other aspects of community life.

[*Semiannual Report of the Secretary of Defense, January 1 to June 30 1954,* General Reference Branch, Center of Military History, Washington, DC.]

The results of this program have been encouraging. Combat effectiveness is increased as individual capabilities rather than racial designations determine assignments and promotions. Economies in manpower and funds are achieved by the elimination of racially duplicated facilities and operations. Above all, our national security is improved by the more effective utilization of military personnel, regardless of race.

●

A noteworthy exception to the general integration to be found on military bases was the operation of schools for dependent children. In an action predating the Supreme Court decision outlawing segregated education, Secretary Wilson integrated the on-base schools. Schools attended by dependents in the local community were not included in this order, and their integration would take many years to complete.

It is desired that appropriate steps be taken to assure that the operation of all school facilities located on military installations shall be conducted without segregation on the basis of race or color. Effective as of the date of this memorandum, no new school shall be opened for operation on a segregated basis, and schools presently so conducted shall cease operating on a segregated basis, as soon as practicable, and under no circumstances later than September 1, 1955.

In the accomplishment of this policy, the following action will be taken:

(a) For each military location on which a school is now operating on a segregated basis, it will be determined whether the local educational agency will be able, under state law, to operate the existing school in accordance with the provisions of this policy. If the local educational agency will not be able to do so, appropriate proposals should be prepared under provisions of Public Law 874, 81st Congress, as amended, to the United States commissioner of education for providing nonsegregated free public education in such school facilities. If the local educational agency will conduct the school, immediate steps will be taken to comply with this policy, and

(b) For military locations on which new schools are being constructed, but the schools are as yet not operating, immediate steps shall be taken to make certain the permit for the operation of the school contains a nonsegregation clause.

[Memorandum, Sec. of Defense Charles E. Wilson for secretary of the army et al., 12 January 1954, subject: Schools on military installations for dependents of military and civilian personnel, General Archives Branch, Washington National Records Center, Suitland, MD.]

This short note from President Kennedy's secretary of defense
put the armed forces on notice that the president was personally
interested in equal opportunity for black servicemen.

The president was very pleased with the honor guard and ceremonial units which were present when he greeted Nkruma.[1]

However, President Kennedy noticed that the units contained few, if any, Negroes.

Would it be possible to introduce into these units a reasonable number of Negro personnel?

[Memorandum, Sec. of Defense Robert S. McNamara for the assistant secretary of defense (Manpower), 13 March 1961, General Archives Branch, Washington National Records Center, Suitland, MD.]

[1] President of Ghana.

●

The integration of the active armed forces introduced an era of
good feelings into the relations between the services and the
civil rights movement. Many from both sides publicly expressed
satisfaction at the new order of things. But the generally
equal treatment and opportunity enjoyed by blacks on the
military reservations only sharpened their opposition to the
discrimination they were forced to endure off-base. The services
professed themselves powerless to combat this form of
discrimination, but by the early 1960s their claims of impotence
only seemed to strengthen the determination of civil rights
leaders to force the Department of Defense to find some remedy.
Men like Congressmen Adam Clayton Powell, Jacob Javits,
and Charles C. Diggs joined with Clarence Mitchell of the
NAACP and the Civil Liberties Union to press the department
for relief. As a result of these protests and because the Kennedy
administration was determined to make its mark in the civil
rights area, Secretary McNamara began in a series of orders
to address the problem of equal treatment and opportunity in
the community.

The purpose of this memorandum is to carry out the directive of the president as set forth in reference (a).[1]

Discrimination based on race, creed, color or national origin by employee recreational organizations is contrary to the purpose and spirit of EO 10925, March 6, 1961.[2]

No employee recreational organization which practices discrimination based on

---

[Memorandum, Sec. of Defense Robert S. McNamara for secretaries of the military departments et al., 28 April 1961, subject: Military and civilian employee recreational organizations, General Archives Branch, Washington National Records Center, Suitland, MD.]

[1] Memorandum from the president, 18 April 1961, subject: Equal opportunity.

[2] Executive Order establishing the President's Committee on Equal Employment Opportunity.

race, creed, color or national origin will be permitted to use the name of, or be sponsored by the Department of Defense. No facility or activity of the Department of Defense will be available to such organization.

The foregoing applies to all facilities and activities of the Department of Defense, including those financed from nonappropriated funds and to all recreational organizations composed of full-time civilian and military personnel in the Department of Defense. This policy is effective immediately.

Action to assure compliance with this policy should be initiated immediately and copies of the implementing instructions issued furnished this office no later than close of business May 15, 1961.

•

The second of these equal-treatment-and-opportunity directives, signed by McNamara's deputy, ordered local commanders to provide integrated "facilities," meaning recreation and living accommodations, for their personnel. It also ordered the commander, acting through command-community relations groups formed for the purpose, to seek the local community's voluntary compliance with the department's equal treatment and opportunity policy. In effect, the secretary was asking his commanders to achieve what the Kennedy administration had been unable to achieve through the courts or in the halls of Congress.

1. The policy of equal treatment for all members of the armed forces without regard to race, creed or color is firmly established within the Department of Defense.

2. Therefore, in those areas where unsegregated facilities are not readily available to members of the armed forces in adjacent or surrounding communities, it is the policy of the Department of Defense to provide such facilities on military installations to the extent possible. In addition, local commanders are expected to make every effort to obtain such facilities off base for members of the armed forces through command-community relations committees.

3. Military police may be used to quell affrays when military personnel are involved but military police will not be employed on behalf of local authorities to support enforcement of racial segregation or other forms of racial discrimination.

4. Legal actions by civilian authorities against members of the armed forces growing out of enforcement of racial segregation or other forms of racial discrimination will be carefully monitored by local commanders. As circumstances warrant, military legal assistance may be provided to assure that members of the armed forces are afforded due process of law.

[Memorandum, Dep. Sec. of Defense Roswell Gilpatric for secretary of the army et al., 19 June 1961, subject: Availability of facilities to military personnel, General Archives Branch, Washington National Records Center, Suitland, MD.]

The services' reserve forces had always lagged behind the active forces in carrying out the Department of Defense's integration policy. While part of the armed forces, the reserve units had strong ties to the local community and reflected the social customs of the areas in which they were organized. Under pressure from civil rights groups, the department acted to eliminate segregation in the reserve units, but the question of segregated National Guard units was left unanswered in 1962.

The problem of assuring equality of treatment and opportunity for all persons in the Army, Navy, Air Force and Marine Corps Reserves has been the subject of a number of past conferences and reports, and is a matter of continuing concern for all of us.

In order to assure that our responsibilities in this area under Executive Order 9981 are carried out, two specific measures are required:

1. The identification of all-Negro and all-white reserve units, and initiation of action to integrate them as rapidly as is consistent with military effectiveness.

2. An overall review of the assignment of Negroes to reserve units to determine if a disproportionate number are assigned to pools. Where this is found to be so, positive measures should be taken, consistent with the military requirements and the skills of the personnel involved, to provide for the assignment of more Negroes to specific reserve units. The proportion of Negroes assigned to units in relation to their total strength in the reserves, while not a mathematical formula which can be applied to action in this area, will serve as a guide for measuring progress.

An initial report of action taken is requested by 1 May 1962. This initial report is to be followed by a series of four reports at quarterly intervals, beginning with the quarter ending 30 June 1962. Each of the quarterly reports should reach this office within thirty days after the end of the quarter. All reports should be addressed to the assistant secretary of defense (Manpower). . . .

[Memorandum, Dep. Sec. of Defense Gilpatric for undersecretary of the army et al., 3 April 1962, subject: Compliance with EO 9981 in the Army, Navy, Air Force, and Marine Corps Reserve, General Archives Branch, Washington National Records Center, Suitland, MD.]

*One of the most accurate and judicious statements of the status
of black servicemen in the 1960s was issued by the US Civil
Rights Commission. The fact that this prestigious agency con-
concluded after a lengthy investigation that discrimination in
the local community affected the morale and efficiency of
black servicemen exerted further pressure on the Kennedy
administration to break out of the traditional limitations
imposed by military policies and take a more active role in
advancing the civil rights of servicemen in the local community.*

CIVIL RIGHTS AND THE MILITARY MISSION

The failure of the Defense Department's first efforts to secure equal treatment for all members of the armed forces is attributable in large measure to the way in which commanders interpret their responsibilities. Most commanders and installation officials see the issues of equal treatment as outside the military mission. They recognize that all servicemen must be dealt with equally while on a military installation, but believe that this responsibility ends "at the gate." To the extent that they must deal with the community beyond the gate, these officers understand their objective to be the attainment of harmonious relations, a goal which will probably be impaired by conflict over race relations. Viewing their position as that of being guests in the community, they believe it inappropriate for the military to serve as a "battering ram" for effecting changes in local customs and mores. And even those who concede that efforts at amelioration are desirable frequently do not believe that they have the necessary authority.

These views of installation commanders are entitled to some weight. But in the United States of 1963, the military mission is not defined in such narrow terms. Today, as Gen. Maxwell Taylor, chairman of the Joint Chiefs of Staff, has said, "The national security program must include national programs in political, diplomatic, military, economic, psychological, and cultural fields which contribute to the stature and prestige of the United States and to the attainment of its national objectives. . . ."

In some places, the civilian community has taken root only after the military installation was established and thus it cannot be claimed that racial practices are protected by traditions which antedate the arrival of the military post.

Finally, the Department of Defense has ample instruments to attain the objectives of equal treatment for all servicemen. It makes decisions on opening, closing, and reactivating military installations. However, in making these determinations it does not discuss with community leaders any steps to prevent discrimination. With respect to existing installations, more flexible instruments are available to base commanders. There is evidence to suggest that where affirmative and imaginative programs of education, persuasion, and negotiation are entered into, they are likely to produce successful results. In North Dakota, for example, a base commander who was disturbed about continuing incidents of discrimination against his men protested to civilian authorities who then worked to secure passage of a public accommodations law. But most base

[*Civil Rights '63, 1963 Report of the U.S. Commission on Civil Rights,* 30 September 1963, Government Printing Office, Washington, DC.]

commanders have not apprised servicemen of their rights under state laws barring discrimination in public accommodations, or in private housing.

Since racial discrimination has an impact on the health, welfare and morale of servicemen at least equal to other unethical or immoral practices, negotiations with local businessmen to attain desegregation can legitimately be backed by the "off-limits" sanction. Where businesses, such as the gate establishments, are heavily dependent on military trade, it is unlikely that it will ever be necessary to employ the sanction. In other cases, the negotiating efforts of military commanders will be part of a national campaign for equal access to public accommodations.

Thus, a policy of securing equal treatment for all servicemen is an essential part of the military mission and commanders have both the responsibility and the means for carrying out such a policy. In the past, they have been hampered by a lack of overall direction from the Department of Defense. Now, however, the secretary of defense has taken steps to provide guidance to base commanders. As noted previously, the directive issued on July 26, 1963, assigned to local commanders the responsibility of fostering equal treatment for servicemen off base. Specific responsibility was placed upon the military commander to oppose discriminatory practices and to recommend use of the off-limits power. As part of this directive, the assistant secretary of defense for manpower was authorized to establish an office to give direction and guidance and to monitor the results of a program designed to achieve this objective.

SUMMARY

Since President Truman's 1948 order desegregating the armed forces, the status of the Negro serviceman has improved considerably. The army, air force and Marine Corps have increased their utilization of Negro enlisted men and the army and air force have a growing number of Negro officers. Only the navy has shown little or no improvement, relying less on Negro personnel during the Korean war than during World War II.

Negroes in the army and air force are used in a wide variety of occupational areas and in higher proportions than in the civilian economy. However, in the navy Negroes are generally used less in clerical, technical, and skilled occupations than is the case in the civilian economy. The problems of the navy are the severely limited number of Negroes enlisting and the lasting effects of the traditional assignment of Negroes to food-service jobs.

With an increasing pool of available manpower, the several services are becoming more selective in their recruitment policies and are using aptitude tests as one means for screening candidates. As yet no test has been developed which takes into account the special background factors of different cultural and economic groups.

With the desegregation of the services, all but a few aspects of racial discrimination were abolished from the military installation. Housing, schools, clubs, stores, and churches on post are all open to personnel without regard to race or color. However, in neighboring communities the Negro serviceman and his family still encounter the traditional patterns of discrimination and segregation. These practices in housing, education, and public and recreational facilities are galling reminders that second-class citizenship has not been completely eradicated, and have a detrimental impact on military morale and efficiency. Despite this, military officials traditionally have not considered community racial practices as matters within their concern although in some cases racial discrimination has been financed, supported, or accepted by the federal government.

In 1963, however, the Department of Defense recognized the adverse affect of these practices on the accomplishment of the military mission and began to assume responsibility for protecting service personnel and their families from segregation and discrimination on and off military installations.

RECOMMENDATIONS

The Commission recommends:

Recommendation 1. That the president direct that corrective action be undertaken in the Department of the Navy to assure equality of opportunity for Negroes to serve as officers and enlisted men and to broaden their occupational assignments and promotional opportunities.

Recommendation 2. That the president request the secretary of defense to reappraise testing procedures currently used by all services in the procurement of enlisted and officer personnel so that they will be validated for performance both in general and for persons differing in educational, economic, regional, and other background factors.

Recommendation 3. That the president request the secretary of defense to undertake periodic reviews of recruitment, selection, assignment, and promotion policies, and of procedures governing reductions in force for officers and enlisted men in each of the services, and to develop such affirmative programs as are required to utilize fully both Negro and white manpower resources. For this purpose, racial statistical data should be maintained for use in electronic data-processing equipment. Racial identification on personnel records should be deleted unless necessary and only then maintained under proper safeguards.

Recommendation 4. That the president request the secretary of defense to discontinue ROTC programs at any college or university which does not accept all students without regard to race or color.

Recommendation 5. That, in view of the Defense Department's firm commitment to a policy of equal treatment off base for all members of the armed forces and its establishment of an office to carry out this objective, the department direct its attention to the following problems:

    a. *The removal of all vestiges of racial discrimination from military installations,*[1] including segregated NCO clubs, segregation and differential treatment of Negroes in social activities, segregated transportation, discriminatory employment patterns in base facilities, and the use of military facilities and services by community organizations which discriminate.

    b. *Ensuring that in dealings with local communities the policy of the armed forces of equality of treatment prevails,*[1] particularly in areas such as armed forces participation in public events or ceremonies, the activities of base social and recreational organizations in the community, the assignment of military police and

---

[1] Emphasis in the original.

other base units to duty in the community, the treatment of servicemen by local law enforcement officials, and the use of segregated facilities in connection with troop movements.

c. *The adoption of an affirmative program to encourage the expansion of housing opportunities available to all military personnel.*[1] The program should include direct negotiations by local commanders for the desegregation of housing developments predominantly occupied by military personnel; cooperation with private fair-housing organizations; utilization of the resources of public agencies enforcing federal, state, and local anti-bias laws and referral of servicemen to housing covered by such laws; initiation of lawsuits pursuant to the housing executive order to desegregate projects receiving federal financial assistance; and revision of the procedures for planning additional military units to take into account discriminatory practices which reduce the supply of housing available to all personnel.

d. *The adoption of an affirmative program to assure equal treatment for all service personnel at places of public accommodation.*[1] The program should include the reorganization of command-community relations committees so that they will be of a more representative character; negotiations with business leaders for desegregation of public accommodations patronized by military personnel; use of the off-limits power where negotiations fail; utilization of state and local anti-bias laws; informing servicemen of their rights as well as their responsibilities and of command efforts to secure desegregation.

e. *The need for prudent negotiations with community leaders to reach agreements assuring equality of treatment for all servicemen before installations are opened, expanded or reactivated.*[1]

Recommendation 6. That the president and the secretary of the Department of Health, Education, and Welfare, in the granting of funds for the construction and operation of schools under the impacted area program, condition such grants upon the receipt of adequate assurances that all children in the district will be assigned to schools without regard to race.

---

[1]Emphasis in the original.

●

Discrimination in family housing was one of the most blatant and widespread forms of injustice suffered by black servicemen. The order against segregation in houses leased by the Department of Defense addressed an important but minor facet of the problem.

Effective immediately, all leases for family housing which are executed on behalf of the United States pursuant to the authority contained in Section 615, Public Law 161–81, as amended, shall contain the following clause:

[Memorandum, Sec. of Defense Robert S. McNamara for secretary of the army et al., 8 March 1963, subject: Nondiscrimination in family housing, General Archives Branch, Washington National Records Center, Suitland, MD.]

It is understood and agreed that the government will assign the desired premises to military personnel in accordance with Executive Order No. 11063, dated November 20, 1962, which provides that housing and related facilities shall be available without discrimination among tenants because of race, color, creed, or national origin.

In addition, effective immediately, listings maintained by base housing offices of available private housing shall include only those units which are available without regard to race, color, creed, or national origin.

Addressees shall ensure implementation of these directives and provide copies to my office.

CHAPTER ELEVEN
ACCOMPLISHMENTS AND FRUSTRATIONS

The Kennedy administration, though opposed to racial segregation, moved slowly to protect black servicemen from the humiliation and inconvenience caused by discriminatory practices in communities near military bases. Until some action was taken, schools in Virginia or Arkansas, for example, continued to bar the children of black servicemen; black air force officers stationed in Nebraska could not find housing except in a segregated area dozens of miles from their duty station. In 1963, acting upon recommendations of the biracial Advisory Committee on Equal Opportunity in the Armed Forces, headed by Gerhard A. Gesell, Secretary McNamara moved against the vestiges of segregation still found on military bases as well as against discrimination in nearby towns and cities both in the United States and overseas.

The Gesell Committee also addressed segregation in the National Guard. Secretary McNamara, who had remained in office when Lyndon B. Johnson succeeded John F. Kennedy, again acted upon the group's findings, but integration was painfully slow in coming to the guard. Indeed, it was the recommendations of yet another presidential committee, the Kerner Commission (headed by Governor Otto Kerner of Illinois), investigating the causes of racial violence in the nation's cities, that prodded the army into making a special effort to recruit blacks into the guard. The government hoped that greater racial balance would avoid the impression that a white National Guard was standing by to suppress urban rioters, many of whom were black.

The armed services made honest, though not always successful, efforts to improve race relations in the military. The army, navy, Marine Corps, and air force followed the Gesell Committee's recommendations in attempting to prevent racial prejudice from affecting recruitment, promotion, and assignment. Programs of education, including the creation of a Department of Defense race relations institute at Patrick Air Force Base, Florida, attempted to create a climate of sensitivity to the hopes and fears of racial and ethnic minorities. The Civil Rights Act of 1964, which outlawed most forms of discrimination, aided the armed forces in combatting racial harassment off military reservations.

These efforts, however, did not ensure racial harmony within the services. Occasional demonstrations and even riots testified to the truth of what various investigatory bodies now reported. Black servicemen believed they were victims of racial discrimination, especially in the administration of military justice. Commanders found it difficult to enforce discipline and at the same time remain sensitive to the concerns of blacks and members of other ethnic minorities. Volunteers from the black community sometimes discovered that the realities of service life scarcely resembled the idealized picture painted by the recruiter. Some black draftees shared the widely held, though statistically erroneous, belief that the number of blacks dying in Vietnam was out of proportion to their number in the army or the general population. In fact, the Vietnam conflict was a poor man's, rather than a black man's, war; economic class, not race alone, determined who would fight. Perceived injustice, rather than statistical data, determined the attitudes of black servicemen.

Conditions changed for the better, as the decade of the seventies came to a close. The Vietnam War ended, and the wounds it had inflicted on American society began to heal. The draft also came to a halt. Even before the nation began its experiment with an all-volunteer force, blacks were enlisting in greater numbers than ever before. Blacks made up almost 12 percent of the army's enlisted strength in 1964, the year that the Gesell Committee completed its work. In 1972, when the draft ended, this share exceeded 17 percent, and in 1979, the year before draft registration resumed, the proportion of blacks among enlisted men approached one third. Military service seemed an increasingly desirable vocation for blacks, so much so that some planners were becoming concerned that the United States soon would have enlisted forces drawn almost exclusively from economically distressed blacks and members of other impoverished minorities but commanded by a predominantly white officer corps.

The idea of creating a presidential committee to investigate
equality of opportunity in the armed services originated with
Adam Yarmolinsky, a special assistant to Sec. of Defense
Robert S. McNamara. Yarmolinsky hoped to improve military
efficiency by eliminating the last vestiges of racial discrimination
not only on bases but in nearby communities where the families
of servicemen lived, shopped, and attended school. The Gesell
Committee[1] came into existence in June 1962; one year later it
issued the first of two reports, this one dealing with conditions in
the United States. Pres. John F. Kennedy, who had given the
committee its formal instructions, declared that the initial report
rightly credited the armed services with making "significant
progress in eliminating discrimination among those serving in
defense of the nation," even as it pointed out that "much remains
to be done, especially in eliminating practices that cause
inconvenience and embarrassment to servicemen and their
families in communities adjoining military bases."

The armed forces have made an intelligent and far-reaching advance toward complete integration, and, with some variations from service to service, substantial progress toward equality of treatment and opportunity. By and large, military bases reflect a clear pattern of integration. Segregation or exclusion of Negroes from barracks or other on-base housing facilities is not allowed. Military messes and all other on-base facilities are open to all personnel without regard to race. Negro personnel serve with whites in almost all types of units and at all levels. Negroes command white and Negro troops. Although the distribution is quite uneven, Negroes have been placed in virtually all of the numerous job specialties and career fields which exist in the various services.

The committee feels, however, that the urgency of the remaining problems faced by Negro military personnel requires that this initial report be rendered at this time, so that corrective action may begin without delay. . . . Negro military personnel and their families are daily suffering humiliation and degradation in communities near the bases at which they are compelled to serve, and a vigorous, new program of action is needed to relieve the situation. In addition, remaining problems of equality of treatment and opportunity, both service-wide and at particular bases, call for correction. National policy requires prompt action to eliminate all these conditions. Equal opportunity for the Negro will exist only when it is possible for him to enter upon a career of military service with assurance that his acceptance and his progress will be in no way impeded by reason of his color. Clearly, distinctions based on race prevent full utilization of Negro military personnel and are inconsistent with the objectives of our democratic society. . . .

Service programs to attract personnel properly emphasize special educational backgrounds and technical training, a need resulting from the increasing complexity of

---

[President's Committee on Equal Opportunity in the Armed Forces, *Initial Report: Equality of Treatment and Equal Opportunity for Negro Military Personnel Stationed within the United States*, June 13, 1963, Center of Military History, Washington, DC.]

[1]Members of the committee were: Gerhard A. Gesell, the chairman; Nathaniel S. Colley, who participated in the initial report only; Abe Fortas, Louis J. Hector, Benjamin Muse, John H. Sengstacke, and Whitney M. Young, Jr.

military operations. Unless Negroes with such aptitudes are encouraged to enter the services, there is the danger that the Negro least attractive to private industry and other career fields—men not always in a position to take full advantage of the opportunity offered by the services—will enter the armed forces. . . .

Special efforts should be made to find and recruit Negroes with the special aptitudes the services now require and affirmative steps should be taken to ensure that no recruiting personnel, consciously or unconsciously, channel Negroes to particular career fields, disregarding their aptitudes.

To increase the pitifully small number of Negro officers, energetic efforts must be made to raise the number of Negroes in the academies and in all other programs which supply officers to the services. . . .

Because of the importance of the assignment of an occupational classification to a new enlisted man, the procedures affecting such assignment, as well as their results, must be carefully and regularly reviewed to see whether they operate to ensure equality of treatment and opportunity for Negro military personnel. When new Negro personnel or applicants are interviewed, they should be made aware of the variety of opportunities available before being required to express preferences for career fields. Special effort should be made to recognize potential capacities of Negroes at the time of recruitment and at other appropriate times, and to encourage their entering, with proper vocational assistance, into career fields which match latent skill.

In addition, continuing efforts must be made to place Negro personnel in as many special and technical career fields and positions of troop command as possible, in order to afford Negro personnel wide training and ensure the fullest utilization of available talent. In this regard, the disproportionate bunchings of Negro personnel in certain service career fields should be reexamined, these personnel retested, carefully advised about other fields for which they are trainable, retrained accordingly and reassigned. . . .

In view of the numerous complaints of discrimination in enlisted promotions and the slight participation of Negroes in the higher NCO ranks, the services should initiate, on a spot-check basis, periodic inquiries into the operation of enlisted promotion procedures, particularly to the higher NCO ranks.

To minimize the possibility that conscious or unconscious discrimination on the basis of race or color may affect the impartiality of the officer promotion system, photographs and racial designations in the folders reviewed by promotion boards should be eliminated. Every opportunity should be taken to appoint Negro officers to serve on promotion boards, in normal rotation. Techniques for assuring that all promotion-board members are free from conscious or unconscious racial bias should be developed. Whenever possible, officers chosen to serve on promotion boards should be chosen from those who have had more than casual experience serving with Negro officers and enlisted personnel. To the extent that similar situations pertain in the enlisted promotion system, like steps should be taken there. . . .

Reference has already been made to the highly successful program of the armed forces to bring about full integration and to the progress made toward equality of treatment and opportunity. More is required. Many of the remaining problems result from the lack of communication between Negro military personnel and the command echelon at bases.

Equality of treatment and opportunity is not the responsibility of any particular official or office in any of the services. Rather, responsibility is service-wide, in the sense that a general policy has been defined by broad directives. As a result, no machinery exists at any particular base by which a given officer is specifically charged with continuing responsibility in this area. There is no satisfactory method of handling complaints. Conditions conducive to discriminatory practices are often not even known to commanders. The Negro serviceman may complain to his immediate superior but it is rare that these complaints reach the attention of the base commander or members of his immediate staff. As problems become severe, they may or may not receive attention at one or more echelons in the command. In sum, there is no affirmative and continuing effort to monitor race-relations problems on base.

An important by-product of the committee's work has been a new awareness, on the part of many of the commanders of bases visited, of the necessity for greater efforts to eliminate remaining obstacles to equality of treatment and opportunity in the armed forces. For example, on visits to bases, committee members noted a number of discriminatory practices. Such practices were often remedied forthwith when brought to the attention of the base commander by committee members. This illustrates the value of expanded communications between Negro military personnel and base commanders. Means must be found to keep base commanders informed of such conditions as they develop. It is clear to the committee that only by fixing responsibility and establishing some means for monitoring these matters, base-by-base, can problems of discrimination, which will inevitably arise from time to time, be cured effectively and promptly.

At the present time, the absence of an effective procedure for dealing with complaints has led Negro personnel to complain to congressmen and to various private groups such as the NAACP[2] and to broadcast letters, sometimes anonymous, to individuals and groups interested in racial matters. The investigation of these letters through the traditional inspector general or Department of Defense channels is often fruitless. These authorities are not geared to handle such problems and too much time elapses, making it difficult to ascertain the facts.

There exists in the minds of many Negro personnel the fear that they will be subject to criticism and reprisal if they raise matters of this kind. Procedures must be developed which eliminate this fear and encourage them to present their complaints. Merely stating that reprisals are forbidden is not enough.

Some complaints will emerge that a specific individual has suffered discriminatory treatment of some kind. Such complaints, involving matters relating to a single person, such as failing to be promoted, cannot ordinarily be investigated without disclosing the identity of the aggrieved individual. This is not true, however, where the complaint discloses a discriminatory condition on base, such as a segregated NCO club. Such conditions can be investigated and eliminated without the need for identifying a particular complainant. . . .

In order to improve the processing of complaints at the base level. . . . an officer should be designated at each base to receive such complaints. This officer must have free access to the base commander or his deputy for the purpose of communicating and discussing complaints of discrimination. Commanders at bases must, of course, be held personally responsible for the effectiveness of the system and for conditions on the base. Discriminatory conditions may exist even where few complaints are made, and the commander should be held accountable to discover and remedy such conditions. . . .

---

[2]National Association for the Advancement of Colored People.

Although the Supreme Court has declared that laws requiring segregation of public schools or other public facilities are unconstitutional, the committee's studies have disclosed that a very substantial number of communities neighboring military bases practice various forms of segregation. Segregation is found in varying degrees throughout the United States. In some communities local laws require segregation; in others the condition derives from custom and the wishes of the local population. The pattern of discrimination and segregation is, of course, particularly noticeable in southern communities, but there are substantial variations from community to community and state to state. Forms of discrimination appear in many northern communities. Discrimination in housing is almost universal. Some bases established in states such as the Dakotas have confronted forms of segregation and discrimination which have much of the same rigidity found in certain southern communities. . . .

It is not surprising, but most discouraging, to have to report that there are bases where Negro personnel confront such intolerable conditions off base that almost any device will be employed to effect a change in duty assignment. Applications for transfer,[3] infractions of rules and a general contempt for the "system" are apt to appear. The effect on service morale and efficiency is apparent. The committee's inquiries, including interviews with many base commanders, made it clear that the accomplishment of the military mission of a base confronted with such conditions is measurably impaired. There was general agreement among base commanders that the morale of both white and Negro troops suffers in the presence of such indignities and inequities. A practical program for dealing with off-base discrimination against Negro military personnel and their dependents is urgently required. . . .

The focal point of any practical approach to this most pressing problem is the base commander.[4] He represents the military in the area. It is his duty to be concerned with the welfare of those under his command. He is in a better position than higher echelons to identify the particular discrimination forms prevalent in the community neighboring his base. On his shoulders should fall the primary responsibility for solving local problems. . . .

RECOMMENDATIONS FOR AN URGENTLY NEEDED PROGRAM

1. The Defense Department and the services must redefine responsibilities, establish goals and provide detailed instructions. . . .

2. Commanders' performance must be rated, monitored and supported. . . .

3. Command training programs and manuals should treat all aspects of discrimination problems and solutions. . . .

---

[3]In order to maintain maximum utilization of manpower, the services generally deny transfers to Negro servicemen when such transfers are requested upon the sole ground that they and their families are suffering racial discrimination in the communities where their places of duty are located. Exceptions may be made for particularly severe cases. [Footnote in the original.]

[4]At some bases, there are commanders senior to the person designated as the base commander. Where this is true, the attitudes of the senior commander are naturally given great weight by the base commander. In such situations, the considerations discussed in the context of the base commander's functions apply with equal force to the role of this senior commander located at the base. [Footnote in the original.]

4. Base commanders must establish biracial community committees and by this and other means lead efforts to reduce discrimination. . . .

5. Where efforts of base commanders are unsuccessful sanctions are available and should be employed. . . .

6. Officials charged with responsibility for equality of treatment and opportunity on and off base should be appointed in the Defense Department and the services. . . .

●

Having completed their investigation of the effect of racial discrimination upon servicemen and their families in the United States, the committee members studied the problem as it arose overseas and in the National Guard, an organization that Judge Gesell's group termed "the only branch of the armed forces which has not been fully integrated." The president's committee, chartered by John F. Kennedy, submitted this last report to Pres. Lyndon B. Johnson about one year after Mr. Kennedy's assassination.

SUMMARY OF OVERSEAS RECOMMENDATIONS

In brief, the committee recommends the following steps be taken to improve equality of treatment and opportunity for Negro servicemen overseas:

1. All recommendations contained in the *Initial Report* dealing with problems of equal opportunity on base within the United States are of equal importance abroad and DoD[1] policies implementing these recommendations should be promptly applied abroad.

2. Vigorous efforts should be made by commanders of overseas bases to eliminate patterns of segregation and discrimination affecting troops off base. Special attention should be paid to taverns, bars and other places of amusement which cater to our servicemen, and to housing. It is particularly urgent to do this where the discrimination reflects attitudes of some of our own military personnel and is not generally practiced by nationals of the host country involved. It is essential that commanders remain in constant touch with conditions surrounding bases overseas and that commanders be closely monitored as to their performance in carrying out responsibilities in this area. If the problem cannot be solved by consultation with local authorities and well-directed use of military police, the development of improved recreational opportunities on base and other similar steps, then the off-limits authority granted by existing DoD directives should be utilized.

[The President's Committee on Equal Opportunity in the Armed Forces, *Final Report: Military Personnel Stationed Overseas and Membership and Participation in the National Guard,* November 1964, Center of Military History, Washington, DC.]

[1] Department of Defense.

3. A continuing review should be made of DoD policies affecting assignment of military personnel to attache, mission and military-assistance-group duty to assure that race is not a factor in determining routine selection for such assignments.

4. The Department of State should take appropriate administrative steps to ensure its full cooperation in carrying out the two preceding recommendations.

THE NATIONAL GUARD

The National Guard is the only branch of the armed forces which has not been fully integrated. Executive Order 9981 establishing the policy of equal treatment and opportunity in the armed services did not apply to the guard.

In addition to the reserves of the four services, the active army and air force are supported by a substantial National Guard organization. The National Guard is organized into units allocated among the states. These units are an important part of our overall organization for national defense. In past wars and periods of crisis, the guard has played an important role and served with bravery and distinction. . . .

Unlike the reserves of the services, which are under purely federal control, the guard has a dual status. In many respects, the rules by which it is governed are provided by Congress under its broad constitutional power over the guard, and by an exercise of rule-making power delegated by Congress to the president. Day-to-day control and supervision, however, are a function of state organizations headed by the state adjutants general, who report to the state governor. Individual guardsmen also have a dual status. Upon joining the guard they take a dual oath and are enrolled as members of the reserve as well as of the particular state guard unit. In addition to their state status, they are thus federally recognized so that they may receive the pay provided by the federal government for participation in the program and are subject to call to active federal duty. . . .

RECOMMENDATIONS AFFECTING THE NATIONAL GUARD

It is clear that discrimination against Negroes exists in the operation of guard units of some states. In some states, for example, there is a complete or almost complete absence of Negroes in officer ranks. Similarly, the participation of Negroes in enlisted ranks in the case of some states is still only on a token basis, a condition that carries special emphasis where such states with a large Negro population and units are not at full authorized strength.

It is impossible to state with complete assurance that equality of treatment and opportunity for Negroes in the guard can be achieved solely by voluntary means. Recent progress in this direction is sufficient, however, to offer some basis for a belief that an attempt to reach this objective by voluntary methods may be successful. This will require an increased and more pointed effort and prompt corrective action when discrimination is disclosed.

The voluntary program now under way should not be allowed to lag. Progress should be closely and frequently checked by responsible authorities. Three immediate steps are recommended:

First, the president should, by appropriate means, make it clear that the national interest requires equality of treatment and opportunity for all persons enrolling or serving in the guard without regard to race, color, religion or national origin. Such a declaration will serve to reenforce the actions of state and federal authorities concerned with this problem. Second, the National Guard Bureau should be provided with more information than is now available as to enrollment, recruitment, assignment and promotion of Negroes. Regular reports should be required from the states in order to provide a basis for more informed and persistent efforts at voluntary compliance. Third, recent changes in guard policies toward Negroes, membership should be widely publicized to attract the interests of Negroes who can meet the high standards and exacting duties of guard membership.

If reasonable efforts to achieve full equality of treatment and opportunity by voluntary means prove inadequate in a given instance it will then be necessary to apply the applicable provisions of the Civil Rights Act. Title VI of that act, Section 601, states:

> *No person in the United States shall, on the ground of race, color, or national origin, be excluded from participation in, be denied the benefits of, or be subjected to discrimination under any program or activity receiving federal financial assistance.*

Since the National Guard is a federally-assisted program, the detailed procedures for implementing this title of the act are available to require the elimination of racial discrimination by the state authorities responsible for their respective guard units. . . .

•

This document enacted the basic program proposed by the Gesell Committee in its initial report. The directive went into effect immediately and required the military departments— army, navy, and air force—to complete by 15 August 1963 outline plans for carrying out its provisions.

I. POLICY

It is the policy of the Department of Defense to conduct all of its activities in a manner which is free from racial discrimination, and which provides equal opportunity for all uniformed members and all civilian employees irrespective of their color.

Discriminatory practices directed against armed forces members, all of whom lack a civilian's freedom of choice in where to live, to work, to travel and to spend his off-duty hours, are harmful to military effectiveness. Therefore, all members of the Department of Defense should oppose such practices on every occasion, while fostering equal opportunity for servicemen and their families, on and off base.

II. RESPONSIBILITIES

A. Office of the Secretary of Defense

1. Pursuant to the authority vested in the secretary of defense and the provisions of the National Security Act of 1947, as amended, the assistant secretary of defense

---

[Department of Defense Directive No. 5120.36, 26 July 1963, subject: Equal opportunity in the armed forces, Office of Deputy Assistant Secretary of Defense (Administration), Washington, DC.]

(Manpower) is hereby assigned responsibility and authority for promoting equal opportunity for members of the armed forces.

In the performance of this function he shall (a) be the representative of the secretary of defense in civil rights matters, (b) give direction to programs that promote equal opportunity for military personnel, (c) provide policy guidance and review policies, regulations and manuals of the military departments, and (d) monitor their performance through periodic reports and visits to field installations.

2. In carrying out the functions enumerated above, the assistant secretary of defense (Manpower) is authorized to establish the Office of Deputy Assistant Secretary of Defense (Civil Rights).

B. The Military Departments

1. The military departments shall, with the approval of the assistant secretary of defense (Manpower), issue appropriate instructions, manuals and regulations in connection with the leadership responsibility for equal opportunity, on and off base, and containing guidance for its discharge.

2. The military departments shall institute in each service a system for regularly reporting, monitoring and measuring progress in achieving equal opportunity on and off base.

C. Military Commanders

Every military commander has the responsibility to oppose discriminatory practices affecting his men and their dependents and to foster equal opportunity for them, not only in areas under his immediate control, but also in nearby communities where they may live or gather in off-duty hours. In discharging that responsibility a commander shall not, except with the prior approval of the secretary of his military department, use the off-limits sanction in discrimination cases arising within the United States. . . .

●

Typical of the objections to the work of the Gesell Committee were the remarks of Sen. John C. Stennis of Mississippi. Although Sen. Barry Goldwater of Arizona expressed doubt that "there is a senator who will defend the directive" that incorporated the committee's recommendations, opposition centered in the south and was voiced by senators like A. Willis Robertson of Virginia, Spessard L. Holland of Florida, and Herman E. Talmadge of Georgia.

Mr. Stennis: Mr. President, those of us who have long insisted that our military people be confined to their historic and traditional roles and missions are greatly

[U.S., Congress, Senate, *Congressional Record,* 87th Cong., 2d sess., 1963, "The Gesell Committee and the Perversion of the Military."]

disturbed by the fact that there has recently been introduced a new, different, and added mission which can only be detrimental to military tradition, discipline, and morale.

This new and previously unheard-of mission is designed to shape our military force as an instrument for social reform and can only result in irreparable injury to the military profession. In addition, it is a grave and serious challenge to the long-established and traditional concept of complete separation of the military from all political matters and activities.

The action of the secretary of defense which I shall discuss is but the latest step in the current massive and widespread assault upon constitutional principles in the misguided and so-called civil rights drive. It is now proposed that the military profession itself be utilized as a driving force in the establishment of a new social and political order which involves race relations and individual associations in off-base areas surrounding our military establishments. . . .

●

Stephen N. Schulman summarized progress since the
creation of his office, formerly the Office of Deputy Assistant
Secretary of Defense (Civil Rights), to help implement
Department of Defense Directive 5120.36, 26 July 1963.

In transmitting the Gesell Report to Secretary McNamara, President Kennedy said "discriminatory practices are morally wrong wherever they occur—they are especially inequitable and iniquitous when they inconvenience and embarrass those who serve in the armed forces and their families." A few weeks later Secretary McNamara replied: "Guided by these words . . . the military departments will take a leadership role in combatting discrimination wherever it affects the military effectiveness of the men and women serving in defense of this country." Shortly thereafter, in July 1963, the secretary put out a Defense Department directive giving the assistant secretary of defense (Manpower)—my boss—the responsibility for promoting equal opportunity in the armed forces. At the same time, he created the office which I now hold and directed the military departments to issue appropriate instructions and regulations to take a leadership role. . . .

As a result, the equal-opportunity program has two parts—on base and off base. Each is important. Obviously, we have more control over the one than the other.

On base, we have proceeded on many fronts. A basic problem has been a lack of awareness on the part of minority youth of the opportunities available for a military career. A program of equal opportunity is obviously not meaningful if minority groups are unaware of it or do not believe it exists with the result of avoiding participation. We have attempted to solve this problem both with respect to officers and enlisted personnel.

For officers, we have encouraged applications of qualified Negro youth to the service academies and in the process have doubled the participation of Negroes at these

---

["The Civil Rights Policies of the Department of Defense," a speech by Stephen N. Shulman, deputy assistant secretary of defense (Civilian Personnel, Industrial Relations, and Civil Rights), 4 May 1965, Office of Deputy Assistant Secretary of Defense (Equal Opportunity), Washington, DC.]

institutions. I might say that the number is still sufficiently small to demonstrate that additional efforts are necessary to ensure that qualified youth are in fact aware of those opportunities. We have sought to improve the ROTC units at predominantly Negro schools and the participation of Negroes in ROTC units at all other schools.

For enlisted personnel, we have reviewed and improved our recruiting literature to assure that it adequately covers our devotion to equal opportunity. We have begun to examine the aptitude tests administered by the armed services to be sure that they do not contain any cultural bias.

Our statistical reports show Negroes entering the enlisted ranks at a rate roughly proportionate to other members in the general population and they are advancing into the upper enlisted grades in increasing numbers. Most significantly, Negro servicemen are reenlisting, becoming careerists, at a significantly higher rate—in some cases two to one—than their white counterparts. This shows that Negroes in the service are aware of the opportunities for advancement without discrimination. The difficulty is in getting the word out to the community.

For both officers and enlisted personnel, we are giving careful attention to assignment procedures to be sure that no discrimination can crop up, and we have paid particular attention to the assignment of Negro officers to the senior service schools, such as the Staff College here at [Fort] Leavenworth [Kansas] and the war colleges, and to those positions of command that are so vital to officer advancement to the highest ranks. In the matter of promotion we have made special effort to eliminate, whenever possible, racial designations in promotion folders and any possible consideration of race by promotion boards. We have also introduced statistical reports which will plot for us the Negro's relative position in the armed services and we intend to make future studies to assure ourselves that the Negro career serviceman proceeds through the same career development patterns as those of his white fellows. . . .

Turning to problems off base, we confront an area in which, as I mentioned, we have less control. The responsibilities of military commanders in the off-base area were defined by Secretary McNamara in 1963 in the following terms:

> *Every military commander has the responsibility to oppose discriminatory practices affecting his men and their dependents and to foster equal opportunity for them, not only in areas under his immediate control but also in nearby communities where they may live or gather in off-duty hours.*

Thus instructed, commanders are thrust into the whole panoply of civil rights; they must seek equality wherever discrimination rears its ugly head—in education, in public accommodations, in recreation, in housing, in all of the areas in which morale and thus military effectiveness may be impaired because of the denial of opportunities otherwise available. They do this in furtherance of their military mission.

The Civil Rights Act of 1964 has been a great help to our off-base program. Implementing it, we have issued specific instructions requiring that legal assistance be given to servicemen seeking their rights under Title II, III, and IV. . . . [dealing with] public accommodations, public facilities, and public education. We have required that all servicemen be informed of their rights under the act, and have instructed commanders to support their personnel who seek to enjoy those rights. Together with other federal departments and agencies, we have issued regulations implementing Title VI—the denial of financial assistance to discriminatory programs. The National Guard and various civil defense programs are the principal activities subject to these regulations. . . .

Commanders have engaged, both before and after the Civil Rights Act, in any number of efforts to promote equality off base at hundreds of installations across the country. We are also requiring efforts to promote equality off base abroad.

Our experience has been varied. We have achieved notable successes. We have also had failures.

In a half-dozen cases, housing developments adjoining military installations have been integrated, and in more than a token fashion, specifically for the benefit of military personnel. In a few cases, trailer parks have been similarly integrated. Others have not.

In the area of public accommodations, our officers have been successful since well before the Civil Rights Act in securing the voluntary desegregation of hundreds of establishments near our bases, sometimes simply by asking these establishments what their policy was. These accomplishments numbered in the hundreds before the Civil Rights Act was passed.

In several areas, the efforts of our commanders have resulted in public-school systems being integrated, mostly—and in a few cases, solely—for the benefit of the children of Negro military personnel. In other cases, our commanders' efforts have produced a speedup in already planned desegregation. Similar instances have occurred with respect to higher education. . . .

●

The first two persons to serve as deputy assistant secretary of defense (Civil Rights), Albert B. Fitt and Stephen N. Shulman, could take credit for providing leadership in several key reforms. These policy changes resulted in a larger number of blacks serving as officers and noncommissioned officers, greater equality of opportunity, and less discrimination on military installations and in nearby communities. As this memorandum conceded, however, a number of problems remained.

Our review of our work indicates that while we have focused attention on the solution of the problems within the purview of our responsibilities, and have made progress along most fronts, we must still address ourselves to many aspects of the problem.

A. Housing: Open and Adequate

The most stubborn problem that we confront in our off-base responsibility to achieve equality of opportunity for minority-group personnel and their families is in the area of housing.

Whereas there have been some breakthroughs in this area, it is the field in which we have our most difficulty. Negro servicemen and their families, like Negroes generally,

---

[Memorandum, Office of Assistant Secretary of Defense (Manpower) for Mr. [Norman] Paul, subject: Policy formulation, planning and action in the Office of the Deputy Assistant Secretary of Defense (Civil Rights), 26 July 1963–26 September 1965, 21 September 1965, Office of the Deputy Assistant Secretary of Defense (Equal Opportunity), Washington, DC.]

are offered the dilapidated, substandard houses in the most undesirable sections of a city and required to pay rents not commensurate with the housing value they receive. Many men are reluctant to move their families to certain communities if at their prior assignment they have been able to find fairly decent living accommodations. The housing problem is difficult in all sections of the country and reflects the national reluctance to deal with this problem in a forthright and meaningful way.

The problem requires special attention. We should carefully assess what commanders have done and where there have been breakthroughs, evaluate their techniques to see if they could be applied to other communities. We must do some creative thinking ourselves and see if there are new techniques that can be applied to this vexing problem. . . .

B. Monitoring and Evaluation

One of the areas of responsibility about which we must admit a serious shortcoming has been that of monitoring the performance of the programs by making periodic visits to field installations. We have required of the military departments periodic reports, but this type of monitoring alone is not sufficient. There are some understandable reasons why we have not done periodic visits to the installations. The flak immediately after the creation of the office was so intense it was considered desirable to abide field visits until such time as congressional criticisms and attacks on the program had subsided. Shortly after this period of amnesty was achieved the civil-rights debate began in Congress and it was deemed prudent not to provide opponents to civil-rights legislation with any ammunition that could be fashioned out of visits to defense installations of an investigating and monitoring nature. By the time the civil-rights debate had concluded we were at the beginning of the presidential election. We thought it politically advisable to remain at home during that period. By the time January 1965 rolled around the administrative requirements of the office, absent of field visits, had reached the point of involving our small staff almost full time. . . .

C. Promotion and Morale

Another problem that creates consternation and at times frustration is the problem of advancement and promotion. . . . We receive complaints from Members of Congress concerning noncommissioned personnel, some sent directly to the president, the vice president and the attorney general, and others directly from the serviceman who knows of the existence of some shop here in the Pentagon where he can address his complaints. . . .

D. Officer Education—Commander Orientation

While some of our commanders have exercised commendable leadership in the area of equal opportunity and equal treatment, others have half-heartedly undertaken this responsibility, while others have been timid and overly cautious, exhibiting the caution that attends dealing with the new and the strange. It is traditional and necessary that a commander establishes effective working relationships with the community, and that all times he has the responsibility to secure the well-being of his men as they live, work and recreate in that community. But it is only since 1963 that we have clearly indicated that along with a concern for the off-base problems of vice and prostitution, disease and sanitation, there are matters of equal opportunity and equal treatment for the men in service and their families. This is a difficult field even for the students and social engineers—the experts—working in the field. It cannot help but present baffling and at times ominous difficulties for the uninitiated. Our service-directed educational programs have done very little in the way of preparing our officers for dealing with these often complicated, subtle and hard problems.

I would suggest and recommend that in order to prepare and support our officers for the more . . . effective discharge of their responsibility for off-base equality of opportunity that we develop education and orientation programs for all our officers and commanders. . . .

F. Officer Procurement: Quality, Quantity and at a Lower Cost

The Negro officer represents a symbol of the degree to which we are successful in achieving equal opportunity and equal treatment in the armed forces. The military departments have already demonstrated their capacity to make progress in this area. Indeed to forge ahead of the rest of the nation. The distance to travel, however, is great. But in achieving our goals we must continue to make input of Negroes into the officer corps—today the Negro officer is 3.4 percent of the army officer complement, 1.5 percent of the air force officer complement, and 0.3 percent of the navy, and 0.4 percent of the Marine Corps.

We propose to continue our program of stimulating and encouraging minority-group youth to utilize the opportunities at the academies. We can say without equivocation that there is no discrimination at the service academies. It must also be said that there is an aspect of this problem that is beyond our direct influence. It is the fact that 86 percent of the appointments to the academies are by congressional appointment.

We believe that there is a heightened sense of concern in the predominantly Negro colleges with ROTC programs, about their deficiencies and the necessity for their improving the quality and increasing the quantity of the input. As far as the limitations of our staff will permit we propose joint visits of one day to the more seriously deficient of these colleges. . . .

G. Ready Reserve and National Guard—Increased Negro Participation

For the ready reserves, we must establish a review procedure, including a statistical reporting requirement, that will ensure equal opportunity in these programs. As we have seen, the Negro participation in the ready reserves was only about 4 percent in 1962, when participation in the active force was 8.2 percent. However, we rarely receive any complaints about reserve practices and there appears to be at least one good reason—the higher active duty retention rate—for a somewhat lower Negro participation rate in this program. On the other hand, though, we can reasonably suspect that, discrimination aside, buddy-type recruiting practices of the ready reserve might tend to perpetuate present racial patterns. We need more data to confirm these probabilities and suspicions.

The National Guard situation is similar to, but somewhat worse than, the ready reserves problem. The guard in the South is just emerging from a nearly completely exclusive pattern—no Negroes at all—and even in northern and western states, Negroes rarely constitute more than 3 percent of the guard population. (Only in a few state guards which formerly contained one or more all-Negro units). Nationwide, as of 1 February 1965, the guard had only 1.3 percent Negro participation. . . .

However far the guard has come, it had the farthest to come; and however good the recently developed procedures for measuring Negro participation, it remains for the guard to go out to the Negro community, erase the "white fraternity" image which it all too often earned, and encourage and recruit Negroes for positions throughout the guard structure.

CONCLUSION

The review of our two years of operation—policy formulation, planning and action—in the civil-rights element of the Office of Secretary of Defense reveals significant advances. The gains have been along many fronts. The steps have been short. The statistical data is quantitatively small, but the quality of the whole effort represents a good product—a good result. This is not to say that discriminatory patterns are entirely eliminated from the military departments, or that commanders have acquired the skills and techniques, and the Civil Rights Act with its lawful requirements has banished off-base discrimination. Essentially, we have initiated a forward movement, have tugged at institutional inertia and have generated momentum in the right direction. It is fair to say that in almost every area of our responsibility, our work is cut out for us. For our office to carry out its responsibilities and for the services to achieve their objectives consistent with our policies[,] all of us, together, must continue to work unceasingly at our jobs.

Our policies are clear. The formulation-of-policy phase of our work is completed. We have embarked on the implementation phase. In this area we have made significant advances, but we can make even more substantial gains given the unqualified support at the highest levels of authority. We need a new thrust, the injection of a new dynamic to generate a heightened spirit of affirmative implementation. We can provide that spirit, that dynamic, that thrust.

At long last, the Department of Defense decided to move against segregated housing in communities with concentrations of service families. The initial step, a means of exerting none-too-subtle pressure on landlords, was a nationwide survey of rental units available to members of the armed forces. In Washington, DC, and its suburbs, the survey would lead to positive action, a test of procedures that might be used throughout the nation.

1. The commanding officer of each installation in the continental United States, having 500 or more military personnel assigned, shall prepare a census of all multiple-housing units meeting the following specifications:

    a. *Location:* within normal commuting distance of the base.

    b. *Type:* Apartment houses, housing developments and mobile courts.

    c. *Size:* Consisting of five or more rental units.

    d. *Significant for Military Occupancy:* Defines as those facilities (1) 40 percent or more of whose units are occupied by military personnel or (2) which by reason of location, accommodations, and price are considered by the commander to be especially suitable for military occupancy.

2. The commanding officer shall determine for each of the above facilities—

    a. Those which are equally available to military personnel. For each of these he shall note those which have adopted a policy of nondiscrimination.

    b. Those which are practicing racial discrimination. . . .

In addition to the above arrangement, I shall shortly appoint a top-level official to serve as the "off-base housing services coordinator" for the Washington, DC metropolitan area, with the following responsibilities:

    a. Conduct the housing census. . . .

    b. Establish a housing referral service, conveniently available to all military families in the Washington, DC metropolitan area. The metropolitan area off-base housing coordinator shall have to direct responsibility for the Joint Housing Office located in the Pentagon.

    c. Arrange for personalized assistance to military families in this area who require help in locating suitable off-base housing.

    d. Work with and through base commanders in this area to obtain community support and affirmative action from governmental officials, leading citizens, civic, religious and other appropriate groups, realtors and others in the community to assure equal opportunity in off-base housing for military families.

[Memorandum, secretary of defense for secretaries of the military departments, 11 April 1967, subject: Equal opportunity for military personnel in rental of off-base housing, Office of the Deputy Assistant Secretary of Defense (Administration), Washington, DC.]

The reserve components, notably the National Guard, remained largely impervious to the Gesell Committee reforms. A number of factors contributed to this condition—the racial composition of the community from which the unit was drawn; "buddy" recruiting that tended to result in new members of the same race as those who brought them into the organization; and the fact, pointed out by Marion Barry, who would become mayor of Washington, that reserve training interfered with the night or weekend jobs that many young blacks needed to supplement their normal incomes. Urban violence in cities with large black populations finally caused the military to make a special effort to "Increase substantially the recruitment of Negroes into the Army and Air National Guard," beyond the 1967 figures of 1.15 and 0.6 percent respectively, a step recommended by the President's National Advisory Commission on Civil Disorders. Rioting thus accomplished what Judge Gesell and his colleagues could not.

The board [headed by Brig. Gen. Robert Williams, assistant judge advocate general, that studied black participation in the Army National Guard and Army Reserve] found that Negroes constitute 11.4 percent of the active army, 1.3 percent of the ARNG[1] and 3.1 percent of USAR[2] units. The board suggested that if Negroes do not appear to be interested in joining ARNG and USAR units, the causes must be sought within both the military and civilian communities. As for the military aspects, it is alleged that recruiting and reenlistment efforts have lagged, that discrimination is practiced, that matters peculiar to the units (geographical distribution, location of training sites, and type of skills required) restrain Negro membership, and that reserve service generally is unattractive today, or is less attractive than service in the active army. Suggested causes to be found within the civilian community include lack of military tradition, belief that the Negro is not truly welcome and unwillingness to be associated with an entity of the "white power structure." There was little overt evidence discovered by the board to support the allegation that active discrimination is a cause for low participation by Negroes in the reserve components. There is no doubt, however, that racial discrimination has existed previously, and that as a result the attitude persists that racial discrimination continues to be practiced in the selection of individuals for enlistment and advancement in the reserve components. This attitude, to the extent that leaders are opinion moulders, influences and reflects the present attitude of the military-age Negro. The comparatively low number of Negroes waiting to join reserve components can be attributed to the same reasons or attitudes.

The Williams Board recommended authorization of an overstrength in each state based upon the available and eligible Negro manpower of the various states, with a goal

---

[Briefing for Gen. William C. Westmoreland, army chief of staff, on Negro participation in the reserve components, n.d. (July 1969), Center of Military History, Washington, DC.]

[1] Army National Guard.

[2] US Army Reserve.

of attaining a national participation rate of 11 percent in both the Army National Guard and the US Army Reserve.

In order to avoid discrimination against non-Negro personnel desiring to enlist in the reserve components, Negro accessions were to be considered as authorized overstrength. . . .

The plan includes increasing the percentage of Negro officers in the reserve components. . . .

Included in the plan is a publicity campaign and recruiting program designed to attain the desired Negro participation. . . .

The Army National Guard designed a test program for the state of New Jersey to determine if Negro recruitment could be increased. This test program extended from August '67 to July '68. The Army National Guard of the state of New Jersey was authorized a 5 percent overstrength. A publicity campaign aimed toward the enlistment of Negroes was prepared which included a complete saturation of the news media to include TV, radio and newspapers, with publicity specifically designed to enhance the National Guard program. In addition, speakers and discussion leaders appeared before local and regional Negro groups to explain the recruiting program and to discuss plans and procedures for further cooperation and dissemination of information on the test program.

At the outset of this test, the various news media reacted with a "tongue-in-cheek" attitude; this attitude changed as the program began to build a head of steam and the news media adopted a cooperative spirit with information being presented in an objective manner. The final results of this program prove conclusively that with a maximum effort, additional Negro recruitment can be accomplished. During the period of the test program, the ARNG enlisted 639 additional Negroes, which was 86.7 percent of the overall objective. Approximately 850 Negroes are currently members of the New Jersey Army National Guard, which represents 6 percent of the overall strength. The percentage of the overall strength at the beginning of the test was 1.7 percent. . . .

In summary, General Westmoreland, it has been proven by the New Jersey test model that Negroes can be recruited in greater numbers than in the past. It is important to point out, however, that the state of New Jersey cooperated fully in this campaign and a maximum effort produced good results. It is possible that we will not experience such a high degree of success in many other states.

*These official statistics, which indicated that the percentage
of blacks killed in battle corresponded closely to the percentage
of blacks in the army, failed to resolve a vexing problem.
Although some scholars, like sociologist Charles C. Moskos,
Jr., have accepted the figures as supporting the proposition
that the poor, regardless of race, were the likeliest to serve and
die, others persist in rejecting this theory, terming the Vietnam
conflict a "black man's war." There is general agreement,
however, that if blacks or any other easily identifiable minority
should suffer a disproportionate share of casualties in some
future war, the effectiveness of the army would suffer.*

NEGRO PARTICIPATION IN THE ARMED FORCES

(As of 31 March 1971)

Over 275,000 Negroes were on active duty with the armed forces as of 31 March 1971; they represented 9.9 percent of our total active duty force. Negro participation was as follows:

Mil Service	Officer			Enlisted			Total		
	Total	Negro	(%)	Total	Negro	(%)	Total	Negro	(%)
Army	155,797	5,480	(3.5)	1,027,911	140,625	(13.7)	1,183,708	146,105	(12.3)
Navy	76,486	518	(0.7)	556,506	29,660	(5.3)	632,992	30,178	(4.8)
Mar Corps	22,322	287	(1.3)	199,671	22,296	(11.2)	221,993	22,583	(10.2)
Air Force	126,958	2,216	(1.7)	627,373	74,745	(11.9)	754,331	76,961	(10.2)
TOTAL	381,563	8,501	(2.2)	2,411,461	267,326	(11.1)	2,793,024	275,827	(9.9)

NEGRO PARTICIPATION IN SOUTHEAST ASIA

(Vietnam, Thailand and Nearby Off-Shore Waters)
(As of 31 March 1971)

Mil Service	Officer			Enlisted			Total		
	Total	Negro	(%)	Total	Negro	(%)	Total	Negro	(%)
Army	31,204	1,027	(3.3)	218,084	28,650	(13.1)	249,288	29,677	(11.9)
Navy	4,022	40	(1.0)	37,268	1,809	(4.8)	41,290	1,849	(4.5)
Mar Corps	1,862	17	(0.9)	16,790	1,785	(10.6)	18,652	1,802	(9.7)
Air Force	4,991	59	(2.7)	58,866	8,383	(14.2)	63,857	8,442	(13.2)
TOTAL	42,079	1,143	(2.7)	331,008	40,627	(12.3)	373,087	41,770	(11.2)

[*Negro Participation in the Armed Forces and in Southeast Asia*, 31 March 1971, Office of the Deputy Assistant Secretary of Defense (Equal Opportunity), Washington, DC.]

NEGRO DEATHS BY HOSTILE ACTIONS IN SOUTHEAST ASIA

(Cumulative through 31 March 1971)

Mil Service	Officer			Enlisted			Total		
	Total	Negro	(%)	Total	Negro	(%)	Total	Negro	(%)
Army	3,092	87	(2.8)	26,636	3,829	(14.4)	29,728	3,916	(13.2)
Navy	211	0	(0.0)	1,157	33	(2.8)	1,368	33	(2.4)
Mar Corps	709	4	(0.6)	12,209	1,594	(13.0)	12,918	1,598	(12.4)
Air Force	596	3	(0.5)	278	20	(7.2)	874	23	(2.6)
TOTAL	4,608	94	(2.0)	40,280	5,476	(13.6)	44,888	5,570	(12.4)

●

*In carrying out Sec. of Defense Melvin Laird's directive to
investigate the effects of racism on the administration of
military justice, a committee, jointly headed by Nathaniel Jones,
general counsel of the National Association for the
Advancement of Colored People, and Lt. Gen. C. E. Hutchin, Jr.,
USA, discovered that subtle forms of ethnic and racial
discrimination were at work. Although the group was not
unanimous in its recommendations—with whites and military
men blaming discrimination upon individuals, while black
civilians believed in the existence of institutional racism—it did
agree on the importance of an impartial system of justice that
was perceived as fair by those subject to it.*

We are learning, for instance, that where once we acknowledged only one manifestation of discrimination, we must acknowledge another, subtly interrelated to the first, but nonetheless discernibly different.

The first is *intentional discrimination.*[1] It is the manifestation with which we are familiar because our attention has been drawn to it most often. The person, persons or groups practicing it do so with the intent of demeaning, harming, disfavoring or disadvantaging another person, persons or group who have race or ethnicity in common. It takes the form of the shouted epithet; segregation of buses or schools, whether by official decree or otherwise; exclusion of individuals or groups from membership in clubs or organizations; the denial of housing choice. It has many expressions but is identified most clearly in an act. We have defined it as a policy of an authority—especially in the context of our study, a military authority—or action of an individual or group of individuals which is intended to have a negative effect on minority individuals or groups without having such an effect on others.

[*Report of the Task Force on the Administration of Justice in the Armed Forces,* 30 November 1972, Office of Deputy Assistant Secretary of Defense (Equal Opportunity), Washington, DC.]

[1]Emphasis in the original.

It is against this manifestation of discrimination—racial, ethnic, religious—that our country has made some strides. Where once it was practiced openly and without apology, it has increasingly become the subject of ethical, moral and legal sanctions. It is this kind of discrimination which the armed forces were among the very first to attack. Neither society nor the military has succeeded in eradicating this manifestation of discrimination. The task force believes that what progress has been made calls not for a slackening of the effort against it but, rather, for a redoubling.

The second manifestation of discrimination is less clear and familiar, at least to nonminority Americans. It is not identified as much by an act as it is by the result of an act or acts or of inaction. It need not be intentional; indeed, a harmful effect may not have been intended. Regardless of whether it can be traced to a single individual, regardless of whether it has its root in a recent event or in history, it nevertheless works to the detriment of minorities and the equality of their opportunities. We have labeled it *systemic discrimination*[1] and defined it as policies or practices which appear to be neutral in their effect on minority individuals or groups but which have the effect of disproportionately impacting upon them in harmful or negative ways.

Understanding the nature of systemic discrimination, we believe, is the key to resolving the paradox of the failure of the military's efforts to eradicate racial and ethnic discrimination from the armed forces. Not unlike other institutions in society concerned with the elimination of such discrimination—religion and government, for example—the military has concentrated on the manifestation which it could identify, that is, on intentional discrimination.

It has, for example, forbidden the use of racial epithets, a form of intentional discrimination. But it has not seen the systemic form of discrimination which is manifested in some of its apparently neutral policies governing the testing of service men and women, the recruitment of minority men and women into its officer corps, or in the assumptions which govern the operation of the various human relations and equal opportunity programs. These policies can characterize a minority serviceman as inferior just as brutally as does a racial or ethnic slur. Like other institutions, the military is now called upon to acknowledge systemic discrimination and move against it. . . .

We have not inquired into the motivation of makers or executors of military policies which are the sources of systemic discrimination. We have been content to study the results of those policies and practices in terms of their effects on minority service-men. In taking this tack, we echo the trend of recent court decisions in cases involving discriminatory action. If the net effect of the action, or inaction, is to discriminate against individuals or groups, the question of intent or motivation need not be considered. The task force concludes that systemic racial discrimination exists throughout the armed services and in the military justice system. No command or installation—and, more important, no element of the military [justice] system—is entirely free from the effects of systemic discrimination against minority servicemen as individuals and as groups.

It is in the policies and practices governing testing, job assignment, promotions and the human-relations programs of the several services that the extremely harmful and discriminatory effects were clearly manifested. . . .

It is enough here to convey our strong conviction of the interrelatedness of these policies and their profound effect upon the lives and military careers of minority-group men and women. The network of effect is as easy to state as it is hard to live with for the

---

[1] Emphasis in the original.

many who must live with it. For many, though not all, it means that a black, Chicano, Puerto Rican, or other minority man or woman comes into the service and is given a series of tests which, we suspect, at best, do a poor job of measuring his basic intelligence and an even worse job of establishing his natural aptitudes. Partly on the basis of those tests, he is given an assignment in which his chances of either rising in the military profession or securing marketable skills to support himself on return to civilian life are markedly reduced. Then, for the period of his service, the human-relations program, which is intended to ease his way through an admittedly difficult and demanding system, proved in many, but not all, cases to be more rhetorical than real.

•

A team of investigators, dispatched to West Germany by Roy Wilkins, executive director of the National Association for the Advancement of Colored People, submitted a report that both sustained "indictments of American society as one characterized by pervasive institutional racism" and offered "considerable hope if we heed its ominous message." The three-man team conducted informal sessions during which they encouraged black servicemen to discuss racial problems. In preparing what Mr. Wilkins termed "a plea by black servicemen for help in making the system work fairly for them," the interviewers sought to "learn from the disenchanted, as well as the contented."

Promotional Discrimination

Nothing short of a dramatic step-up in the rate of promotions and a revision of the career-assignment practices will assure black servicemen that the military is not adhering to a discriminatory double standard. From the views of the Negro soldiers and airmen with whom our team talked, . . . it should be abundantly clear that blacks know where the problem is and what remedial steps must be taken.

So grave and pervasive is the problem that we urge the following:

1. Adoption of an armed forces "Philadelphia Plan"[1]; and
2. A thorough reexamination of the Armed Forces Qualification Test in light of the declaration by the United States Supreme Court[2] that a test, which has the effect of excluding Negroes from certain jobs and is not related to job performance, is illegal. . . .

Administration of Justice

Integrity is the cornerstone of an effective system of military justice. It is essential that not only the system be fair, in fact, but that those subject to it *believe*[3] in its integrity.

[*The Search for Military Justice: Report of an NAACP Inquiry into the Problems of the Negro Serviceman in West Germany*, 1971, National Association for the Advancement of Colored People. Reprinted by permission.]

[1] In effect, a quota system to compensate for past discrimination.

[2] Griggs vs. Duke Power. [Footnote in the original.]

[3] Emphasis in the original.

One's perception of the system is as real as the system itself inasmuch as persons are prone to act and react on the basis of their perception of that system. . . .

Pretrial Confinement

The dramatically high rate of pretrial confinements by the army in West Germany is contrasted by the remarkably low rate found in the air force. We learned . . . of the feeling that is widely shared by Negro soldiers, i.e., that officers use the pretrial gambit as a cover for leadership failure. The informality of the process invites abuse.

We urge, therefore, that more formality be required and that standards be constructed to protect both the rights of enlisted men, and at the same time preserve the power to incarcerate in cases that warrant it. . . .

Administrative Discharges

A key to reduction of the disturbingly frequent use of Chapter 10 and 212 discharges[4] from the armed services is the education of senior noncommissioned officers and junior-grade officers on the subject of culture and race. Another key requirement is the providing of counsel in whom the affected soldiers have confidence. . . . [such as] NAACP lawyers and nonwhite law students.

The recently announced program by the Department of Defense requiring all men in the armed forces to attend classes in race relations, under the direction of the Defense Race Relations Institute, will go a long way toward minimizing incidents that lead to the confrontation offenses. These incidents are often the first steps along the road to more serious disciplinary problems, leading to a court martial or punitive discharge or both. . . .

Housing

Without question the most pervasive problem confronting Negro soldiers in West Germany is that of housing. Regardless of rank or age of the servicemen, there were strong feelings expressed about the discrimination being practiced by Germans against the black soldiers. It, more than any other problem, caused blacks to regard Germany as an unfriendly country and to wonder aloud why they should be stationed there. . . .

Recreational Opportunities

Many of the confrontations that have taken place between black and white troops occurred in connection with off-duty recreation, either on or off base. Racial polarization appears most pronounced during these times as groups of whites and blacks vie for control of recreational facilities such as enlisted men's and NCO clubs. Efforts to use off-base clubs have led to clashes between blacks and whites growing out of attempts of club operators to exclude Negroes.

---

[4]Administrative discharges.

What appeared to some as the effect of subtle racism impressed others as resulting from a lack of discipline. In blaming "permissiveness" for racial outbursts on two naval vessels, a House subcommittee nevertheless made the useful observation that actions not racially motivated could be perceived as discriminatory. The resulting discontent, unless understood and dealt with, could result in violence. In reacting to the complaints of one race or group, however, a commander might easily give the impression of injustice toward another.

Immediately following air operations aboard the *Kitty Hawk* on the evening of October 12, 1972, a series of incidents broke out wherein groups of blacks, armed with chains, wrenches, bars, broomsticks and other dangerous weapons, went marauding through sections of the ship disobeying orders to cease, terrorizing the crew, and seeking out white personnel for senseless beating with fists and with weapons which resulted in serious injury to three men and the medical treatment of many more, including some blacks. While engaged in this conduct some were heard to shout, "Kill the son-of-a-bitch; kill the white trash; wipe him out!" Others shouted, "They are killing our brothers."

Aboard the USS *Constellation,* during the period of November 3–4, 1972, what has been charitably described as "unrest" and as a "sit-in" took place while the ship was underway for training exercises. The vast majority of the dissident sailors were black and were allegedly protesting several grievances they claimed were in need of correction.

These sailors were off-loaded as part of a "beach detachment," given liberty, refused to return to the ship, and were later processed only for this *minor*[1] disciplinary infraction (six hours of unauthorized absence) at Naval Air Station, North Island, near San Diego. . . .

Opinions

1. The subcommittee is of the opinion that the riot on *Kitty Hawk* consisted of unprovoked assaults by a very few men, most of whom were of below-average mental capacity, most of whom had been aboard for less than one year, and all of whom were black. This group, as a whole, acted as "thugs" which raises doubt as to whether they should ever have been accepted into the military service in the first place.

2. The subcommittee expresses its strong objection to the procedures utilized by higher authority to negotiate with *Constellation*'s dissidents and, eventually, to appease them by acquiescing to their demands and by meting out minor nonjudicial punishment for what was a major affront to good order and discipline. Moreover, the subcommittee stresses that the actions committed aboard that ship have the potential for crippling a combatant vessel in a war zone. . . .

[U.S., Congress, House, Committee on Armed Services, *Report by the Special Subcommittee on Disciplinary Problems in the U.S. Navy,* 92d Cong., 2d sess., 2 January 1973.]

[1]Emphasis in the original.

Discrimination or Perception?

During the course of this investigation we found *no substantial evidence*[1] of racial discrimination upon which we could place true responsibility for causation of these serious disturbances. Certainly there were many *perceptions*[1] of discrimination by young blacks, who, because of their sensitivity to real or fancied oppression, often enlist with a "chip on their shoulder." Those young blacks, who enter the service from the ghetto with a complete black awareness, probably for the first time find themselves immersed in a predominantly white society which, in civilian life, they had come to mistrust. These young men are subject to being easily led—as was the case in the *Constellation* uprising where about fifteen agitators orchestrated the entire affair. . . .

The Communications Gap

With communications a primary tool, and beginning with the *very first*[1] exposure to the recruiting system, we are convinced that a much better mutual understanding of racial matters, the needs of the service, and the requirements of good order and discipline can be achieved in the navy, as well as in the other services. For example, it is wrong to mislead a young recruit in a low mental group with respect to his opportunities for attending service school or "learning a trade" while in on-the-job training—particularly on a ship. His chances are limited and he must clearly understand this from the beginning, though examples abound that with superior effort he can advance to the fullest extent. While some degree of incompetence, inexperience or low intelligence can be absorbed in duties ashore, there should be no compromises aboard ship. Unquestioned discipline, instant response to orders and an acceptable standard of performance are absolutely essential to the operation of a naval vessel. This every man must understand clearly. It is not a racial consideration.

So, too, with the untrained recruit who reports to a ship only to find himself swallowed up in mess-cooking for three months, followed by what seems to be an endless period of compartment cleaning or chipping paint in a deck division. This experience is accompanied by serious trauma after the excitement and high sense of accomplishment in recruit training. Many blacks view this as an injustice and a breach of faith. In reality it is routine and a fact of life in duty afloat—a situation that every recruit should understand.

Similarly with questions of discipline. There is much misconception among young blacks with regard to the theory of punishment. They do not seem to understand that a poor disciplinary record or a history of poor performance is considered when meting out punishment for an offense—particularly at Captain's Mast (nonjudicial punishment). This "complaint" occurs if a white and a black are punished for the same transgression and the white receives a lesser punishment because of a better record of prior conduct. All personnel must receive careful explanation of the system and be advised further that the same system obtains in comparable civilian proceedings.

Polarization

The vast majority of blacks and whites are fine members of the military and go about their daily routines doing their jobs quietly and effectively. It appears that the

---

[1]Emphasis in the original.

militants and agitators comprise but a small minority of the black membership of units inspected during this inquiry. But apparently there is a polarization of the races developing in many quarters which is most distressing.... Although this tendency manifests itself typically during off-duty hours, in the mess hall, and in making berthing arrangements, it certainly is not stunted by convening ad hoc councils and committees composed of all black members to provide guidance to command on racial matters. It can encourage a white sailor to view this polarization as a threat to his own security....

●

The US Army, Europe, surveyed racial attitudes in forty-six company-sized units of various types and in a variety of locations. The project elicited almost fifteen hundred valid responses from whites, blacks, and Hispanic-Americans, both enlisted men and officers.

The principal conclusions are:

1. There has been a significant reduction in mistrust of racial groups different than one's own among both black and white enlisted men.

2. Friendly associations among men of different races appear to have declined slightly.

3. Perceived commitment on the part of the army to achieve equal opportunity has increased.

4. Enlisted personnel feel that the emphasis on equal opportunity and improvement of race relations by their immediate leaders has declined.

Conclusions one and two, as well as conclusions three and four, appear inconsistent. A possible explanation is that the expansion of race-relations programs in the past year, particularly education programs, has accounted for the increase in racial understanding and in perceived commitment by the army to achieve equal opportunity.

On the other hand, these programs have made racial problems more visible by increasing awareness and recognition of racial tensions and discrimination, thus accounting for the unfavorable trends in conclusions two and four. It is probable that because of the EO[1] programs, incidents of discrimination and racial tension that went unnoticed in the past are currently recognized as such.

5. Race-relations programs focus attention on racial problems. Consequently, attitudes concerning the existence of racial problems will in the short run suggest that race relations are deteriorating. What in fact may be occurring is, because of increased awareness, subtle forms of discrimination and covert racial tensions are being recognized as such.

6. About one-half of the enlisted personnel have had classroom instruction on race relations.

[USAREUR (US Army, Europe) Race Relations: Attitude Trends, June 1972–March 1973, Office of Deputy Assistant Secretary of Defense (Equal Opportunity), Washington, DC.]

[1]Equal Opportunity.

7. About one-half of the officers have taken part in race relations seminars and human relations councils.

8. About one-third of all white enlisted men and about 40 percent of all black enlisted men have attended seminars and councils.

9. The majority of soldiers feel classroom instruction, seminars and councils increase understanding and reduce tensions.

10. Officers and white NCOs feel: relations between soldiers have improved; understanding and efforts to promote understanding on the part of leaders have increased; and discrimination in job assignments, promotions and punishment have decreased.

11. Both white and black personnel in grades E1–E5 feel: relations between soldiers have deteriorated; understanding and efforts to promote understanding have decreased; and discrimination in job assignments, promotions and punishment has increased.

INDEX

A

Abolitionists, 19–20, 28, 40–41
Adak, Aleutian Islands, 164
Adams, John, 7
Adjutant General, 49, 59, 111, 126, 221, 262, 267
Advisory Committee on Negro Troop Policies, 121–26
Aerographers, 141
Affirmative action programs, 321–22, 329, 342–43
Agriculture, 1, 38
Air base security battalions, 279
Air base service squadrons, 282, 298
Air cargo resupply squadrons, 279
Air Command and Staff School, 281
Aircraft carriers, 141–42, 272, 274
Airdrome defense battalions, 279
Air Force Headquarters, 280–83, 298–99, 301
Air Force Letter (35-3), 249–51, 297, 299
Air police units, 282
Air Staff, 176, 245, 295
Air stations, 147
Air Training Command, 249, 280, 282, 284, 297
Air University, 229
Air War College, 281
Alabama, 50
Alexander, John H., 52
Alexander, Sadie T. M., 242
Alexander, William, Lord Stirling, 8
All-volunteer force, 326
Allen, Cleveland G., 67
Alnavs, 253, 273
American Civil Liberties Union, 316
American colonies, 1–5
American Expeditionary Force: 78, 82–84, 86, 89; cables, 81–82
American Freedman's Inquiry Commission, 30, 32
American Red Cross, 116–17. *See also* Red Cross Clubs
Ammunition depots, 147, 185, 187, 232, 272
Ammunition handlers, 175
Anderson, Gen. T. J., 25
Andrews, Walter G., 237, 239

Antiaircraft artillery mechanics, 291
Antietam Creek, Maryland, 20, 25
Anti-Lynching Bill, 109
Apprenticeship training, 106
Aptitude, 189, 198, 207, 212, 217–18, 221–23, 252, 254, 257–58, 269–70, 277, 279, 284–85, 289, 292, 328, 347–48, 350
USS *Arctic*, 184
Arkansas, 49, 325
Armed blacks, fear of, 1, 3, 20, 41, 46, 71
Armed Forces Qualification Test, 347
Armistice (World War I), 87
Armored Force, 113
Armored School, 290
Armored units: 761st Tank Battalion, 209
Armorers, 217
Army Field Forces, 265
Army General Classification Test, 172, 197–98, 200, 212, 217–18, 221–23, 257, 263–64, 270, 274, 288–89, 292, 307–08. *See also* Armed Forces Qualification Test
Army General Staff. *See* War Department, General Staff
Army Ground Forces, 123, 126, 174, 179, 213–17
Army and Navy Journal, editor of, 66
Army of Occupation, 209–10
Army Personnel with the Air Force (ARWAF), 225, 299, 301
Army Regulations: (615–368 and –369), 219; (600–629-1), 284–85, 308
Army Service Forces, 123, 126, 217
Army Service Forces Study Concerning the Participation of Negro Troops in the Postwar Military Establishment, 174–79
Army Talk, "Why a Uniform?," 228
Army of Tennessee (Confederate States of America), 40
Army War College, 91, 285–86
Arnold, Rear Adm. Burr E., 304
Arnold, Gen. Henry H., 98
Arsenals, 106–07, 109
Artificer Branch, 140–41
Artillery: 65, 104, 125, 194–95, 285; Fifth Artillery, 50; 30th Field Artillery Battalion, 209

H

I